FORTY YEARS

THE SAGA OF BUILDING

THE SALT LAKE TEMPLE

FORTY YEARS

 THE SAGA OF BUILDING

THE SALT LAKE TEMPLE

MARK HENSHAW

**DESERET
BOOK**

SALT LAKE CITY, UTAH

Library of Congress Cataloging-in-Publication Data

Names: Henshaw, Mark, 1970– author.
Title: Forty years : the saga of building the Salt Lake Temple / Mark Henshaw.
Description: Salt Lake City, Utah : Deseret Book, [2020] | Includes bibliographical references and index.
Summary: "A history of the planning and construction of the Salt Lake Temple of The Church of Jesus Christ of Latter-day Saints, which took forty years to build"—Provided by publisher.
Identifiers: LCCN 2020005925 | ISBN 9781629727509 (hardback)
Subjects: LCSH: Salt Lake Temple—History. | Salt Lake City (Utah)—Church history. | Salt Lake City (Utah)—Buildings, structures, etc.
Classification: LCC BX8685 .H46 2020 | DDC 246/.958332—dc23
LC record available at https://lccn.loc.gov/2020005925

Printed in the United States of America
Publishers Printing, Salt Lake City, UT

10   9   8   7   6   5   4   3   2   1

WHAT WE OBTAIN TOO CHEAP, WE ESTEEM TOO LIGHTLY: IT IS

DEARNESS ONLY THAT GIVES EVERY THING ITS VALUE. HEAVEN

KNOWS HOW TO PUT A PROPER PRICE UPON ITS GOODS.

THOMAS PAINE

The American Crisis

CONTENTS

FOREWORD

BY JACOB W. OLMSTEAD, PhD

A s you begin this book, you might be asking yourself why you are reading a foreword by somebody you've never heard of. Let me answer that question. I am a historian who works for the Church History Department of The Church of Jesus Christ of Latter-day Saints in Salt Lake City. In December 2011, I was asked to help the department better understand the construction of the Salt Lake Temple. I spent thousands of hours going through the vast holdings of the Church History Library. Others in and out of the department also scoured the archives and the temple itself to learn what happened to the temple after its dedication—changes over time to carpeting, paint color, furnishings, artwork, and so on. This research has ultimately been used to help guide decisions about the preservation and restoration of the temple.

My research uncovered many previously unknown stories about the temple's construction. It also clarified several stories that had achieved mythic status among the Latter-day Saints. It has been my hope to share these stories with those interested in the history of the Salt Lake Temple. In time, I became aware of Mark Henshaw's work. As I read his manuscript, I was delighted to learn that he had written the kind of book I felt should be written for the temple—and, more important, what the temple deserved. Mark had done an impressive amount of research to understand the construction of the temple and, significantly, how it was interwoven into the events in the lives of the Latter-day Saints. With Deseret Book's help, it has been my privilege to work with Mark to fine-tune some of the details about the temple's construction and suggest a few new stories that reveal its value.

Most readers of this volume will have some idea of the major plot points in the story of the building of the Salt Lake Temple: it was difficult to move the stone from the mountains, the construction took a long time, and it required a great deal of faith and sacrifice to get it done. That is all true. And yet, when Latter-day Saints, as well as those of other faiths, stand in the presence of this temple, they know intuitively that those facts don't quite explain the value of this building. It somehow means more than that.

Permit me to share a couple of stories that for me help capture the meaning of the Salt Lake Temple. When the Latter-day Saints arrived in the Salt Lake Valley in July 1847, they really had nothing. They were destitute. They had wagons, some cattle, seed, and little else. But they did have their faith. The day following Brigham Young's arrival was the Sabbath day. Thomas Bullock, the official clerk for the first pioneer company, briefly recorded that Apostle George A. Smith offered the first Sabbath-day sermon in the valley. He wrote, "Elder G. A. Smith preached about the House of the Lord being established on the tops of the Mountains."[1] Isaiah 2:2 would have been the text for that sermon. In these verses, the Old Testament prophet, who lived more than 2,500 years before the Saints arrived in the Salt Lake Valley, prophesied that "in the last days, . . . the mountain of the Lord's house shall be established in the top of the mountains, and shall be exalted above the hills; and all nations shall flow unto it." This sermon, among other events, suggests to me that the temple was central to the Saints' purpose in

---

1. Will Bagley, *The Pioneer Camp of the Saints: The 1846 and 1847 Mormon Trail Journals of Thomas Bullock* (Spokane, WA: Arthur H. Clark, 1997), 238.

establishing a city and a people centered on the Lord and His gospel. In this they followed the pattern established by Joseph Smith. But what is more astounding is the notion that these Latter-day Saints, who had nothing, intended to fulfill this Old Testament prophecy in preparation for the Lord's return. That vision, that purpose, that faith drove the pioneers forward to do something truly extraordinary. As you read this book, the magnitude of the Saints' devotion to achieve this goal will become clearer.

A second meaningful event took place about five and a half years later, during the groundbreaking ceremony for the temple. By this time, a much larger group of Latter-day Saints had gathered to hear the words of their Church leaders and to take turns scooping shovels full of frozen dirt out of the ground. During Brigham Young's comments, he rehearsed the events in the history of the Church that had brought them to that point, including the adversity that had come to the Saints in Ohio, Missouri, and Illinois, but also "how they had been led by an overruling Providence to this consecrated spot." The Saints had taken steps into the darkness and were now enjoying the first shimmers of morning light. Following President Young's remarks, two bands gathered to the center of the temple plot and played a "soul cheering strain" of the old Scottish folk song "Auld Lang Syne."[2] On this occasion the Saints remembered with a song the old times and the old friends, but also rejoiced in the beginning of a new era in Church history. And the Salt Lake Temple was at the center of this new era for the next forty years. This era has continued with the temple at the center, as the Lord's prophets and apostles gather to the Salt Lake Temple to receive direction for the building of His kingdom on the earth.

These kinds of vignettes offer valuable insight into how much the Salt Lake Temple meant to the Latter-day Saints. They provide a window

---

2. John D. T. McAllister, Journal, February 14, 1853, 3-6, Box 1, Folder 3, Church History Library, Salt Lake City, Utah. With some alterations, McAllister's account is based upon the report of the event made in the *Deseret News* (*Weekly*), which subsequently appeared in the *Millennial Star*.

into the thoughts, emotions, and devotion exhibited during the building saga. In them we can find a kinship that will bless each of us on our own spiritual journey and in our efforts to build the Lord's kingdom.

Mark Henshaw's work to weave together many vignettes and story lines also allows the reader to step back and take in a much larger picture of the significance of the Salt Lake Temple. To me, the story of the Salt Lake Temple reveals the absolute supremacy the Saints placed on the ordinances and covenants that are housed and delivered in the house of the Lord. It was at the core of everything they did. Collectively, they had no other thought than to demonstrate their willingness to do the Lord's will. *Forty Years: The Saga of Building the Salt Lake Temple* shows that this was not an easy road. It took time, it took patience, it took sacrifice. But this was the kind of work that made them Saints. They were refined by this process. The history of its construction imbues the Salt Lake Temple with meaning for a global body of Latter-day Saints. The value of this story transcends direct ancestral connection or geography.

Like the spired temple itself, the story of its construction pulls our gaze upward to the heavens.

PREFACE

As of this writing, The Church of Jesus Christ of Latter-day Saints has one hundred fifty operating temples in forty-three countries. Seventeen more are under construction or renovation, and thirty-four others have been announced. The Church does not lack for resources to build or maintain these holy buildings. The entire cost of construction for each one is allocated before groundbreaking—the Church does not take out loans or mortgages to fund construction, which usually takes only a few years once begun. When obstacles to construction arise, whether physical, legal, or political, the Church can call on highly educated and experienced men and women to work through the problems. For most Latter-day Saints, the hardest part of temple building is waiting for the prophet's announcement of where new temples will be built and hoping one will be constructed close to home.

It was not always so. The Church's first temples were erected only with great difficulty. Most of the Saints lacked experience or training in constructing anything larger or more refined than a rustic farmhouse. By all rights, designing and building any large house of worship should have been beyond them. Added onto that lack of general knowledge was their poverty. Most Saints had to work constantly for their daily bread and had little to donate to a building fund. Many could give only their time and labor, which became an even greater challenge as hostility against the Church increased over the years. Mobs combined repeatedly to deny the Saints use of the temples they worked so hard to build. They had access to the Kirtland Temple for less than two years before enemies and apostates drove them away. They spent five years building the Nauvoo Temple, and persecution from their neighbors forced them to dedicate it in sections so they could put parts of it to use even before it was finished. Once that temple was completed, they were privileged to use it for just four *months* before mobs forced them in 1846 to evacuate the city they'd built up from swampland. An arsonist burned that temple a few years later. The Saints would not have access to another completed, fully functioning temple again for thirty-one years, when, in 1877, Brigham Young dedicated a house of the Lord in St. George, Utah.

———•·•·•———

I point out this bit of history for a reason. With so many temples available to most of the Latter-day Saints in the world, I worry that we may not fully appreciate their eternal worth. It's human nature that we lose sight of the value of things that cost us nothing to acquire or use. I became painfully aware of that tendency in myself in recent years. Living in Northern Virginia, I would attend the Washington D.C. Temple a few times each year, but I could be dissuaded from making the trip if traffic were heavy or some other inconvenience arose. Then the Church closed the temple for a multiyear renovation. Suddenly, the closest temple to me was in Philadelphia, a three-hour drive by car. Attending the house of the Lord became an all-day affair.

In the back of my mind I was aware that, compared to traveling the same distance on foot or in a horse-drawn wagon, three hours in a climate-controlled car posed no great inconvenience. Brigham Young would not have been sympathetic to complaints about having to spend a few hours in freeway traffic. Early Saints were driven, hounded, arrested, attacked, jailed, and sometimes killed for their beliefs. If the hardest trial we endure to attend the temple is sitting in a car for a few hours, we have no cause to complain.

Realizing my own weakness, I decided that I wanted to understand better what my ancestors had endured to gain access to a temple. I already knew a fair amount about early Church history, but I knew little about the period after the Saints reached the Salt Lake Valley. I did know that the Salt Lake Temple had taken decades to build, but I did not know why. So I started to research the subject. I found any number of scholarly articles and books on the subject, but none that told a narrative history of the Salt Lake Temple. I watched the Church's hour-long movie *The Mountain of the Lord,* but I saw that, of necessity, it gave only brief treatment to events that must have been prolonged and complex. So, being a novelist with training in historical research and analysis, I decided to write the narrative myself. This book is the product of that effort.

In a sense, the main "character" of the story is the Salt Lake Temple itself. It is the focal point, so the people and events described in the pages that follow are those which had some notable effect on its construction. Some major events, such as the United States Civil War, are described only briefly because they shaped the environment in which the temple was built and not because they had an immediate, direct impact on the construction itself. Others, such as the US government's campaign to eliminate plural marriage in Utah in the 1880s, did have such an impact but had their origins decades in the past. Rather than spring these events on the reader fully formed and break up the larger narrative with repeated flashbacks to explain where such hard left turns really started, I've tried to keep the narrative as linear as possible and follow the most important threads from the start. So readers may wonder why, in a story about the Salt Lake Temple's construction, I have spent time talking about disgruntled Judge William Drummond's bitter letters to a Washington newspaper and government officials; or Elder Rudger Clawson's trial for "unlawful cohabitation." For such diversions, I ask the reader's patience and promise that if they will stick it out to the end, they will see how each thread fits into a larger tapestry of events that eventually had serious impacts on the Saints' effort to build what is now the most iconic house of the Lord.

—————•••————

It is my hope that this history will help readers come to appreciate the magnitude of the challenges those early Saints faced to build the Salt Lake Temple, and thus the depth and intensity of the faith required to overcome those obstacles. Understanding that, I believe, will help us properly value the worth of temples. I think those early Saints would be deeply gratified by that, because they did not build temples just for themselves. They also built them for us. The greatest way we can honor their labors is by entering into the house of the Lord as often as we're able, not letting ourselves be deterred easily for truly minor reasons, and performing the work for which those temples were built.

In writing this story, I have made every effort to ensure accuracy of facts. The only changes I have made to quotations is to standardize the spelling so modern readers would not be taken out of the narrative by the creative arrangements of letters so common in early America. Any errors of fact or interpretation of the facts are purely my own.

MARK HENSHAW
June 9, 2019

CHAPTER 1

HERE WILL BE THE TEMPLE OF OUR GOD

SATURDAY, JULY 24, 1847

Brigham Young was lying in the bed of a wagon, having been severely ill for the last twelve days, when he saw the valley for the first time.[1] He was forty-six years old, short and quite stocky, a carpenter by trade and physically robust; but "mountain fever" could put even the strongest men flat on their backs. Several diseases fell under that generic name because they all produced high fever, severe head and body aches, deep pain behind the eyes, chills, nausea, and vomiting. Colorado tick fever was one of the least severe of these illnesses, usually passing in a few days after the onset of the symptoms, but Brigham had been down for almost two weeks, suggesting that he may have contracted the more serious Rocky Mountain spotted fever. If so, it was remarkable that he was still alive. That strain persisted for weeks, and the fatality rate was high owing to the inflammation of the heart, lungs, and brain or the kidney failure it produced. The only known treatments were home-brewed remedies and rest, but sleep was hard to come by in a wagon on the plains. Summer days were bright and hot, and Brigham would have felt every bump in the road as the wooden wheels rolled over the uneven land. And he wasn't alone in his suffering. Thirty-seven other Latter-day Saints traveling with him had also contracted the fever—a full quarter of the company. But they did not have the luxury of time to grant the sick much rest.[2]

They'd needed 111 days to cover 916 miles from their last home in Winter Quarters, just across the Missouri River near present-day Omaha, Nebraska. That worked out to an average pace of just over eight miles per day, and that was threatening to create a crisis. More wagon trains were following and would arrive in staggered numbers throughout the late summer and early fall—too late to plant enough crops to carry the Saints through the winter. Those who reached the valley first needed to start up the farms that would feed everyone else coming in behind. They had to grow a large amount of food in a short time, and everything they'd heard about the Salt Lake Valley suggested the land there was no good for farming. Explorers had been mapping the region for decades, including famed trapper Jim Bridger, who had first seen the Great Salt Lake in 1824; and John C. Frémont, who had explored the area just a few years before. Their published reports suggested that the Saints' destination was a barren place with few trees and little useful vegetation of any kind. A mountaineer by the name of Goodyear met the company while he was heading back east and shared his recent tale of having just wintered north of the valley. He "had tried the experiment of sewing [sic] grain and vegetables in a small way. But he too, was unable to give . . . any hope; on the contrary, he told of hard frosts, cold climate, difficult to produce grain and vegetables in any of this mountain region."[3] The Saints were undaunted. They had faith and were hard workers, always a potent combination, and their labor supply would receive regular infusions of fresh strength. It was their supply of time that was shrinking. This lead company needed to break ground soon or the winter of 1848 would be a hungry one for hundreds of people.

Then, on July 12, the mountain fever struck Brigham when the company was still 116 miles outside of the valley, near the present-day border of Wyoming. Rather than hold up the entire company while the sick members recuperated, Brigham ordered Elder Orson Pratt to take a group of forty-two men and push ahead the final 116 miles. They were to cut a road through the timber and brush in the canyons, find a site in the valley to settle, and start planting.[4] Pratt's advance team reached the valley on July 21 and found a suitable location to start farming. The main body of the company, which hadn't given the sick members much time at all to recover, joined them by nightfall of the twenty-third. Only Brigham and the other sick travelers were still straggling behind as Pratt's group tried to break ground and start planting crops on the twenty-third. On the morning of the twenty-fourth, Brigham and the last of the company finally were closing in on the valley. The thermometer read ninety-six degrees Fahrenheit.

The driver of Brigham's makeshift ambulance was Wilford Woodruff, another member of the Quorum of the Twelve Apostles. Forty years old and a fellow New Englander—he'd grown up in Connecticut—he may have felt a particular empathy for his friend's suffering. "Spotted fever" had killed Wilford's own mother in 1809 when he was fifteen months old. But all he could do to alleviate the discomfort Brigham was enduring in the back was to reach their destination as quickly as the trail would allow. The end was close, and Wilford spurred the horses on until they reached "Big Mountain."

It was there that both men saw the Great Salt Lake Valley for the first time in their lives. The landscape didn't quite fit the description of the barren waste they'd been told to expect. "We gazed in wonder and admiration upon the vast valley before us . . . ," Wilford wrote, "with the waters of the Great Salt Lake glistening in the sun, mountains towering to the skies, and streams of pure water running through the beautiful valley. It was the grandest scene we had ever beheld till this moment. Pleasant thoughts ran through our minds at the prospect that, not many years hence, the house of God would be established in the mountains and exalted above the hills; while the valleys would be converted into orchards, vineyards, and fruitful fields, cities erected to the name of the Lord, and the standard of Zion unfurled for the gathering of nations."[5]

Brigham Young.

Wilford Woodruff.

Brigham, though still sick, was equally moved by the sight. "I ascended and crossed over the Big Mountain, when on its summit I directed Elder Woodruff, who had kindly tendered me the use of his carriage, to turn the same half way round so that I could have a view of a portion of Salt Lake Valley," he later wrote. "The spirit of light rested upon me, and hovered over the valley, and I felt that there the Saints would find protection and safety."[6] According to Wilford, Brigham's actual words were less eloquent. Brigham pushed himself up with some effort, supporting himself on his arm, and he looked out at the valley opened up before them for several long minutes. "It is enough. This is the right place," Wilford recalled him saying. "Drive on." Then he lay back down in the wagon and Woodruff urged the horses forward.[7]

So it was that the man who would begin the forty-year construction of the Salt Lake Temple and the man who would finish it, both future Presidents of the Church and prophets of the Lord, entered the valley together—one driving the wagon, the other stretched out in the back, a weak and bedridden passenger.

◆ ◆ ◆

At the moment that first company of pioneers reached the Salt Lake Valley, the members of The Church of Jesus Christ of Latter-day

Saints—the label of "Mormons" was an unfriendly slur bestowed on them by their enemies—were mostly homeless, a diaspora of 16,000 people spread across two continents that Brigham and his fellow Apostles were trying to bring together. They hadn't always been so. In fact, they'd built several settlements since Joseph Smith Jr. had established the Church seventeen years before in Palmyra, New York. But each time they moved somewhere new, the longtime residents of the area grew hostile as the Saints—with their strange religion and talk of angels, revelations from God, and modern scripture translated from gold plates—grew in numbers. Mobs formed over and over, and the Saints became repeated targets of violence.

For anyone ignorant of Joseph's revelations and teachings, such hostility might have been surprising. At first glance, the young church seemed little different from the Protestant denominations around it. But the Saints believed that the original gospel of Jesus Christ, along with the priesthood authority to perform saving ordinances in His name, had been lost through apostasy and persecution after the New Testament period. They rejected the Nicene Creed and other long-held Christian teachings, believing that the original gospel and priesthood authority could be recovered only through revelation from God to prophets He would call and upon whom He would bestow authority to act in His name. Joseph, they believed, was such a prophet, and the evidence of his divine calling was the Book of Mormon, a book of new scripture on par with the Bible itself. That was all pure blasphemy to the Saints' Protestant neighbors.

Then Joseph announced in December 1832 that the Lord had commanded the Saints to build a temple at their settlement in Kirtland, Ohio. The concept of a temple was not unknown to any Christian even moderately familiar with the Bible. The earliest of these was the tabernacle that Moses had built in the desert, the plans for which were laid out in significant detail in the Old Testament book of Exodus.[8] Five hundred years later in Jerusalem, King Solomon built a more permanent structure that was desecrated, damaged, and rebuilt several times over the centuries as Israel warred with her neighbors. King Herod rebuilt and expanded it, a project that was ongoing through Jesus Christ's entire lifetime, but the Romans razed that structure to the ground in 70 AD during the Great Jewish Revolt. The scattered Jews had not built any comparable structure since, nor had any Christian denomination. In two thousand years, no religious group had erected any structure that was uniquely designated as the "house of the Lord," the very place where God Himself might come to commune with His people or where they could perform uniquely sacred rites.

Some of the more hostile neighbors vowed that they would never let the temple be finished. Despite the opposition, the Saints began construction on the building the following June, in 1833. The plan, which Joseph and several others had seen in an open vision, was ambitious. The structure would be very large—three stories high, fifty-five feet wide, and sixty-five feet long. The first two levels would be assembly halls where hundreds of Saints could gather for instruction, or that could be subdivided by the use of curtains to create separate rooms for smaller groups. The top floor would house administrative offices and other rooms used for teaching classes or any other purpose as needed. The walls were composed of sandstone and covered with a bluish-gray stucco plaster created by mixing crushed glass and crockery into a cement that was applied to the exterior.

Construction was slow, however, and persecution affected the pace of the work. Brigham Young later noted, certainly with a hefty bit of literary license, that the laborers worked "holding the sword in one hand to protect themselves from the mob, while they placed the stone and moved the trowel with the other."[9] Estimates of the final cost vary widely, but it was likely $100,000 or more, much of it having come in donated labor and goods—almost $2,500,000 today, adjusting for inflation. The building took three years to complete and was finally dedicated on March 27, 1836.

They had little time to use the temple, as it turned out. Many of the

Saints suffered economic reversals during the national financial crisis of 1837 and the ensuing recession. Joseph's leadership became a focal point for their frustration and anger, and some became bitter enemies who joined the ranks of the persecutors. The environment grew so toxic that most of the Saints were forced to flee Kirtland, and by July 1838, almost all of them were gone, having left behind that first temple.

———— • • • ————

Saints had been settling in Missouri as early as 1831, so Joseph went there. He arrived on March 14, 1838, with Emma and their three children, and in his wake came another influx of Saints. They and the Missourians had already clashed several times before, and now Joseph's presence and the increasing numbers of Saints began to arouse the Missourians' hostile feelings again. In the midst of the growing turmoil, Joseph announced that he had received another revelation commanding the Saints to build a temple at Far West. To comply with the commandment, they laid the cornerstones for another house of the Lord on July 4, 1838, as part of an Independence Day celebration. But at the same gathering, Sidney Rigdon gave an intemperate speech in which he declared:

> That mob that comes on us to disturb us; it shall be between us and them a war of extermination, for we will follow them, till the last drop of their blood is spilled, or else they will have to exterminate us. . . . No man shall be at liberty to come into our streets, to threaten us with mobs, for if he does, he shall atone for it before he leaves the place, neither shall he be at liberty, to vilify and slander any of us, for suffer it we will not in this place. . . . We this day then proclaim ourselves free, with a purpose and a determination, that never can be broken, "no never! no never!! NO NEVER."!!!![10]

Within days, copies of the speech found their way into the outsiders' hands, and they were enraged by the tenor and contents of the entire discourse. The friction between the Saints and the Missourians finally broke into open violence on August 6, 1838, when a mob tried to stop a group of Saints from voting in Gallatin. A riot broke out, and from that day on, vigilante mobs began raiding and burning the Saints' homes and taking prisoners, some of whom died in their custody. A few Church members responded in kind, which usually resulted in further reprisals. Any hope for peace evaporated as the violence increased in frequency and scale, and some of the Missourians vowed that the Saints would never be allowed to build the temple.

Joseph appealed to Governor Lilburn W. Boggs for relief, but Boggs declined to intervene. Convinced that the government would not help, the Saints tried to defend themselves. Governor Boggs responded with Missouri Executive Order 44, stating that "the Mormons must be treated as enemies, and must be exterminated or driven from the State if necessary for the public peace—their outrages are beyond all description."[11] Boggs then dispatched 2,500 militia, led by Major General Samuel W. Lucas, to Far West, the largest Latter-day Saint settlement in Caldwell County, to enforce the order.

Lucas and his force surrounded Far West, where he ordered the Saints to surrender their leaders and their guns and to pay restitution for damage done to Missouri settlers' property and the cost of deploying the militia. Joseph and other Church leaders were arrested, the Saints' weapons were confiscated, and the militia proceeded to ransack Far West, seizing property and killing livestock for sport. There were claims of physical assaults on Latter-day Saint men and rapes of women by the soldiers. Joseph, his brother Hyrum, and others were remanded to the ironically named Liberty Jail, where they spent five miserable months in an unheated basement cell during the winter of 1839.

Leaving Far West and the site of the unbuilt temple behind, the Saints evacuated northeast, crossing the Mississippi River into Illinois and settling in the swamplands of Commerce. Suffering from exposure and malaria spread by the mosquitos in the marshes, they set out again to build a safe haven. They drained the swamps and began to erect new homes and businesses. Joseph rejoined the Saints in the spring of 1839 after a sheriff tasked with transporting him and the other prisoners from the jail to another city decided of his own accord to let them all go. In an act of hope, Joseph renamed their new home Nauvoo—a Hebrew word meaning "beautiful place." Its location at a prominent bend in the Mississippi River made it a prime site for riverboat traffic, and the economy boomed.

In response to a revelation from the Lord, Joseph and several other Church leaders left for Washington, D.C., in late October to petition the US government for redress of the Saints' losses in Missouri.[12] They arrived a month later, on November 28, and found some cheap lodging west of the Capitol on the corner of Missouri and 3rd Streets.[13] Wasting no time, Joseph and his small party—accompanied by John Reynolds, former governor and now congressman from Illinois—went to the White House and asked to meet with the president of the United States, Martin Van Buren.

That was the one and only request of Joseph's that was granted. Elias Higbee, one of Joseph's traveling companions, reported:

> We were immediately introduced into an upper apartment where we met the President and were introduced into his parlor, where we presented him with our Letters of introductions;—as soon as he had read one of them, he looked upon us with a kind of half frown and said, "what can I do? I can do nothing for you,— if I do any thing, I shall come in contact with the whole State of Missouri."[14]

Van Buren was very much a states' rights politician. As far as he was concerned, the "Mormon War"[15] had been an internal state matter for Missouri to resolve as Governor Boggs saw fit. But Van Buren's constitutional opinion in this particular matter was reinforced by his electoral vulnerability. He was an unpopular president, much disliked in Washington and the country at large, and he would need Missouri's electoral votes in the coming election of 1840.[16] So his self-declared inability to act legally coincided neatly with the outcome he wanted politically, producing a double-barreled refusal to help. The Saints never received restitution for their losses, and Boggs's extermination order remained on the books until 1976.

———•·•———

The revelation that sent Joseph to Washington also contained a commandment for the Saints to build another temple in their new home. This one would be an even more ambitious project than its predecessor in Kirtland. Like the first temple, the house of the Lord in Nauvoo would have two large assembly halls for public gatherings, but it would be a larger building, four stories high. It would also have a greater purpose than the Kirtland Temple. That first temple had functioned largely as a chapel on Sundays and a school and office building during the rest of the week. The Nauvoo Temple would be used for some of those functions too, but it would also be used for the practice of baptisms, "endowments," and other sacred ceremonies not open for viewing by curious or hostile outsiders.

The temple was only partially constructed by the late spring of 1844 when a group of apostates and other enemies to the Church set up a print shop in Nauvoo itself and started a broadsheet called the *Nauvoo Expositor*. It ran exactly one issue, on June 7, 1844, heavily critical of Joseph Smith personally, professionally, and religiously—to the point of vitriol. The city council declared it a public nuisance under Nauvoo's libel ordinance and moved to shutter the establishment. The press was broken up, the metal type scattered, and other materials confiscated or destroyed. The reaction was immediate and explosive. The threat of mob violence rose to such a degree that Joseph declared martial law on June 18 and called out all 5,000 members of the Nauvoo Legion to protect the city.

Illinois governor Thomas Ford decided that the danger merited his personal intervention. He traveled to the nearby town of Carthage, a few miles southeast of Nauvoo, and declared that the Prophet needed to stand trial for his actions. Joseph did not believe that he would live to see a courtroom once he was taken into custody, but he ultimately decided to surrender himself to the state authorities. On June 25, he was booked on the charge of inciting a riot and released on $500 bail; but the same judge then immediately charged him with treason—a crime for which bail was impermissible—and ordered him held at the Carthage Jail, a two-story brick structure. He was imprisoned along with his brother Hyrum and Church leaders John Taylor and Willard Richards.

The afternoon of June 27, a mob of more than one hundred men, faces painted black, stormed the jail. Hyrum was killed first when a rifle ball penetrated the wooden door to their room and struck him in the face. Joseph died next, taking multiple rounds, which knocked him out of the window to the courtyard two stories below. Taylor was shot in the knee, arm, and hip, but ultimately survived. His watch broke against the wooden floor when he fell, marking the moment of the assassination precisely—5:16 p.m. Richards suffered a bullet graze to his ear but was otherwise unharmed.

No one was ever convicted of the murders of Joseph and Hyrum.

———•—•—•———

Based on his history alone, Brigham Young seemed like an unlikely choice to be Joseph's successor. He was, like Joseph, a New Englander born into a family of poor Vermont farmers, the ninth of eleven children born to John and Abigail Howe Young, and likewise seemed "doomed to the necessity of obtaining a scanty maintenance by his daily labor."[17] He was fourteen when his mother died in 1815, and he left home not long after to make his own way. He stood five foot ten, with brown hair and blue eyes. His daughter Clarissa, who idolized her father, said that he had "a high brow that was broad and intelligent, a long straight nose, and a chin that denoted character and firmness."[18] He was clean shaven until middle age; the long beard immortalized in so many photographs wouldn't come until decades later. In his manners, Brigham was courteous until angered, at which time his language could turn harsh and even coarse on occasion. He was unpretentious perhaps for the same reason that he was not talkative in private—he had almost no formal schooling. In 1859, Horace Greeley, the famed author and founder of the *New York Daily Tribune*, interviewed Brigham for two hours and reported, "He spoke readily, not always with grammatical accuracy, but with no appearance of hesitation or reserve, and with no apparent desire to conceal anything, nor did he repel any of my questions as impertinent. He was very plainly dressed in thin summer clothing, and with no air of sanctimony or fanaticism." Greeley added that Brigham seemed "to enjoy life, and be in no particular hurry to get to heaven."[19]

Brigham's lack of education also created an expectation that he would make his living with his hands. He became a journeyman carpenter, a cabinetmaker, a glazier, and a blacksmith. His skills in those trades were sound enough to earn him a living and enable him to marry Miriam Works when he was twenty-three, though there was nothing about him that promised he would ever be more than a common laborer or prominent beyond his hometown. But the faith that he shared with Joseph would lead Brigham to take up Joseph's mantle and would make him just as famous as the martyred prophet—and just as despised in most quarters.

———•·•———

Brigham had first heard of the Book of Mormon in 1830 when his sister, Rhoda Green, obtained a copy from Samuel Smith, Joseph's brother. But his conversion was not immediate. He spent the better part of two years studying the book and the Church's doctrine. It wasn't until April 14, 1832, that Brigham finally united with his new faith. He was baptized by immersion in his own millpond, which was probably a physically unpleasant experience, the day being cold and snowy.[20] Miriam, his wife, was likewise baptized three weeks later, but their time in the Church together was short. She died of "consumption"—possibly tuberculosis—later that year on September 8, leaving Brigham a widower and single father of two young daughters, ages six and two. The bereaved little family was taken into the home of fellow Saint and close friend Heber C. Kimball, whose wife, Vilate, helped care for the girls.

In that same month, Brigham traveled to Kirtland, some two hundred miles away, and there he met Joseph Smith for the first time. Brigham found him chopping wood in the forest with his brothers. The fact that the Prophet did not hold himself above common labor but instead was willing to work with his hands alongside his fellows endeared him to the new convert. Joseph invited Brigham to join him and other Church leaders for dinner, and they spent the evening conversing about religious matters. Thus began a friendship between the two men that would endure through all the troubles that followed. Brigham developed an unswerving loyalty to Joseph that went unshaken even when the Prophet made mistakes and proved himself as imperfect as other men. "He was called of God; God dictated him, and if He had a mind to . . . let him commit an error, that was no business of mine," Brigham later explained. "It was not my prerogative to call him in question with regard to any act of his life. He was God's servant, and not mine."[21]

That belief led Brigham to stand against anyone who denounced the Prophet, including dissidents and apostates. On one occasion, a group of disaffected Saints declared in a public meeting that Joseph should be deposed as President of the Church and another man installed in his place. Brigham opposed that proposal almost to the point of fisticuffs.

> I rose up, and in a plain and forcible manner told them that Joseph was a Prophet, and I knew it, and that they might rail and slander him as much as they pleased, they could not destroy the appointment of the Prophet of God, they could only destroy their own authority, cut the thread that bound them to the Prophet and to God and sink themselves to hell. Many were highly enraged at my decided opposition to their measures, and Jacob Bump (an old pugilist) was so exasperated that he could not be still. Some of the brethren near him put their hands on him, and requested him to be quiet; but he writhed and twisted his arms and body saying,

"How can I keep my hands off that man?" I told him if he thought it would give him any relief he might lay them on.[22]

Nor was Brigham's readiness to defend his friend restricted to Church meetings. During the years in Kirtland, another Latter-day Saint named Hawley came to town and declared that God had rejected Joseph as a prophet.[23] Not content to lambast just the Prophet, he "went through the streets of Kirtland one morning, after midnight and cried 'Woe! Woe! Unto the inhabitants of this place.'" Brigham set out to confront the man.

> I put my pants and shoes on, took my cowhide, went out, and laying hold of him, jerked him round, and assured him that if he did not stop his noise and let the people enjoy their sleep without interruption, I would cowhide him on the spot, for we have the Lord's Prophet right here, and we did not want the devil's prophet yelling round the streets. The nuisance was forthwith abated.[24]

Brigham was not in Nauvoo when the mob murdered Joseph at nearby Carthage. He was in Boston and didn't hear of the event until three weeks later; but he recounted that at the hour the mob was storming the jail, "I felt a heavy depression of spirit, and so melancholy I could not converse with any degree of pleasure."[25] He dismissed the accounts he read in the newspapers, not trusting the press to accurately report anything with regards to Joseph. It was only when he received letters from other Saints in Nauvoo that he accepted the reality of his friend's death.

———— • • • ————

In mourning, the Saints continued building the temple. That must have come as an unwelcome surprise to their enemies, who hoped Joseph's death would have dissolved the Church. But once again, Brigham recalled, it was "by the aid of sword in one hand, and trowel and hammer in the other, with firearms at hand, and a strong band of police, and the blessings of heaven, the Saints, through hunger, and thirst, and weariness, and watchings, and prayings so far completed the Temple, despite the devices of the mob."[26] They finished the house of the Lord on May 1, 1846, almost two years after the Prophet's assassination in Carthage Jail.

When their enemies realized that the majority of the Saints weren't going to disperse, but had united under Brigham's leadership as the senior Apostle in the Quorum of the Twelve, the threat of violence rose again and, just as in Missouri less than a decade before, the government itself moved against them. The Illinois state legislature revoked Nauvoo's charter in December. All city assets were placed in receivership, the courts disempowered, and, worst of all, the Nauvoo Legion disarmed and dissolved. With no military force to protect the city and outlying farms and settlements from vigilante raids, Brigham knew that the Saints could not stay in Nauvoo.

He counseled with the Twelve and many other men, including the Council of Fifty, as to possible sites where the Saints could go to build a settlement. Texas and California were both considered, as was the Pacific Northwest. But Brigham needed to know the mind and will of the Lord on the matter. He took the question to the Lord in fasting and prayer, and he was not disappointed. His answer came in a vision of his dear friend now dead, the Prophet Joseph. Joseph showed Brigham a flag on a hill and said, "Build under the point where the colors fall and you will prosper and have peace."[27]

Their destination would be the Great Salt Lake, which was technically part of the Mexican territory Alta ("Upper") California. He told the Saints to prepare to abandon Nauvoo, but they needed time, and their enemies were impatient. He managed to negotiate a deadline of May 1846 for the Saints' evacuation, but violence again arose in areas outlying the city, and by the start of 1846, the situation had again become intolerable. Despite a lack of supplies, many of the Saints began to flee the city in February and head west across Iowa. The exodus accelerated when temperatures plunged below zero, freezing the Mississippi River solid and allowing those with wagons to drive across and those without to walk instead of waiting for ferries to shuttle them to Montrose, Iowa.

Thomas L. Kane, a lawyer and abolitionist who was a friend to the Saints, described their departure years later in a speech he presented in Philadelphia. "The people of Iowa have told me," he said, "that from morning to night they passed westward like an endless procession. They did not seem greatly out of heart, they said; but, at the top of every hill before they disappeared, were to be seen looking back, like banished Moors, on their abandoned homes, and the far-seen Temple and its glittering spire."[28] The final landmark that the Nauvoo emigrants saw as they crossed was their temple, sitting on the highest point of the city, rising above the river, another house of the Lord abandoned to their enemies.

———•·•———

Most of the Saints were poorly prepared for a journey to the nation's western frontier and beyond. Their non-Mormon neighbors knew that they were evacuating Nauvoo, so rather than pay a fair market price for land, homes, or anything else, all they had to do was wait and they could acquire everything for pennies on the dollar, if not for free—what the Saints couldn't sell or load in their wagons simply got left behind. Then heavy rains during the spring and summer had flooded Iowa's rivers and plains, turning the state into a swampy morass that took the poorly equipped Saints months to cross. By the time they reached the Missouri River, Brigham had decided it better to settle there until his people could gather and organize themselves and acquire the resources they would need for the rest of the journey. So they established a settlement they called Winter Quarters just across the Iowa border, where more than seven thousand Saints endured the Nebraska snowstorms in covered wagons, log cabins, mud hovels, and even some nearby caves.

Despite the US government's refusal to deliver any redress for their property losses of the previous years, Brigham had petitioned for government aid to support the exodus. With the assistance of their friend

Thomas Kane, a deal was eventually struck with President James K. Polk—the Saints could receive aid if they would enlist "a few hundred men" in the army to help fight the war with Mexico that Congress had declared the previous May. It was not a purely altruistic arrangement. Polk recorded in his diary that "Col. [Stephen W.] Kearny was . . . authorized to receive into service as volunteers a few hundred of the Mormons who are now on their way to California, with a view to conciliate them, attach them to our country, and prevent them from taking part against us."[29] The Saints would get money, blankets, guns, and other supplies useful for pioneers heading west; the United States would be reassured that the Latter-day Saints—whom the US government had thoroughly alienated by a decade of inaction—wouldn't help the Mexican army.

Most of the Saints were skeptical of the offer, but Brigham saw an opportunity and agreed. Still, he wasn't one to let the president think that the Latter-day Saints' loyalty could be easily bought with a few supplies. In his letter to Polk accepting the bargain, Brigham let the president know that the Saints' view of the government remained decidedly unfavorable.

> We would esteem a territorial government of our own as one of the richest boons of earth, and while we appreciate the Constitution of the United States as the most precious among the nations, we feel that we had rather retreat to the deserts, islands or mountain caves than consent to be ruled by governors and judges whose hands are drenched in the blood of innocence and virtue, who delight in injustice and oppression.[30]

Still, the deal was struck. Each member of the battalion was paid $42 in advance, all of which they gave to the Church for use in buying supplies. The unit marched nineteen hundred miles to Los Angeles, arriving on July 16, 1847, just a week before Brigham's wagon company reached the Salt Lake Valley. The men never fought a single engagement against the Mexicans, though twenty died from exposure or injury. Eighty men reenlisted for another six months of military service, bringing the total of salaries earned to $30,000, most of which they gave to the Church.

The late fall of 1846 and the winter of 1847 were hard, even by Iowa standards—the temperature on January 18 dropped to twenty degrees below zero[31]—and Brigham felt the strain of having to lead so many people with so few resources. By January, he had lost so much weight from the stress that his clothes no longer fit his otherwise stocky frame. Determined to start west as soon as possible, he hoped the advance companies could be ready to leave by the middle of March, but the snow was still falling, the rivers had not thawed, and needed supplies remained short, and so his own group did not leave until April 9. He made it less than twenty miles, camping at the Elk Horn River, before he was called back to address Church business. It was not until April 14 that Brigham finally left Winter Quarters for the Great Salt Lake Valley.[32]

Though Brigham had finally reached the valley, another two days passed before he could muster the strength to start walking around. He wanted to begin exploring this new home where he hoped the Saints would find solitude and protection from their enemies. He told Wilford Woodruff and the others, "If the people of the United States will let us alone for ten years, we will ask no odds of them."[33] But they would not make it ten months if they could not grow enough food to feed both the Saints already here and the ones yet to arrive before the end of the year. The advance company had set up camp two days before, a short distance from what is now Temple Square, and started getting crops planted. The topsoil, if it could be called that, was hard to plow, and the men built a dam on the later-named City Creek to flood the ground so they could soften it up. By the afternoon of July 24, they had six acres of potatoes and vegetables in the ground.[34] A thunderstorm "that reached nearly over the whole valley" broke out later that evening, watering people, animals, and the fledgling crops, and perhaps giving the leader of the Saints a wanted omen that they wouldn't all starve to death in the coming months. [35]

They rested on the twenty-fifth—a Sunday—doing no work beyond cooking some rations, thereby giving Brigham another day to recuperate. The pioneers convened Sabbath services twice that day. Apostles George A. Smith, Heber C. Kimball, and Ezra T. Benson preached in the morning; Wilford Woodruff, Orson Pratt, and Willard Richards took those duties in the afternoon. Standing first, Elder Smith apparently used the book of Isaiah, chapter two, verse two as his text.

> And it shall come to pass in the last days, that the mountain of the Lord's house shall be established in the top of the mountains, and shall be exalted above the hills; and all nations shall flow unto it.

"The mountain of the Lord's house" was a temple, he explained to the congregation, and here they would build it in the Rockies, in a city that would sit at one of the highest elevations on the continent—the "top of the mountains" indeed.[36]

On the twenty-sixth, Brigham resumed his exploration of the area. He took with him Heber C. Kimball, Willard Richards, Orson Pratt, George A. Smith, Amasa Lyman, Ezra T. Benson, Thomas Bullock, and Wilford Woodruff, his erstwhile ambulance driver. They walked "north of the camp about five miles and climbed to a hilltop—the very place, as it turned out, that Brigham had seen in vision back in Nauvoo. This, they saw, was "a proper place to raise an ensign to the nations."[37] From the vantage point of Ensign Peak, they surveyed the valley with a telescope. They were now "in a new holy land, with its . . . Dead Sea, its River Jordan, Mount of Olives, and Galilee Lake."[38] They had their own Jerusalem to build.

They descended from the hilltop and eventually returned to the camp. Later that day, about five in the evening, Brigham was walking with Wilford, going around the grounds near the camp, when they reached a point between the two primary creeks that ran through the area. There, Brigham stopped. The senior Apostle raised his cane and stamped it into the dry, hard dirt of the valley floor.

"Here," he said, "will be the temple of our God."[39]

SHALL WE NOT BUILD THE LORD A HOUSE?

For three years, since Joseph Smith's death, Brigham and the Quorum of the Twelve had been concerned with the safety of the Saints, the planning and logistics of the trip to the valley, the daily grind of the journey. Now they were safe from the mobs and indifferent or hostile governors and militias. The only immediate threats were native tribes, wild animals, and foul weather—minor troubles compared to the dangers they'd come through. They could finally start building a permanent home. They did not even have a settlement yet, just wagons, a few shelters, and some seeds in the ground. But they believed a city would rise here, filled with Saints living in peace. And no matter how far the city grew in any direction, toward the mountains or the Great Salt Lake or any other point they could see, the temple would be at the spiritual and literal center of it. Wilford recalled decades later that, determined not to lose that precise spot of Brigham's emphatic proclamation, he had scrounged up a nearby stick and used a rock to hammer it down into the divot where the senior Apostle had planted his cane.[1]

Brigham and Wilford returned to the proposed temple site two days later, on the twenty-eighth, around three o'clock in the afternoon. The rest of the Apostles joined them around five, and all agreed, in a fit of exhilaration, that this central "temple block" should cover forty acres. (They would eventually reconsider and reduce that number to a more manageable ten.) At eight that evening, they assembled the other priesthood brethren in the camp and called for a sustaining vote on whether to remain in the valley or look for another location, perhaps one that might offer better conditions for farms and settlements. They voted to stay.

With that decision made and sustained, Brigham, Wilford, and the other Apostles returned to the long list of more immediate matters demanding their attention. It was fortunate that they had considerable experience building cities. The Prophet Joseph himself had drawn up a "plat for Zion" in 1833, a design for a city unit one mile square divided into forty-nine square lots laid out on a perfect grid. The three central lots were reserved for temples, storehouses, offices, and any other facilities the Church required. When one plat was fully occupied, they could lay out another adjacent to it, repeating the process as necessary during the city's growth so that it would remain neat and organized. Nauvoo had risen from a swamp in just a few years using Joseph's plan.[2] They would use a version of that proven system here. The city, they decided, would have ten-acre blocks laid out on a perfect grid that lined up in the four cardinal directions, each with lots measuring ten rods by twenty, covering an acre and a quarter of land. Brigham wanted only one house on each lot, built in the center so that "if they took fire they would not burn up their neighbors."[3]

Building a temple here would require the support and resources of an entire community of thousands of Saints, and the Great Salt Lake Valley was not just going to give them what they needed to survive. Making this valley into home would take all of their labor and leave them none to spare for building another house of the Lord for some years.

Brigham's first great worry was food. His company had started planting crops, but it was already late July in a region where visitors had seen winter come early and snow could fall by the foot. It was very possible that they had simply arrived too late to get enough fields sown and harvested to guarantee full stomachs through the spring for themselves and those Saints still coming that year. Even if the weather cooperated, it would take constant labor to reach that quota, so they worked in shifts, breaking ground in plot after plot. By the end of July, after one week of hard labor (the Sabbath excepted), they had "thirty-five acres planted in corn, oats, buckwheat, potatoes, beans, and garden seed."[4] Soon it was eighty acres.[5] They would keep the plows tilling the ground for weeks, and when the season finally turned too cold to plant fair-weather crops, they planted winter wheat—875 acres of it—so they could harvest grain in the early spring before they started again with corn, potatoes, and the rest.[6]

Brigham's other immediate problem was ensuring that his people had protection from the weather and possibly the natives. Wagons served as homes just fine on the trail, but Rocky Mountain winters and potentially hostile neighbors called for more than a canvas tarp as a roof and walls. Brigham's advance party had not suffered any raids by native warriors on the journey from Winter Quarters, which was fortunate. But the Utes, who lived to the south, had now started approaching the Saints' camp, looking to satisfy curiosity and trade goods. There were also Shoshone tribes to the north. The early meetings with the Utes had been peaceful, and perhaps the local tribes would prove to be kind neighbors, but the Saints planned on building their cabins together and surrounding them with a wall for protection in case the natives decided not to be friends.

Then, once the first winter was past, they would start building up the city in earnest, and that would require buildings other than cabins. They would need stables, barns, offices, shops, and schoolhouses, hundreds upon hundreds, as quickly as they could build them. That would require mills to process lumber and blacksmith shops to manufacture nails, saws, and carpentry tools of every kind. They would need coal pits to stoke the forges, brickyards, cooper shops, and supply stores; granaries to store their wheat; grain mills to grind it into flour; and bakeries to turn it into bread. All of those structures required bricks and wood, as quickly as they could make the former and harvest the latter. In the case of lumber, that was going to be problematic. The valley floor wasn't just hard and dry—it was also largely devoid of trees. In every direction out from the encampment, there was "nothing to vary the scenery but rugged mountains, the sage bush, and the sunflower."[7]

Brigham had seen plenty of trees in the canyons while riding in. He sent out exploring parties, and they quickly confirmed that the eastern canyons had "an abundance of good timber, principally pine, balsam fir and a little cottonwood," but "access to the same [would be] very difficult."[8] They would have to haul their fallen trees some six miles back to the valley in wagons pulled by ox or horse teams.[9] "It is an uphill business to go into these canyons and get wood, to say the least," Brigham described the task with considerable understatement.[10] He directed that there be a "company appointed to make a road into the canyon, to facilitate the procuring of timber."[11] Teams were assembled and sent up into the spaces between the mountains, and "lumber was made in the canyons, or from logs drawn thence, with whip-saw, through the entire winter," cold and snow notwithstanding.[12] The logging operation was also a danger to life and limb at times—Elder George A. Smith was struck in the head by a heavy log that he and Wilford were unloading from a wagon. "It was a great mercy he was not killed," Brigham recorded.[13] Smith apparently shrugged it off, but there would be many more injuries to come.[14] Building a city was not without its hazards.

It didn't take long to figure out that they wouldn't be able to retrieve trees in sufficient quantities for everyone to have a log cabin before the weather turned cold. The only alternative was to start making bricks, so Brigham gave the word to "commence building our houses for those who were to tarry through the winter of dobies [adobe bricks] instead of timber."[15] They promptly set up an "adobe yard" to manufacture crude blocks for building shelters, but figuring out the formula for making a sound brick took some experimentation. The clay used contained some type of alkali that reacted in the presence of water, causing the first bricks they produced to swell and crack—or even "explode"—when the rains fell.[16] They had to make several test batches to find a usable formula, but by August 5 the yard was producing bricks that held together in a storm.[17] Of the 1,671 Saints who reached the valley that year, many of them would spend their first months living in those rough adobe shelters.

— • • —

The first death in the valley was not one of the men hauling wood, hunting food, exploring the ravines and passes, or trading with natives. On August 11, at about five o'clock in the afternoon, three-year-old Milton Therlkill was found floating lifeless in Irrigation Pond, behind the City Creek Dam. The loss of their child apparently was more than the family could bear. "The grief of both of the parents was great but that of the agonized mother baffles all description," one bystander wrote. "She laughed, wept, walked to and fro, alternately refusing all attempts at consolation from her friends, being, apparently unable to become resigned to her domestic and melancholy bereavement."[18] The Saints were not strangers to the deaths of children. Joseph Smith himself had lost five, four being stillborn or passing away shortly after birth. Brigham would lose thirteen during his lifetime.

The boy was laid to rest the next day in a lot near the adobe yard, with Orson Pratt conducting the funeral.[19] A few days later, with young Milton's death still on his mind, Brigham himself addressed the Saints and offered a consoling message about the priesthood and the doctrine of eternal families. He delivered his message while standing under a brush bowery, the first structure of any kind erected on what the Saints would later call the "temple block."[20]

"As soon as we get up some adobe houses for our families," Brigham assured the first settlers, "we shall go to work to build another . . . "[21]

Brigham was being overly optimistic, but he had reason to feel cheerful. By late August, the first rough wood cabins and adobe homes were up, and the adobe yard and logging operations were producing enough building materials to ensure the Saints would have enough shelters to stay warm, if not especially comfortable, until the spring. More than a hundred acres of crops were under cultivation, and City Creek provided fresh water for drinking, bathing, and irrigation. They'd made enough progress that Brigham felt he could return east to help his own family make their journey. He had already counseled others who'd left for that reason to "not give way to a hurrying spirit, not letting your spirits run away to Winter Quarters before your bodies can arrive there"; but he too needed to hurry. [22] The soonest he could hope to cover the distance back to Iowa was two months. If he tarried much longer, he risked getting caught out in some early snowstorm on the Midwestern plains.

He still needed to address a few items of business before he could leave. On Sunday, August 22, at about 2:00 p.m., the Saints in the valley gathered at the bowery on the temple block. "It was a pleasant day," one of the attendees wrote, "though thunder could be heard in the distance . . . and it probably rained considerably in the mountains."[23] With a storm pending, Brigham stood and presented the issues at hand. Someone needed to take charge while he was gone—and he would be gone for a year—so he moved that John Smith, uncle to Joseph and Hyrum, be appointed in Brigham's absence to oversee the growth of the settlement. Then Brigham made a second proposal, approval of which would echo on to the present: he moved that "we call this place the Great Salt Lake City of the Great Basin, North America." Both votes were unanimous.[24]

The truth was that they had no official authority to name the city— every one of the Saints there was, literally, an illegal immigrant. As far as the governments of the earth were concerned, the valley, the mountains, everything they had seen and surveyed was *Mexican* land. (Those same governments could not have cared less that native tribes had been living in the region for centuries and also called it home.) Still, Brigham probably was not terribly worried about that particular legality. Even if Mexico's ruler, General Antonio López de Santa Anna, objected to the Saints' presence (assuming he even knew they were there), he wasn't in a position to do anything about it. He'd been waging war with the United States for more than a year, and the conflict was not going in his favor. US troops, including the Mormon Battalion, had occupied the Mexican provinces of Alta California and Nuevo México with only minor opposition. Now, US soldiers led by General Zachary Taylor had invaded Mexico both overland, crossing the Rio Grande river to the north, and by sea, having landed men under the command of General Winfield Scott on the eastern coast near Matamoros and Vera Cruz. Santa Anna was fighting and retreating toward Mexico City on two fronts. The war would surely end soon, and many US leaders were calling for the annexation of the occupied territories, if not all of Mexico. The generally accepted prediction of "Manifest Destiny"—the idea that the United States would inevitably expand its borders to the Pacific Coast—was fueling such talk. The only real questions were how that would occur and how soon it would be accomplished.

Brigham knew something about the progress of the war. The Mormon Battalion had reached San Diego in January of 1847, then spent time building Fort Moore in Los Angeles and performing occupation duties until the unit mustered out of the army just a few days before the first Saints entered the Salt Lake Valley. Many of the former soldiers had been coming to the valley in their own slow and weary trickle, and they almost certainly shared the news of the war they'd heard before leaving California. Brigham may have listened with polite interest to their tales and reports, but how interested he was in such current events is uncertain. He recorded no war gossip in his journal, even on days when he noted that members of the battalion had reached the settlement. "The Twelve met with the officers of the battalion and held a lengthy council," reads one entry. "All the brethren met at 8 p.m. when praise to God for the safe return of so many of the battalion . . ."[25] What the former soldiers said in the council is unknown. Instead, Brigham filled his short daily accounts with notes on the progress made building up their new homeland. He was certain that the Salt Lake Valley would be their land of inheritance and a temple would be built upon it, and that conviction did not stem from secondhand news, however accurate, that the US was winning the war with Mexico. His written entries reveal Brigham's certainty that the Lord had prepared and reserved the valley for His people, and so wars, diplomacy, and treaties between nations were of no consequence. The Lord had shown him this place in a vision before, so the Lord's people would settle here, no matter whether Mexico, the United States, or native tribes wanted it otherwise.

———— ◆ · · ◆ ————

Brigham, Wilford, Heber C. Kimball, and several others left for Winter Quarters on August 26, the following Thursday, around ten o'clock in the morning. Others had started out earlier, some as early as nine, and the prophet's group was among the last to leave that day.[26] They shouted a good-bye to the families that were going to tarry through the winter.[27] Then they made their way back up the trail along which they had first come a month before. They traveled fourteen or fifteen miles that first day and camped for the night by a spring.[28] The journey back took a little more than two months. The weather was mostly cooperative, but the native tribes along the route were not. A group of Sioux stole between forty and fifty horses and mules during the night of September 9, and another tribe stampeded their animals twelve days later as they prepared to depart their campsite at Big Timber Creek.[29] Brigham and his men tracked down the thieves, who returned all but two of the animals after "learning that we were whites and friendly."[30]

Brigham's fears about getting back to his family before winter set in were well founded. The first snowstorm of the season caught them on October 24, but it was not severe enough to delay their arrival at Winter Quarters a week later.[31] Brigham reported:

We drove into the town in order, about an hour before sunset. The streets were crowded with people to shake hands as we passed through the lines; we were truly rejoiced to once more behold our wives, children, and friends after an absence of over six months, having traveled over 2,000 miles, sought out a location for the Saints to dwell in peace, and accomplished the most interesting mission in this last dispensation.[32]

Referring to the members of his current pioneer company, Brigham reported, "Not a soul of our camp died, and no serious accident happened to any, for which we praise the Lord."[33]

◆ · · ◆

Miles behind Brigham, a serious obstacle to the temple's construction was developing in the form of William Weeks, Church architect. Weeks was a Massachusetts man, born in 1813 to a Quaker family living in Martha's Vineyard, and he learned architecture from his father. They moved to Chicago in 1835, and Weeks joined the Church sometime soon thereafter (the exact date is unknown). But he was in Missouri for the persecutions there, and he ended up in Illinois with the main body of the Saints after their expulsion, courtesy of Governor Boggs's extermination order.

When the Prophet Joseph announced in Nauvoo that the Lord had commanded them to again build a temple, he invited any men with architectural skill to offer designs for the planned structure. Weeks submitted a proposal, and Joseph was so taken with it that he bear-hugged the architect and exclaimed, "You are the man I want." Together, they worked out the final plans, with Joseph describing the building and the features that he had seen in vision and Weeks turning the descriptions into professional blueprints. At times they clashed over details. At one point, Joseph insisted on circular windows, but Weeks tried to dissuade him on the grounds that "round windows in the broad side of a building were a violation of all the known rules of architecture and [he] contended that they should be semicircular—that the building was too low for round windows." Joseph cared nothing for the "known rules of architecture." "I have seen in vision the splendid appearance of that building illuminated," he told Weeks, "and will have it built according to the pattern shown me."[34]

After Joseph's death, Weeks followed Brigham and the Twelve, but his relationship with the senior Apostle apparently was rougher than the one he'd enjoyed with Joseph. Still, Brigham wanted the young architect to go to the valley that first year to assist in making plans for another temple as soon as possible. "Just as soon as I find the spot I want Bro[ther] Weeks to dig deep and lay the foundation of the temple for I intend by the help of my brethren to build a temple unto the Lord just as soon as the Saints by a united exertion can complete it," Brigham explained.[35] Weeks arrived in the valley on October 2, more than a month after Brigham had started out on his return trip—and it was at that point that William Weeks rebelled.

Why he was disaffected is unknown, but he seems to have been unhappy with the strict rules Brigham had established for the crossing. Whatever his reasons, on October 6, the architect and three others took their families north and set up their own camp without getting approval from "Uncle John" Smith, the man Brigham had left in charge. Smith tried to persuade them to come back to the safety of the main settlement, which the disgruntled group agreed to do, but only after "all of them had made use of harsh remarks, [that they] 'did not like so much bondage, etc.'" And despite their promise to rejoin the settlement, Uncle John had to send a second party out to retrieve them ten days later. Weeks and his companions wintered with the Saints, but their bitterness was still undiluted when spring came. They left the valley for the East as soon as the weather permitted.[36] Weeks refused all entreaties to rejoin the Saints, and he declared that they could never build the new temple without him. Brigham disagreed, assuring the people that "we can build a temple without his assistance although he [Weeks] says we cannot."[37]

Weeks and his wife, Caroline, left for Wisconsin, taking all the architectural drawings and blueprints for the Nauvoo Temple with them. Brigham felt that Weeks had left him and the Twelve no alternative, and they excommunicated the Weeks family in October 1848, leaving the Church without an architect. They had a few years yet before they would be able to start building a temple anyway, so the vacancy was not immediately critical for that project. But Brigham eventually would need to find some competent man to fill the post before they could begin.[38]

＊＊＊

Leading a mass migration away from a settlement, even one as crudely built as Winter Quarters, was no easier than building a new city from scratch. But now Brigham had made the journey to the valley once and understood the precise obstacles that any company would face during the crossing. He also had developed considerable skills as an organizer during the Zion's Camp march of 1834; serving with the Apostles on a two-year mission to Great Britain, from 1839 to 1841; gathering the Saints to Illinois while Joseph was in Liberty Jail; and leading their people to Winter Quarters after Joseph's death. If there was anyone in all of the United States prepared to lead an exodus of this magnitude, it was Brigham Young.

His first priority was simply to bring together as many Saints as possible to Winter Quarters before the spring. They were spread across the whole of North America, from California to New York, with a substantial number in Canada. Others lived in Australia and on islands of the Pacific, and large numbers were in Great Britain and the other countries of Europe. Many, if not most, were poor, and the costs of acquiring passage and supplies for such a trip would be serious obstacles. But Brigham had faith that the Lord would make the emigration possible, no matter how far the Saints had to come or how meager their means. "Let all the Saints in the United States and Canada gather to the same place [Winter Quarters] by the first spring navigation," he urged in his first epistle to the Church as its prophet and president. "To the Saints in England, Scotland, Ireland, Wales, and adjacent islands and countries, we say, emigrate as speedily as possible to this vicinity . . . and to all Saints in any country bordering upon the Atlantic, we would say, pursue the same course; come immediately and prepare to go West."[39] Those who could were asked to bring additional supplies that would be useful to everyone developing their new valley home. Brigham exhorted them to carry

> all kinds of choice seeds, of grain, vegetables, fruits, shrubbery, trees, and vines . . . also, the best stock of beasts, bird, and fowl of every kind; also, the best tools of every description, and machinery for spinning, or weaving, and dressing cotton, wool, flax, and silk, . . . and the same in relation to all kinds of farming utensils and husbandry, such as corn shellers, grain threshers and cleaners. . . . So far as it can be consistently done, bring models and drafts, and let the machinery be built where it is used, which will save great expense in transportation, particularly in heavy machinery, and tools and implements generally.

The valley's isolation ensured that anything the Saints lacked in the early years would have to be grown, scrounged, or crafted from whatever materials they could find. Tools and labor-saving machinery of every kind would be both needed and scarce, so anything the emigrants could bring early on would be a great blessing.[40]

But Brigham wanted them to bring more than just the tools of their trades. He asked them to also bring tools for the *mind*.

> It is very desirable that all the Saints should [secure] at least a copy of every valuable treatise on education—every book, map, chart, or diagram that may contain interesting, useful, and attractive matter, . . . and also every historical, mathematical, philosophical, geographical, geological, astronomical, scientific, practical, and all other variety of useful and interesting writings, maps, &c., . . .
>
> We have a printing press, and any who can take good printing or writing paper to the valley will be blessing themselves and the Church. We also want all kinds of mathematical and philosophical

instruments, together with all rare specimens of natural curiosities and works of art that can be gathered and brought to the valley, where, and from which, the rising generation can receive instruction.[41]

The Saints in the valley were living in cabins and adobe huts, and already Brigham was thinking about schoolhouses, universities, and museums. Other settlers not driven by religious zeal might have found his request for books and scientific instruments to be premature when the Saints still lacked comfortable homes or a steady supply of food. As another of the Church's leaders recalled some thirty years later:

> One would suppose that it would have been a long time before the subject of education would have received any attention from a community situated as the pioneers of the valley were for many years after their arrival here. But such was not the case. Stripped and bare; scattered and peeled; forced to flee in to the heart of a dreary desert, more than a thousand miles from the borders of civilization, and more than that distance from the nearest mart where a school book could be purchased, to their eternal credit it is recorded that they did not, for a moment, forget the subject of the education of their youth.[42]

Although building schoolhouses and other institutions of education so early on would add "to their toil and poverty, they dreaded ignorance and its effects more than these, and did all in their power to dissipate it from their midst."[43]

Like so many of his other decisions related to the exodus, Brigham's call for educational books, maps, and tools was grounded in gospel doctrine. The Lord had once commanded the Saints, "Seek ye diligently, and teach one another words of wisdom; yea, seek ye out of the best books words of wisdom; seek learning, even by study and also by faith."[44] Joseph had repeated those words in the dedicatory prayer of the Kirtland Temple, asking the Lord to grant that "all those who shall worship in this house" could receive such instruction.[45] So a temple was not just a house of worship—it was a place of *education*. The Lord had revealed that "the glory of God is intelligence, or in other words, light and truth."[46] But "intelligence" wasn't just knowing a long list of all the facts in the universe; it was a perfect understanding of truth versus error, and experience gained by applying that knowledge and understanding to life's challenges. God wasn't "the greatest of all" simply because He *knew* more than any other being; rather, it was because His matchless knowledge and power were governed by the "excellency of the character of God."[47] His "character, perfections and attributes" were pure and impeccable beyond human understanding.[48] No disciple, no matter how devoted, could develop a perfect character on par with the Master's in this life, no matter how hard he tried. But a devoted disciple could become *ever more like* the Master, if just a little at a time. One first had to acquire knowledge through study; then sift out the truth from error through revelation from the Lord; and then finally acquire intelligence—develop one's own character and righteous attributes through experience by applying that learning in righteous ways. It was a doctrine that transformed academic study into a spiritual activity that reaped eternal rewards. "Whatever principle of intelligence we attain unto in this life, it will rise with us in the resurrection," Joseph had explained.[49] Knowledge and personal character, whether good or evil, were two things that carried over into the next life. So the Saints wanted their city to be more than just a place of physical refuge or of commercial industry. It needed also to be a place of high learning, with schools and a university for secular studies and the temple for receiving revelation and instruction from heaven. Neither form of education would be complete without the other in Zion.

It was this doctrine that led to Brigham's final request in the epistle, a plea for the Saints to bring materials to the valley for the temple.

> Let all Saints who love God more than their own dear selves—and none else are Saints—gather without delay to the place appointed, bringing their gold, their silver, their copper, their zinc, their tin, and brass, and iron, and choice steel, and ivory, and

precious stones; their curiosities of science, of art, of nature, and every thing in their possession or within their reach, to build in strength and stability, to beautify, to adorn, to embellish, to delight, and to cast a fragrance *over the House of the Lord;* . . . whether it be in precious jewels, or minerals, or choice ores, . . . manifested in carved work; or curious workmanship of the box, the fir and pine tree, or any thing that ever was, or is, or is to be, *for the exaltation, glory, honor, and salvation of the living and the dead, for time and for all eternity.* (Italics added.)[50]

Brigham had seen the valley for himself, and he knew there were materials there to build the walls of a temple; the Saints could make bricks and quarry stone from the mountains for that. But was there material to decorate a temple inside? Shouldn't a temple have as fine or better an interior as any mansion on earth? That meant the finest metals, woods, fabrics, and stonework. Perhaps search parties might find gold, silver, copper, and other metals and materials in the canyons suitable for that purpose, but whatever could not be found there would have to be brought in overland. Whatever the Saints could bring themselves would contribute to making the house of the Lord a fitting residence for the Savior, who they hoped would visit His people.

———————

Brigham and the Twelve also addressed another task that December, one that had been long delayed. Joseph Smith had been killed more than three years before, and the First Presidency had dissolved upon his death. Now Brigham felt it was finally time to reorganize the presidency so that the Twelve could devote their full time and energies to their unique roles as "special witnesses of the name of Christ in all the world."[51] He summoned all of the Apostles present at Winter Quarters to meet in Orson Hyde's cabin on Sunday, December 5, where they unanimously sustained Brigham as the second President of the Church. He chose Heber C. Kimball and Willard Richards to be his counselors, and the Twelve voted to sustain them as well.[52] A few weeks later, Brigham convened a general conference of the Church at Miller's Hollow.[53] More than a thousand Saints met in a new log tabernacle that offered only twenty-four hundred square feet for the congregation. (The close quarters probably helped keep the building warm in the frosty Iowa air.) On December 27, in the afternoon, Elder Orson Pratt stood and delivered a discourse on the mission of the Twelve. "If there is no First Presidency, it confines the Twelve too much to one place," he explained. "They cannot have their eyes on the distant parts of the earth." Amasa Lyman agreed, adding that the Twelve needed to not be "cooped up in Salt Lake City," dealing with administrative matters.[54] He was perfectly happy, it seemed, to have Brigham be the one "cooped up" in the valley to manage Church business.

When the speakers were finished, Brigham's call as prophet and President of the Church, with Heber C. Kimball and Willard Richards as his counselors, was laid before the Saints assembled in the building. The sustaining vote was unanimous, and the Church again had a prophet at its head.

— • · • —

The Latter-day Saints were fortunate that the winter of 1848 was not a hard one in the Salt Lake Valley. The season was mild, with only occasional light falls of snow, not enough to interfere with plowing and sowing of winter wheat. By the spring they had 5,133 acres of land tilled, with 872 sown with winter wheat.[55] Even so, they still did not have food in the abundance they needed. Families had to ration their flour, and wild sego and parsnip roots scrounged from the valley floor became frequent additions in their meals, later joined by thistle tops.[56] It was no king's feast, but no one starved to death. Wool for clothing was scarce, and moccasins were adopted as shoes wore out.[57] One sawmill was up and running, with three more in various stages of construction, and harvesting and processing of wood continued throughout the season.[58] The fort covered ten acres and was sufficient to keep the natives outside, but not mice, which invaded the compound in whole colonies.[59] Heavy spring rains penetrated the leaky roofs of cabins and adobe shelters, which had been built almost flat and so didn't shed water.

The following summer saw the invasion of crickets that threatened the new city's survival. The crickets were not new to the area. In fact, the Ute tribes harvested and stored them as a source of winter food.[60] But now it was the insects doing the eating. Hordes devoured every plant in their path, sparing nothing, and the Saints were facing a potential famine for a second winter in a row. Then came the seagulls in early June in numbers as countless as the crickets, gorging themselves, flying off and purging their stomachs, then returning for more.[61] Enough crops were spared to yield a good harvest that year. The Saints considered the seagulls' arrival to be an act of heavenly intervention.

A second reason to celebrate occurred that summer when the Treaty of Guadalupe Hidalgo went into effect. Santa Anna had indeed lost the war when the US Army, led by General Winfield Scott, seized Mexico City. The price for that failure would be steep. In a meeting with US negotiator Nicholas Trist at the old Basilica of Guadalupe at Villa Hidalgo (today within Mexico City's limits), three Mexican representatives signed the treaty on February 2. Among its several provisions, the treaty ceded California and all of the territory now forming the states of Utah, Nevada, New Mexico, and most of Arizona and Colorado. The agreement went into effect on July 4, 1849, and so, on Independence Day, the Saints were again living on US soil.

———— · · ————

Brigham returned to the valley in September, arriving on the twentieth. He moved his family into the cabins he had built before departing the year previous, and the remainder of the year for him and the other inhabitants of Great Salt Lake City was relatively uneventful. The next several years promised to be a repeating cycle of planting, building, and harvesting, with Great Salt Lake City expanding at a steady rate as Saints came west from Winter Quarters and east from California; but the planned temple would remain a distant hope. The day-to-day struggle to build Great Salt Lake City was still consuming most all of the people's energy. To undertake a full-scale building project to erect the house of the Lord that Brigham had seen in vision would have been an unsupportable strain on the people and the economy, but he did want to make some moves toward construction.

Those first real steps came on October 1, 1848. The Saints were holding Sunday services under the bowery at the temple site. Brigham was delivering the afternoon sermon when he announced that their "first efforts to build a temple would be expended in erecting a large wall around the Temple Block." The Saints supported that motion and another to construct a "Council House," their first public building, and they sustained Daniel H. Wells as the superintendent for the projects. They would have to build both the wall and the Council House with "tithing labor." The Church was in no position to pay anyone for their work.

⋅—⋅⋅—⋅

Those first tentative steps were interrupted by one piece of news that reached them soon after. The Nauvoo Temple had been in their enemies' hands since the mobs had driven the Saints from their former home. Now the word came that an arsonist had set fire to the building on October 9, 1848.

> About 3 o'clock (in the morning) fire was discovered in the cupola. It had made but little headway when first seen, but spread rapidly, and in a very short period the lofty spire was a mass of flame, shooting high in the air, and illuminating a wide extent of country. It was seen for miles away. The citizens gathered around, but nothing could be done to save the structure. It was entirely of wood except the walls, and nothing could have stopped the progress of the flames. In two hours, and before the sun dawned upon the earth, the proud structure, reared at so much cost—an anomaly in architecture, and a monument of religious zeal—stood with four blackened and smoking walls only remaining.[62]

Brigham considered that a better fate for the holy edifice than to see it polluted by the Church's enemies. "We were not permitted to enjoy that house, we were not permitted to continue receiving blessings there," he recalled. " . . . the enemies of God's kingdom were upon us, and we were compelled to abandon it and our homes, and it fell a sacrifice . . . and it was burned with fire—probably a better fate than to have it stand and be defiled by the wicked."[63]

Some years later, Apostles George A. Smith and Erastus Snow visited Nauvoo, inspected the temple's burnt-out ruin, and learned the details of its destruction from Lewis Bidamon, who had married Joseph's widow Emma. Bidamon explained that "the inhabitants of Warsaw, Carthage, Pontusuc and surrounding settlements in consequence of jealousy that Nauvoo would still retain its superior importance as a town and might induce the Mormons to return, contributed a purse of five hundred dollars which they gave to Joseph Agnew in consideration of his burning the temple; and that said Agnew was the person who set the building on fire."[64]

Any hopes that some few Saints might have entertained of ever reclaiming the Nauvoo Temple were crushed. Nor would they have a new temple for years—they did not even know when they would be able to start building one. It seemed that the Saints would just have to go without the blessings of a temple for a decade or longer.

Brigham had a ready, if temporary, solution to that problem. Joseph Smith had performed the first temple ordinances years before the Nauvoo Temple had been completed—he'd conducted them in the upper room of the Red Brick Store in Nauvoo.[65] Brigham had been in that first group and had seen that, when circumstances required, the Lord would allow His people to perform temple ordinances in other buildings and places until a temple was available. The Council House that the Saints were going to build could serve that dual purpose. The lower chambers would be devoted to secular purposes, housing the seat of government, the courts, a territorial library, and classrooms for the

University of Deseret. The upper rooms could be used for temple work. It would not be a dedicated house of the Lord, but it would suffice for a time until the Saints could do better. So, one month after the Nauvoo Temple was destroyed by fire, the Saints started to dig out a foundation for the Council House, their seat of government, house of learning, and temporary temple.

———•·•·•———

January of 1849 arrived, along with the news that gold had been discovered at Sutter's Mill in Northern California, which would spark the "gold rush," drawing tens of thousands of Americans west. It would be an economic boon for the Saints, as Great Salt Lake City became a critical way station for travelers heading to California. Weary travelers hoping to find wealth further west sold off tools and luxury items at bargain prices to the Saints to make room for other supplies.

With their economy growing and their homes free from the threat of mob violence, the Saints in the valley finally were enjoying a peace, solitude, and security that they had hardly ever known in all the years since the Church had first been organized. In a personal letter made public to the British Saints yet to cross the Atlantic, Elder Parley P. Pratt of the Quorum of the Twelve described life in the valley, telling his readers:

> All is quiet, stillness. No elections, no police reports, no murders, no war in our little world. . . . A meeting, a dance, a visit, an exploring tour, an arrival of a party of Trappers and Traders, a Mexican caravan, a party arrived from the Pacific, from the States; from Fort Hall, or Fort Bridger, a visit of Indians, or, perhaps, a mail from the distant world, once or twice a year, is all that break upon the monotony of our peaceful life. . . . Oh what a life we live! It is the dream of the poets actually fulfilled in real life. *Here* we can cultivate the mind, renew the spirits, invigorate the body, cheer the heart and enoble [sic] the soul of man.[66]

This was the peaceful existence that Joseph had always been hoping and praying the Saints might enjoy. But, as previously, their peace and solitude were short-lived.

In the months since the Treaty of Guadalupe Hidalgo had taken effect, Congress had taken no action to organize a territorial government over the lands acquired from Mexico, so the Saints took the initiative to establish it themselves. They convened a three-day convention beginning on March 8, 1849, and held an election four days after it ended to choose their political leadership. Brigham Young, of course, was elected governor. Willard Richards became secretary of state; Heber C. Kimball would be the chief judge, with Apostle John Taylor and Newel K. Whitney, Presiding Bishop of the Church, becoming associate justices.[67] The settlers also drafted a provisional constitution that would have looked familiar to any US citizen of the time. Modeled after the US Constitution, it began with the preamble, "We, the people, grateful to the Supreme Being for the blessings hitherto enjoyed, and feeling our dependence on Him for a continuation of those blessings, do ordain and establish a free and independent government, by the name of the state of Deseret."[68] They prepared a copy to submit to Congress and attached a lengthy petition—literally, for it was twenty-two feet long and contained 2,270 names—asking "that the state of Deseret be admitted into the Union on an equal footing with other states, or such other form of civil government as your wisdom and magnanimity may award to the people of Deseret."[69]

Congress did not cooperate. The national legislature was at loggerheads over slavery's expansion into the territory acquired from Mexico. Each new state would expand the US Senate by two seats, so Southern officials wanted every new free state to be balanced by a new slave state to prevent a pro-abolitionist majority from developing. Most of the Saints were either New Englanders or Midwestern northerners—both regions largely opposed to slavery—or from Great Britain, which had outlawed the whole institution in 1834. Deseret almost certainly would have entered as a free state. So, with California's admission as a free state practically a given, the Southern senators weren't about to allow another free state in before a slave state was admitted. Newly elected President Zachary Taylor gave his blessing to Congressional inaction on the Saints' petition, asserting that "no material inconvenience will result from the want, for a short period, of a government established by Congress, over that part of the Territory."[70]

In private, President Taylor was less neutral in his choice of words regarding the Saints' political hopes. He declared "before twenty members of Congress that he would veto any bill passed, state or territorial, for the Mormons, —that they were a pack of out-laws, and had been driven out of two States and were not fit for self-government," or so heard Almon W. Babbitt, one of the Saints' envoys to Washington. Babbitt went to the White House to confirm the report. "I went to [the president] in person . . . and charged these sayings upon him and he owned that he had so said; and tried to reason with me in relation 'to the absurdity of the Mormons asking for a State or Territorial government.'"[71] But Taylor died suddenly on July 9 of "cholera morbus" (an intestinal ailment), which some Saints might have found convenient, if not downright providential.

It was Senators Stephen A. Douglas of Illinois and Henry Clay of Kentucky who negotiated an end to the impasse. Douglas had met Joseph Smith during the Saints' time in Nauvoo and developed a friendly relationship with the Prophet. He had also publicly called for Joseph Smith's murderers to be found, arrested, and tried after the Prophet's death. Douglas apparently still had a good opinion of the Saints, and so he and Clay worked out the Compromise of 1850. Among other provisions, California would be admitted as a free state but New Mexico and Deseret would receive only territorial status. Douglas also decided that the Saints' territory should be named *Utah* after the Ute natives who had lived in the region long before the Saints arrived. The name change probably seemed a minor point to Douglas, but to the Saints, it was another example of the national government's disregard for them.

On September 9, 1850, Congress finally passed the compromise as a bill titled "An Act to establish a Territorial Government for Utah" and sent it to the new Chief Executive for his approval. President Millard Fillmore was more favorably disposed toward the Saints than his predecessor had been—he had coincidentally grown up in the Finger Lakes region of upstate New York, not far from Joseph Smith's home in Palmyra—and he signed the bill on the twentieth. It was not the statehood that they wanted, but the truth was that being designated a territory really was no slight. Many regions were given the same status as a kind of tutorial period during which they could learn how to govern themselves. Statehood would surely come in time.[72]

That done, Fillmore had to appoint officials to govern the new territory. John Bernhisel, the Saints' other envoy to Washington, urged the president to appoint men who were already settled in the area. "The people of Utah cannot but consider it their right, as American citizens to be governed by men of their own choice, entitled to their confidence, and united with them in opinion and feeling," he told Fillmore.[73] In plainer terms, he was asking the nation's leader to select only members of The Church of Jesus Christ of Latter-day Saints, who effectively constituted the entire population of the region. But Fillmore was fairly certain that the US Senate would not confirm a list of nominees composed entirely of Saints. In the end, he split the difference. Four appointees were Saints, including Brigham Young, who would be the first territorial governor and Superintendent of Indian Affairs; Seth M. Blair, nominated to be US attorney; Joseph L. Heywood for US marshal; and Zerubbabel Snow for associate justice of the territorial supreme court. But the territorial secretary, two Utah Supreme Court justices, and the "Indian agent" would be outsiders.

—————•·•—————

The Saints finally learned on October 15 that they would be a territory, not a state, much to their disappointment, if not disbelief. Nor were they pleased to learn that their territory would be called Utah, not

Deseret, and that President Fillmore had appointed several outsiders to government posts. But they had a sanctioned government and the governor they wanted, and that, it seemed, was enough for the moment. In gratitude, and perhaps in a small bid to curry some of the political goodwill in Washington that was always in short supply, they established the new territorial capital of "Fillmore" 150 miles south of Great Salt Lake City and named the county in which it was located "Millard."[74] The legislature of Deseret was dissolved and replaced by the new Utah territorial legislature, and Brigham Young was sworn in as the territorial governor on February 3, 1851.

————— • • —————

The Council House was nearly finished by then. The Saints, including Brigham himself, had been laboring steadily on it for more than a year, and it was complete by April of 1851 except for a few finishing touches. Brigham didn't consider that reason to hold back, and the first temple ordinances were performed at 11:00 a.m. on April 16. The "upper room," as they called the second story, could not accommodate large numbers, so priority was given to Saints who had been called on missions and would be absent for a few years. Brigham and the other leaders kept the upper room working throughout the summer, trying to accommodate as many as wanted to come. But this was all a temporary arrangement, acceptable only so long as they were pushing ahead to build a real temple. Exactly when that would begin, no one knew. The Saints were still dealing with the basics of building up a city in the wilderness, and, in that regard, the United States government was proving to be more of a hindrance than a help.

————— • • —————

Several of President Fillmore's appointed judges did not arrive until early August, and, despite receiving cordial welcomes that included dances, dinners, and gifts, hard feelings developed very quickly. The causes were apparently both secular and religious. On the secular side, every man seemed to have his own personal reasons; on the religious side, the key issue appears to have been the Saints' institution of plural marriage. It had been generally known for several years that Brigham and other Apostles had more than one wife, but they hadn't taught the doctrine openly. That was irrelevant to these newly arrived government servants, as Territorial Secretary Benjamin D. Harris's wife proved when she denounced the Saints as "hardly better than animals."[75]

In early September, Associate Judge Perry Brocchus approached Brigham on behalf of the group with an unusual request—he wanted to address the Saints during one of their religious meetings. When Brigham asked what the subject of the address would be, Brocchus, oddly and perhaps disingenuously, said that he did not know. Despite that suspect answer, Brigham agreed to the request, perhaps hoping that such a concession might be a first step toward healing the breach between the political officials and their religious constituents.[76]

The following Monday, September 8, 1851, the second day of a conference of the Church, Brocchus appeared in the bowery with Harris, Chief Justice Lemuel Brandenbury, and several other government officials. There were hymns and prayer, and then the prophet introduced Brocchus to the congregation. Brocchus offered thanks for the warm welcome the Saints had given him and those behind him. "He bore testimony of the peacefulness of the inhabitants, their fellowship, peace and love one towards another. . . . He expressed his indignation and abhorrence of the scenes which transpired, in driving the Latter-day Saints from Missouri and Illinois," the *Deseret News* later recounted.[77] The newspaper's report, in fact, terminates almost there, short and almost perfunctory, giving no indication that the speaker had delivered any offensive remarks. Perhaps the paper's editor had thought censoring out the rest of Brocchus's address was the better part of discretion. The journals of Saints present at the conference did the judge no such favor.

After his remarks of gratitude and "disapprobation" of the persecution the Saints had suffered, Brocchus denied that the US government had injured them in any way. The mobs' violence toward the Saints had all been "private wrongs," and "the President could not lay a private wrong before Congress. To those states [the Saints] should look for redress." The federal government was powerless to help them against such enemies, so the Saints' anger toward Washington was unfounded.[78] That rankled enough, but if Brocchus had closed his remarks there, the meeting likely would have ended quietly. Brocchus kept going, however. "Much was said by the speaker which was calculated to stir the blood of the people and offend them," Wilford Woodruff recorded, and there was no topic more calculated to "stir the blood" of this particular audience than plural marriage.[79] Brocchus denounced the doctrine and told the women in the audience that they needed to start "practicing virtue."

That was too much. Implying that the women of the Church were ladies of low morals was more than Brigham could let pass. Given his usual fighting spirit, his restraint in letting Brocchus finish was notable, but the prophet was on his feet as soon as the judge was done. He denounced Brocchus as "either profoundly ignorant or willfully wicked."[80] "I am indignant at such a corrupt fellow as Judge Brocchus coming here to lecture us on morality and virtue. . . . Ladies, and gentlemen, here we learn principles and good manners," and Brocchus had displayed neither so far as Brigham was concerned. "It is an insult to this congregation to throw out such insinuations," he declared.[81] Then Brigham stopped short. He had more to say to the judge, but he would say it in a more appropriate setting. As for the conference itself, which went on for two more days, Brigham later called it "one of the best I ever attended."[82]

It was the only one Brocchus ever attended. Within a week, rumors were flying that Brocchus, Brandenbury, and Harris were planning on leaving for the East. Having had some time for his temper to cool, Brigham tried making peace with the men. He sent Brocchus a letter on September 19 and, in a triumph of hope over experience, he invited the judge to address the Saints again.

> I propose and respectfully invite your honor to meet our public assembly at the Bowery on Sunday morning next at 10 a.m. and

address the same people from the stand that you addressed on the 8th inst.[ant] at our General conference. And if your honor shall then and there explain, satisfy or apologize to the satisfaction of the Ladies who heard your address on the 8th, so that those feelings of kindness which you so dearly prized in your address can be reciprocated by them, I shall esteem it a duty and a pleasure to make every apology and satisfaction for my observations which you as a gentleman can claim or desire at my hands.

As a further incentive to draw Brocchus to the meeting, Brigham added in a postscript that the judge could "be assured that no gentlemen will be permitted to make any reply to your address on that occasion."[83] The prophet would keep his seat this time.

Brocchus's reply was immediate. In a letter dated the same day as Brigham's invitation, Brocchus declared that his first speech had been "the result of deliberation and care," a direct contradiction to his original claim that he didn't even know what topic he would be discussing. Nonetheless, he said that "at the time of the delivery of my speech, I did not conceive that it contained anything deserving the censure of a just-minded person."[84] Brocchus had nothing to apologize for, in his opinion.

Brigham disagreed with that assessment, to put it mildly. "You . . . deliberately planned a speech to excite the indignation of your hearers to an extent that would cause them to break the bonds of propriety." In plainer terms, Brocchus had wanted to incite a verbal riot at least, perhaps a physical altercation at worst. Why did Brigham think so? Something that Brigham had heard, no doubt from Elder Albert Carrington, who had traveled with Brocchus to the valley: "It is reported on pretty good authority that [you] made [a declaration] . . . substantially as follows: 'If the citizens of Utah do not send me as their delegate to Washington, by God, I'll use all my influence against them and will crush them. I have the influence and power to do it, and I will accomplish it, if they do not make me their delegate.'" And the proof that Brocchus had made the claim was the provocative speech he'd delivered.

That alone "proved that you harbored these malicious feelings in your heart."[85] "I wonder not that you should excuse yourself from the attempt or 'decline appearing again in public on the subject,'" Brigham concluded.[86]

Brocchus didn't bother to answer. He and the others had already decided to leave their posts and the valley to return east. Territorial Secretary Benjamin Harris also announced that he would be taking with him the $24,000 in gold—more than $700,000 in today's dollars—that Congress had sent to fund territorial government operations, as well as the territorial seal used to grant an official imprimatur to the governor's legal acts.

Brigham moved to block Harris from taking the seal or the funds and, with the territorial legislature's support,[87] he ordered US marshal and Church member Joseph L. Heywood to secure all government papers and property and to arrest Harris if he refused to hand over the money. Harris refused to comply, claiming that he answered only to the US government.[88] Why he didn't answer to the territorial governor— Brigham—who was also a presidential appointee, he never explained. Two days later, Brigham appealed to the Territorial Supreme Court, but he could hardly have expected an impartial answer, given that two members of the three-judge court were Brocchus and Brandenbury.[89] When they didn't respond for two days, Brigham filed a petition to compel their verdict; the three men had fled the valley by then.

The day after the "Runaway Officials" left, Brigham dictated a letter to President Fillmore giving his interpretation of the events leading up to their abdication.[90] "I am . . . satisfied that it was and is the intention of [Brocchus, Brandenbury, and Harris] to utterly subvert and overthrow the government of Utah."[91] But he assured the president that he, the legislature, and all remaining government officers would "discharge faithfully every duty" and that he would be grateful for any counsel that Fillmore might offer. The runaways wrote their own report to the president, which denounced Brigham specifically and the Saints generally as seditious. Their lives had been threatened, they said, and the Saints were "inexorable in their hatred, and are ready and willing to plot the destruction of their liberal benefactor [the United States government]."[92]

The affair landed on the desk of US Secretary of State Daniel Webster. After much deliberation, he ordered Judge Brocchus and the others to either return to their duties in the Utah Territory or resign. They all resigned. Their posts went unfilled until 1853, and although some people thought the appointment of new officials would put an end to the affair, the allegations that Brocchus, Brandenbury, and Harris had circulated would not be so quickly forgotten.

———— • • ————

While the scandal of the "Runaway Officials" was still unfolding, work on the temple block had continued unabated. By the late spring of 1851, the space was no longer vacant. The newly established Public Works Department had set up shops there, housing blacksmith, carpentry, and other trades that provided tools and materials for construction projects throughout the city. That and the block's central location made it the industrial hub for the city as it grew outward, as Brigham had always planned for it to do, but most of the ten acres remained unoccupied. The temple site's centrality also made it the most convenient place to hold large public meetings. Those had been growing in size and frequency as the population of the city swelled—hence a larger bowery had been constructed, which offered a speaker and a few others shade from the sun but no other protection from the vagaries of the climate. It was an open pavilion built "by the simple method of putting poles into the ground at short intervals, making the framework of a roof—also of poles—and covering it over with branches, sagebrush, or whatever else [was] available."[93] It had a dirt floor, crude benches, and no walls, which one congregant liked because "it was easy to see what was going on outside, and this might be entertaining if the sermon was dry."[94] But the open sides also let the summer heat punish any congregation gathered there and made the building virtually unusable during the winter, and

49

the roof wasn't watertight for any season. So when the general conference that began on April 6, 1851, had to be postponed a day "on account of the heavy rains" that leaked through the bowery ceiling onto the assembled Saints,[95] Brigham decided that enough was enough. He called for the construction of a tabernacle on the temple block's southwest corner.[96]

The building's architect was Truman Osborn Angell. Truman was actually Brigham's brother-in-law—his sister Mary Ann had married Brigham after the prophet's first wife, Miriam, had died in 1832. He was not quite a decade younger than Brigham, the third son born in Rhode Island to James and Phebe Angell. And, like Brigham, he had learned carpentry and joinery as a teenager. But his father's cruelty toward his mother drove Phebe to move in 1831 to New York near the Pennsylvania border with Truman and Mary Ann in tow. There, all three of them learned of the restored gospel and were baptized: Truman in January 1832 and Mary Ann soon after. Mary Ann moved to Kirtland, where she met and married Brigham. Truman eventually came to Kirtland in 1835 with his wife, Polly, and he used his training and talents as a joiner to assist in the construction of the Kirtland Temple.

Truman suffered terrible financial losses in Kirtland during 1838, which reduced his family to utter penury, but his testimony remained firm enough that he decided to follow Joseph and the rest of the Saints to Missouri that year. The day of their departure, Truman's total assets were "a rickety wagon, a balky horse, not a penny in my pocket, a family to feed and a thousand miles to go,"[97] he later wrote. He earned money by working odd jobs as the family traveled. They succeeded in reaching Missouri, but they were there less than a year before they were forced to run for their lives from the mobs. They made their way to Nauvoo, and there Truman was called to be the superintendent of joiners on the Nauvoo Temple. In that capacity, he worked closely with Church architect William Weeks and was introduced to the rudiments of architecture.

After Joseph Smith's death, Truman remained loyal to the Apostles

—a decision likely influenced by his
personal relationship with Brigham,
the new leader of the Church after
the martyrdom. He left Nauvoo with
the rest of the Saints in 1846 and
settled at Winter Quarters, where
he and Polly would eventually bury
three of their children: their ten-year-
old daughter, Martha Ann; their only
son, two-year-old Truman Carlos;
and a newborn girl named Almirah.
Truman himself became very ill while

Truman Osborn Angell.

bringing his family across Iowa, and he remained sick throughout the
entire winter. He recovered by the spring of 1847 and joined Brigham's
first expedition to the valley that year.[98] The expedition had been subdivided into "companies of ten," and Truman and Brigham had been in
the same company.[99] He too returned to Iowa in the fall and brought his
family across to the valley in 1848.

Truman probably had no expectation of spending his life as anything
more than a farmer, carpenter, and missionary, but William Weeks's
departure had left the Church without an architect. That was no serious problem early on, when the Saints were focused mostly on building homes, barns, and shops. Those required no specialized knowledge
of construction beyond what any experienced carpenter learned on the
job. But an architect's services became necessary as the need grew for
more specialized buildings such as the Council House, and of course
the temple construction could not proceed very far until an architect
was commissioned. As the superintendent of joiners during the Nauvoo
Temple's construction, Truman had apparently absorbed more than a
little architectural knowledge. So Heber C. Kimball had urged Brigham
to select Truman to replace William Weeks. After some consideration,

Brigham accepted his friend's recommendation and appointed Angell to the post on January 26, 1850, at a salary of three dollars per day.

It was a very different kind of occupation for a man more accustomed to manual labor, and one that he found mentally taxing. "I have always been since my manhood a hard-working carpenter and Joiner with my own hands," he wrote in one of his short journals. "But it is a trifle to labor with one's own hands [as compared] to the labor of the mind. While one tires the extremities, the other wearies the man in his whole system."[100] Nor was he an obvious choice for the position—he had no formal training in the discipline, and his handwriting, as evidenced by his personal journal, was hideous. "God has not made me mighty with my pen," he admitted.[101] But, untrained and ill-prepared as he may have felt for the job, he seems to have taken pride in his designs and disliked seeing the credit for them go to others. In a fit of frustration, he vented his spleen to his journal, grousing:

> I never saw a station as responsible as the architect calling has to be—so trampled on he is not known among the common people; this makes him much trouble. After he has watched over his plans and seen them carried out the committee that can't do it has all the credit for it and this kills the spirits of a man or hurts me more than all the mobbing I ever had to pass thru in my life.[102]

Maybe it was facetious to say that the mobs of Missouri and Illinois had inflicted less pain than watching other men take credit for his work. Still, Truman was not one to turn down a Church calling. Brigham set him apart as the Church architect exactly one week after Truman had recorded those contrary feelings on the pages of his personal history in his nearly illegible handwriting.

The first buildings he designed were not complicated structures, and Truman drew heavily from architectural pattern books in the territorial library. The Council House was a simple square with a cupola on top, a very similar pattern to the courthouses found back East in several states along the US frontier; and the "Adobe Tabernacle" was not significantly

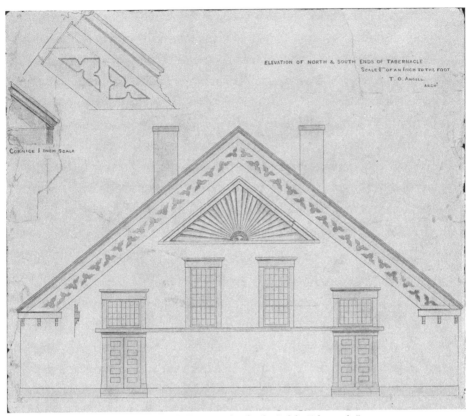

Truman Angell's elevation plan for the "Adobe Tabernacle."

more complex. It was a rectangle, 126 feet long and 64 feet wide—giving it a little more than 11,000 square feet of floor space—with a gable roof that ran the full length of the building. Its lone innovation was in the trusses needed to support the ceiling, which rose 60 feet into the air. Truman tested them by building small models before ordering their full-scale construction. The tabernacle was identical on the north and south ends, with two doors for entry and large windows above them and to the side to illuminate the interior. A triangular wooden cut of the rising sun rested above those for decoration. The interior was, for the most part, an open hall. The congregation sat on tiered benches that surrounded a lowered dais on three sides. The entire hall descended down below ground level, possibly to help cool the building during the summer. It was made of sun-dried clay brick and so was called the Adobe Tabernacle during its lifespan, but its simplicity in design and materials was a boon for construction. Construction began on May 21, 1851, and was completed in less than a year.[103] Two thousand five hundred Saints could fit under its roof, making for tight quarters, but they were out of the weather, at least. In future years it would be torn down, replaced by an Assembly Hall, but for two decades, it served its purpose quite well. As for Truman's own skills, his journal records no self-serving judgments that he considered himself an expert architect—but that first tabernacle he designed in 1851 was proof that he was at least a competent one.

———————•——•——•———————

Near the end of the year, a Christmas festival was held for the "public hands" who were government employees of the city and the territory. As the territorial governor, Brigham was a "public hand" himself, and he attended the event. But in his capacity as the prophet, he took the opportunity to deliver a short address to those present. "There are none to make us afraid, far from our persecutors, far from the turmoil and confusion of the old world," he reminded them. Perhaps gesturing to Christmas treats and dishes laid out on tables for the festival, he asked: "Has not the Lord poured out His blessings upon you to surpass all former times? Your barns and presses are filled with fine wheat, and other productions of these valleys; your tables groan under the abundance of the blessings of the Almighty. Is there room for one complaint or murmur by this people? No!"[104]

With that said, he turned his thoughts in another direction. Perhaps the temple had been weighing on his mind of late, or maybe the topic simply came to him in the moment. But in either case, he shifted the subject in an instant, without warning or transition.

Brethren, we are the Lord's and all we possess; and I have determined, by the help of the Lord and this people, to build him a house. You may ask, "Will He dwell in it?" He may do just as He pleases; it is not my prerogative to dictate to the Lord. But we will build Him a house, that if He pleases to pay us a visit, He may have a place to dwell in, or if He should send any of His servants, we may have suitable accommodations for them. I have built myself a house, and the most of you have done the same, and now shall we not build the Lord a house?[105]

The Saints in the room responded "aye," and suddenly Brigham seemed to break out of whatever reverie had driven him to talk of temple building. "I will not interrupt your enjoyments by saying more," he apologized. Then he shared a parting thought that seemed almost a promise. "Though, on such an interesting occasion as this," he added, "much more might be said."[106]

***

The year 1852 arrived, and the winter months passed into spring. The Adobe Tabernacle was completed and dedicated with a lengthy prayer offered by Willard Richards during the first session of the April general conference.[107] On the third day of the conference, April 8, Brigham gave an extended discourse on the need to build a temple, showing now that the subject had, in fact, been weighing on his mind all along. Some work had been done on building the wall around the temple block, which he saw as important to creating a sacred space where those attending the house of the Lord would eventually feel separated from the world outside. Still, Brigham offered no specifics about when a groundbreaking would take place or when construction on the temple might start. In fact, he noted that the Church had some significant debts that needed to be paid, implying that those were a hindrance to getting the temple project under way, and he exhorted the congregation to help pay them off.[108] The conference adjourned after four days, nothing else on the subject of the temple being said.

***

It was not long after the April conference that events took another dramatic turn. After four years in self-imposed exile, William Weeks returned to the Salt Lake Valley. He had spent some time in Wisconsin before settling down in Iowa, and, feeling repentant, was rebaptized somewhere along the way. If he was hoping to resume his previous duties as the Church architect, learning of Truman's appointment to that post must have come as an unpleasant surprise. After all, Weeks could make a solid claim to being the only man living who had any practical experience designing a house of the Lord. But there are no records suggesting he thought about challenging Truman's qualifications for the position. Not only had Truman filled the job for two years at that point, he'd filled it quite admirably. He hadn't yet produced a design for a temple, but he'd worked on a number of homes and other buildings that were now testaments to Truman's professional abilities. And Brigham may not have been anxious to trust the job of drawing up plans for the new temple to someone who had already absconded once with the blueprints for the last one. So Brigham did not offer Weeks his old job back. In fact, there's no record that Brigham ever utilized the man's architectural skills again in any capacity.

The former Church architect decided to leave Great Salt Lake City, and he moved his family south to Provo. He never left the Church again, but neither did he ever enjoy an association with its senior leadership, as he once had. In later years, after his death on March 8, 1900, Weeks's daughter could not recall her father ever expressing any frustration that he was given no role in designing the Salt Lake Temple—but neither is there any evidence that Weeks did so much as lift a single spade of dirt to assist in its construction.[109] The first Church architect's days of leading the design and construction of temples was over.

—— • · • ——

The summer of 1852 drew to its close and the harvest season was under way when, in August, Brigham called a special conference, almost a month earlier than the usual time. The first day was spent organizing a wave of missionaries to travel abroad. One hundred three men received calls to serve from the tabernacle, with some learning of their calls when they were announced at the pulpit, as was frequently the custom in those times. The fields of labor included Africa, Australia, Europe, the United States, Canada, and the Pacific Islands.

If the members returning for the second day expected the sermons to continue with that theme, they were surely surprised. Missionary work drew hardly a mention. Instead, they received a discourse from Orson Pratt that would affect the course of the Church for decades, and it was apparently as much a surprise to him as it was to his audience. "It is quite unexpected to me brethren and sisters," he started, "to be called upon to address you this forenoon; and still more so, to address you upon the principle which has been named, namely, a plurality of wives."[110] At Brigham's request, the Apostle stood and delivered the first public sermon on the doctrine of plural marriage.

That some Church leaders had been practicing plural marriage was no great secret, either to the Saints or to the world at large. Pratt said as much, telling the congregation that "it is well known [to you] that the Latter-day Saints have embraced the doctrine [of plural marriage] as a part of their religious faith."[111] But no one—not one Apostle, not Brigham, not Joseph himself—had ever preached it openly from the pulpit until that morning. Joseph had told a few close friends in private that the Lord had revealed the principle to him while he had been engaged in a revision of the Bible. Joseph had offered no specific date, though it could well have come during 1830 while he was revising the Old Testament—perhaps while he had been poring over the story of Abraham, who had been husband to both Sarah and Hagar; or that of Jacob, who had married both Leah and her younger sister, Rachel.[112] It was part of the larger revelation on celestial marriage, Joseph explained, which taught that the union of a man and woman could endure into the eternities if performed in the temple by one holding the sealing power of the priesthood. Joseph had freely taught the doctrine of eternal marriage, but he'd been very reticent to teach or practice the principle of plural marriage, knowing the hostility it would stir up. That foot dragging, he admitted, had earned him visits from angels three times between 1834 and 1842, each time commanding him to institute the practice. Evidence suggests that Joseph quietly obeyed after the first instance, marrying one plural wife; but it ended in separation, and Joseph apparently made no move to try again for some time. But, according to Joseph, the Lord was insistent. "God commanded me to obey it," Joseph explained later. "He said to me that unless I accept it and introduce it and practice it, I, together with my people, should be damned and cut off from this time henceforth."[113]

Joseph obeyed and began teaching plural marriage in private to a relatively small number of his close associates. It was a hard doctrine that many struggled to accept, including Brigham himself. "I was not desirous of shrinking from any duty, nor of failing in the least to do as I was commanded, but it was the first time in my life that I had desired the grave, and I could hardly get over it for a long time," Brigham admitted.[114] He was not alone, and for some time the number of Saints practicing the doctrine was relatively small. By the time Joseph was martyred in 1844, fewer than thirty men and fifty women had entered into plural marriages.[115] The numbers rose over the years, and about two hundred men and five hundred women were practicing it three years later when Brigham first entered the valley.

Joseph's concerns about the public reaction had been well-founded. Plural marriage was denounced in every quarter in the harshest terms by politicians and clergy alike. But didn't the Constitution's First Amendment guarantee freedom of religion to all sincere believers? Didn't that protect them in the practice of plural marriage, no matter what the public thought of it? Orson Pratt proposed an answer to that question in his address:

> I think . . . that the constitution gives the privilege to all the inhabitants of this country, of the free exercise of their religious notions, and the freedom of their faith, and the practice of it. Then, if it can be proven to a demonstration, that the Latter-day Saints have

actually embraced, as a part and portion of their religion, the doctrine of a plurality of wives, it is constitutional. And should there ever be laws enacted by this government to restrict them from the free exercise of this part of their religion, such laws must be unconstitutional.[116]

Orson was a fine scientist, but he was not a very good constitutional lawyer, as events in subsequent years would prove.

When the next session of conference convened later that day, Brigham shared his testimony of Joseph's prophetic calling, and then called on Thomas Bullock to read the original revelation on celestial marriage in its entirety.[117] For many of the Saints, it was the first time they heard the doctrine in the original language that Joseph had recorded in 1843. It also put the official stamp on what had, to that day, been a private practice. Plural marriage was, from that point forward, a public doctrine of the Church.

———◆·•·◆———

Two months later, the Saints again came together on the sixth of the month in the tabernacle to hear the prophet and the Twelve preach in general conference. Brigham was suffering from some kind of respiratory ailment and apologized that he would not be able to speak at length. He spoke less than ten minutes, only setting out an agenda for the remainder of the conference. Construction of a temple was at the top of his list. "I have a few texts to give to the brethren, who may speak upon some of the items I wish to be laid before this Conference . . . ," he started. "The first I have noted is a question: Shall we commence to build a Temple next spring, in order that we may receive our endowments more fully? There are many in this congregation who are aware, that we do not give all the endowments, neither can we, legally, until we build a Temple."[118] His illness kept him from elaborating much more. He took a few moments to discuss the wall being erected around the temple block, mentioned a few other issues, and then sat down.

Despite Brigham's laying the question on the table, there was very little discussion about it for most of the conference. Heber C. Kimball was the man who finally put it to a vote. He called the question during the following day's morning session.

> I do not know whether you have any desire to have a temple built or not. Have you reflected upon it, that we may go to with our might, our means, our substance and with all we have to build a house to the Lord, to build fonts that we can attend to the ordinances of salvation for ourselves, our children, our fathers and mothers both living and dead? What do you say? If you say we shall do so raise your right hands.[119]

All hands went up. "It is clear they will have a temple, Brother Brigham," Kimball reported.[120] But that was all that he or anyone else said about it that day.

It was not until the final day of the conference, October 9, that the topic arose again—and again, it was Heber who broached the subject. When his turn at the pulpit came in the morning session, he gave the most detailed public address on the topic on record since the Saints had entered the valley five years earlier.

> The subject President Young wished me to speak of is in regard to our temple, which we shall soon commence to build—what course we shall take, and what kind of materials it shall be built of; whether we shall build it of the stone that is got in the Red Butte Canyon, or of adobies, or of the best stone we can find in these mountains, . . . inasmuch as we intend to build a house unto the Lord for him to accept, for his angels to come to as ministers to give instructions, I can feel, myself, as though we are perfectly able to build one, of the best kind of materials from the foundation to the tip top. We are able, and we have strength and union, and we have bone, and marrow, and muscle, and we are able to commence it next year.[121]

He then went off on some tangents about the situation of the Saints in the valley and their ability before finding his way back to the issue at hand:

> I want a vote from the congregation concerning the temple, whether we shall have it built of the stone from Red Bute [sic] or of adobies, or timber, or of the best quality stone that can be found in the mountains. . . . I put the motion which is before you, that we build a temple of the best materials that can be furnished in the mountains of North America, and that the presidency dictate where the stone and other materials shall be obtained.

As before, the vote was unanimous.[122]

Elder George A. Smith followed Heber and declared that "if we build of the best [material available], the Lord will open the way for it to be got"; but of the choices available—timber, brick, stone—he favored stone. Elder John Taylor declared that, whatever the material they chose, the cost and distance involved in obtaining it were irrelevant. Stone would be more expensive than adobe brick, he admitted, but he observed that "in England and France, they fetch their stone for public buildings from a great distance, and at an immense expense, and if the Gentiles do it, in the name of God and common sense I say, we must be a poor miserable set of beings, if we cannot do the same." There was consensus among the Twelve and the congregation that nothing less than the best material available would do.[123]

Brigham finally offered his own opinion on the subject that evening at the final meeting of the conference. Whatever had been ailing him before seems to have eased, as his discourse was considerably longer than the few remarks he'd offered in the first meeting. As it turned out, Brigham was not in favor of building the temple of stone. "I am inclined to offer a chemical argument," he said, "with regard to the material for building a temple in our present circumstances." Of all the construction materials available in the valley—he listed off stone, sandstone, limestone, and adobe brick—"which do you think will stand the longest?" he asked.

After time and erosion had worn away the other materials, a temple built of adobe brick would not only still stand, but would be in better condition than at the first day it was built. We have proof of this. Go into Egypt, for instance, and you will find the monuments, towers, and pyramids, that were erected in the days of Joseph, and before he was sold into Egypt; they were built of what we call adobies, clay mixed up with straw . . . they had bid defiance to the wear of ages, and they still remain. But you cannot find a stone column that was reared in those times, for they are all decayed.[124]

The prophet was arguing for a brick temple, though he did admit they might cover it with a stone veneer. But lest anyone get lost in the details of his historical and chemical lessons about the durability of various building materials, he stated his opinion in flat, unmistakable terms.

According to my present views, there is not marble in these mountains, or stone of any kind or quality, that I would rather have a building made of than adobies. As for the durability of such a building, the longer it stands the better it becomes. . . . I give it as my opinion that adobies are the best article to build it of. I do not fear the expense, neither do I care what you build it of; only when it is built, I want it to stand, and not fall down and decay in twenty or thirty years.[125]

And with that, Brigham ended his address and the meeting.

The conference adjourned the following day. In neither of the final two meetings did any of the speakers take up the question of the material they would use to build the temple. Brigham had stated his opinion, and the Saints were accustomed to deferring to the prophet's decisions. So the congregation could be forgiven if they left the tabernacle that afternoon believing that the house of the Lord they would soon construct would be made of adobe bricks.

CHAPTER 3

THE VISION
OF IT WAS THERE

I t is not clear whether Brigham's "chemical argument" had been a case of the prophet thinking out loud or if he had truly settled the issue in his own mind. Besides the durability of brick, which Brigham had extolled, there were other considerations in favor of choosing adobe. Access to the raw materials was one. The clays and binders for adobes were within easy reach, but timber would have to be collected and hauled in from miles away up the canyons. Production capacity and cost were others. The Saints had been building up brickyards close to the city for more than five years now and had the means to make adobes in quantity for even large buildings. The tabernacle itself was made of them, a fact that likely hadn't escaped the notice of the congregation when Brigham was extolling the virtues of the brick. But timber would first have to be processed in mills that were farther away and couldn't turn out the same linear feet of lumber as fast as the brickyards could turn out an equivalent amount of adobes. And fabricating stone was a process that didn't even play on the same time scale. The best stonecutter might need several days to cut a single rough block from a mountainside or a boulder; a wagon team would be needed to haul it by ox- or horse-drawn cart to the construction site, with travel time varying by the distance and the weight of the cargo; then a stonemason would need days more to chisel the block into the designated shape, depending on the size of the stone and the complexity of the design. Getting a single rough block out of a quarry and into a building wall could easily take weeks. And for both timber and stone, the greater distance, slower processing, and added manpower all meant an increase in the total cost the Church would have to bear.

Given the temple's proposed size, adobe appeared to have all the advantages. It was easier and faster to manufacture, it was durable, and it could be made in quantity close to the temple block. So building a brick temple was an entirely logical course, and Brigham, Truman, and others discussed it seriously.

No matter the logic of it, there was at least one person among the leadership who was not settled on the idea of a brick temple—Wilford Woodruff. In fact, he was quite certain the temple would *not* be made of adobe, no matter the advantages, cost, or convenience it offered. His conviction rested not on purely rational arguments. It stemmed instead from a nighttime vision that he deemed a personal revelation from the Lord. Decades later he explained:

> Before we came to the Rocky Mountains, I had a dream. I dreamed of being in these mountains, and of seeing a large fine looking temple erected in one of these valleys which was built of cut granite stone. . . . And whenever President Young held a council of the brethren of the Twelve and talked of building the temple of adobe or brick, . . . I would say to myself, "No, you will never do it;" because I had seen it in my dream built of some other material.[1]

In spite of his conviction, Wilford seems to have kept his dream to himself whenever Brigham and the rest of the Twelve discussed construction materials. He may have politely favored granite or some other stone during those meetings, but there's no evidence that he tried to invoke a personal revelation in an attempt to steer his leaders in a different direction. The Lord Himself had once dictated that "thou shalt not command him who is at thy head, and at the head of the church."[2] If the Almighty wanted His house to be made of granite, He would share that detail in due time with the prophet, and He wouldn't go through a middleman, even another Apostle, when He did it. So Wilford said nothing that would have fostered disunity between himself and Brigham, whether publicly or in private.

◆ • • ◆

For all the discussion of bricks and wood and stone, not one spade of dirt for the temple foundation had been turned as 1852 drew to a close. Barely a week after the conference, Brigham stated his expectation "to be able to lay [the cornerstones] at the next ensuing April conference."[3] But the construction materials were not the only detail still undecided; the temple's whole design was not just unsettled but largely unstarted.

Brigham spent that winter dividing his attention between settling territorial matters and addressing Church affairs, but he decided in January of 1853 that it was time to talk with Truman Angell in detail about the temple that he had seen in vision. He marched over to the architect's office and sat down with his brother-in-law and also assistant architect William Ward and gave them the design. Ward recalled:

> The design was formulated in the following manner: Brigham Young drew upon a slate in the architect's office a sketch, and said to Truman O. Angell: "There will be three towers on the east, representing the President and his two Counselors; also three similar towers on the west representing the Presiding Bishop and his two Counselors; the towers on the east the Melchisedek Priesthood, those on the west the Aaronic Priesthood. The center towers will be higher than those on the sides, and the west towers a little lower than those on the east end. The body of the building will be between these and pillars will be necessary to support the floors. Angell then asked about the height, and drew the following vertical section according to Brigham's instructions. The basement 16 feet high to contain the font. The first story twenty-five feet high

between the pillars but between the pillars and sidewalls fifteen feet high, leaving room for a tier of rooms above the side aisles about ten feet high below the second floor. The second story like the first. The construction of the roof was left to Mr. Angell.[4]

It was enough for a start, and the architect set to work immediately.[5] He found the project all-consuming. "My attention has been engaged on the designs of a Temple and this burdens the mind so much as to cause a neglect in writing every day in a journal," he wrote.[6] Truman had most of the dimensions worked out by February 12, 1853, and his plan was not timid.[7] The building would be 186½ feet long including the towers, and a little more than half as wide, at 98 feet. Factoring in the towers that would jut out beyond the walls at the corners and centers on both ends, Truman worked out the total area at 21,850 square feet. That was half again what the Nauvoo Temple had covered and very nearly double the footprint of the Kirtland Temple, and starting with the vertical heights that Brigham had mandated, it was practically a given that every one of the spires capping the six towers would be taller than the lone steeples atop either of the earlier temples. The Saints had never attempted to build something so large. It would have been an ambitious project for a well-heeled church in a major city with easy access to tools and materials; for a poor community in a large frontier settlement not six years old, such an undertaking might have seemed downright delusional. A temple of that size would be by far the largest building in the territory—the largest west of the Mississippi and east of California.

Just getting the cornerstones laid down would be an accomplishment. Given the proposed size, the temple would be very heavy no matter what material Brigham ultimately chose for it. So the foundation would need to "depress into the earth, at the east end, to the depth of 16 feet, and enlarge all around beyond the lines of the wall 3 feet for a footing," by Truman's calculations.[8] Excavating that much dirt with nothing better than muscle, pickaxe, shovel, and spade would take months. When to start? The weather was already turning colder, and snow had been known to fall in the valley as late as May.[9] To meet Brigham's April conference deadline, the Saints would have to break ground immediately, and that would add an extra measure of difficulty to the task. The earth had never been particularly soft even during the summers, such as when they'd first arrived in the valley and had to irrigate to soften the terrain enough to start planting seeds. Now they would have to attack almost the very same patch of ground, working in near-freezing and sub-freezing temperatures, maybe during snowfall, to dig down more than a dozen feet, remove tons upon tons of soil and rock hardened by the cold, and cart it all away in wagons and wheelbarrows.

———— • · • ————

The Saints turned that first spade of dirt on February 14, 1853, a Monday. It was a clear day and cold, for there had been sharp frosts for several nights preceding the event. There was snow on the ground. The masses began to assemble at the temple block starting around ten o'clock that morning, Brigham and the other Church leaders with them. They watched as Truman and Jesse W. Fox conducted a last-minute, hour-long survey of the site. By the time they finished, "several thousand" people had gathered around the "hollow square" the surveyors had marked off on the ground. Brigham took up a place along the east survey line, climbed aboard a small buggy where he could be seen, and began to address the crowd in a loud voice "so as to be heard distinctly in all parts of the vast assembly."[10]

"If the congregation will give me their attention, I will detain them but a short time," he began. "Suffice it to say, to this congregation, that we shall attempt to build a temple to the name of our God. This has been attempted several times, but we have never yet had the privilege of completing and enjoying one."[11] He was hardly exaggerating. If he was counting from the day the Kirtland Temple was dedicated to the day Joseph had had to leave Kirtland for the last time, the Saints had "enjoyed" that first building for a little more than twenty-one months, but they'd needed thirty-two to build it. The Nauvoo Temple's history was even more lopsided. They'd been able to use parts of that building during its construction, but having only four months to enjoy the final product hardly seemed like just compensation for five years of labor, especially given how the Church's enemies had treated the structure afterward.

Some in the crowd might have expected Brigham to have been bitter about such losses, but if the prophet felt any such emotion in his heart, he made no show of it. He had not been reminding his audience of their labors and losses to stir them up to anger. Instead, he had been preparing them to hear a very different doctrine that morning.

> It is for us to do those things which the Lord requires at our hands, and leave the result with Him. It is for us to labor with a cheerful good will; and if we build a temple that is worth a million of money, and it requires all our time and means, we should leave it with cheerful hearts, if the Lord in His providence tells us so to do. If the Lord permits our enemies to drive us from it, why we should abandon it with as much cheerfulness of heart as we ever enjoy a blessing. It is no matter to us what the Lord does, or how He disposes of the labor of His servants. But when He commands, it is for His people to obey. We should be as cheerful in building this temple, if we knew beforehand that we should never enter into it when it was finished, as we would though we knew we were to live here a thousand years to enjoy it.[12]

Obey God, work hard, and leave the rest to the Almighty was Brigham's counsel.

They were, perhaps, not the most reassuring words. If he was going to ask the Saints to labor on yet another temple that their enemies might seize from them, could he not give them some reassurance that such a project was actually a directive from the Lord? Had Brigham received a revelation that they were to build a temple here in this place? Brigham did not say so, but he assured the audience, "The Lord wished us to gather to this place, He wished us to cultivate the earth, and make these valleys like the Garden of Eden, and make all the improvements in our power, and build a temple as soon as circumstances would permit."[13] Moreover, they didn't need a specific commandment to build a temple any more than they needed one to "accumulate [their] daily bread," to pray, or to pay their tithing, which would be the means by which the construction would be funded.[14]

Then he returned his remarks to the Saints' recent history.

> Let us revert for a moment to the past, to the years we have spent in toil and labor, though very agreeably. Seven years ago to-morrow . . . I crossed the Mississippi river, with my brethren, for this place, not knowing, at that time, whither we were going, but firmly believing that the Lord had in reserve for us a good place in the mountains and that He would lead us directly to it. It is but seven years since we left Nauvoo, and we are now ready to build another temple. I look back on our labors with pleasure.[15]

They had lost every city and settlement, all of the temples and homes they had ever built, but now they had Great Salt Lake City, and that was a cause for rejoicing as far as the prophet was concerned.

Brigham then directed his remarks to the part of the crowd that may have felt disconnected from the events he'd been recounting for the last half hour. Many in the audience were converts from Great Britain and other countries of Europe who had not experienced the sufferings of their American brothers and sisters. Immigration into the valley had been constant over the previous years, and for those who had come later, the Church's history with the mobs was primarily academic. Those newcomers would see their share of trials in the building of this temple, Brigham assured them, but they should look upon those challenges with faith and good cheer.

> Here are hundreds and thousands of people that have not had the privileges that some of us have had. Do you ask, what privileges? Why, of running the gauntlet, of passing through the narrows. They have not had the privilege of being robbed and plundered of their property, of being in the midst of mobs and

death, as many of us have. Only be faithful, brethren and sisters, and I promise that you shall have all such privileges as shall be for your good.

Brigham may have been injecting a small bit of humor into the proceedings with his talk of being robbed and plundered as a privilege; if so, any laughter that resulted must have turned to nervous laughter as he assured the newer immigrants that they would not be deprived of any such "blessings."

> You need not be discouraged or mourn because you were not in Jackson County persecutions, or were not driven from Ohio, Missouri, and Illinois, and stripped, robbed, and plundered of all your property. Do not mourn and feel bad, because you were not in Nauvoo; have no fears, for if the word of the Lord is true, you shall yet be tried in all things, so rejoice, and pray without ceasing, and in everything give thanks, even if it is in the spoiling of your goods, for it is the hand of God that leads us, and will continue so to do.[16]

Brigham's remarks that morning had been a call to happiness no matter how hard the task ahead might prove to be. Brigham had started by urging the Saints to be obedient to God and cheerful through persecution and trials, and he ended it on the same note. His words were more appropriate for the occasion than anyone could have known at the time, as events in the coming years would prove. The discourse he shared during that half hour on that cold February morning, standing on a buggy, his breath likely visible in the air, may have been the most prophetic message he ever gave in public.

—•·•—

Heber Kimball was the next man to ascend the buggy. He was Brigham's counselor in the First Presidency and had been chosen to offer a prayer over the site. He began asking heaven for a blessing on Brigham for "length of days and wisdom to see the work completed which was then commenced" and that the Apostles and other "associates in the ministry" and their families might have all of the spiritual and temporal blessings God might see fit to grant. He prayed for the Saints to be gathered, Israel to be rebuilt, Zion redeemed, the Lamanites restored, and the gospel to "go to all nations." He then turned the subject of his appeal to the temple itself.

> The ground for the Temple was consecrated to the MOST High God; to be a Holy Place; where no unclean thing should ever approach; calling upon his Heavenly Father to protect it from every thing that was evil; and that he would bless the Architect, the Superintendent, the Foremen and all the laborers on the Temple, with wisdom, and understanding and knowledge, and perseverance in the midst of all difficulties, and their wives, and children . . . that they might be faithful to the end and receive their blessings in the Temple; and that the angels of heaven might descend and visit them in that house, and dwell therein, and that God himself might meet his servants there, and administer to them.[17]

Heber appears to have continued on for some time. The *Deseret News* journalist covering the event noted that "it seemed he knew not when to stop, till his lungs failed him, and he said Amen."[18] The crowd shouted "amen" after, though the reporter's account leaves it unclear whether their "joyful hearts" were due to the contents of Heber's prayer alone or the fact that it was finally over.

After Heber's extended benediction, the leaders of both the Church and the city walked to the southeast corner, the traditional location during those times for the cornerstone of any major building. Breaking that ceremonial first piece of ground proved troublesome. The frost of the previous days had done its work, and the terrain refused to break apart. Heber started into it with a pickaxe, followed by the Quorum of the Twelve.[19] At that point, the ground finally was broken up enough from the hacking and pulling for Brigham to extract a piece of earth about a foot square and six inches deep.[20] Someone from the crowd tossed a single silver dollar, which fell onto the small patch of rock-hard dirt. No one claimed it, and Heber declared that it was "a good token, and means would not be wanted to build the Temple."[21] Brigham scooped up the hardened dirt on his shovel to toss it aside, but the crowd was pressing in close around him and he had nowhere to put it. He raised his spade into the air. "Get out of my way," he announced, "for I am going to throw this." The crowd was packed in tight enough that it took a minute for them to move aside and open a space for the prophet to finally pitch the shovel's contents away. He then "declared the ground broken for the Temple, blessed the people in the name of the Lord, and dismissed the assembly."[22] Some members of the crowd "rushed to the hole to get a chance to throw a little dirt out," but most of the multitude dispersed to their homes. With the masses finally gone, the first workers proceeded to dig in earnest.[23]

—— • • • ——

From that moment, the excavation proceeded in haste, with dirt being hauled out as fast as the cold, daylight, and available labor would allow. Brigham had decided that he wanted to lay the temple cornerstones at the next conference, which was scheduled to open on April 6. That deadline gave the Saints exactly forty-three days—there would be no work done on any Sabbath—to dig. It was apparent that six weeks would not be enough time to empty out the entire square that Truman had marked out. Instead, long trenches would be dug out, twenty feet wide and sixteen feet deep. The north-south trenches would measure 193 feet, the east-west trenches 125.[24] Those dimensions would require the men to remove more than 200,000 cubic feet of dirt weighing more than 80,000 tons; to meet their goal, they would have to cart away almost 1,900 tons of dirt each day.

As if the math weren't daunting enough, the weather continued to give them trouble. The temperatures were relatively mild for the season, but storms rolled in repeatedly. Snow fell again twice within the week after the groundbreaking ceremony, and several more times throughout that month and the next. One storm in late March started at seven in the morning after a night when "the wind blew a perfect hurricane, roaring and howling dismally"; it was leaving knee-deep drifts by noon. Many nights were frosty, but the temperatures sometimes rose above freezing during the day, leaving the laborers to hack at frozen earth in the morning and then shovel cold, wet dirt and rocks by the afternoon as the sun warmed the ground and melted the snow and ice.[25] The same cycle of snow falling and melting also kept the city streets muddy, making travel to and from the temple block by wagon a more troublesome affair.

But the math, cold, and snow together were no deterrent. "Many hands are busy, and have been since Monday noon, excavating the ground for the Temple," the *Deseret News* reported five days after Brigham had thrown out that first bit of hard dirt.[26] All men and boys who were physically capable were asked to spend one day in every ten digging at the site on the temple, and those who donated their labor according to that schedule were called "tithing hands." For several years, the public works had used such free labor, in which tradesmen donated one day out of every ten and applied their skills to projects for the community. For a volunteer system, it had proved effective and was doing so again. Somewhere between 150 and 200 men and boys could be found working on the site on any given day, loading up more than a dozen wagons that hauled away the dirt they shoveled out.[27] There were enough such hands working daily that it was clear that a foreman was needed.

Brigham and Wilford Woodruff were dining with fellow Apostle Ezra T. Benson on the twenty-first, a week after the digging commenced, and sometime during the meal the prophet asked Wilford to oversee the excavation.[28] He accepted the job. He spent his first day as overseer training with Daniel Wells to make sure he had a firm grasp on his responsibilities and drawing up rosters of the laborers' names. He also spent time visiting Truman Angell to see the temple plans, such as they were, to ensure that the crews weren't clearing the foundation too short or long in its length or width.[29] The architect had spent most of this time since the groundbreaking working on the building design but had been

73

forced to deal with constant interruptions. Working for both the Church and the city meant that he was constantly being pulled away to manage other civil construction projects, such as the city arsenal.[30] But the foundation plans were developed sufficiently to guide Wilford in his responsibilities as an overseer, and he started his new assignment at the temple block the following morning. He "found it a busy place" and spent most every workday thereafter on the site until the foundation was ready for the cornerstones.[31]

———•—•—•———

There are no records indicating exactly when Brigham made his decision about what construction material to use for the temple proper, but there seem to have been no doubts about what they would use for the foundation itself. During his speech at the groundbreaking, Brigham had taken a brief moment to exhort the men in the crowd to build a railroad track to "the quarry." "We cannot commence to lay rock here without time, and we cannot get the stone for the foundation [until] the railroad from this place to the quarry is completed," was all he had said about the matter at the time.[32] He had not specified which quarry because there was only one to choose from—the Red Butte Canyon quarry. John Sharp, a recent emigrant and coal miner from Clackmannanshire, Scotland, had discovered a large bed of good-quality red sandstone four miles east of the city in 1850. He and his brothers Joseph and Adam set up a quarry to recover the material, and they'd been pulling stone from it for the temple block wall ever since. By then he had developed a strong friendship with Brigham, who contracted with the three brothers to recover stone for the public works projects.

The city council also passed an ordinance in 1851 to incorporate the Red Butte Railroad Company to transport the sandstone from the quarry for use in public buildings. The plan had been for ox teams to pull the cars east up the canyon to the quarry, where the sandstone would be loaded and the car coasted back down to the temple block under the control of a brakeman.[33] But two years later, the railroad to the quarry remained unfinished. The roadbed had been graded, and many of the timbers and rails were laid out on the shoulders of the trail, but the actual chore of laying the four miles of track had not been completed. Brigham's comment in conference about finishing the spur started a furious effort to lay that track, but that was not going to be finished in time. They would have to haul the cornerstones by ox and wagon. They needed only four stones, albeit large ones, for the coming ceremony, but once the cornerstones were laid, they would need the sandstone in volume, and hauling it all by wagon teams would require more time and manpower in the form of teamsters.

On March 29, 1853, Brigham and Daniel H. Wells mounted up in the prophet's buggy and took a trip to the quarry. Wells was the public works superintendent over the shops on the temple block and had been appointed as a "committee of one" to oversee the temple's construction. The reason for their trip is unknown, but Brigham had had a conversation with Truman about the foundation stones just the day before, which might have spurred the prophet's desire to visit Sharp in the quarry.[34] Brigham may have just wanted reassurance that everything was on track to have the cornerstones in place within the week. The recent snowstorms had made a sloppy mess of the dirt streets in the city, so doubtless the two men could imagine what the storms might have done to the rougher trails up the canyons, where snowfall was often heavier than in the valley. Even the most experienced oxcart driver would struggle to navigate through trails of mud and melting snow with a heavy wagon laden with a few tons of rock. If anything could endanger Brigham's planned schedule for the cornerstone ceremony, it was the late-season snows.

Any such fear was ultimately unfounded. As it turned out, the rail spur wasn't needed to get the cornerstones out of the canyon, and on the following Saturday, April 2, the southeast and northeast cornerstone were delivered, with the remaining two stones arriving at the temple block sometime the following Monday or Tuesday.[35] The deliveries had cut the timing a bit close, so perhaps there had been some difficulties. Each block was cut roughly two feet by four by six. With the average weight of a sandstone block being 150 pounds per cubic foot, each block would have pressed the scale at 5,400 pounds, or nearly two and three-quarter tons. That was more than enough weight to push a heavy wagon down into the mud created by the snowmelt, and it would have required a powerful ox team or several very strong horses to pull it out— but the Sharp brothers managed the feat. Brigham could sleep on the eve of the ceremony assured that the stones were in place in the trenches that Wilford and the tithing hands had been laboring steadily to open.

———— • • • ————

Wednesday, April 6, was a mild spring morning. Winter finally seemed to have broken, and for a few days the Saints had enjoyed a run of warmer weather. "The sun, the sky, the atmosphere, the earth, appeared neither too cold nor too hot nor lukewarm," Brigham later reported. "All seemed filled with life; adapted to each soul, to cheer and make happy every individual of the many thousands of aged, middle-aged and youth, who had assembled from the near and remote parts of the inhabited valley."[36] Those thousands of people would have come that morning for conference in any case, but they all must have felt a special investment in the proceedings. They'd been waiting for this day since they had fled Nauvoo and left that temple behind eight years ago. The seven-week dig on the foundation had been the first chance the rank-and-file members had had to start building a temple again, and their response to that opportunity had been impressive. "The digging of the earth, preparatory [to the laying of the cornerstone] cost from seven to ten thousand days' labor beside many teams,"[37] the *Deseret News* asserted. It was no exaggeration. An average daily labor force of between 160 and 230 men working forty-four full days works out to exactly the number of man-days reported—and it was only the smallest beginning of what they knew would ultimately be required. They had only carved out four trenches, the sides of a rectangle they needed to completely hollow out—more dirt several times over than they had removed in the last seven weeks—before they could start the real construction work on a building that would be larger than many of them had ever seen. It was staggering to contemplate, which the newspaper did anyway.

If it cost 10,000 days digging to prepare to lay the foundation stones, how many days' work will it require to complete the excavation for the walls; erect the edifice, and finish the wall around the Temple Block, the stone being yet in the mountains, unquarried; the timber yet growing in the canyons; the lime in the stone, and kilns unbuilt; and not wheat enough in the Lord's Store House to feed the laborers on the Public Works, one week? Add to this, the preparing of the public grounds, the building of fonts, and planting of shade and fruit trees, &c., thereon, and a tabernacle capable of convening twenty, thirty, or fifty thousand people; and then say, what have you to do, to finish the work which is now before you to be done on the Temple Block alone?[38]

But those were all concerns for tomorrow and the years to come. Today was a celebration.

Brigham opened the general conference of the Church at ten o'clock in the Adobe Tabernacle. He talked for only a few minutes to note the progress of the Church since its founding precisely twenty-three years before. He returned to his seat, and a choir stood to sing "On Mountain Tops in Latter Days" as a prelude to Elder John Taylor's opening prayer. The choir followed with another hymn, "Come All Ye Saints of Zion." Then, when the last verse concluded, the Saints exited the building and engaged in an activity never before witnessed before in any general conference of the Church—they staged a Sabbath-day *parade.*

A color guard took the lead carrying the United States flag; they also carried another blue-and-white flag featuring stars, stripes, and the embroidered words *Kingdom of God* across it.[39] The Nauvoo Brass Band came next. Founded in 1842 to accompany the practice drills of the Nauvoo Legion militia, that unit had marched directly in front of the funeral wagon carrying the bodies of Joseph and Hyrum Smith after their murders at Carthage Jail in 1844. Next followed a twenty-piece band led by Dominico Ballo, a Sicilian convert who was both a graduate of Italy's Milan Conservatory and former bandmaster of the US Military Academy at West Point. Another military guard stepped in behind Ballo's band, and a small group of singers followed the soldiers. Then came Brigham and his counselors in the First Presidency, Heber C. Kimball and Willard Richards, along with "Uncle John" Smith, the presiding patriarch. The rest of the Church leaders fell in line after that—the Quorum of the Twelve Apostles, the Presidency of the Quorum of Seventy, and other senior and local leaders. Nearing the end of the line came Truman Angell, the architect, and a number of workmen selected to represent their various classes of profession; a final military guard brought up the rear.

The parade route wasn't long, to be sure. The Adobe Tabernacle sat on the southwest corner of the temple block, and the excavated trenches were centered along the north side—a direct distance of a few hundred feet, though the parade line may have taken a somewhat more circuitous route for the benefit of the Saints who hadn't been able to cram into the tabernacle. In any case, depending on the precise path they took, it's quite possible that the first marchers arrived at their destination before the last in line even started walking.

When the trailing members of the parade line finally arrived and the bands finished playing, the military units that had marched took up station in a line between the crowd and the trenches. It was a precautionary measure to keep anyone from falling accidentally into the man-made, sixteen-foot-deep ravine, depth enough to seriously injure any unlucky Saint who might go over the side. There was also some concern about the crowd surging forward—perhaps as the people behind tried to move in for a better view—and pushing the entire front line of celebrants into the long hole all at once. No doubt Brigham didn't want to see a mass accident going down in Church history as one of the notable events of this particular day.

The choir sang an opening hymn, and, as the music faded to quiet, the crowd looked to the prophet. For some reason, Brigham decided against addressing the congregation—he may have been ill and was trying to save his voice. Whatever his reason, he remained silent, and Thomas Bullock stepped forward to deliver an oration in Brigham's place that the prophet had written in advance of the occasion. Bullock was a British convert to the faith, having been baptized in late 1841. He'd immigrated to Nauvoo soon thereafter and was Joseph Smith's clerk for much of the year before the Prophet's death at Carthage. He'd continued on as a clerk for Brigham and the Twelve as the Saints went west, and now he would speak on the prophet's behalf. He stepped forward and in his British accent addressed the crowd, speaking from a text probably written by Brigham. "This morning we have assembled on one of the most solemn, interesting, joyful, and glorious occasions, that ever has, or will transpire among the children of men," he began. "And I congratulate my brethren and sisters that it is our unspeakable privilege to stand here, this day, and minister before the Lord, on an occasion which has caused the tongues and pens of prophets to speak and write for many scores of centuries which are past."[40] Moses had constructed a portable tabernacle that housed the ark of the covenant until God revealed to Solomon a pattern for a permanent temple to shelter it, he explained. That temple was built, destroyed, rebuilt, desecrated, purified, expanded, and destroyed again; and since that time, there had been no temple on the earth where God could visit His people and teach them His ways. At that point, Bullock preached the apostasy of the ancient church and its latter-day restoration through Joseph Smith. The Lord had commanded Joseph to build a temple in Kirtland and revealed the pattern for it as He had done for Moses and Solomon. "Without revelation, Joseph could not know what was wanting, any more than any other man," he explained, and it was only with divine assistance that that temple was completed.[41]

At that point, the Saints who had been the earliest converts must have thought back to days when the Kirtland Temple had been taken out of their hands. Others who had come later may have thought instead about the Nauvoo Temple, which their enemies had desecrated and reduced to a pile of charred rubble. It had all been worth it, Bullock assured them.

> The preparatory ordinances there [in the Kirtland Temple] administered, though accompanied by the administration of angels and the presence of the Lord Jesus, were but a faint similitude of the ordinances of the House of the Lord in their fulness; yet many, through the instigation of the devil, thought they had received all, knew as much as God, apostatized, and have gone to hell; but be assured, brethren, there are but few, *very few* of the elders of Israel, now on earth, who know the meaning of the word *endowment*; to know they must experience, and to experience, a Temple must be built.[42]

All of their work and sacrifice in building two houses of the Lord, and all they would do now to build a third, was to enable the Saints to receive that endowment. But if "very few" Saints understood what an endowment was, those who didn't could not see all of their past work, sufferings, and losses through an eternal perspective. What was an endowment? Bullock's written text explained the concept in plain terms.

> Your endowment is, to receive all those ordinances in the House of the Lord, which are necessary for you, after you have departed this life, to enable you to walk back to the presence of the Father, passing the angels who stand as sentinels; enabled to give them the key words, the signs and tokens pertaining to the Holy Priesthood, and gain your eternal exaltation in spite of earth and hell.[43]

And there it was—to return to God's presence, the Saints had to take part in ordinances that could be performed only in the temple. It was that simple. They'd had the use of the finished Nauvoo Temple for only a few months to perform those ceremonies. Were they ready to try again?

Brigham's pugilistic nature came through the written words that Bullock shared with the crowd. "These are questions for you to answer. If you say yes, you have got to do the work, or it will not be done. We don't want any whiners about this Temple," he warned them. "If you cannot commence cheerfully, and go through the labor of the whole building cheerfully, start for California, and the quicker the better," he charged them in his usual blunt style. Do the work with a smile or leave the valley. The prophet wanted the shirkers out, and he had no sympathy for anyone who wasn't ready and willing to devote full energies to the project.[44]

Ending the discourse, Bullock's written speech took on a softer tone. "We dedicate this, the South-East Corner Stone of this Temple, to the Most High God," he announced. Then, hearkening back to Elder George A. Smith's first sermon in the valley almost six years before, he concluded the oration. "May it remain in peace till it has done its work, and until He who has inspired our hearts to fulfil the prophecies of his holy prophets, that the House of the Lord should be reared in the '*Tops of the Mountains*,' shall be satisfied and say it is enough."[45]

Just as when they had first broken ground here not quite two months before, Heber C. Kimball followed Bullock's oration with an extended prayer, though this one was moderately shorter. When Kimball was done supplicating heaven, the choir sang again, this time performing a song written by Eliza R. Snow. Eliza was the sister of Apostle Lorenzo Snow, a former plural wife of the Prophet Joseph, and one of the most respected and highly accomplished women in the entire Church. Born in Massachusetts in 1804, Eliza was the second of seven children; she was ten years older than Lorenzo. Their parents were unusual in that they were farmers by occupation but also educated enough that Eliza's father qualified for professional work. They sought to give their children the same strong education they enjoyed, and Eliza was learned enough to work in her father's office when he served as the local justice of the peace for a time. She and several other members of the Snow family joined the

Church in 1835, and Eliza immediately moved to Kirtland, whereupon she donated her entire inheritance to the building fund for the temple there. She shared in all of the persecutions of Ohio and Missouri, and suffered more than most when a brutal assault at the hands of mobbers during the "Mormon War" left her unable to bear children.

Eliza was a truly gifted poet who had published almost two dozen compositions before her baptism into the restored Church. Her output was prodigious and lasting—she would go on to write ten poems that would later be set to music and published in the Church's hymnal. But most of those still lay in the future. For this day, she had composed a set of verses, now set to music and titled very simply, "The Temple."

> Our Era this day number three years and twenty,
> And lo! A great people inhabit the West;
> The Lord God of Abra'm, the great God of battles,
> Who leads forth to vict'ry, appointed our rest.
>
> Chorus
> The Temple, The Temple—we'll build up the Temple,
> A court of salvation—iniquity's rod—
> A glorious beacon—a light on the mountains—
> A portal for angels—a threshold for God.
>
> The stone of the corner—the Temple's foundation
> In peace, in the City of Brigham are laid;
> In the chambers of Israel, the ground that is sacred,
> Where righteousness triumphs—where truth is obey'd.
>
> Glad tidings of joy to the spirits in prison,
> To the Saints of all countries and Isles of the sea,
> For a Temple of God in the midst of the mountains;
> And joy in the courts of the highest will be.
>
> Rejoice all ye meek—all ye contrite in spirit
> For Zion's redemption is now drawing near;
> And the vail will be rent, and the Saints resurrected,
> The kingdom in heaven will shortly appear.

The Lord whom ye seek will soon come to his Temple,
The covenant messenger who ye desire;
He'll purify Israel as god in the furnace,
Consume the dross with unquenchable fire.

Sing aloud hallelujah to God the Eternal:
To him be all excellence, glory and worth,
And blessed be Brigham and Heber and Willard,
His authoriz'd agency here upon earth.[46]

The choir finished Eliza's hymn, and the Nauvoo Brass Band started another song, which they played through as Brigham led the group to the southwest corner of the foundation. Edward Hunter, the Presiding Bishop of the Church, delivered the oration this time, and he began by congratulating the people on making it thus far despite the persecutions of the past. Hunter even took a few moments of personal privilege to taunt the Saints' old enemies—who, mercifully, were a thousand miles out of earshot.

> Let all people, sinners, mobocrats, and devils, learn from experience, that persecution, plunder, robbery, rapine, murder, and expulsion from home and country, will not win. They have effectually tried it, and it has as effectually failed, every time. Please take notice! and devise some new scheme the next time, wherein you can feel some assurance, that you may possibly succeed; and we have the pleasure of not being plundered, murdered, and disfranchised, in the same way. Tax your inventive genius, for some broad scheme, to destroy God's people from the face of the earth.[47]

It would all be for naught, he assured the crowd. The temple would be built anyway. All they had to do was to throw themselves into the work. "Bring forth the materials for building; stone, lime, and sand; lumber and timber; the pine, the fir, and the cedar; the iron and steel; the silver, gold, and precious stones; to ornament, make beautiful and glorious the place of His presence, whose excellence surpasses the understanding of the children of men."[48]

When Hunter had finished, one of his counselors, Bishop Alfred Cordon, stepped up to pray over the cornerstone. Cordon was a British convert from Liverpool, a potter, and a reformed heavy drinker by his own admission. It had been his struggle with alcohol and the death of a young daughter that had turned him to religion, and he'd first heard the restored gospel from a woman, Mary Powel. Sister Powel had explained the restoration to Cordon, and he was baptized shortly thereafter. He preached as a missionary with Wilford Woodruff, Willard Richards, several other Apostles, and Brigham Young, and he apparently shared some of their more hard-edged views about what should happen to the wicked who persecuted the Saints. The sentiments that Cordon offered in prayer matched those that Hunter had shared in his discourse. After he asked the Lord to take notice of all those who would labor on the temple, that they might be blessed and protected, he requested an equally powerful cursing on their enemies. "Let every person that shall put forth their hand to prevent this thing from being accomplished, sink into oblivion, and may His power wither [them] like the gourd of Jonah," he implored.[49]

The choir sang again, and the crowd shifted to the northwest corner as the band played another martial tune. John Young, president of the high priests quorum, spoke standing atop the stone. Young promised that he had not written his talk out in advance and so spoke off-the-cuff, delivering the shortest address of the day. His testimony was filled with exclamations of happiness that he had lived to see this event and hope that he would live to see the capstone placed on the temple—but his joy was tinged by a moment of foreboding. "I very well know, that, at the commencement of the Temples that have heretofore been built to the name of the Lord by this people, the devil has always moved his artillery with greater power and activity at that time," he warned the audience. "This is the foundation of the fourth Temple that the Latter-day Saints have laid; and I pray that we shall all feel nerved up with power, to accomplish the great and glorious work which we are called to perform."[50] After thus asking the Saints to gird up, Young returned to happier thoughts and thanked God that there was a prophet on the earth and shared his feeling that "while these stones were being laid, that the angels of God were round about us."[51]

Following the pattern, Elder George B. Wallace followed with a short prayer. Wallace was a New Englander, born in New Hampshire in 1817, and had joined the Church in 1842. He had been one of the first captains of a pioneer company and had led 232 Saints to the valley in the summer of 1847. Shortly thereafter, Brigham had called him on a mission to the British Isles, which Wallace had completed the previous summer.[52] Wallace prayed that the temple foundation would be "firm as the foundations of the everlasting hills that cannot be moved" and "that the superstructure which shall be reared upon it may never be shaken." Then he added a request that hearkened back to Brigham's explanation of the temple endowment, asking that "the people may receive their blessings therein, to qualify them to pass through the vale into celestial happiness."[53] He asked for heaven's blessings on the laborers who would build the house of the Lord and on the audience.[54]

The northeast cornerstone was the last, and it was Elder Parley P. Pratt of the Quorum of the Twelve who ascended the stone to address the assembly. Pratt was from New York, a Baptist originally, though he later admitted that he'd never been fully satisfied with the doctrines of that denomination. He'd been a farmer in Ohio as a young man until early August of 1830, when, at the age of twenty-three, he felt a powerful call to preach the gospel. He and his wife, Thankful, ten years his senior, sold their farm at a loss and started to make their way back to Albany. During one leg of the journey, aboard a ship traveling the Erie Canal, Parley had another strong feeling—that he should disembark at Newark—so he told his wife to continue on while he obeyed the prompting. He met "an old Baptist deacon by the name of Hamlin" who had a copy of the Book of Mormon, which he loaned to Parley.[55] "I opened it with eagerness, and read its title page," he recorded in his autobiography. "I then read the testimony of several witnesses in relation to the manner of its being found and translated. After this, I commenced its contents by course. I read all day; eating was a burden, I had no desire for food; sleep was a burden when the night came, for I preferred reading to sleep. As I read, the spirit of the Lord was upon me, and I knew and comprehended that the book was true, as plainly and manifestly as a man comprehends and knows that he exists."[56] Determined to meet the book's translator, Parley made his way to Palmyra, New York, where he met Joseph Smith's brother Hyrum. It was Hyrum who explained the book's origin and introduced Parley to the restored gospel. Parley was baptized shortly thereafter on September 1, less than a month after he had left his farm to preach. He was called to the apostleship in 1835 and during his life proved to be one of the Church's most eloquent missionaries and prolific apologists.

His discourse that day was unlike any of the three that had preceded it. Pratt started by quoting Isaiah: "And when they shall say unto you: Seek unto them that have familiar spirits, and unto wizards that peep and mutter—should not a people seek unto their God for the living to hear from the dead?"[57] The world of the living, Pratt said, seeks communication with the dead and has turned to all manner of false mediums to accomplish it—but "it becomes the saints to be able on this, as on all other subjects, to judge correctly and understandingly, by their knowledge of the principles of true philosophy, and of the laws of God and nature," he explained.[58] Pratt launched into an extended discussion of the subject, driving to the point that such communication with the spiritual world occurred in one way only—through revelation from God to His prophets. Joseph Smith had been the first prophet in modern times to receive that privilege, and through him, the Lord had revealed the ordinances of the temple and the priesthood authority needed to perform them. "Ye are assembled here to-day and have laid these Corner Stones," Pratt declared, "for the express purpose that the living might hear from the dead; and that we may prepare a holy sanctuary where 'the people may seek unto their God; for the living to hear from the dead;' and that heaven and earth, and the world of spirits, may commune together."[59] To that end, the temple was needed so the Saints could enjoy a communion with the spirit world that the rest of humankind sought after but could not have. Then, like the speakers before him, Pratt took the opportunity to warn the people that the devil himself would try to stop them from building the temple. A fight was coming, he assured them—in fact, it had already begun. "From the moment the ground was broken for this Temple, those inspired by him [Satan] have commenced to rage; and he will continue to stir up his servants to anger against that which is good; but if we are faithful, the victory is ours."[60] And with that assurance, he ended his discourse.

Elder Orson Hyde, a fellow Apostle, offered the final prayer. He confessed to the Lord: "Our merits and demerits have been open to thy view; and our wisdom and folly have not been hid from thine eyes. Thou hast comprehended our strength and our weakness, our joys and our sorrows; and also our sufferings and persecutions for thy name's sake and the martyrdom of thy servants!"[61] It was an admission that the Saints had made their share of mistakes along the way, but he pleaded for heaven's help to be with them anyway as they built up the house of the Lord. "Whosoever, Oh, Lord, shall bless and aid the building of this Temple with their faith, goodwill, and means . . . and in the confidence and favor of God and his servants; and may the blessings of this Temple be extended unto them," he pleaded. At the finish, he asked for the construction to be "speedily erected and finished" so that the completed house of the Lord might "prove a beacon light to the nations who are floating on the sea of time in a dark and cloudy day."[62]

When Hyde ended his prayer, the choir sang again, and the crowd turned back to the prophet. "Brethren and sisters, I bless you in the name of Jesus Christ of Nazareth, and pray my Father in Heaven to encircle you in the arms of his love and mercy; protect us until we have finished this Temple, receive the fulness of our endowments therein, and then build many more," he said.[63] And with those words, Brigham dismissed the crowd.

Five years, eight months, and thirteen days after the first Saints had entered the valley, the cornerstones for the Salt Lake Temple finally had been laid.

— • · • —

The conference reconvened in the Adobe Tabernacle an hour later, at three o'clock. Brigham chose not to spare his voice this time. He was clearly in a good mood as he joked early on that the change in the unfavorable weather of the past weeks to the clear, temperate morning they had enjoyed was proof that "the devil has been sent on an errand another way and has forgotten himself. I do not think, however, he need trouble himself much about the world, for he has them secure enough. Perhaps he may have slept a little too long, as he has not been here on this notable day."[64] Then he apologized that not everyone had been able to hear the orations and prayers on the stones—which should have been predictable, given the size of the crowd and the location of the speakers deep in the trenches—but he assured them that those speeches would be printed for all to read.

Then, without preamble, he spoke of doubts about the project that had been laid before him. "Do you suppose we shall finish this temple, Brother Brigham?" he repeated the question. His answer was surprising. "I do not know, and I do not care any more about it than I should if my body was dead and in the grave and my spirit in Paradise," he assured them. "I never have cared but for one thing, and that is, simply to know that I am now *right* before my *Father in Heaven*. If I am this *moment*, this *day*, doing the things *God requires* of my *hands*, and precisely where my *Father in Heaven wants me to be*, I care no more about tomorrow than though it would never come."[65] Whether they could finish the temple wasn't his concern. All he knew was that it was his duty and theirs to start, and that they had done. How did he know it? He revealed an answer that surely must have surprised the audience. "I am not a visionary man, neither am I given much to prophesy," he admitted.

> I scarcely ever say much about revelations, or visions, but suffice it to say, five years ago last July I was here, and saw in the Spirit the temple not ten feet from where we have laid the chief cornerstone. I have not inquired what kind of a temple we should build. Why? Because it was represented before me. I have never looked upon that ground, but the vision of it was there. I see it as plainly as if it was in reality before me.[66]

It was an open declaration that he had seen the temple in vision, not once, but many times. As evidence that he was not speaking in some kind of exaggerated eloquence—which had never been his style anyway—he offered the Saints their first small description of its design. "It will have six towers, to begin with, instead of one," he said, a notable difference from the single spires of the Kirtland and Nauvoo Temples. He also added a prophecy, which surely sounded preposterous, about other rooftop features that future temples would have. "The time will come when there will be one [spire] in the center of Temples we shall build, and, on the top, groves and fish ponds. But we shall not see them here, at present."[67]

They still had to build this temple first.

CHAPTER 4

THE WORKS
OF THE ANCIENTS

The conference ended on Saturday, but work on the temple foundation didn't start for another two months, mostly due to the weather. Winter died out slowly—there was a crop-killing frost as late as mid-May—and spring rains were unusually frequent and heavy. The repeated storms combined with melting mountain snow raised the rivers in the valley to flood stages higher than any the Saints had seen. Some of the bridges over the larger rivers were swept away. Mail delivery from the eastern United States was delayed as the carriers had to wait until the waters receded,[1] and several Saints elected to the territorial legislature were unable to reach Great Salt Lake City to attend to government business.[2] City Creek, the closest waterway to the temple block, overflowed its normal channel on East Temple Street, "tearing the road to pieces" and threatening several homes.[3] Men were called away from their regular labors to help save the structures, slowing the temple construction for a short time.

The weather finally settled down, the days warmed up, and by June conditions were ripe for work to resume on the foundation. Cut sandstone would soon be needed in bulk. The choice of which quarry to draw from was already settled, so all that was left was to work out the particulars of a legal arrangement with the Sharp brothers. It didn't take long for Brigham to approve a deal, and the Church issued the first contract for the temple construction project. The Sharps agreed to deliver sandstone from the Red Butte Quarry to the temple site at a cost of $11.00 per cord, with teamsters earning $1.50 to $4.00 per wagonload. By mid-June they were delivering twenty-six loads of sandstone per week,[4] enough for construction to start, and masons and tithing hands began laying blocks on June 13, starting at the southeast cornerstone.[5] For the first year, most of the quarried stone went not into the temple foundation but into the fifteen-foot wall around the temple block, which was only one-quarter finished as of the cornerstone ceremony.[6] That project was an integral part of Brigham's plan for the temple, but it had the beneficial side effect of helping create jobs for some arriving immigrants who had no immediate prospects for employment.

While the temple foundation and the wall were going up that spring, Brigham's attention was diverted from Church matters in general and the temple in particular as Native Americans of the territory started to threaten settlements to the south. Relations with most of the tribes had been generally peaceful for three years now, and a fair amount of trading had gone on between the white settlers and their neighbors. Generally good feelings prevailed if not actual trust, but one group was a serious threat. The Timpanogo were a group of Shoshone led by a chief named Walkara, or Walker, as the Saints called him. He was, first and foremost, a notorious horse thief. That was hardly unknown in the West—native tribes had pilfered cattle and horses from more than one company of Saints crossing the plains from Winter Quarters—but Walkara's reputation for thievery was notorious even among the tribes. He was a duplicitous man, acting friendly toward the white settlers one day and ugly the next. When the Saints had first entered the valley, a council of braves had met to determine how to treat the newcomers. Walkara had argued for a massacre. The younger braves had sided with him, the older braves and chiefs with a leader named Soweite, who had argued that perhaps the Saints, like the Utes, had been driven to the mountains for refuge. The council had split, and only when Soweite had flogged Walkara with a whip did the council choose the peaceful route. Given that history, when Brigham heard that Walkara had expressed a desire to "live at peace and be a brother"[7] to the territorial governor, his expressed opinion toward Walker was anything but brotherly. "It is enough for me to know that Walker dare not attempt to hurt any of our settlements. I care not whether he loves me or not. I am resolved . . . not to trust his love any more than I would a stranger's," Brigham declared.[8]

Then the news came that there was "a horde of Mexicans, and outlandish men who are infesting the settlements, stirring up the Indians with guns, ammunition, etc."[9] Walker had given the Saints no serious problems of late, but Brigham was sure that the chief wouldn't need much encouragement to become openly hostile. If Walker's gun suppliers were agents of the Mexican government, stirring up an insurrection could be cause for war. As the US government's chief executive in Utah, Brigham did not want to act rashly, but he wanted the Saints protected and the truth uncovered. To that end, he ordered William M. Wall, captain of the Provo Military District, to take a force of thirty men and patrol the southern territories, interviewing settlers and natives alike to find out what was going on.[10] The governor was hoping for peace, but if Wall's detachment found that Walker and his followers were engaged in open hostilities, then Brigham would use the full military power at his command to "preserve peace, quell the Indians, and secure the lives and property of the citizens of the Territory."[11]

Captain Wall was well known to Brigham. Tall and well-built, with a heavy beard, he had been an occasional wrestling partner to the Prophet Joseph during the Nauvoo days. [12] He'd also been a lieutenant in the Nauvoo Legion by age twenty-three, and, by age twenty-nine, a captain of fifty in a pioneer company that crossed the plains in 1850. Now thirty-one, he was an experienced military officer. He led his detachment out of Provo, forty miles south of Great Salt Lake City, on

April 24. In less than a month they traveled five hundred miles through Millard, Iron, and Washington Counties and found neither Mexicans nor Chief Walker. Most of the natives whom Wall met were friendly, and, in fact, were openly desirous to have the governor's help in putting down Walker's horde. Discussions with several tribes revealed the real story. Walker and his followers were indeed getting arms and ammunition from Mexicans, but the Mexicans weren't gifting the guns for the purpose of inciting violence and undermining US control of the territory. Rather, Walker and his men had been raiding the other tribes for the express purpose of stealing their children, whom they sold to the Mexicans for the illegal arms. Chief Walker was a slave trader.

The child slave trade between Mexicans and native tribes was already known to the Saints, and slavery was still legal in the region, courtesy of the Compromise of 1850 that had given Utah its territorial status. Some of the settlers had bought kidnapped children to save them from being murdered, as the slavers were known to kill the children they could not sell; but the Saints' benevolence only encouraged Walker to kidnap more children. So Brigham decided that this particular form of human trafficking had gone on long enough. In his view, there was only one way to deal with such men, which policy he explained in his usual blunt manner. "If he [Walker] becomes hostile and wishes to commit depredations upon the persons or property of this people," Brigham declared, "he shall be wiped out of existence and every man that will follow him."[13] Then he ordered all of the slave traders out of the territory and called up the militia to enforce the ban by force of arms if necessary.

Walker was undeterred. All he needed was a provocation, which came on July 17, when a settler living near Springfield intervened to stop one of Walker's men from beating his own wife. A fight ensued, and the settler killed the brave. Walker demanded that the Saints kill one of their own to make restitution. They refused, so on July 18, a group of Walker's men killed Alexander Keel, a settler in Payson, fifteen miles southwest of Provo on the east side of Utah Lake. They also stole twenty-four head of cattle and horses.[14] Thus started a war between the whites and the natives that would stretch the rest of the year.

The conflict threatened to take another serious turn for the worse when, a few months later, a group of Utes massacred Captain John W. Gunnison of the US Army Corps of Topographical Engineers and seven other men near Sevier Lake. A company of emigrants traveling from the States to California had passed through Fillmore and fired on members of the Corn Creek Tribe who had come to their camp at Meadow Creek looking to trade for food and clothes. The Americans killed one native and wounded two, and they took guns and a horse left behind. Local leaders intervened and the confiscated property was returned, but the three sons of the dead warrior would not be placated. They attacked Gunnison's party and killed him and seven others. Corn Creek Chief Ka-no-she helped restore the peace, pleading for the Saints to accept that the massacre had been the independent action of the aggrieved sons. Brigham agreed that the native tribes should not be "censured unjustly, nor any blame rest where it does not belong."[15]

Both sides cooperated to keep the event from fueling larger hostilities, but Walker's depredations continued for seven more months. By the time Brigham, Walker, and Chief Ka-no-she formalized a peace treaty the following spring, nineteen settlers and an unknown number of natives had been killed.

On October 16, a little after two o'clock in the afternoon, a wagon train emerged from the mouth of Emigration Canyon above the city and made its way down into the valley. It was a Sunday, fair and cool. Many of the Saints were attending Church services in the Adobe Tabernacle, the second meeting that would be held that day in the building. The new immigrants had left Council Bluffs, Iowa, four months prior, late in the emigration season but not dangerously so if they made good time. Led by Appleton M. Harmon, the group numbered about 300 in all. The sight of a group of pioneers emerging through the pass was not unusual.

Wagon trains were arriving on a fairly regular basis now, courtesy of the Perpetual Emigration Fund Company that Brigham had established to help indigent Saints cross the plains. Nor was it unusual that most of the group were from England, Scotland, and Wales. The impressive success that missionaries had been enjoying in Great Britain for years had resulted in a constant stream of Saints traveling across the Atlantic to Utah throughout the summer and fall.

One member of this particular wagon train was a rather young Scotsman, age nineteen, who would have a profound effect on the temple now under construction. He was, in fact, a teenager when he walked into Great Salt Lake City, and there was nothing particularly remarkable about him. James Campbell Livingston was born on December 2, 1833, in Lanarkshire, Scotland. His mother died when he was just five, and a cholera pandemic claimed both his father and stepmother in 1849, leaving James and his siblings—three brothers and two sisters—as orphans. Their grandmother took in the six Livingston children, and the oldest boys, James and his brother Charles, worked to support the family. It was just a year later that Latter-day Saint missionaries introduced them to the Book of Mormon, and the entire family was converted to the gospel and baptized.

British Saints were encouraged to come to Utah and lend their efforts to build up the territory and the temple, but it was not until May 1853 that any of the Livingston children would be able to go. James, not yet twenty, left his siblings in the care of their grandmother while he sailed to the United States. Impoverished British Saints often sent one or more family members ahead to establish themselves in Salt Lake or another settlement, earn funds to help the rest, and prepare a home where the family could land when they finally were able to make the trip. James's journey followed that model. Most of his siblings eventually followed their older brother and made their way to Utah, but James traveled first and without family.

He sailed on the merchant vessel *Falcon* from Liverpool to New

Orleans, where he boarded a riverboat. That steamer carried him up the Mississippi to Keokuk, Iowa, where the Saints maintained an outfitting station to equip emigrants for the cross-country trek to Salt Lake. Nauvoo, now mostly empty and a shadow of its former self, sat on the opposite side of the river, and James took a few days to go across and see the city the Prophet Joseph had built. He eventually made his way to the Mansion House, Joseph's former home and still the residence of the Prophet's widow, Emma Smith Bidamon, and her second husband, Lewis. At their invitation, James spent the night in their home, which had been built to serve as a hotel. Emma and Lewis apparently took a liking to the young Scotsman and gave him a personal tour of the city during his stay. He saw the now-closed shops, stores, and homesteads that the Saints had once owned, some of which had been the property of Brigham, Wilford, and other Apostles—but one site made a particular impression on the teenager. "The Temple had been burned but part of the walls were standing, and we were much interested even in the ruins," he remembered.[16] Remaining residents of Nauvoo and surrounding townships had carried away much of the rubble from the site and used it in new homes and buildings, but there was enough left to fire James's imagination.

He and the rest of his company pushed on from Keokuk in mid-June and reached their destination just before winter set in. "I arrived in Salt Lake City October 16, 1853 having been seven months on the journey," James recalled later. "I traveled from the Mississippi River and drove an ox team the entire distance walking and fording rivers and streams. The Lord blessed me by sea and by land for which I was very thankful especially for the good health I enjoyed."[17] But his health was about all he had to his name. He had no family in the city to take him in, no job to pay his way, and no property but what little he'd carried from Scotland. Nor was there anywhere for him to ply the trade he'd worked back in Scotland— Harmon's report to Brigham listed the young man as a "colier," a coal miner, which was problematic, as there were no mines of any kind in the valley.[18] Brigham had actively discouraged mining from the beginning because he didn't want the Saints to contract "gold fever" and abandon jobs producing needed goods in the hopes of finding quick wealth. Fortunately for James, he was not the first emigrant to arrive virtually destitute. His plight was common, and it was normal practice for the Saints already established in Salt Lake to take new emigrants into their homes until their guests could find lodging and gainful employment.

James C. Livingston.

In the case of young James Livingston, the family that took him in was that of Brigham Young himself.

Within a few days, Brigham put James to work building a road in City Creek Canyon to facilitate the retrieval of timber, which was still a scarce commodity. James could wield an axe or a shovel, or drive a team of oxen, just as well as the next man; cutting roads was a task that any day laborer could perform. The young Scot stayed on that project only two weeks, as James or someone else—possibly Brigham—decided that the Scot was better suited for a different profession. By the end of the month, he'd been shifted to a job more to his liking. James went to work as a stonecutter in the Red Butte Quarry for the wage of two dollars per day. The temple cornerstones had already been laid by the time James reached Salt Lake, but the foundation and the wall around the temple block were still in the early stages. James certainly would have cut some of the sandstone that went into both. He worked through the early winter in November and December until the quarry closed for the season just before Christmas. He returned to work when the quarry reopened in late February the next year.[19] His new trade agreed with him. It would, in fact, be his career until he died.

It would be as a stonecutter that James Campbell Livingston would make his contribution to the building of the Salt Lake Temple, and it would earn him a storied place in the building's history that few others would match.

——— · · ———

The Saints could have used more James Livingstons. The Council House was proving to be a weak substitute for a real temple. The fact that it was serving two masters, with the first floor dedicated to public work, made it difficult to sustain the spiritual atmosphere that should have attended the temple ordinances taking place upstairs on the second. The building was crowded and noisy much of the time, there were some issues with the construction, and the space available really was too small.[20] But there was no real temple on the horizon to replace it. It was clear by this point that even getting the temple's foundation up to ground level was going to take several years, and the entire building perhaps a decade or more, at the rate things were moving.

So Brigham decided that the Church would have to build a dedicated facility of some kind to attend to the work. They broke ground for what they would soon call the Endowment House on August 4, 1853.[21] Truman Angell was the designer, and the plan was quite simple: a two-story, rectangular, adobe-brick building that, by all appearances, could have been mistaken for a residential home—except that it would sit on the northwest corner of the temple block. It would be smaller than the Council House, at thirty-four feet by forty-four feet, but the entire space would be devoted to temple ordinances. It would take only a year to build and would eventually have amenities that the Council House lacked, such as a baptistry of hewn stone in the lower level. The interior arrangements would also be designed, arranged, furnished, and decorated with the endowment ceremony in mind. It would not be a house of the Lord, but it would be more suitable than the Council House's top floor, and so, until the temple was finished, however long that would take, it would have to be enough.

———·—·—·———

Another major problem was threatening to stretch out how long building the temple was going to take—Truman Angell's mental health. He had been working on the temple designs as much as his constitution and other responsibilities allowed. He was using books on architecture available to him for reference, drawing off the patterns and elements he found there, but he was proud of the design he was developing on the page and thought that the overall design was unique enough that he could call it his own. "The finishing touches are quite original," he wrote.[22] But the unrelenting work was beginning to take a toll on his mind and spirit. In one journal entry, he complained that "all I feel to regret about is that I can't do more, but designing is a hard study for me and wearies me as mowing used to do, for if I stick too close to it, it affects my nerves."[23] Still, he pushed forward as best he could. By August of 1854, the design had progressed sufficiently that he was able to publish a letter in the *Deseret News* offering a wealth of detail about the temple that was still very much on the drawing board. Answering questions from the curious and impatient was growing tedious enough that he hoped the printed description would "obviate so many questions being asked by various individuals."[24] After listing off the temple's basic dimensions, the composition of the foundation, the width of the walls, and other facts, he did offer some details not previously known—most notably, a description of the planned towers. All that had been known about them was what Brigham had said in conference: that there would be six of them. Truman explained:

> These [corner] towers are cylindrical . . . within which stairs ascend around a solid column four feet in diameter, allowing landings at the various sections of the building. These towers have each 5 ornamental windows on two sides, above the basement. The two center towers occupy the center of the east and west ends of the building. . . . The east center tower then rises 40 feet to the top of

battlements; the west center tower rises 34 feet to the top of battlements. All the towers have spires, the details of which are not decided on.[25]

He also gave a rough layout of the interior rooms on each floor, and even listed some of the exterior symbols that would be chiseled into the walls, including the sun, the planets, the moon in various phases, and the constellation of Ursa Major. Then, after going on for almost two thousand words of tedious and dry exposition filled with heights and lengths and widths, Truman seemed to weary of his own letter and brought it to an abrupt close. He ended it with a prickly line that warned away those curious and impatient Saints who had driven him to publish the letter in the first place. "For further particulars," he told them, "wait [until] the house is done, then come and see it."[26] Anyone not satisfied by the considerable details he'd given would just have to suffer through his silence until the temple was complete, and then the building could answer their questions by itself.

The article's publication may have brought him some relief, but his duties gave him none. He was pulled constantly in three and four directions as he oversaw the simultaneous construction of other buildings in various stages, including a large home for Brigham (today called the Beehive House), which also served as the governor's mansion and a Church office; another combined house and office for the Church historian; a school; a sugar factory; a fort for one of the southern settlements; and a penitentiary. Even sharing the burden with William Ward, Truman was still overloaded, and though he might have successfully deflected the public's curiosity for a time regarding the temple, he still had to deal with government officials who took issue, and not always calmly, with some of his designs. In one case, Judge Zerubbabel Snow, associate justice of the Territorial Supreme Court, came to Truman's office demanding he alter the proposed blueprint for a schoolhouse. Whether out of impatience, professional pride, or pure architectural necessity, Truman declined, and Snow took the man's obstinacy badly. "I withstood him,"

Drawing of the Salt Lake Temple by William Ward.

Truman recounted, "and I found him much puckered up in his feelings, and, I unpuckered him as much as I could."[27] How much "unpuckering" he managed to perform, Truman didn't say, but he clearly operated better as an architect than a peacemaker.

Despite the demands on his time and energy, by May 8, 1855, he had made enough progress to hand over a completed set of "bills & specifications for the temple foundation" to Alonzo Raleigh, chief mason of the public works.[28] That came none too soon. Work on the foundation had proceeded at a ferocious rate. Later that summer, on July 23, after just two years' labor, the temple foundation was completed. The stones laid down in those first layers were called *ashlars,* and each layer was referred to as a *course.* By Raleigh's calculations, the workers had set down 101,056 cubic feet of ashlars weighing 7,478 tons in total—almost 15,000,000 pounds. They had been cut by hand, hauled by wagon, then laid and cemented in place in each course with mortar made from lime and sand applied between the courses.[29] The top course of ashlars would be cut precisely enough to establish a level horizontal surface on which to put down a layer of smooth flagging stone ten feet wide. It was upon the flagging that the temple's walls would rest.

There was every reason for the Saints to believe that they would have a temple again before too many more years passed, and they could now see what the building would look like once finished. By August, Truman's exterior design was advanced sufficiently that Ward was able to make a perspective drawing of the planned temple's complete exterior. (Truman lacked that particular skill.) Brigham liked the drawing so much that he hung the framed work in his office.[30]

—————

May 5, 1855, was a frigid day. A hard freeze the night before had left a half inch of ice on all of the standing water in the city—not that the cold of previous weeks had slowed the laborers of the public works down a whit. After almost eight years, they'd become accustomed to doing their tasks in cold weather, as they had done the past winter on the "temporary temple" that Brigham had commissioned on the temple block. They had finished their work on that structure a few days before, and now the prophet was ready to dedicate the Endowment House, as it was soon called, and open the building to the Saints. They would again be able to participate in temple ordinances.

Brigham had, in fact, allowed the place to be used before he arrived—five men and three women went through at eight o'clock that morning to take part in an endowment ceremony. Once they were finished, Brigham went to the upper room of the house, where, at ten o'clock, he met several Apostles and other Church leaders, including Wilford Woodruff, Heber C. Kimball, Orson Pratt, Daniel H. Wells, Ezra T. Benson, and a few others. They talked for forty-five minutes, and then Brigham asked Elder Benson to begin the dedication with a prayer. "After other ceremonies," which were not recorded, Brigham then asked Heber to offer the dedicatory prayer. The oration was extensive, as was Heber's usual practice, and he prayed over every room and the individual materials used in the building's construction. When he was finished, Brigham declared that "the house was clean and [he] named it 'The House of the Lord.'" Thus finished, they wasted no time in putting the Endowment House to work. At eleven fifteen, the Apostles began conducting temple ceremonies, which ran through the afternoon until a quarter past five.[31] For the first time since they'd left Nauvoo nine years before, the Saints had a building dedicated to the ordinances of salvation. It was a temporary arrangement, a "temple pro tem" that was nothing special to see, but they could attend to ceremonies they believed necessary for salvation while they worked on their permanent temple, no matter how long that project would take.

—•··•—

Whatever optimism was created by the dedication of the Endowment House and the publication of Truman Angell's plans for the true temple suffered a hard blow after the summer of 1855 closed and the weather turned cool. The farmers had enjoyed a good harvest for the last four years, with crops increasing each season enough to create a moderate surplus; but a drought, unusually hot weather, and another plague of grasshoppers brought that happy streak to an end. Harvest yields were reduced by up to two-thirds in some settlements. To keep the livestock fed, the ranchers led their herds up to Cache Valley in northern Utah, where they could graze on untouched grasslands. But the winter there proved to be the most severe one since the Saints' first entry into the valley. Cattle died from exposure, exhaustion, and starvation. By the time spring came, half of the livestock in the territory had perished, according to estimates.[32] Thirty-five thousand Saints were facing a famine. They would be living off the previous years' surplus that they had stored and what they could grow in their own gardens until the first harvest. To assist the most destitute among them, Brigham called on the Saints to fast for twenty-four hours on the first Thursday of every month and deliver the food saved to the ward bishops. These "fast-day offerings" were distributed to the families most in need of assistance.[33] Brigham also made the decision to suspend the temple construction for the year. Every hand would be needed in the fields to ensure that there was enough food grown to sustain the population for the next winter.

Brigham also had another announcement regarding the temple that was surprising to everyone except Wilford Woodruff. "We have abandoned the idea of using adobies in the walls of that building, and intend to use granite," Brigham declared from the pulpit in March.[34] Precisely when Brigham and his counselors made the decision to use granite is not known, but it was sometime in mid-1854 or early in 1855. Brigham's "chemical argument" for bricks had given way to the reality, discovered through some experimentation, that adobe walls as high as Truman's design called for were impossible to build. Even with the foundation built to handle brick walls eight feet thick, the overall weight would be more than the adobes in the bottom layers could bear. They would be crushed. So the Church leaders would either have to scale down the size of the temple to reduce the weight or abandon adobe brick as the building material.

So they turned to granite, which had the compelling advantages of greater structural strength and near indestructibility even when subjected to extremes of temperature and moisture. And there was no shortage of it nearby. There was a considerable quantity of granite—actually quartz monzonite, a dense igneous rock often confused for granite—in Big Cottonwood Canyon, nineteen miles to the southeast, and the samples retrieved from there had a striking appearance. There was more in Little Cottonwood Canyon farther south, just lying on the ground in enormous boulders. But granite would come with serious challenges. Just cutting the blocks in the quarry down to size for transport would require a significant number of stonecutters to hammer and split rock, along with blacksmiths to craft, repair, and hone the tools. Teaching unskilled men the basics of splitting boulders down to manageable sizes was doable, as many a prison jailer could attest, but even with skilled men, it would still be a much slower and more labor-intensive task than making adobe brick.

Still more stonecutters would be needed at the temple site, and these men would need to be experienced and skilled. They would be carving individual stones into the proper shapes and executing detailed design work to decorate the building's facade. Even assuming there were enough such men in the territory, it would be slow and tedious labor, as shaping a single stone could take days or weeks of careful work for even an experienced stonecutter. And once they were shaped, lifting the enormous stones into position would be no small feat of engineering. Adobe bricks were light enough to be moved and laid by one man or a few, but placing granite would require the same kinds of construction derricks the workers had used to put down the sandstone foundation, and they would have to use them with practically every stone in the structure all the way up. So choosing granite for the construction material would add countless man-hours to the project and delay the building's completion by years.

Transporting the stone would be the other serious challenge. The Saints could have made adobe bricks within a stone's throw of the temple site, but hauling large granite stones almost twenty miles would be a major undertaking. Teamsters could move a block of sandstone from the Red Butte Quarry to the temple site in a single day—a trip so short that they had finally decided that finishing that railroad spur to Red Butte wasn't worth the money or the trouble, not to mention the potential danger. Trying to stop a flatcar with no engine, moving at speed while hauling several thousand pounds of stone, was a risky feat, to say the least.

But moving granite from the southern canyons to the city would take several days, assuming that rain or snow hadn't turned the roads muddy or impassable. That meant the builders would need several times as many teamsters, wagons, and oxen if they wanted to maintain daily deliveries of stone. They didn't have many reinforced wagons designed to haul heavy cargo, and it was doubtful the light wagons they had available could handle the weight of granite stones. And regardless of the kinds of wagons they used, the Saints would need to improve and maintain the north-south road between Salt Lake and the southern canyons, with all the toil and expense that would involve.

A railroad line between the two points would be the ideal solution. Railways were impervious to all but the most extreme weather and required relatively little maintenance. A single flatcar driver would be able to transport even the heaviest granite blocks from the quarry to the temple site in a matter of hours. Replacing all those teamsters and oxen with a handful of drivers would reduce the transportation costs by a considerable amount. It was the ideal answer to the problem—except that the up-front costs of building a rail line were far more than the Saints had to spare at the moment in either money or labor.

Perhaps an easier solution, they decided, would be a canal. Brigham and the other Saints who had lived in New England in the early days of the Church would have remembered the Erie Canal, which cut a 363-mile path through the state to connect the Great Lakes with the Hudson River in Albany, New York, opening a waterway to the Atlantic. Its construction had taken only eight years, and once it was complete in 1825, boats towed by pack animals had been able to haul far more passengers and cargo in a shorter time and for less money than by any other method. It had been an economic boon to every area through which it passed, and a fair number of Saints had traveled its length back and forth. A canal here would offer all of the same benefits, and it could easily be fed from the seven canyon creeks that poured their waters into the Jordan River. It would provide easy access to water for irrigation and power to drive sawmills and gristmills. The benefits looked endless, and the Saints could enjoy them soon. If men could build the Erie Canal in eight years, surely the Saints could build a twenty-mile canal—less than one-tenth the length—in far less time than that.

The Territorial Legislature took up the proposal and issued a land grant for its construction. The *Deseret News* reported:

> The Governor and Legislative Assembly of the Territory of Utah, during the last session, granted to Brigham Young, Isaac Chase and Feramorz Little, and their associates and successors, the right to make a canal from Big Cottonwood creek to G. S. L. City, and a strip of land one mile wide on the East and a half mile on the West side of the canal for its entire length. This work is designed to be permanent, and will be constructed for the purpose of boating granite rock from Big Cottonwood for the Temple and for building up this City, and from the abundant supply of water, will afford great facilities for bringing the adjacent valuable land into a high state of cultivation and for propelling machinery of all descriptions.[35]

Brigham wasted no time once the grant was approved; he had surveyors mapping a route for the canal by the end of April. He hoped to have the canal ready to start moving granite by June of 1856, the following year.

Wilford's vision that the temple would made be of stone, not brick, would come true, even if the beginning of its fulfillment would have to wait another year.

———— ◆ · · ◆ ————

For his part, three years of serious physical and mental effort expended on the temple, in addition to whatever physical labor Truman was exerting on his own home and land, were straining the Church architect to his limits. By the winter of 1856 his health was failing him, and he was unable to work for months. His absence from the architect's office did not go unnoticed on Brigham's part. Concerned, and despite feeling ill himself,[36] he invited Truman to dinner on the first of April. The prophet's brother-in-law clearly needed a vacation, and sometime during the evening, Brigham asked Truman whether he might be agreeable to visiting Europe. Truman admitted that his responsibilities "were very fatiguing and crowded upon me farther than I could attend to them, and that I did desire temporary relief."[37] So Brigham approved a missionary tour across the Atlantic for the beleaguered architect. To that end, Truman went to Brigham's office a few days later to be set apart in that calling and to receive a blessing. The prophet and his counselors laid hands on Truman's head, and during the prayer, Brigham gave the Church architect a second mission to perform during his foreign travels.

> You shall have power and means to go from place to place, from country to country and view the various specimens of architecture that you may desire to see, and you will wonder at the works of the ancients and marvel to see what they have done; and you will be quick to comprehend the architectural designs of men in various ages, and you will rejoice all the time, and take drafts of valuable work of architecture and be better qualified to continue your work and you will increase in knowledge upon the temple and other buildings and many will wonder at the knowledge you possess.[38]

The blessing made it clear—this would be a change of scenery, but it would be no vacation. The purpose of Truman's sabbatical would be "to visit the works of men a preaching as I go at the same time view the old cathedrals . . . and seek to improve the art of building if the experience can be got more externally than at home."[39] Sharing the gospel was the universal duty of all missionaries, and whatever Truman could do in that regard would be appreciated, but it would be a secondary activity for him on this journey. Europe's architectural tradition was both ancient and rich—its religious buildings in particular—and he was to study it so he could apply the lessons learned to the temple blueprints. The large churches and cathedrals of Great Britain had impressed Brigham during his time there, and he hoped Truman might feel the same and draw liberally from their designs.

Within the week Truman was setting his affairs in order. "I remained about home in the city endeavoring to make my family as comfortable as

I could," he wrote, "arranging the various plans and designs I had made of the Temple, and other buildings, and giving instructions concerning them to the various foremen, that they might be prepared to carry out the same, and gathering together such provision and raiment as I could, which seemed necessary for my journey."[40] His assistant William Ward was left in charge of architectural responsibilities relating to the temple that might arise in his absence. Truman arranged for his family's maintenance and care, and gave them a blessing of peace. He also found the time to pen a letter to Brigham, expressing his gratitude for the opportunity to travel and his confidence in the prophet's counsel.

> I should neither do justice to you, or my own feelings, by leaving this place without first expressing my gratitude to you for your kindness, patience, and long-suffering toward me. And what have I done for you in return for the many blessings you have bestowed upon me? Nothing. I have seen the hand of our Heavenly Father in all your moves; the Most High has in you truly a friend on this Earth, another such a sample cannot be found in Israel, much less among the gentiles. . . . I do most assuredly know, that the counsel of the Lord is in you, to a much greater degree than can be found in any other man, and the few cases wherein I have allowed myself to differ in opinion from you, have always caused me hours of regret.[41]

It was a letter that expressed deep gratitude such as Truman rarely put on paper. One reason for that was the self-admitted diffidence that had been a defining trait of his since his childhood. In this instance, and in defiance of that shyness and lack of confidence, he clearly spent time choosing his words with great care to express some of the most heartfelt emotions he ever recorded.

Truman left home for the eastern United States on April 21, three weeks after Brigham had issued the invitation to travel abroad. He was in ill health when he left, suffering from a "nervous weakness" that he couldn't seem to shake, but he'd been under the weather so often that it was hardly a deterrent for him. Nor would he be traveling alone.

He would be part of a company of forty-five people led by Abraham O. Smoot, the chosen captain, and Apostle Ezra T. Benson. They assembled near the mouth of Emigration Canyon and spent a very cold night outside. Brigham came the next day to see them off. He charged them to live their religion and offered some counsel Truman didn't record, blessed the company, and bid them farewell.[42] The company crowded into their fourteen wagons and moved out.

It took almost two months to travel the 1,160 direct miles to St. Louis, Missouri. Arriving on the twelfth of June, Truman had walked most of the way because of the limited wagon space, and the company had spent nearly a week trapped in place by a late snowstorm that had caught them eleven days out from the valley.[43] But having finally left the frontier behind, Truman tarried in that city for less than a week before buying passage to New York by rail. He made that 870-mile trip in four days, arriving on June 21, no doubt better rested than his thousand-mile walk across the plains had left him. From New York he made his way to Boston, and on July 2, he bought passage on a steamship bound for Liverpool. Most of his traveling companions had dispersed in St. Louis, but a few reconvened with Truman on the ship, including Elder Ezra T. Benson, Apostle and scientist Orson Pratt, and Brigham's older brother Phineas. "We were a happy company," Truman reported, and the journey across the ocean appears to have done nothing to disturb their congeniality.[44] Truman made no note of any storms or other contrary events during the passage, the Atlantic crossing was relatively swift, and they arrived in Liverpool eleven days later, on July 13, with the ship pushing up the Mercy River and "firing off two guns" to announce the vessel's arrival.[45] The Custom House Officer boarded the ship, searched their baggage, and cleared the small company of Saints just before midnight to enter the country. Despite the late hour, they secured a horse-drawn cab that carried them to the home of Elder Franklin D. Richards, the presiding Apostle over the Church's British Mission, who met them at the door.

After settling in for a few days in Liverpool, which would act as his home base throughout his travels, Truman boarded a train to Birmingham to attend a Church conference at President Richards's invitation. The ninety-mile trip took him a little over seven hours, he reached the city by midafternoon, and the conference itself lasted for three days. If the architect spent any of his spare time looking at the buildings of Birmingham, he didn't record it in his journal, but he seems to have been in good spirits. During one of the meetings he bore his testimony of the gospel and shared his hope that his time in Great Britain would renew his mind and body. "I . . . stated that my business had tended to wear me down in body and that by casting all off for a season, I was in shape to . . . return invigorated and refreshed."[46] To support him during his travels, Orson Pratt suggested and the leadership agreed that Elder John Kay should accompany Truman and act as a guide.

The conference adjourned on June 23. Truman and his companion boarded a train the next morning, and they were back in Liverpool for dinner. The following morning, he started his architectural studies simply by spending several days walking around the city to "look at their best buildings."[47] No structure impressed him enough to merit listing in his journal by name, and he was ready to look elsewhere by the end of July. Rather sensibly, he booked passage to the city that hosted England's greatest buildings: London itself. Surely, if the United Kingdom had anything to offer in the way of superior architecture, he would find it there. He arrived on the fourth of August, settled in, and spent a few days visiting with local Church leaders, some of whom acted as tour guides for the visiting missionary. The first object of his study was the London Monument, a Roman Doric column 202 feet tall designed by Sir Christopher Wren and erected in the 1670s as a memorial to the Great Fire of London that had destroyed the homes of tens of thousands in 1666. Truman ascended the spiral staircase to the viewing gallery, which allowed him to review the broad sweep of the city. The building intrigued him, and the scene laid out before him at the top impressed him enough that he tarried for a while. "We looked at the Metropolis as far as our eyes would extend and time would permit," he wrote. [48] His choice of one of the tallest structures in London as his first stop suggests that he likely spent some of his time in the gallery considering which buildings he wanted to see next.

The following day he took a steamer up the River Thames destined for Woolwich. He passed London Bridge and many prominent buildings within view from the ship's deck, including the residence of the Bishop of Canterbury, Westminster Abbey, the Houses of Parliament, St. Paul's Cathedral, the Wellington Monument, the Tower of London, and "other things too numerous to mention."[49] Whatever awe Truman may have felt for these famous structures after seeing them from a distance, he began to sour on them after some closer observations. His first such review was a tour of the Houses of Parliament. He was thoroughly unimpressed. "I shall not make any lengthy notes of them," he wrote later, "but I must say that it was burdened with ornaments till it became sickening. I had to think the object of decorating so much was to excel rather than to display anything like a reasonable taste."[50] He felt a similar distaste for the National Gallery, and the Tower of London earned nothing more than a passing mention that he'd visited it. The Crystal Palace,[51] constructed in Hyde Park to house the Great Exhibition of 1851, was the first building that he appreciated. It was enormous, covering almost a million square feet. The superstructure was wood and cast iron, with walls and ceiling of plate glass that let sunlight flood the interior, earning the building its name. Truman stayed there most of the day, seven or eight hours by his own estimation, and he went back and visited it a second time a week later. "I will not attempt to pretend to describe it," he wrote, "but sum it up by saying it is intended to exhibit the genius of England as well as to exhibit many foreign articles from other nations. And it is a grand affair."[52]

Westminster Abbey did not draw the same compliments after Truman's visit; he did feel that it "exhibited the genius of men but there was something about it very inanimate."[53] He and Elder Kay attended several theaters, but they all appeared nearly identical to his eye, with "little difference"[54] to distinguish them. They visited another of Sir Christopher Wren's buildings, St. Paul's Cathedral, considered the designer's greatest work. Truman was underwhelmed. After a meticulous tour of the building "from bottom to top," he had decided that "the most I could say of it was that it was a national show, and when the people want to make a show with their money, such buildings may be built, that can be easily matched."[55] There was a difference between architectural excellence and opulence, he thought, and the British were constantly mistaking the latter for the former as far as Truman was concerned. Accordingly, when he wrote an August report to Brigham about his trip to date, he mentioned none of the buildings he had seen; instead he filled the pages with talk of missionary work and how he handled those who challenged his testimony of the restored gospel. With the exception of the Crystal Palace, which had dazzled him and the rest of Europe, Truman preferred American simplicity. The United States was too young a country to have constructed buildings so large, elaborate, intricate, and ornate; even the best structures back home were smaller, simpler, and cleaner in their designs. The result was that his criticism of the buildings he was seeing now grew in direct proportion to their complexity.

He decided to expand his search. As a side mission, he'd been seeking out information on sugar refineries so he could help build a similar facility back in Utah, and he'd heard that there was one in Ireland. He wrote a letter of inquiry to a Church member there, who confirmed that there were three. So on August 29, he got out of bed at five o'clock in the morning and boarded the train for Liverpool, where he spent the month of September before taking a steamboat to Belfast. From there he made his way to Dublin. The trip was fruitful for him with regard to learning about the Irish process of sugar making, but less so for his review of the city's buildings. He visited the Phoenix Park and Zoological Garden, the Duke of Wellington Monument, and the Sarah Bridge, but a little more than two weeks of searching there produced nothing more interesting to him than a month in London had. "The architecture of these places was not very remarkable," he noted. [56] It was so unremarkable to him, in fact, that his next letter to Brigham, an eight-page dispatch, was devoted to describing a method of converting beets into sugar. There was not one mention of any of the famed Irish buildings he'd toured.[57] He returned to Liverpool, again unmoved and unimpressed by what he'd seen.

Truman made his way to Manchester in late October, which city he found to be a mixed architectural bag, but even that was an improvement. He thought the Free Library there was worth a few lines in his notebook, noting that "the building or rooms were nearly similar to one of our chambers in the Plan of the State House, Utah Territory."[58] To find that his own designs were similar to those being drawn up by more professional architects must have felt encouraging. But after that hopeful beginning in this new city, he returned to form after touring one building that he simply called the "Old Church," possibly the Manchester Cathedral. It was "a dark, gloomy scene."[59] He described the exterior gargoyles as "hobgoblins" and thought the interior was depressing, but he at least credited the builders for the "immense deal of labor bestowed on it."[60] He appreciated the hard work that went into its construction, even if all of that well-meaning effort had produced an edifice that he didn't find spiritually uplifting.

After three months of touring, most of what he'd seen in Great Britain had struck him as drab, dark, and ostentatious, with little real variation in design. He had Brigham's blessing to travel to any country in Europe, so Truman returned to London and obtained approval to visit France from that country's consulate. He boarded a steamer midmorning at London Bridge on November 19 and set foot on French soil at Dieppe eight hours later—and probably for the first time in his life, he found himself surrounded by people who spoke a foreign tongue. The strange language came as a bit of a shock. "We find ourselves in a land where our native tongues are not worth much to help us,"[61] he wrote. In England

and Ireland, for all their faults, at least he hadn't needed an interpreter just to travel around, much less to preach the gospel and minister to the Saints. Here he was practically illiterate. Undaunted, he managed to find his way to Paris within a day, where he followed his usual practice of taking a walking tour of the city. "The streets were mostly narrow but quite clean, the most popular streets containing fanciful buildings,"[62] he recorded. He needed half a week to make the rounds, which included stops at the Royal Palace, the tomb of Bonaparte, and the home of the current Emperor Napoleon.

Four days of that was apparently enough, and from Paris he traveled by train to Le Havre, 109 miles to the northeast in the Normandy region along the Atlantic Coast. There he found an English hotel a few miles from the train station, but whatever delight he initially felt at being in more familiar surroundings disappeared quickly. The inn proved to be an uncomfortable place to lodge, where the proprietor didn't light fires for his guests' warmth, which Truman noted was a general practice in the country. "The Saints in Zion should be thankful to the Lord, for the poor in Salt Lake are a thousand times more comfortable than they are in this town," Truman decided. "My heart sickens at the horrors seen in this hemisphere."[63] And Le Havre did nothing to raise his spirits in the following days. He found one theater he considered beautiful but nothing else. He went on to Saint-Lô, where he described the people as "a rude-looking set";[64] then to Jersey in the Channel Islands off the French coast. There he found an ancient fortress he referred to as "Oxgud Castle,"[65] which he thought was "a miserably poor place."[66]

France was proving no more fruitful than Great Britain for his studies. He was ill, possibly because the innkeepers stubbornly refused to heat their inns, a problematic issue given his weak constitution. The worldly cultures surrounding him were nothing like the religious society the Saints had created back home, and he could neither understand nor make himself understood to anyone without someone else to speak for him. All of these factors drove Truman to his decision to leave France.

After three days on the island of Jersey, he booked passage on a steamer for England, with any thoughts of touring the rest of Europe now abandoned, or at least delayed until the spring. He would spend the winter in England and wait to visit the continent again until the cold weather was no longer an issue.

Truman passed December and January 1857 in and around London, ministering to the British Saints while he searched out other examples of architecture to study. He visited Greenwich College and noted that the buildings there had required considerable labor to put up like the Old Church he'd seen in Manchester—but, as with St. Paul's Cathedral, he thought them gaudy, "burdened," he said, overdone with the intricate details and flourishes that Truman disliked.[67] Truman toured the Greenwich Observatory, the British Empire's center of astronomical studies and the site through which the prime meridian ran, but he had more praise for the scientific equipment he found there than for the buildings that housed it. Only one building that he saw during that winter season drew real admiration from Truman—the Hereford Cathedral. "It was built in a masterly style of architecture," he wrote, some of the highest praise that he'd offered to any structure he'd seen during the entire trip.[68]

Any plans he may have been making to visit other cities were abandoned when the mail arrived on January 27. Truman received three letters from his family back home. Elder Orson Pratt had received a letter from Brigham containing a single sentence that cut Truman's sabbatical in Europe short:[69] "We wish to have Bro. Truman O. Angell return early in the spring."[70] The sabbatical was over. How much time he and Brigham had originally expected him to spend in Europe is unknown, but the letter had been written on October 30, 1856, barely six months after Truman had left. No explanation was given for the recall, and to reach Great Salt Lake City by "early in the spring," he would have to leave Europe very soon.

If Truman was unhappy about the sudden end to his mission, he never wrote of it. He'd spent more time nursing his health and preaching than he had studying architecture. He was sick again by this time and not sleeping well, which likely fueled the sense of severe depression he was feeling—indeed, he'd suffered repeated bouts of melancholy, which may have influenced his negative feelings toward so many of the buildings he saw. He had seen enough of Great Britain to expect that he wasn't going to find anything novel or radically different from the intricate and ornate buildings he'd seen already, and he was in no shape to travel around the rest of Europe before spring. But above all else, the prophet had asked him to come home, and Truman would respond.

Truman started his preparations for the trip across the Atlantic. He had the time to tour a few more buildings, and he did some shopping for supplies that were likely hard to acquire back in the valley, including paint and brushes, a six-shooter, a gun belt, and one hundred rounds of ammunition that he'd purchased from a British arms dealer.[71] On February 13, a little more than two weeks after he'd received the news of his recall, Truman boarded a steam packet bound for the United States.[72] The return voyage took three days longer than his initial crossing months earlier, but it was uneventful, and Truman landed in Boston on March 1. Winter was still in full force in Massachusetts, with a blustery snowstorm greeting him as he set his feet on his native soil again. He lingered there a week before boarding the train for Brooklyn, New York, and then another to St. Louis. It was there that he found a possible reason for the abrupt end to his mission: William Ward. His assistant, to whom he had entrusted the responsibility of all work related to the temple in his absence, had left both the Church and Great Salt Lake City and moved to St. Louis. Ward left no written explanation for his disaffection, but it had apparently happened before Brigham wrote his October letter asking Truman to come home. Ward was now the second Church architect to walk away, but, unlike William Weeks before him, Ward had at least not absconded with the temple plans in an act of spite. Those were back in the valley in the office he and Truman had shared, and his reception of Truman in St. Louis was friendly, suggesting that whatever had driven Ward away had not also turned him bitter. But regardless of the circumstances of Ward's defection, if he was here in Missouri, then there was no Church architect back in the valley. It was now April, and winter in Utah was ending, so the temple construction could resume, but the Saints needed someone qualified to oversee it.

Truman made his way to Independence, Missouri. There he joined a small wagon train of twelve people led by Apostle George A. Smith, and they rolled west on the first of May. They suffered an immediate delay when, on their second day out, three mules wandered off. They could have left the animals behind—every wagon train lost livestock to death, Native Americans, and wandering—but a member of the search party also disappeared, and it took two days to track him down. After recovering both man and beasts, they suffered no other significant delays along the trail. They enjoyed fair weather and avoided Indian troubles, which enabled them to make exceptionally good time, averaging almost forty-five miles per day and traversing fifty-five miles in one twenty-four-hour stretch. The pace was exhausting, but, unlike on the prior journey, there was room enough for Truman to ride in the wagons. Even so, as they entered the Utah Territory, Truman was hardly eating and was suffering from frequent nightmares, robbing him of what rest he could get. It was fortunate that he did not have to suffer long. His traveling company entered the valley on May 29, 1857, after covering the twelve hundred miles from Independence in just twenty-seven days.[73] "Found all my family well and in good spirits," he wrote in his usual understated fashion, though Truman himself had been neither well nor in good spirits for some time.[74] Despite that, he considered himself far better off in the company of family and the Saints than in any place he had seen over the last year. In thirteen months, he had traveled 16,579 miles by his own calculation—some ten thousand by ship, almost twenty-five hundred by wagon or on foot, the rest by train—to see places considered wonders of the world. To Truman Angell, none of them were nearly so beautiful as his home in the Rocky Mountains.

———•·•———

While Truman was making his way back, work on the canal needed to transport the temple granite was under way, but it was moving at a slower pace than Brigham wanted to see. He made an inspection tour in mid-March in the company of Surveyor General Jesse W. Fox and several others. The group was "much surprised by the great amount of work done at the deep cuts, heavy grades and wide ravines; and were highly pleased with the zeal and energy manifested by the laborers."[75] It was evident, however, that the canal would not be done by June as Brigham had imagined. Daniel H. Wells, called to the apostleship the January past, put out the call for more laborers from the pulpit two weeks later.

> The Big Cottonwood canal should be finished to facilitate procuring rock for building the Temple. Much labor has already been expended upon it, but it requires still more. The brethren have been very diligent in this matter, but we expect that we shall have to call upon them for further labor on that work. . . . Will you lend your aid in this enterprise? Will we complete it this season, that we may boat rock for the Temple? This will be proved by your acts, as well as by your faith.[76]

Even without the canal, Brigham hadn't been content to wait. The temple footings were ready for the walls, so the prophet had directed that the project resume in early March when the weather had finally warmed enough to allow it. Men were dispatched to Big Cottonwood Canyon, teamsters had returned with the first granite stones, and a team of stonecutters had started shaping the rough blocks for eventual placement in the temple's basement walls.[77] Retrieving the blocks had been difficult but not complicated. Granite boulders of all sizes littered the canyon floor, so once they were cracked down to size, it was mostly a matter of raw muscle and basic engineering to get them into wagons. It did indeed take the teamsters four days to haul one load, and there was a shortage of stone-cutters available to finish the stones once they arrived. In addition to asking for more men to help dig the canal, Daniel Wells had asked for more stonecutters to present themselves and lend their skills to the work. "Are there but few in the country? If so, men can soon learn the trade," he assured the congregation.[78] There would be jobs for anyone willing to work.

The labor shortage actually insulated the project from what would have become a series of serious and growing problems. William Ward's unexpected departure had created a void of leadership, and by the time Truman arrived in late May, the workers had been doing their business for seven weeks without an architect to direct the labor. The lack of skilled stonecutters and the slow process of dressing rock saved the work from grinding to a halt, but within a few months they would need someone to provide them with precise patterns and other guidance to keep them on course. Truman arrived before that became an issue and saved them that particular headache. Even better, he let it be known that he hadn't seen anything in Europe that inspired him to change the temple's design in any significant way, so there was no need to stop the quarrymen or the stonecutters in order to redraft the plans. The workers kept moving without any added delays coming from the architect's office, and they were ready to lay the first cut stones within seven weeks of Truman's return.

Placing the first stones for the basement walls was not so momentous as the laying of the cornerstones had been, but there was public interest in the event. The fifteen-month delay in the project had left the Saints with considerable pent-up anxiety to see *some* progress made. They'd built the entire Nauvoo Temple from start to finish in a little over five years—and that in the midst of fierce persecution. Here, working on this new temple, they'd invested tens of thousands of man-hours over four years and there was, as yet, no part of the temple even visible above the ground level. So the laying of the first basement stone was cause for a minor celebration. Brigham came to watch the event, bringing with him a small company of other leaders and a reporter from the *Deseret News* who recorded the events for the Saints at large.

> On the morning of Thursday, June 18, and in company with President H. C. Kimball, we visited the foundation of the Temple, upon the N.E. Corner of which, brother Edward Parry was laying the first stone in the basement story under the supervision of A.H. Raleigh, foreman of the mason work. All along the foundation walls, huge stones, averaging about two tons in weight, were strewn in readiness for being placed in their positions, while numerous stone cutters were busily occupied in shaping the rude blocks from the quarry. [79]

There were no parades, no hymns sung, no prayers offered or speeches made that morning, just a group of witnesses who came to watch the moment and see the construction grind to a start again. "How cheering this news to every one striving to aid in accomplishing the great design of our being here," one observer wrote.[80] But there would be little significant work done on the temple this year. The crop failures and other troubles that had shut down the work when Truman had first left for Europe had not been entirely resolved. It would take years to rebuild the herds that had been decimated by the previous winter's brutal weather, and after the meager harvest of the previous year, they desperately needed this season's crop yields to improve. On top of that, the Church had little money to pay the laborers on the temple block. So Brigham reported to the Saints: "We were compelled to suspend operations upon the Public Works, until we could pay our debts and somewhat replenish our means. Since harvest we have partially resumed, but will not commence laying stone upon the Temple until next Spring, when we hope to prosecute that work with much vigor."[81]

The following month marked the ten-year anniversary of the Saints' entry into the valley, and Brigham was not going to let that day pass with anything less than a grand celebration. The accomplishments of the last decade really were significant enough to merit a holiday. Where there had been nothing before 1847, now Great Salt Lake City's population numbered more than ten thousand people. It was the second largest city west of the Mississippi; only San Francisco was larger. They were a US territory with a government and a governor filled almost entirely by their own people and led by men they considered inspired of God. On the whole, they were largely self-sufficient. There was agriculture and industry of every kind producing every needful thing, and what luxuries they couldn't make themselves, emigrants bound for California often sold them at bargain prices to free up space in their wagons for more critical supplies. They were building a canal that would accelerate commerce along its banks as the Erie Canal had done for New England. They were free to practice their religion as they saw fit, with only occasional interference by government officials, but that was hardly an annoyance compared to their past troubles in Missouri and Illinois.

On July 23, one day shy of the ten-year mark when he himself had ridden into the valley in the back of Wilford's wagon, Brigham led an enormous company to Big Cottonwood Canyon, where they would camp in preparation for the observance the following day. He led "the long line of carriages and wagons, which easily passed up the now comparatively smooth ascent, made so at great expense by the Big Cottonwood Lumber Company, and began to reach the camp ground at the lake at about 11 a.m." By late afternoon, more than twenty-five hundred people had arrived for the party. Six brass bands were there, including Captain Ballo's, which played throughout the day as Saints arrived from around the area. The Nauvoo Legion had sent its own band as well as units of artillery and infantry.[82] The lumber company had constructed three boweries with planked wooden floors for the Saints to use in the festivities. The planned gala promised to be the largest celebration of any kind since the Saints had laid the temple cornerstones. Similar events were planned in other settlements of the territory, including Pleasant Grove, Provo, Cedar City, Nephi, and Manti.

The start of the festival on the morning of the twenty-fourth could have been mistaken for a worship service. A choir sang "On the Mountain Tops Appearing" and was followed by Elder George A. Smith, who offered an opening prayer. Four flags of the United States were raised on "two of the highest peaks in sight of the camp and on the tops of two of the tallest trees." At 9:20 a.m., the Nauvoo Legion fired a cannon three times, then again at 10:15, which was followed by a military parade staged by the infantry. And with that, the celebration was in full swing, with "programs, singing, dancing, and visiting" throughout the camp.[83]

Around noon, a group of four exhausted and dirty men rode into the campground: Bishop Abraham O. Smoot, Elder Judson Stoddard, Judge Elias Smith, and Orrin Porter Rockwell. Smoot and Stoddard had crossed the plains from the Missouri River to the valley in just twenty days—besting Truman Angell's speedy time by a solid week—to bring the most unwelcome news the Saints could imagine. "They informed us that the United States had taken away the mail contract [and] that a new governor [and] judges & 2,500 troops would start for Utah soon," Wilford Woodruff wrote.[84] Brigham, Wilford, and other Church leaders took the conversation into a tent, where they asked the messengers for every bit of information they could get.

The mood in Brigham's tent must have been the polar opposite of the celebration going on outside. He allowed the celebration to continue through the afternoon. Perhaps he was still discussing the situation with Wilford and the others, or he simply may not have wanted to disturb "the gaiety of the scene," to give the Saints a few more hours to enjoy the day before telling them what he knew. After a few hours, Brigham finally went out to speak to the assembled crowd and told them what was coming. "After the first shock there was little or no confusion. [Brigham] told the people to go on with their merrymaking, and the day's festivities ended with a dance, as had been originally planned."[85] The music played on, but the Saints' spirits must have been far less cheerful than they had been that morning.

The question now was how they would respond to this sudden move. They'd lived through a time once before when a government had sent an army against them. Now it was happening again, and surely they must have thought that the situation had the potential to be the Missouri persecutions repeated on an even larger scale. This invasion would not be a state governor letting a militia full of hostile civilians run rampant. These coming troops would be trained, disciplined regular soldiers. Some likely would have seen battle in Mexico. The general leading them surely would be a hardened veteran of that war, with considerable experience leading men into combat and imposing military rule on an occupied population. The governor they were escorting would become the territory's military commander-in-chief, and he might be as hostile as Lilburn Boggs had been, for all they knew.

Would Brigham ask them to fight? If he called out the Nauvoo Legion to fight a pitched battle, scores of men would die, and the nation would take it as evidence that the Saints were indeed in a state of rebellion against their country. The nation's president would likely send more and more soldiers until the Saints were defeated. Their leaders would be jailed, their property seized. They would lose their city, and they would never get to finish their temple, "the erection of which was the pinnacle of all their fondest hopes and dreams."[86]

Would the prophet ask them to leave their homes again as they had done in Ohio, Missouri, and Illinois? They would still lose their cities, homes, farms, and temple. And where would they go this time? If they tried to stay in the United States, wouldn't the army just follow them wherever they went? Would Canada or Mexico allow tens of thousands of refugees to cross their borders? Would the United States even let them go?

Could they petition the government in Washington for relief? They'd gotten no help from the federal government when Joseph had pleaded with Martin Van Buren to give the Saints protection and justice. The current president, James Buchanan, clearly was against them—sending thousands of troops to the valley without warning was proof of that. If the president was listening to men like Judge Perry Brocchus, then he doubtless imagined that Brigham was a villain. If so, communication from Brigham could be seen as the desperate attempt of an evil man to escape justice and cling to power. Would Congress be any more willing to believe their petition? Given all that the Saints had heard from their delegates in Washington, that seemed doubtful.

Brigham's decision was unequivocal. "We have built cities in the East for our foes to occupy; our very temples have been desecrated and destroyed by them but with the help of Israel's God we will prevent them enriching themselves with the spoils of our labors in this mountain retreat," he told his friends.[87] If the Saints were forced to flee, they would not just leave their homes and settlements to the invaders. They would destroy everything they had built, and their enemies would have come a very long way at very great expense for nothing. That said, Brigham conceded the possibility that the new governor could be coming in peace and should be given the chance to prove his intentions. "If the governor [and] officers wished to come [and] would behave themselves well they would be well treated," he announced. But if they did not behave themselves well, he "felt determined no more to submit to oppression either to individuals, towns, counties, states or nation."[88]

The day that Brigham had first entered the valley in 1847, sick and lying in Wilford's wagon, he had declared that "if the people of the United States will let us alone for ten years, we will ask no odds of them."[89] Ten years later to the day, the statement looked truly prophetic. Brigham's deadline was up, and it was the United States government "asking odds" of him and his people—and they didn't know why. "The Saints were at a loss . . . to understand why an army of such proportions should be descending upon them."[90] All of the possible motives for the invasion that they could imagine were hostile. All of the outcomes they could envision—war, military occupation, evacuation—looked bleak.

Perhaps the Lord would still deliver them from their enemies, and they would be able to stay without bloodshed. But until the Lord's will became clear, Brigham and the Saints would prepare to fight.

CHAPTER 5

TRUST IN GOD AND KEEP YOUR POWDER DRY

The Utah Expedition officially began on May 28, 1857, when Winfield Scott, General-in-Chief of the United States Army, issued a military circular ordering the assembly of 2,500 troops and the supplies necessary for them to march from Fort Leavenworth, Kansas, to Great Salt Lake City. The order was short, just twelve paragraphs long, but the soldiers who read it that day would have realized that Scott was organizing the largest military operation since the Mexican War had ended. One-sixth of the entire army would assemble and march almost fifteen hundred miles west, not for the purpose of expelling a foreign enemy, but to suppress, they were told, a revolt among their fellow citizens. At least, that was what US President James Buchanan imagined. "This is the first rebellion which has existed in our Territories," Buchanan would say later that year, "and humanity itself requires that we should put it down in such a manner that it shall be the last."[1]

Buchanan's decision to send the army into Utah was grounded in two major factors. The first was the intense pressure heaped on him to resolve a toxic political problem that left him little bandwidth for tackling an alleged rebellion by the Saints two thousand miles away. The "peculiar institution" of slavery had divided the United States since the days of the Founding Fathers, defying all attempts by even the most talented leaders in the nation's history to resolve. And as the country expanded west, the debate over slavery's expansion into the new states admitted to the Union became the key battle in that political war. The Missouri Compromise of 1820 had banned slavery west of the Mississippi River and north of the 36° 30' parallel, Missouri excepted; but Southern Congressmen resisted, believing that law would eventually render them a permanent minority on Capitol Hill. So Senator Stephen A. Douglas had proposed the Kansas-Nebraska Act of 1854, which both organized those two territories and granted each the right to settle through an election whether to allow slavery in their borders. That established the principle of "popular sovereignty," letting each new state decide for itself whether to accept slavery.

That policy was failing to keep the peace, and Kansas was the case in point. Pro-slavery and abolitionist settlers alike were burning buildings, destroying print shops, murdering each other, and raiding jails to free their own when arrested. One abolitionist, John Brown, caught the nation's attention when he, his three sons, and four henchmen massacred five pro-slavery settlers in a single night. The Browns invaded the men's homes, marched them outside at gunpoint, killed them, and mutilated their bodies with swords. Abolitionists back East called Brown a hero. "Slavery was a sin, and the wages of sin was death. God had ordained Brown to smite the wicked," they believed;[2] but Brown was a murdering villain to Southerners and pro-slavery advocates in Kansas and Missouri. Sheltered by friends and emboldened by his supporters, he began planning a more ambitious raid—an attack on the federal armory at Harper's Ferry, Virginia, in an attempt to spark a large-scale slave rebellion.

Nor was the violence restricted just to the western frontier. On May 20, 1856, Charles Sumner, a Republican from Massachusetts, stood in the well of the United States Senate on Capitol Hill and delivered a potent anti-slavery speech in which he denounced fellow senator Andrew

Butler of South Carolina, one of the coauthors of the Kansas-Nebraska Act. Two days later, South Carolina Representative Preston Brooks, a Democrat and a cousin of Butler's, entered the senate chamber flanked by fellow Southern Congressmen Laurence Keitt and Henry Edmundson. Brooks approached Sumner, who was seated at his desk. "I have read your speech twice over carefully," Brooks told the senator. "It is a libel on South Carolina, and Mr. Butler, who is a relative of mine." Brooks then proceeded to beat Sumner mercilessly with his cane, wooden with a metal head. Blinded by blood flowing from a gash in his scalp, Sumner flailed about, unable to defend himself. Brooks continued beating his victim until his cane broke in half. Several senators rushed to Sumner's aid, but Keitt drew a pistol and held them at bay. Brooks then took up the cane's broken half with the metal head and renewed his assault until Sumner was knocked unconscious. Brooks collected himself and walked away with his accomplices following behind.[3]

In a sense, the US Civil War was already under way, the United States' survival as a single nation was an open question, and the election of 1856 was largely a referendum on disunion. Buchanan won that election mostly because he'd managed to avoid saying anything in public about slavery. He'd spent the last few years in London as the US Ambassador, which had kept him out of the debate. He came out in favor of popular sovereignty, which both got him elected and crippled his ability to address the nation's political divisions—no matter how badly popular sovereignty was failing, Buchanan couldn't abandon it, fueling the drive to disunion. All he could do was try to put out the political brush fires as quickly as possible wherever they erupted.

If Buchanan hadn't been desperately trying to hold the country together, the second driving force behind his decision to dispatch the army to Utah might not have gained so much attention. As it was, the strain on the president acted as a catalyst for it instead. The simple fact was that James Buchanan, like most everyone in Washington, was prone to uncritically accept just about any slander regarding the Saints. So when the president heard that a rebellion had broken out in Utah, he apparently never stopped to question whether it was actually true. To be fair, it didn't help that the charge was coming from a personal and political friend of Buchanan's, William M. F. Magraw.

In 1856, Magraw was responsible for servicing federal mail route No. 8911 between Independence, Missouri, and Great Salt Lake City. It was a lucrative contract to hold. Magraw's compensation was initially set at $14,400 annually, a hefty amount, but he petitioned for $40,000 and cited the distance and dangers of raids by Native American tribes along the route. Congress went as high as $36,000, but it's questionable whether he would have gotten his raise had the legislature known of his performance. Magraw did not keep a regular delivery schedule, and when he did show up, entire mailbags of letters were missing or destroyed—he would carelessly let them get soaked during river crossings and didn't usually bother to fish out any that fell out of his wagons. Frustrated, the Saints openly questioned whether Magraw's performance issues weren't intentional, and they were elated when the news came that Congress was going to reopen the contract and accept bids from other carriers.

The B. Y. (Brigham Young) Express Company won the new competition with a bid of $23,000, one-third less than Magraw was getting and only a little more than half of what he'd demanded. Embittered at the loss of his government salary, Magraw returned to Independence, Missouri. There he wrote a vitriolic letter to President Franklin Pierce, but the timing of the letter was suspect. It was dated October 3, just a month before the presidential election, and Pierce wasn't on the ballot. So the outgoing president almost certainly wasn't Magraw's intended audience. More likely, it was the frontrunner, James Buchanan.

The substance of Magraw's letter was that the Utah Territory had devolved into a murderous theocracy led by Brigham, who was a religious despot. Magraw declared:

> There is no disguising the fact, that there is left no vestige of
> law and order, no protection for life or property; the civil laws of
> the Territory are overshadowed and neutralized by a so-styled ec-
> clesiastical organization, as despotic, dangerous and damnable,
> as has ever been known to exist in any country. . . . [Utah resi-
> dents] are set upon by the self-constituted theocracy, whose laws,
> or rather whose conspiracies, are framed in dark corners, promul-
> gated from the stand of tabernacle or church, and executed at mid-
> night, or upon the highways, by an organized band of bravos and
> assassins, whose masters compel an outraged community to toler-
> ate in their midst.[4]

There was a ready remedy for the situation, Magraw claimed. The people of Utah were being oppressed, so give them some outside assistance, and the people would rise up against Brigham. As for his own motives in writing the letter, Magraw sought to assure his reader that he was being purely dispassionate. "I have endeavored to discard all feelings arising from my personal annoyances in the Mormon country, but had desired to lay before you the actual condition of affairs."[5]

On April 21, 1857, a second letter denouncing Brigham and the Saints appeared in the *Daily National Intelligencer* in Washington. It was signed "Verastus," but Magraw was almost certainly the author. It testified to the same atrocities as Magraw's earlier letter; it used similar language as Magraw's earlier letter; and the *Intelligencer* described the writer as "a respectable citizen, who lately spent twelve months in the Salt Lake Valley, engaged in business connected with the transit of the mails through the Territory."[6] There was one difference between the letters, though. Verastus did not just issue a vague call for general outside assistance to overthrow Brigham. Instead, he called for the US government to send 5,000 federal troops, one-third of the entire federal army, to do the job.

In short order, another letter filled with similar accusations against Brigham and the Saints arrived in Washington. The author was William Wormer Drummond, an appointee of outgoing President Franklin Pierce to the Utah Territorial Supreme Court. Drummond had lasted less than a year on the job when his troubled family situation had come to light—his "wife" was actually a prostitute named "Skinny" Ada Carroll for whom he'd abandoned his real wife and five children back in Illinois. Some Church members had dug into his past when the judge had started inviting "Mrs. Drummond" to sit on his lap at the bench while he lambasted Saints in court for the practice of plural marriage. When his adulterous relationship with Ms. Carroll and the existence of his still-legal wife and children became public, the Saints avoided Drummond's court like he was a plague carrier. Drummond also created more problems for himself when he sent a servant to assault a "Mormonized Jew" named Levi Abrahams who spoke publicly (and truthfully) about the judge's questionable character. Abrahams survived, and both Drummond and his servant were arrested and charged with assault and battery with intent to commit murder.

That was enough for the judge. He posted bail to get out of jail and then fled to California, where he wrote his nasty letter to Jeremiah S. Black, US Attorney General, in which he accused Brigham and others of the most serious crimes imaginable. Brigham and "all male members of the church" were members of "a secret oath-bound organization committed to defying the Federal Government's authority." Federal officers were "constantly insulted, harassed, and annoyed." Brigham was interfering with the courts, and to hide such activities, "the records, papers, &c., of the supreme court have been destroyed by order of the Church, with [Brigham's] direct knowledge and approval." Drummond also added murder to the list of charges, accusing Brigham of inciting the Corn

Creek Tribe natives to slaughter Captain John W. Gunnison and his party back in 1853.[7]

Anticipating questions as to whether he could back up his claims with evidence, Drummond preemptively explained, "I could, sir, if necessary, refer to a cloud of witnesses to attest the reasons I have given, and the charges, bold as they are, against those . . . but I shall not do so, for the reason that the lives of such gentlemen as I should designate in Utah . . . would not be safe for a single day." Anyone who could support his claims had to remain anonymous, he explained, so the only answer, Drummond argued, was to overthrow Brigham and the Church by force. As long as Brigham was governor, attempts to administer justice in Utah would be "madness and folly," with federal officers in danger of being "murdered for doing their duty, and not recognizing Brigham Young as the only law-giver and law-maker on earth."[8]

Church members in the East published their own letters refuting the accusations, to no effect. The more serious and bold the charges against Brigham and the Saints, the more the public and the politicians in Washington seemed willing to believe them. The Saints' practice of plural marriage left them with no public defenders. The Republican Party had been founded just two years before on the express promise of stomping out the "twin relics of barbarism," slavery and polygamy. The Democrats—Buchanan's own party—were divided over the first of those twin relics, but they were united with the Republicans in condemning the second. Senator Stephen Douglas, whom the Saints had considered a friend, demonstrated that fact when he declared that they were guilty of "treason and crime, debauchery and infamy" and that it was the duty of Congress to "apply the knife and cut out this loathsome, disgusting ulcer."[9] It was now clear that so long as plural marriage was an open doctrine, taught in public from the pulpit, the Saints would have no friends in Washington, and their protests of innocence would carry no credibility at all.

With Buchanan helpless to stop the murders in "Bleeding Kansas" that were fueling the runaway drive toward disunion, some of his political allies thought that he might head off the problem by focusing the country's attention on another villain, one that all Americans could despise. The Latter-day Saints seemed custom-made to play that role. To that end, Robert Tyler, son of former US President John Tyler, the chairman of the Democratic Executive Committee of Pennsylvania, sent a letter to Buchanan explaining the potential strategy.

> Phila: April 27, 1857
> My dear sir:
>
> The public mind is becoming greatly excited on the subject of Mormonism. The Popular Idea is rapidly maturing that Mormonism (already felt slightly in our large Northern cities) should be put down and utterly extirpated.
>
> I believe we can supersede the Negro-Mania with the almost universal excitements of an Anti-Mormon Crusade. Certainly it is a subject which concerns all the Religious Bodies & reaches every man's fireside with a peculiar interest. Should you, with your accustomed grip, seize this question with a strong fearless & resolute hand, the Country I am sure will rally to you with an earnest enthusiasm & the pipings of Abolitionism will hardly be heard amidst the thunders of the storm we shall raise. Were I President I would put down & cast out this hideous imposture equally at War with Conscience, Reason, & Philosophy, at all hazards. I would take the ground that the case was anomalous & altogether exceptional, without the limits of ordinary Constitutional treatment. . . . The eyes & hearts of the Nation may be made to find so much interest in Utah as to forget Kansas.[10]

If Buchanan ever replied to Tyler's communication, the letter has been lost to history. Whether Buchanan's subsequent course was influenced by Tyler's view cannot be known, but it seems unlikely that Tyler would suggest such a course if he didn't strongly believe the political support for it would be there. He was suggesting that the administration target an unpopular minority for political reasons and that the public would allow Buchanan to wave aside any questions about legality on the grounds that the Latter-day Saints' religious practices were so abhorrent as to place them beyond the bounds of constitutional protections.

In any case, it is clear that Buchanan accepted Magraw's and Drummond's accusations as true and so believed there was only one possible course of action: to send a military force to Utah to reassert federal authority. If tens of thousands of Saints there were more loyal to a religious leader guilty of such heinous crimes, just replacing Brigham as governor would accomplish nothing. Any new governor's authority would have to be enforced by the United States Army. So, less than a month after Tyler sent his letter to the president, Buchanan gave the order enabling the Utah Expedition. The newly formed "Department of Utah"[11] would be assigned a force of "not less than 2,500 men,"[12] to be drawn from the US Army's 2nd Cavalry Regiment, 5th and 10th Infantry Divisions, and one battery from the 4th Artillery Regiment.

The question of who would command the "Utah Expedition" shouldn't have been difficult to answer. There weren't that many officers who had the required combination of rank, experience, and ability. But the army lacked a retirement system, so career officers rarely left regardless of age, physical condition, or any other reason—Winfield Scott himself was seventy years old and weighed nearly three hundred pounds. The result was an officer corps in which the most senior members were the least able to take field command, and men lower down were rarely promoted simply because positions matched to the ranks they deserved rarely opened up. Now most of the officers with the necessary rank were physically incapable, and those who were capable lacked the rank. So when President Buchanan asked Secretary of War John B. Floyd for names, Floyd responded that it wasn't a long list. "[General William S.] Harney is really the only general officer—[Albert Sidney] Johnston alone excepted—who has the physical capacity to conduct such a campaign as this."[13] Buchanan accepted the first recommendation.

William Selby Harney was born in 1800 in Tennessee and joined the army as a teenager in 1818. He earned his reputation leading raids during the Black Hawk War and other campaigns in the 1830s. He was a fighter, though he tended to fight his fellow officers as much as the enemy and so had endured four courts-martial—but he'd been efficient in dealing harshly with Native Americans, so the promotions kept coming. He was considered one of the nastiest characters in the entire army. One subordinate recorded in an official war department cable that Harney's character "is anything but enviable, being notorious for profanity, brutality, incompetency, peculation, recklessness, insubordination, tyranny and mendacity."[14]

Upon learning of the assignment, Harney boasted that any campaign against the Saints that he led would start with the summary arrest and execution of Brigham Young and the entire Quorum of the Twelve Apostles, possibly followed by a repeat of "the daring deed of the Roman Titus who captured and laid waste Jerusalem" after reaching Great Salt Lake City.[15] But elation over his new command died quickly when he learned of a private arrangement that President Buchanan had made with Kansas Governor Robert J. Walker. Harney was the commanding officer at Fort Leavenworth, and Walker didn't want the general leaving for Utah while violence between settlers in his state was still a threat. Buchanan allayed Walker's fears by promising that Harney would be staying put. "General Harney has been selected to command the expedition to Utah, but we must continue to leave him with you, at least until you are out of the woods. Kansas is vastly more important at the present moment than Utah," the president promised the governor.[16] When July arrived, Buchanan kept his word. As the infantry marched out of Fort Leavenworth on July 18 for Utah, all Harney could do was watch them go.

Harney did not surrender easily, and he took his case straight to Secretary of War Floyd. He argued that "everything here [in Kansas] is quiet, nor is there any probability that I shall be needed"—wishful thinking, given recent events.[17] He also claimed that "My knowledge & experience of that country [Utah] will do much towards smoothing the way upon [the troops'] arrival, to a correct & proper understanding with the people, among whom they are to serve."[18] That was an outright lie. Harney had never seen the Utah Territory, and he wanted to hang Brigham upon arrival, which wouldn't have been conducive to "smoothing" anything between the Saints and his soldiers. In any case, his arguments went nowhere. On August 28, Floyd released General Order No. 12: "It being deemed inadvisable to detach Brevet Brigadier General Harney from service in Kansas, Colonel A. S. Johnston, Second Cavalry, is assigned to the command of the Utah expedition, and will proceed to join the same without delay."[19]

Born in Kentucky in 1803, Albert Sidney Johnston was three years younger than the man he was replacing; unlike Harney, Johnston was highly regarded within the army. Johnston graduated high in his class at West Point Military Academy in 1826 and, like Harney, served in the Black Hawk War. Johnston resigned his commission after that and moved to Texas, but he returned to service to fight for that territory's independence from Mexico. He was promoted to brigadier general in command of the entire Texas army within a year and became the Secretary of War for the new republic that had secured its freedom. Texas joined the Union in 1845, and Johnston rejoined the US Army to fight in the Mexican War, albeit at a lower rank than he'd enjoyed in the Texas Army. Having distinguished himself in two armies, he enjoyed an acclaim that was practically universal—his selection to lead the Utah Expedition was proof. "I consider it highly complementary to you to be selected for this service over others more convenient & accessible," wrote one of Johnston's friends, another highly regarded soldier and fellow army colonel, Robert E. Lee.[20]

Under General Scott's orders, Johnston would not be under the command of the new territorial governor—a Southerner named Alfred Cumming—but would be responsible for maintaining a cooperative and

General Albert Sidney Johnston.

cordial relationship with him. The army would not act as a *posse comitatus*—a domestic police force—unless the governor requested military assistance. When so asked, the orders explicitly stated that "in no case will you, your officers or men, attack any body of citizens whatever, except on such requisitions or summons [from the governor], or in sheer self-defense."[21] After all of the directions laying out authorities and treatment of civilians, the order also contained one bit of guidance that would prove problematic in the coming months. "It is not doubted that a surplus of provision and forage, beyond the wants of the resident population, will be found in the valley of Utah; and that the inhabitants, if assured by energy and justice, will be ready to sell them to the troops. Hence no instructions are given you for the extreme event of the troops being in absolute need of such supplies and their being withheld by the inhabitants."[22] Scott was anticipating that the Saints would be compliant capitalists once faced with a military force ready to suppress any rebellious outbursts, but if the Saints refused to sell whatever supplies the soldiers needed, "the necessities of such an occasion would furnish the law for your guidance."[23] "Do what you have to do," in other words.

During his week at Leavenworth, Johnston also met the new territorial governor, Alfred Cumming. A Georgian by birth, Cumming was a short man, morbidly obese, with a head that was small around the top, leading Elder George A. Smith to suspect on first inspection that the new governor "had more chops than brains."[24] Fifty-six years old, he

had gray hair, and his face was
so ruddy that people could
tell at a distance that he was
a heavy drinker.[25] But he was
a capable executive despite
that love of alcohol. Cumming
had gained national prom-
inence while serving as the
mayor of Augusta in his home
state during a yellow-fever ep-
idemic that struck the city in
1854. Now he had accepted
the appointment to oversee a

Governor Alfred Cumming.

despised people in a frontier land—but, unlike many, Cumming seems
not to have had any special animus toward the Saints. To the contrary,
he seems to have wanted to gain their support. "He did not want to govern a people, if they did not want him," he was reported to have said.[26]
While that may not have been strictly true—the Saints clearly wanted
Brigham Young to be their governor—Cumming was at least resolved to
respect their constitutional rights.

———— • • • ————

By the time Albert Sidney Johnston set out for Utah, Brigham Young
had been preparing for the army's arrival for almost two months, considering his strategy and organizing his people. If the US Army entered the
valley looking for a fight, "there shall not be one building, nor one foot
of lumber, nor a stick, nor a tree, nor a particle of grass and hay that will
burn, left in the reach of our enemies," Brigham had declared from the
Adobe Tabernacle pulpit.[27] In his role as governor, Brigham published
a broadside to the "Citizens of Utah" to mobilize the resistance. "We
are invaded by a hostile force who are evidently assailing us to accomplish our overthrow and destruction," it began. "The Government has
not condescended to cause an investigating committee or other person

to be sent to inquire into and ascertain the truth, as is customary in such cases." [28] There was no arguing that point. Buchanan was acting solely on the word of angry men bent on hurting the Saints who had refused to tolerate their misbehavior. In Brigham's mind, a policy based on such false assumptions was unconstitutional, so the Saints were justified to act in self-defense.[29] Acting on those grounds, Brigham issued a three-part declaration of resistance against the coming army.

> 1st:—To forbid, in the name of the People of the United States in the Territory of Utah, all armed forces, of every description, from coming into this Territory under any pretense whatever.
>
> 2d:—That all the forces in said Territory hold themselves in readiness to march, at a moment's notice, to repel any and all such threatened invasion.
>
> 3d:—Martial law is hereby declared to exist in this Territory, from and after the publication of this Proclamation; and no person shall be allowed to pass or trespass into, or through, or from this Territory, without a permit from the proper officer.[30]

It seems unlikely that Brigham actually thought the law empowered him to order the coming army to stay out of the Territory. Federal forces acted under the command of the president of the United States, and Brigham surely knew that. He might have hoped that once faced with an order not to enter the territory, the general might feel *some* need to parlay and send an emissary to investigate the situation—exactly what Buchanan should have done in the first place. But peace through diplomacy also seemed unlikely. The US government had already declared the Latter-day Saints in rebellion and Brigham Young a criminal. Negotiations require trust, and there was precious little of that on either side. So the army would march ahead, and if the Saints shed the soldiers' blood, even in self-defense, the US government would consider that confirmation that the testimonies of Drummond and Magraw and every other enemy of the Saints was true.

If the Saints were not to be occupied, scattered, or perhaps destroyed as a church, they would need some divine help—but theirs was a practical religion that taught divine help would come after the people had done what they could do for themselves. In this case, that meant resisting unjust oppression, as they saw it. And if their faith alone weren't enough to lead them to that decision, their own history showed that attempts to negotiate with armed mobs didn't end well. So, with faith and experience as his guides, Brigham saw no reason to repeat the experiment of trying to bargain at gunpoint with their enemies for the Saints' lives and property. They would resist to buy time—for what, exactly, they did not know—and then they would "stand still, and see the salvation of the Lord."[31]

◆ ⋅ ⋅ ◆

That property for which Brigham absolutely would not bargain included the temple. It was no secret that the Saints were building it, and history had taught them what to expect when their temples fell into the hands of their enemies. Two thousand soldiers could tear out the stone foundation in a matter of a few days if so ordered. But even if the army left it alone, would they let the Saints work on the building unmolested? That seemed too much to hope. This was a problem Brigham would have to study out in his mind if it became apparent that the Saints could not keep the army out of the valley.

Before that unwelcome moment approached, there was one more bit of work Brigham wanted to see done on the Lord's house. Years before, in Nauvoo, the Saints had erected the Nauvoo House mansion by commandment of the Lord. "I command you . . . to build a house to my name, even in this place, that you may prove yourselves unto me that ye are faithful in all things whatsoever I command you. . . . And now I say unto you, as pertaining to my boarding house which I have commanded you to build for the boarding of strangers, let it be a delightful habitation for man, and a resting-place for the weary traveler, that he may contemplate the glory of Zion," the Lord had said.[32] When they had laid the southeast cornerstone of that building, the Prophet Joseph had deposited the original manuscript of the Book of Mormon inside the stone to preserve it for a future generation to find.[33] Brigham thought to do something similar here. It was a frequent practice of the times to include record stones in important buildings; perhaps the prophet wanted to perform a public act symbolic of the Saints' faith that the Lord would not let the army eject them from their city and that they would go on to finish their temple.

Whatever his reasons, on August 13 he summoned a small assembly to meet at the temple site to "make a deposit of the works published by the Church of Jesus Christ of Latter-day Saints."[34] The appointed hour was six o'clock in the evening, and the last of the group had arrived by six-thirty. The Church leadership was represented by the First Presidency; Wilford Woodruff, John Taylor, Erastus Snow, and Franklin D. Richards of the Twelve; and Jesse C. Little, a counselor in the Presiding Bishopric. Others invited included John Lyon, superintendent of the Endowment House; Truman Angell; Alonzo H. Raleigh, foreman of the public works masons, and three of his craftsmen; Albert Carrington, editor of the *Deseret News*; and, oddly, Henry W. Maiben, a thirty-eight-year-old British convert who was a stage actor.[35]

What words Brigham or others offered were not recorded. Fifteen minutes after the group came together, Brigham "packed the books in a stone box two and a half feet long, twenty inches deep, and one foot seven inches wide." Wilford kept a detailed list in his journal of the contents, which included copies of the Book of Mormon in English and five other languages; the Doctrine and Covenants; the Pearl of Great Price; several volumes of the Church's periodicals, including the *Latter-day Saints Messenger & Advocate*, *The Times and Seasons*, and the *Millennial Star*; a hymnal; two volumes of the *Journal of Discourses*; numerous English and foreign-language books and missionary tracts authored by members of the Quorum of the Twelve; portraits of the First Presidency and the Apostles; and a volume of Eliza R. Snow's poetry. Wanting to preserve elements of their secular history as well, they added the Constitution of the State of Deseret, the entire legal code of the Utah Territory, records of the Resolutions, Acts & Memorials passed by two sessions of the territorial legislature, and samples of gold coinage minted in the valley. It took the better part of an hour to finish loading the materials into the stone coffer—perhaps the men took turns examining the books and papers individually before they were laid down. When they were all loaded, "the lid was put on, soldered with lead & covered with plaster [of] paris & turned bottom side up & set in the South East Corner." The hollow stone was placed on the flagging stones, to become part of the first course of stones that would make up the temple walls.

With the box sealed and placed, the group joined in prayer, offered by Brigham, to call upon the Lord to protect the time capsule.[36] He did not address heaven for very long.

"O God our Eternal Father, we ask thee in the name of Jesus Christ that thou will bless this deposit which we have made in the foundation of this temple," he began.

> We dedicate all these books, papers, records and history unto thee O Lord our God. And I pray in the name of Jesus Christ, Our Father in Heaven that thou wilt preserve this deposit . . . that it may endure that no mildew or decay may come upon it until it shall come forth for the benefit of the House of Israel and thy people that it may be a benefit unto them. . . . Preserve these records . . . to come forth in the own due time of the Lord.

He pleaded with the Lord to protect His people from their enemies; to give the Saints "power to finish this temple even to the top stone"; to bless the land that it would continue to provide the food and water the Saints needed; and to bless the Indians that they would be converted to the gospel.[37]

Brigham finished the oration, and the group dispersed, the cornerstone now holding written treasures that would remain inside for almost

140 years before another generation of Saints would open it to see what was inside.

————— ◆ · ◆ · ◆ —————

The same day Brigham was helping preserve Church documents and relics in the cornerstone, orders were going out fast and furious to the Nauvoo Legion to prepare to meet the army and keep them out of the valley. To carry out that defensive campaign, Daniel H. Wells, Brigham's counselor and the Legion's commanding officer, directed Major General George D. Grant of the Great Salt Lake Military District to call up four hundred men under the command of Colonels James Cummings and R. J. Burton. The Legion responded, and within days several units were equipped and moving east toward the approaching army.

Supporting the Legion was the Public Works Department. All labor was suspended for the duration on the temple, the canal, the Red Butte Quarry, and other construction projects. That freed the public works craftsmen not marching in the field to turn their skills toward the manufacture of military supplies. Their efforts enjoyed the full support of the militia, as Daniel H. Wells was both the Legion's commander and still the head of the public works. So the blacksmiths and other workers began turning out guns, bullets, and various types of ammunition for cannons. They erected a chemical laboratory in an unused sugar factory and successfully began mixing their own gunpowder. A new shop on the temple block was set up just to make pistols and managed to produce twenty every week—not a significant number, but an accomplishment nonetheless.[38] It's questionable how long the public works could have kept the Legion supplied with weapons and ammunition in the event of a protracted conflict, but their efforts were evidence of the public spirit supporting Brigham's decision to resist.

————— ◆ · ◆ · ◆ —————

First contact between the Saints and the army came on August 31. James Cummings and R. J. Burton reported that one of their units stationed in Emigration Canyon had encountered a small force of thirty men and ten wagons led by one Captain Van Vliet that was en route to the city. Van Vliet had shared his plan to "reach Salt Lake on the 9th of Sept and leave there on the 15th of the same month. . . . He said he was going to Salt Lake to meet the governor and to purchase some building material."[39] The Saints warned Van Vliet away, but he pushed ahead anyway and arrived in the city on September 8.[40]

Stewart Van Vliet was a New Yorker and West Point graduate, class of 1840, where he'd served as First Captain of Cadets over a group of "plebes" (first-year students) that included Ulysses S. Grant. Van Vliet finished ninth in his class of forty-two and found himself assigned to an artillery unit during the Seminole Wars. Like most of the soldiers of his generation, he'd fought in Mexico; he remained in the army after and fought against the Sioux.[41] Now forty-two, he was the quartermaster of the Utah Expedition and had pushed out ahead of the main body to buy supplies and gather intelligence. The coming army was counting on the supplies he'd been tasked to secure, but he decided not to risk his own men. Personally fearless, as he'd demonstrated several times in battle against Mexicans and Native Americans, Van Vliet ordered his company to hold its position while he proceeded on to Great Salt Lake City alone.

Van Vliet was granted a meeting with Brigham the evening of the captain's arrival. Notwithstanding the soldier's claims of benign intent, Brigham recounted the Saints' history of persecution and told the officer "that now the United States were about to pursue the same course, and that, therefore, he and the people of Utah had determined to resist all persecution at the commencement, and that the troops now on the march for Utah should not enter the Great Salt Lake valley."[42] Having drawn that line for his guest, Brigham invited Van Vliet to meet with other leaders the following evening. The captain agreed.

Van Vliet received a cordial reception the following day from the First Presidency, the Twelve, and a hundred other citizens.[43] He reciprocated with a letter of introduction, which Daniel H. Wells read to the group twice. Unfortunately, the document, authored by General Harney, ended up doing more harm than good.

> The Government of the United States have decided to form the Territory of Utah, into a Military Department. . . . The great distance to be passed over, with the shortness of the season in the Rocky Mountains, have urged the expediency of placing the troops on the march, and they are now en route to some suitable position in Utah, the better to protect the interests with which they have been charged.[44]

Nothing in the letter was untrue, but there was no mention of rebellion or a new governor. Harney was claiming, in essence, that several thousand men were marching to the Great Salt Lake City to deal with no pressing issues whatsoever. His innocent explanation for the expedition seemed like an intent to deceive, perhaps to lull the Saints into a sense of complacency.

Alarmed by that interpretation, Van Vliet tried to convince his hosts that the army's mission was only to install the new governor, not to wage war. Brigham replied that he was convinced of his guest's sincerity, but that the officer didn't know the intentions of his own government as well as the prophet did.[45] Van Vliet persisted, trying to persuade his hosts that their course would lead to disaster.

> I told them plainly and frankly what I conceived would be the result of their present course. I told them that they might prevent the small military force now approaching Utah from getting through the narrow defiles and rugged passes of the mountains this year, but that next season the United States government would send troops sufficient to overcome all opposition. The answer to this was invariably the same: "We are aware that such will be the case; but when those troops arrive they will find Utah a desert. Every house will be burned to the ground, every tree cut down, and every field laid waste."[46]

He did not change their minds, but the Saints' calm manner during the conversation convinced Van Vliet that they were not asking for a fight. "I am inclined . . . to believe that the Mormons will not resort to actual hostilities until the last moment," he wrote in his official report.[47] There was no bloodlust here that Van Vliet could see. Brigham even gave Van Vliet the exact position of his line in the sand—the Saints would take no offensive action as long as the army advanced no farther than Forts Supply and Bridger.[48] That was a welcome bit of information because Van Vliet thought the Saints were in a highly defensible position. Emigration Canyon in particular was narrow and rugged, and a "small force could hold [it] against great odds," he asserted.[49]

Van Vliet spent the next week visiting with several families to see whether the defiant attitude was general throughout the city. It was, but the "cordial" manner and "greatest hospitality and kindness" that Van Vliet received made an impression on him. He met with Brigham before leaving to return to the army, at which time the soldier expressed his conviction to the prophet that the Saints "had been misrepresented and that he would hurry back to Washington to use his influence in favor of the Territory." Brigham was grateful to hear it. "I believe that God sent you here and that good will grow out of it. I was glad when I heard you were coming. If we can keep peace for this winter, I feel sure that something will occur to save the shedding of blood."[50] That said, Van Vliet would have to leave empty-handed. "The governor informed me that there was an abundance of everything I required for the troops, such as lumber, forage, &c., but that none would be sold to us," Van Vliet reported.[51] His mission to secure supplies was a failure. With that settled, the captain left Salt Lake for Camp Winfield, the army's temporary base on the Ham's Fork River about thirty miles northwest of Fort Bridger.

———◆·◆———

While the army had been slogging forward, the Nauvoo Legion had been improving the natural defenses of Echo Canyon, the primary route into the valley, by erecting rock walls, digging out trenches, and preparing ditches and dams to flood the road. Against defenses thus fortified, Albert Sidney Johnston would have needed overwhelming forces to push through to Great Salt Lake, and he just didn't have them. There were more than a thousand Legionnaires in the field now, which number was very nearly equal in size to Johnston's entire force. Winfield Scott had called for twenty-five hundred troops, but the actual total that had reached the territory by early October was far less—well under two thousand men.[52] There was also a thirty-mile gap between some of the units, with supply wagons strung out on the road in between. Those were the Legion's primary targets, and the army was almost helpless to defend them because virtually all of Johnston's Army was composed of foot soldiers and a few cannons. Johnston had almost no mounted units at his command.

The army was composed of three branches: the infantry, the artillery, and the cavalry. The infantry, composed of foot soldiers, was the largest of the three and made up the hammer fist of the army. But the need to travel on foot made the infantry slow and ponderous, and an enemy on horseback could race around them with impunity. The second branch, the artillery, was equally slow, as it required horses and mules to move at all. Cannons were used primarily to break down enemy fortifications and defend one's own; trying to shoot men on horseback at long range with those weapons would have been like trying to shoot flies with muskets. The army's third branch, the cavalry—also called "dragoons"—had the mobility and speed to conduct reconnaissance, carry communications, raid the enemy's supply lines, and defend its own.

Winfield Scott had assigned the 2nd Cavalry Regiment under the command of Colonel Philip St. George Cooke to Johnston's Army, but General Harney had held them back. Cheyenne natives had attacked the cattle drive that was to keep the troops fed during the winter and made off with 824 beef cows. Declaring that "infantry is useless against mounted Indians," Harney diverted the 2nd Cavalry to Fort Laramie to guard against further raids and hadn't replaced them. That left Johnston without any dragoons. That single order of Harney's, more than anything else, was what allowed the Nauvoo Legion to keep the US Army out of the valley that season.[53]

———•··•———

Major Lot Smith of the Nauvoo Legion was only a month younger than the Church itself. Born on May 16, 1830, in Williamstown, New York, Smith had only known life as a Latter-day Saint. He was not a relative of the Prophet Joseph, but he might as well have been, given the devotion he would later show to the faith. His family had joined the Church early on, and the young Lot had witnessed the persecutions of Ohio and Missouri while he was still a child. He was barely a teenager when the mobs had driven his family from Nauvoo, and his mother had died in Iowa soon after. Smith joined the Mormon Battalion the same year as his mother's passing; the long march to California was his introduction to the military life. He learned the skills, discipline, and demeanor of a soldier during that long walk, all of which he put to use a few years later when he joined the Nauvoo Legion and was called to fight Chief Walker and his band of warriors.

The US Army had trained him to perform infantry duty, but in the decade since, Smith had developed into a highly skilled equestrian, perhaps the best in the Legion. Recognized by Brigham and his commanding officers as a fearless soldier, a skilled horseman, and a solid leader, by the fall of 1857, twenty-seven-year-old Lot Smith had risen to the command of the very kind of cavalry unit that Albert Sidney Johnston was so keenly missing. And with no enemy dragoons to stop him, Major Lot Smith and his unit of twenty Legionnaires would need only one night to cripple Johnston's entire force.

The military maxim that an army marches on its stomach applied as much to Johnston's soldiers as anyone, and with the Utah Expedition strung out in a line dozens of miles long, Major Smith saw an opportunity to punch the US Army in the gut. He took his unit on a ride around the ponderous infantry toward the wagons rolling along a fair distance behind. They weren't hard to find, and after sundown on October 4, Major Smith and his men captured and burned three long supply trains filled mostly with food. The first went up in flames with no resistance. Unable to tell in the dark how many troops Smith was leading, the wagon masters had assumed it was a large force and surrendered their supplies without firing a shot. The officer leading the second train, a Captain Simpson, was willing to fight but found out the hard way that his teamsters lacked his bravado. Simpson was ahead of his train when the Legionnaires moved in. While his raiders captured the wagon drivers in the rear, Lot Smith approached Simpson and demanded the captain's sidearms.

"No man ever took them yet, and if you think you can, without killing me, try it," Simpson replied.

Smith declined to shoot him. "I told him that I admired a brave man, but that I did not like blood—you insist on my killing you, which will only take a minute, but I don't want to do it." He marched Simpson back to the train, where the captain realized that his troops had been disarmed.

"I see you have me at a disadvantage, my men being disarmed," Simpson admitted.

Smith, feeling his oats, offered to give Simpson a fight if he wanted one. "I replied that I didn't need the advantage and asked him what he would do if we should give them their arms," he said.

"I'll fight you!" was Simpson's answer. But Simpson's men declined. "We came out here to whack bulls, not to fight," one of them answered for the group.

"What do you say to that, Simpson?" Smith asked.

"Damnation," the captain replied, now angrier with his own men than with Smith's. "If I had been here before [Smith's unit arrived] and they had refused to fight, I would have killed every man of them."[54]

Before sunrise the following morning, Smith's unit had burned seventy-four wagons in all. The fires consumed more than a ton of ham, forty-six tons of bacon, almost eighty-four tons of flour, and varying amounts of bread, coffee and tea, sugar and molasses, candles and soap, and, perhaps most demoralizing of all, a generous amount of whiskey.[55] Smith's raiders also ran off with more than half of the army's cattle and wiped out most of the forage supply for the draft animals hauling what few supplies were left.[56] The army still had clothing, Sibley tents, and other nonconsumables; but much of the soldiers' and animals' food was now gone. [57]

<hr />

Johnston, who was still on the plains, learned of all this from dispatches carried back to him by couriers. Looking down at the inches of fresh snow that had fallen on the eighteenth of October, he decided that the army could not mount a campaign now before the weather became an insuperable obstacle.[58] "It is now manifest that before the force can be united the autumn will be too far advanced to move with a probability of success," he decided. "Our most potent enemy at present is the snow."[59] It was time to concentrate the army and establish winter quarters. Johnston brought the entire expedition together at the Ham's Fork River, which took almost two weeks. There he found his advance companies suffering from the lack of supplies created by Lot Smith's night of destruction. He decided to outfit the men for winter operations before moving again, but that created a two-day delay, which resulted in considerable suffering. Just after Johnston's men started their march for Fort Bridger, a vicious blizzard overtook them. "The snow storms raged with short intermissions after it commenced, for several days during which time it was exceedingly cold. The thermometer ranged from ten degrees above to sixteen degrees below zero," Johnston reported. Men developed frostbite. Because they were unable to find shelter for the animals, the bitter temperatures killed hundreds of their remaining oxen, mules, and horses.[60] With draft animals now in short supply, and getting shorter by the day, the men had to haul half their wagons forward each day, stop, unhitch the oxen, and lead them back to pull up the wagons left behind the day before. The quartermasters struggled to save enough beef cows to ensure the troops would have something to eat through the rest of the winter, but the snow, wind, and lack of timber prevented them from kindling campfires. One soldier writing home to his wife recorded that they had

> no fire except what we could make from the sage bushes. It was awful. Never was [sic] men more exposed or had a harder tour of duty. You see our animals have no corn, and the grass, what little there is, is under the snow. . . . When all these things are [taken] into consideration you will come to the conclusion that we are having a pretty hard time. We are.[61]

In fair weather, disciplined troops could easily march thirty-five miles in two days, but this storm cut that down to fifteen. Johnston's men did not see their new home until the late evening of November 17. In the dark, the stone walls of Fort Bridger finally took shape through the haze of the falling snow. The fort was actually two compounds. The first was a square, one hundred feet long to a side, with walls fifteen feet high and five feet thick at the base. The second enclosure was smaller, a rectangle eighty by one hundred feet, with shorter walls that reached up only seven feet. A picket fence surrounded several acres of grazing land for horses and cattle, enough to contain all the animals they now had left. This would be home for the next six months, and they were happy to see it—but their frustration rose again when they entered the facility. The walls and the fence, as it turned out, were all that remained of the place. Lot Smith's raiders and other Legionnaires had already been there, put the torch to the outpost, and turned all of the buildings inside into charred husks. The stone walls could shield the troops from the wind, but that was all the protection the fort offered now.

——— • · · • ———

Colonel Philip St. George Cooke, his dragoons, and Governor Cumming finally arrived at Fort Bridger two days later, on November 19.

The same storm that had punished Johnston's infantry had caught the mounted troopers, too, and the nighttime temperatures had bottomed out at forty-four degrees below zero. Cooke's men had lost almost half their mounts to the blizzards, and the 200 horses they had left were dying from exposure and lack of forage.[62] The storm had turned half of the cavalry into infantry. Johnston saw that even when spring arrived, he still would not be able to launch his campaign until the army resupplied him with horses, mules, and other animals to replace the losses they'd suffered the past two months.

Johnston was not one to complain. "The troops have borne the hardships and privations of the march with patience and cheerfulness, and continue in fine health," he reported.[63] Those privations would last for months. Soldiers would have to take wagons miles out into the countryside to retrieve firewood. Worn-out shoes and boots had to be replaced with moccasins homemade from the hides of their dead animals. Flour was scarce, salt nonexistent, and all other rations were tightly restricted. Just keeping the morale in camp from sagging into depression would be one of the great challenges of Johnston's career.

There was no help for it but to take it on. The colonel renamed their burned-out fortress "Camp Scott" to honor the US Army's commanding general, and, that done, Johnston's army settled into winter quarters.

The winter in Great Salt Lake City was considerably more comfortable than what Johnston and his men were enduring 120 miles to the northeast. When Brigham heard that Johnston's army would not try to enter the valley that season, he recalled the Nauvoo Legion except for a rotating guard of fifty men to keep watch and guard the passes throughout the winter. Two weeks later, another heavy storm filled the canyons with deep snows, and Brigham recalled another forty men, leaving just ten. That small lookout force, to be relieved weekly by replacements, was deemed sufficient to give warning should any unit of Johnston's army make a move toward the valley.[64]

Johnston's army had been held back, and the entire Nauvoo Legion had, quite literally, not had to fire a single shot. The Saints saw it as a miracle and evidence of Brigham's calling as a prophet. "We can now clearly see the hand of God made visible here, in our behalf concerning the campaign of our enemies against us this season past," one observer wrote years after.

> Pres[ident] Young testified unto the people in the name of God if they would be united with him in their faith, prayers and works that the enemy would not have power to come into our vallies [sic], that the Lord would hedge up their way, and we should not be called to shed their blood, neither should they have power to shed ours. . . . The Lord fought our battles and hedged up the way of our enemies . . . the storms and cold killed their horses, mules and cattle by hundreds, so that . . . they [were] obliged to stop and spend the winter in the storms of the mountains. . . . Through this whole scenery of alarm of war and the approach of the enemy, Pres[ident] Young has been as calm and serene as a morning in May.[65]

Captain Van Vliet, the quartermaster, arrived in Washington in November and reported directly to President Buchanan, but the president's belief that there was a rebellion in Utah was unchanged. He reported it as fact in his State of the Union address the following month and warned Congress not to underestimate the Saints' "frenzied fanaticism." The remedy, he argued, was to raise four new army regiments and march into Utah "with such an imposing force as to convince these deluded people that resistance would be vain." That was the best manner, he said, "to convince them that we are their friends, not their enemies."[66] Peace and friendship through superior firepower was his policy.

However, Buchanan soon found himself going through his own kind of winter suffering. The Utah Expedition was a very expensive undertaking, so reports of the army's struggles and losses, joined with the Saints' continued insistence that they'd never been in rebellion, led Congress to start asking some uncomfortable questions. Van Vliet—whose loyalty wasn't in question—was insisting there was no rebellion. So why had Buchanan believed there was? Why hadn't he sent investigators out before deploying the army?

Buchanan did not have good answers, and he found himself trapped in a growing controversy of his own making. The army would have to move when spring arrived or it would starve. Should the president just bring them home? That would be a de facto admission that Buchanan's judgment had been poor and that he wasn't a careful steward of the country's blood and treasure. And given the Saints' successful campaign to keep the army at bay, such a move would also be a concession that the federal government lacked the ability to control the territory. But if he ordered the army forward into Utah, was he risking an unjustified "effusion of blood"? Van Vliet said the Saints were prepared to receive a new governor, but they didn't want him forced on them at gunpoint—hardly an unreasonable position. So was Buchanan provoking the very rebellion he said he was trying to suppress? And if armed warfare broke out, the army would need more men and supplies. Buchanan would have to double down and send additional resources even as the justification for the entire expedition was eroding. What Buchanan really needed was a third option.

That option was Thomas L. Kane, the Saints' old friend.[67] The idea of a mediator between the Saints and the government was floated, and one of Buchanan's confidants recommended Kane as a possible candidate. Buchanan was not optimistic that anyone could negotiate peace with Brigham Young, but, given his alternatives, the president kept an open mind. He met Kane at the White House the day after Christmas, and Kane declared himself willing to make the attempt. His health was poor, but he was restless and ambitious, and the challenge appealed to his sense of adventure. He was also, quite literally, the only man for the job. There was no one else both acceptable to the government and trusted by the Saints. So Buchanan gave his blessing to the peace mission, though not his official sponsorship. He did furnish Kane with letters of introduction to facilitate his passage to Utah, but the text confirmed Kane's independence from the president. If negotiations were going to fail, as Buchanan expected they would, he did not want the failure to be laid on his doorstep.[68]

Kane left for Utah early in the new year. Traveling under the pseudonym "Dr. Osborne," he took a steamer down the coast to Panama and crossed the isthmus by rail to the Pacific Coast. He boarded another ship there for California, where he traveled overland through San Bernardino and Las Vegas, finally reaching Salt Lake on February 25. Brigham called in his counselors in the First Presidency and the Quorum of the Twelve to receive Kane in the early evening that very day and discuss whatever intelligence their visitor could provide.[69] Kane asked those present to "enlist [their] sympathies in behalf of the poor soldiers who are now suffering in the cold & snows of the mountains and . . . render them aid and comfort and to assist them to come here and to bid them a hearty welcome into [their] hospitable valley." He also reported that Captain Van Vliet had been a staunch advocate for their cause in Washington and "had done a great deal in [the Saints'] behalf." The politicians were not as united behind the cause of "putting down Utah" as Brigham had supposed. Of course, there were hostile critics, but there were also many who "said [the Saints] were a poor persecuted people and ought to be helped instead of being persecuted."

Brigham indicated his willingness to accept the new governor, but he did not want the army coming into Great Salt Lake City. Emotions were running too high on both sides, and sooner or later, someone would do something foolish. If one Saint or soldier fired one shot, they would all find themselves in a shooting war, no matter how much Brigham or Albert Sidney Johnston might want to avoid it. Then, Brigham ended the meeting by expressing his gratitude for Kane's efforts. "You have done a great work and you will do a greater work still," the prophet told him.[70]

Kane stayed in Salt Lake to recover from his journey until March 8, when he set out for Fort Bridger, but Brigham placed about as much hope in Kane's mission as Buchanan did. There was still every reason to think the army would march on the city and occupy it, and Brigham remembered perfectly well how a government army had treated his people in Missouri. He would not ask the Saints to submit to that again; he vowed to take a different course.

> Rather than see my wives and daughters ravished and polluted, and the seeds of corruption sown in the hearts of my sons by a brutal soldiery, I would leave my home in ashes, my gardens and orchards a waste, and subsist upon roots and herbs, a wanderer through these mountains for the remainder of my natural life.[71]

He shared his sentiments with the First Presidency, the Twelve, and the leading officers of the Nauvoo Legion in a special "Council of War." They agreed with him, so Brigham put the question to the people three days later in a Sunday meeting in the Adobe Tabernacle.[72] By a public vote, the people agreed that they did not want a war in their city. "I am in favor of leaving here without fighting," said Mary Ann Young, one of Brigham's wives. "I am very comfortably situated, but I would be sorry to think that one good brother's life was lost in defending my home. I would rather leave peaceably."[73]

The decision made, the Saints began preparing to leave the following day, and wagons began rolling south within the week.

———— • • ————

There was the question of what to do with the temple. The Saints had laid only the foundation and two and a half courses of stones in the basement walls, but they considered those parts no less holy for being unfinished than a fully constructed temple would have been. What to do with it? Leave it to be desecrated? Albert Sidney Johnston would have to be an extraordinarily spiteful man to order thousands of soldiers to tear out the stone walls of an incomplete religious site, but they'd seen such men leading those kinds of willing mobs before.

Whoever came up with the idea is not recorded, but the prophet settled on a plan to bury the foundation. That would be no trivial task. Five years ago, the Saints had dug up more than 80,000 tons of dirt to open the trenches for the cornerstones and foundation. Meeting the six-week deadline for the cornerstone ceremony had required hundreds of workers to haul away some 1,900 tons of dirt almost every day from the middle of February to early April. That was just to open the four trenches for the walls. Now the Saints would have to haul a significant portion of that dirt back to the temple block, plus what they'd excavated from the square between the walls. Nor did they know how long they had to complete the job. It was March now. The snows would begin to melt soon, and when they did, Johnston's army would start to move. So the Saints would have to haul more dirt in less time than ever before, and they would have to do it while they were making their other preparations to abandon the city.

Brigham gave the order. The uncut stones would be cached in the basement, and the whole of it covered with dirt. The public works shops would be torn down, and everything inside the four walls around the temple block would be removed. By the twenty-fifth of March, the workers were "caching the cut stone in the East wall of the temple foundation, [and] also ploughing around the temple foundation to cover it with earth."[74] When the soldiers arrived, the whole temple block would look like a farmer's freshly plowed field, with no obvious clue as to where the temple foundation was inside the walls. If Albert Sidney Johnston found out or already knew what would be under all that dirt and still wanted to tear it apart, the Saints wouldn't be able to stop him. But if he and his men truly had that kind of burning desire to demolish the foundation, they would have to dig up much of the temple block just to find it, then spend weeks more digging the foundation out before they could even begin to tear it apart.

———— • • • ————

The trip from Great Salt Lake City to Fort Bridger was 113 miles, much of it through the snowfall that had filled up the mountain passes.

Brigham had sent a security escort with Kane, but as they finally approached the federal camp, the emissary decided to approach the pickets alone. His decision proved wise. An overexcited guard challenged the approaching traveler and then shot at him without giving Kane time to reply. He missed, and Kane responded by breaking the stock of his rifle over the picket's head. The soldier thus disarmed, Kane politely asked the young man to escort him to Governor Cumming's tent, or so the story goes.[75]

Cumming greeted him kindly enough, but Johnston and his officers were less welcoming—there was at least one serious attempt to arrest Kane as a spy. They sorted the matter diplomatically, and Kane presented his case to the governor. The accusations against the Saints were false, he said. There was no rebellion. The Saints weren't happy about being governed by someone they hadn't chosen, of course, but Brigham was prepared to accept his replacement and the people would follow, on two conditions. First, the army should not escort the governor into Great Salt Lake City; second, no soldiers were to be quartered in any civilian settlement. Brigham wanted to keep the people and the army separated. If Cumming would accompany Kane back to Great Salt Lake City to meet Brigham, the matter could be resolved without any further resistance.

Governor Cumming decided to take Kane at his word and go with him into the city. The letter Kane bore from Buchanan proved that the president had approved Kane's mission, and Kane's personal sacrifices in making the trip during this season at his own expense while ill spoke well of his character and motives. Johnston protested. If Kane was wrong, Cumming would be delivering himself as a potential hostage into the hands of traitors to the country. If Brigham Young really was ready to submit, he could have ordered the Nauvoo Legion to stand down. They hadn't killed anyone, that was true, but they were still mobilized. But Cumming was undeterred, and Johnston had no authority to prevent the governor from acting as he saw fit.

—•—•—•—

Back in Washington, Buchanan's misery in his handling of the expedition had been increasing by the day since Kane left. As the news of the army's troubles continued to trickle in, Congress had launched an investigation into the affair. The House of Representatives issued a formal request to Buchanan for

> the information which gave rise to the [Utah Expedition], the instructions to the army officers in connection with the same, and all correspondence which has taken place with said army officers, with Brigham Young and his followers, or with others, throwing light upon the question as to how far said Brigham Young and his followers are in a state of rebellion or resistance to the government of the United States.[76]

As requested, Buchanan delivered the documents—and there, on the second page, was an admission that the president would have preferred not to make. Secretary of State Lewis Cass had searched the administration's files and reported that "the only document on record or on file in this department, touching the subject of the resolution, is the letter of Mr. W. M. F. Magraw to the President."[77] What had been rumor before was now official—Buchanan had launched the largest military operation of the decade against an unpopular minority on nothing more than the uncorroborated word of a political friend hostile to the very people now facing invasion and occupation. Judge Drummond's testimony was also public knowledge, but invoking him was no help. His accusations were even more extreme than Magraw's, his motives equally suspect, and he was guilty of moral turpitude. When Van Vliet's reports and the Saints' claims of loyalty to the country were added to the mix, the president's lack of due diligence became a political scandal worthy of its own title: "Buchanan's Blunder."

As spring approached, the pressure on Buchanan to resolve the crisis became immense, but his fundamental dilemma hadn't changed a whit. Every option seemed likely to do him and the Democratic Party severe political damage. One Republican senator, Simon Cameron of

Pennsylvania, said he would vote in favor of Buchanan's request to authorize new regiments to fight in Utah because he thought Buchanan was destroying the Democratic Party, and granting the request for troops would hurry the process of political self-immolation along. "If there was no war [in Utah] before, they have provoked one now," he said. "They have expended millions upon millions of dollars in a fruitless endeavor to give power to themselves. I wish them to have the responsibility of it, and not the party to which I belong."[78]

Buchanan understood that when one's political enemies thought cooperating with the opposing party was the surest path to beating it, the time had come to change course. But two thousand miles removed from the arena of action, Buchanan had virtually no control over anything. Unless he was prepared to recall the army—and he wasn't—then he was, for all practical purposes, a helpless spectator. He really had only one last bit of leverage that might entice Brigham Young to come to the negotiating table: the offer of a presidential pardon.

Buchanan drafted a lengthy statement designed to give him a way out while saving political face. Making no mention of his own failure to investigate before sending the army, he excoriated the Saints for the mess and accused them of sedition and treason. It was the Saints' hatred for the US government that had brought the nation to this point, he said. They were levying war against their country under the deluded notion that this was all a "crusade against [their] religion. . . . This rebellion is not merely a violation of your legal duty; it is without just cause, without reason, without excuse," Buchanan declared. (Brigham might have added "without existence.") "You never made a complaint that was not listened to with patience. You never exhibited a real grievance that was not redressed as promptly as it could be." Those were jaw-dropping claims to the Saints. The fact that they were even in Utah was itself a testament to the federal government's failure to redress their grievances.

Then, casting himself in a merciful light, Buchanan toned down his scathing language to make his pitch.

Being anxious to save the effusion of blood, and to avoid the indiscriminate punishment of a whole people for crimes of which it is not probable that all are equally guilty, I offer now a free and full pardon to all who will submit themselves to the authority of the federal government. If you refuse to accept it, let the consequences fall upon your own heads. But I conjure you to pause deliberately, and reflect well, before you reject this tender of peace and good will.

Then he returned to his fire-breathing rhetoric. Those who rejected his mercy could "expect no further leniency, but look to be rigorously dealt with"; the army would remain in Utah until the Saints manifested "a proper sense of the duty to which they owe this government."[79] With that, he chose two peace commissioners and sent them and his message on their way.

— • • —

Cumming's trip with Kane to Salt Lake took one week exactly, and they arrived on April 12. The governor's reception was as Kane had promised. He was given a Legion escort to his temporary residence, and city officials and prominent citizens joined with him for the last leg of the journey. Brigham met with Cumming later the same day, and the two men shared a cordial conversation. After Brigham left, one of Cumming's hosts asked whether the prophet had struck him as a tyrant. "No, sir," Cumming answered. "No tyrant ever had a head on his shoulder like Mr. Young. He is naturally a very good man. I doubt whether many of your people sufficiently appreciate him as a leader."[80]

Cumming tested the waters for several days, then sent word to Johnston—the Saints had received him as the territory's chief executive without resistance. In his report back of May 2, he confirmed:

I have been everywhere recognized as Governor of Utah; and, so far from having encountered insults or indignities, I am gratified in being able to state to you that, in passing through the settlements, I have been universally greeted with such respectful attentions as are due to the representative authority of the United States in the Territory. . . . The Territorial seal, with other public property, has been tendered me by William H. Hooper, Esq., late Secretary *pro tem.* I have not yet examined the subject critically, but apprehend that the records of the United States Courts, Territorial Library, and other public property, remain unimpaired.[81]

No rebellion, no destruction of federal property, not a single insult leveled in his direction. It was the second piece of good news that Johnston had received in a month, the first being his brevet promotion to brigadier general on April 10.

But Johnston still planned on bringing the army into Great Salt Lake City, even if he wasn't going to station them there, and that led to an event that Cumming found astonishing. Following through on the plan Brigham had presented before, almost the entire population of the city began to abandon their homes. By early May, hundreds of wagons were moving south. Some carried families hauling personal property, food, and supplies. Others were driven by Church teamsters evacuating machinery, the Deseret News print shop, Church records and papers, and other equipment. Truman Angell packed up the architect's office and carried away his tools and the temple blueprints. "The people, including the inhabitants of this city, are moving from every settlement in the northern part of the Territory. The roads are everywhere filled with wagons loaded with provisions and household furniture, the women and children often without shoes or hats, driving their flocks they know not where," Cumming reported.[82]

The workers had covered the temple block by early May, and now it looked little different than it had before the groundbreaking in February 1853. "The temple foundation is cached, the public shop[s] removed, except what is required to be retained in operation in order to fix wagons, shoe animals, make boxes, etc.," Brigham reported.[83] The temple had, for all practical purposes, been erased from the earth. It was a kind of magic trick they were trying to pull off, making four years of hard work disappear, but every Church member passing by the site knew the secret lying sixteen feet beneath the illusion. How long it would stay buried, no one knew, but staring at that level field of freshly tilled dirt, some must have wondered whether their enemies hadn't successfully managed to stop them from finishing a temple yet again. Indeed, given Brigham's claims that the devil got riled up whenever a temple was started, they could have been forgiven for wondering whether that building, now buried, hadn't brought Johnston's army to their door.

——— · · ———

Cumming left for Fort Bridger on May 13 to retrieve his family, a month and a day after he'd first entered Salt Lake. When they returned a few weeks later, the "Move South" was very nearly complete. The governor found the entire city abandoned, gardens and orchards loaded with straw, and the only Saints left in town were those assigned to arson duty. Cumming entered his temporary home and there found Elder William Staines, his host, sitting at the table with lunch spread for his visitors. Cumming's wife, Elizabeth, asked Staines about the empty streets, and he responded by explaining the plan to burn the city if the army tried to occupy it. Mrs. Cumming began to weep. "Oh! Alfred, something must be done to bring them back!" she exclaimed to her husband. "Do not permit the army to stay in the city. Can't you do something for them?"

"Yes, madam," Cumming replied. "I shall do all I can, rest assured. I only wish I could be in Washington for two hours; I am persuaded that I could convince the Government that we have no need for troops."[84]

He was as good as his word. Cumming spent several days on horseback, riding up and down the exodus line and pleading with the people to return to their homes, but it was futile. If the army was coming into the city, the Saints were leaving. The property they were leaving behind was not worth suffering a possible repeat of their Missouri troubles, as they saw it.

When asked what, if anything, could bring the Saints back to their homes, Brigham said "the greatest inducement to go back to Great Salt Lake City would be to build the Temple."[85]

———•··•———

Brigham was in Provo on June 1 when he received a military dispatch containing unusual news. An army deserter had come into one of the Nauvoo Legion's camps and reported that ex-governor Lazarus Powell of Kentucky and US Army Major Benjamin McCulloch—Buchanan's delegation—were at Fort Bridger and wanted to speak with Brigham Young. Had the president only taken that step a year before, the current trouble could have been avoided entirely. As it was, Brigham was in no rush to sit at the negotiating table. He was not the one looking for an easy end to the trouble, especially if it involved suffering a military occupation to quell a "rebellion" they'd never staged. This was Buchanan's mess to clean up, and Brigham wasn't going to give up cheap concessions.

McCulloch and Powell convinced General Johnston to keep his army at Fort Bridger until after their meeting with Brigham. At that word, Brigham, the First Presidency, and several of the Twelve saddled up to ride north on the tenth of June. Leaving at four o'clock in the morning, they reached Salt Lake in a day.[86]

They convened with Powell, McCulloch, and Governor Cumming in the Council House the next morning at nine o'clock to "effect an amicable adjustment of the 'unfortunate difficulties' existing between the General Government and Utah." The discussions lasted all day, and Buchanan's proclamation, with its vitriolic language, was no help. The president was trying to salvage his political situation from a massive error, and the prophet actually seemed to feel some small bit of pity for the chief executive's situation. "Buchanan, poor fellow, is gone already," Brigham told a friend.[87] But any soft feelings Brigham might have held clearly were tempered by the document's many slanders—forty-two, to be precise, they counted them. Brigham was also unimpressed by Buchanan's offer of mercy.

> I thank President Buchanan for forgiving me, but I really cannot tell what I have done. I know one thing, and that is, that the people called "Mormons" are a loyal and a law-abiding people, and have ever been. Neither President Buchanan nor any one else can contradict the statement. It is true, Lot Smith burned some wagons containing Government supplies for the army. This was an overt act, and if it is for this we are to be pardoned, I accept the pardon.[88]

But after many hours, Brigham finally said the words that the commissioners had been hoping to hear. "Will [I] submit to constitutional principles? I reply, I will." Then turning to those on his side of the table, he tried to offer some reassurance. "Will they hang you, Bro[ther] Brigham?" he asked rhetorically. "Don't be concerned, brethren, we have to do right and God will sustain us." Then he added one last bit of counsel that perhaps made McCulloch and Powell just a bit nervous: "Trust in God and keep your powder dry."[89]

It was enough. Powell and McCulloch wrote to Johnston, reporting that

> the chief men of the Territory . . . will yield obedience to the Constitution and laws of the United States; that they will not resist the execution of the law . . . that they cheerfully consent that the civil officers of the Territory shall enter upon the discharge of their respective duties and that they will make no resistance to the army of the United States in its march to the valley of Salt Lake or elsewhere.[90]

The army could march to Great Salt Lake City as soon as it could get under way. Cumming issued his own proclamation, declaring that under the president's pardon all offenses committed during the recent hostilities were forgiven.

Cumming's first report to General Johnston—that the Saints had received him amicably as the new governor—arrived in Washington on June 9, a little more than a week after Powell and McCulloch arrived at Johnston's winter camp. So while both sides were sitting around a Council House table working out their differences, back in Washington the president was busy declaring victory. "There is reason to believe that our difficulties with the Territory of Utah have terminated, and the reign of the Constitution and laws has been restored," he told Congress the next day.[91] His declaration probably spurred some private sarcasm at his expense—Cumming's letter made it clear that the "reign of the Constitution and laws" among the Latter-day Saints hadn't needed restoring in the first place. In any case, the public could now turn its gaze away from Utah, and Buchanan's mass pardon guaranteed that there would be no trials to draw the public's attention back to it. The Utah Expedition could fade in significance compared to the unrest over slavery. Buchanan had always thought that managing that problem was far more important anyway. Slavery was splitting the country like a wedge in a log, so he would gladly take this resolution to the Utah affair and swallow the political embarrassment if it let him turn his full attention back to the task of fending off a civil war.

On June 13, after seven months encamped at Fort Bridger, General Johnston and his army finally marched south, traversing the 113 miles in just under two weeks. They "came not as conquerors into Zion," one historian wrote after the fact. What once was "expected to have been a triumphal entrance . . . with all the pomp and circumstance of glorious war" was, in the end, an event witnessed by almost no one.[92] A military correspondent traveling with Johnston recorded his observations of the army's passage through the empty city.

> It was one of the most extraordinary scenes that have occurred in American history. All day long, from dawn until after sunset, the troops and trains poured through the city, the utter silence of

the streets being broken only by the music of the military bands, the monotonous tramp of the regiments, and the rattle of the baggage wagons. . . . The only visible groups of spectators were on the corners near Brigham Young's residence, and consisted almost entirely of Gentile civilians.[93]

One of the officers in the column offered a shorter, more telling description—"It was substantially a city of the dead," he said.[94] The army rode through the quiet streets, looking at the homes and buildings, every man alone in his own thoughts. Colonel Philip St. George Cooke, Johnston's cavalry chief, had led the Mormon Battalion overland to California a decade earlier during the Mexican War. Now he took off his hat and rode with his head uncovered as a show of respect for the Saints he had commanded then, though none of those men were present to see his gesture.[95]

The army took most of the morning and much of the afternoon to pass through the city. They marched to the Cummings' new home and, as ordered, serenaded the governor as they stepped past. The rest of the day they sang "One-Eyed Riley" as they marched, a bawdy Irish barracks tune that would have confirmed every fear Brigham had about the soldiers bringing vice and immorality with them into the territory.[96] The soldiers camped that night two miles from the city "on a dusty meadow by the river bank" of the Jordan.[97] They resumed their march the following morning and finally settled forty miles south in Cedar Valley, near the present-day town of Eagle Mountain. There they established Camp Floyd, named for the Secretary of War who had given his full-throated support for the expedition from the beginning. As Brigham had insisted, the permanent camp for Johnston's army was located a fair distance from any settlement. Utah Lake sat between the new military outpost and the closest towns, Provo and Lehi.

———•·•·•———

Governor Cumming visited Brigham in Provo on the evening of June 29. Great Salt Lake City had been abandoned now for more than a month, and, with Johnston's army safely settled in the distance, Cumming hoped the Saints might be ready to come back. Brigham's message to the Saints the next day was fewer than twenty words: "All who wish to return to their homes in Great Salt Lake City are at liberty to do so." That evening, around six o'clock, Brigham mounted up in his own wagon and began to ride north. Cumming rode with him, as did Heber C. Kimball, Daniel H. Wells, George A. Smith, Amasa Lyman, and Albert Carrington. A company of thirty men led by William Wall provided a military escort for the group.[98] They reached Salt Lake at four o'clock in the morning after "a pleasant night's ride."[99]

Within a few weeks, the Saints were in their homes again. For the first time in almost a year, life in Great Salt Lake City became normal again . . . or nearly so. The temple block had been the center of industry for the city for ten years. Now the public works were gone, and the temple foundation sat buried and out of sight, waiting for Brigham's order to start construction on the house of the Lord again.

CHAPTER 6

THIS IS MY REVELATION

Brigham Young's concerns about the army sowing "seeds of corruption" among the Saints proved accurate. Salt Lake was not completely free of alcohol, gambling, and prostitution—no large city ever is—but now the influx of soldiers into the region fueled the growth of the vice industry. The largest military expedition in a decade had been an irresistible lure to civilians who often followed military camps and looked to make a profit off the soldiers' less virtuous pastimes. Teamsters brought profanity, gamblers brought cards and games of chance, and everyone brought alcohol. After the army established Camp Floyd, saloons and houses of fornication opened nearby. Throughout the rest of 1858, soldiers on leave made their way into Provo, Salt Lake, and other settlements, where they drank, gambled, and brawled. A few gunfights resulted in fatalities. Before the year was out, a hostile group began publishing an anti-Mormon newspaper titled the *Valley Tan* that followed in Judge Drummond's footsteps and accused Brigham and others of treason and murder. The Saints had avoided war that year, but there wasn't much peace in the valley when Christmas passed and the New Year began.

The weather had scarcely started to warm when a new conflict threatened to break out, courtesy of Associate Justice John Cradlebaugh, one of Buchanan's appointees to the federal bench. In March 1859, Cradlebaugh, not content to merely decide cases brought before him, decided to take an active hand in making sure that the cases he wanted to decide would, in fact, be pursued. He ordered investigations and prosecutions, and he called on General Johnston to send a contingent of soldiers to Provo to back up his authority. He justified the request on the grounds that his investigations would produce "a great many prisoners, and as there is no jail, it [would] be a great expense to keep them, so he [thought it] best to have a company of soldiers to guard them."[1] Johnston granted the request and sent a company under the command of Captain Harry Heth to Provo. Cradlebaugh put them to use. The soldiers rode out to round up suspects, searching homes and farms, and those who were found were arrested, taken to Provo, and kept in tents under guard until their day in court. Cradlebaugh's interrogations of the witnesses were openly hostile. "It is another Missouri Military mob court," Brigham reported in his usual blunt manner.[2] Outside the building, the soldiers "established a camp in the city and posted pickets who antagonized the citizenry by demanding all passers-by identify themselves at point of bayonet." By night, "the soldiers were nearly all gloriously drunk, and the officers, ditto."[3]

Mayor B. K. Bullock of Provo petitioned Cradlebaugh to order the troops out of the city. Cradlebaugh refused and had Bullock arrested. Believing that the judge was engaged in tyrannical persecution under the thin cover of the law, armed Saints came to the city in droves. Captain Heth called for reinforcements, and Johnston sent them. The number of soldiers deployed in Provo eventually neared a thousand, including a battery of artillery. Following the situation from afar, Brigham speculated that Cradlebaugh's "reign of terror" was a deliberate attempt to provoke the conflict they all had so narrowly avoided the previous year.[4] Governor Cumming personally asked Johnston to withdraw the men. Johnston, believing the Saints to be guilty of a number of crimes, refused. Cumming appealed to President Buchanan, and the commander-in-chief sided with the governor over the judge. The troops were ordered back to Camp Floyd, and US Attorney General Jeremiah Black banned federal judges in the territory from employing soldiers as court bailiffs and jailers.

With hostile magistrates thus defanged in some measure, life in Provo returned to normal, but two facts were evident. First, General Johnston, his soldiers, and the federal judges shared the "popular prejudice" and ugly feelings toward the Saints that were so prevalent back East.[5] And second, while the Saints may have been able to keep their homes, the isolation and peace that Brigham and his people had mostly enjoyed for ten years was well and truly gone.

* · · ·

Brigham was not happy about that prospect, but there was no help for it; and despite the language of his antigovernment railings, the prophet was not one to obsess over circumstances that he could not change. The tenuous peace with the army was about the best they could expect, and there was work to be done. "The barren stretch of a roughly plowed field" inside the temple block could never have been far from Brigham's thoughts. He lived nearby and would have seen the wall around the site most days, a reminder of what was waiting for him inside. By early December, he felt the work needed to push forward, and so he paid a visit to Wilford Woodruff. Wilford had been called as the Church Historian and so was spending much of his time in the Historian's Office, where he was preparing a history of Joseph Smith for publication. Brigham told the Apostle to set the manuscript aside for a time and raised the subject of restarting construction on the temple. "I think we must commence it next spring, uncover the foundation," he said.[6] That would be welcome news for the Saints, but Brigham confided to his old friend that the stonemasons had warned him of a potential problem with the foundation. The sandstone blocks needed to be cut and laid perfectly level in the limestone mortar between courses to bear the weight of the granite walls that would be stacked on them. That required the masons to use a level to check the alignment of each stone to keep it in horizontal line with the rest of the stones in the tier. Truman Angell had such a tool, known to be accurate. But the masons told Brigham that Alonzo Raleigh, the foreman, had demurred from using Truman's implement in favor of his own homemade—and apparently defective—level. The false readings from the device had led to the stones being improperly laid. Truman confirmed the problem on December 7. Enough dirt had been removed for him to take a measurement of the exposed basement walls, and he found sections that were two inches off level.

Years before, once Raleigh had realized there was a problem, he'd directed the masons to fashion wedge-shaped stone shims to insert into the horizontal seams to straighten the next tier. It was a solution that had no prayer of working. The foundation stones weighed in at two tons apiece, never mind the weight yet to come from the stones they would be adding to build up the walls. The wedges surely would be pushed out of place or crushed, and the foundation would again settle out of alignment, putting unimaginable stress on the wall above. "I shall have to take up one tier of rock all over the foundation, for Brother Raleigh appears as though he wished to destroy that Temple," Brigham told Wilford. "One quarter of an inch settling of that building would crack it from top to bottom. . . . I do not know as Brother Raleigh realizes what he is doing but it appears to me that he is trying to destroy the architecture of that building."[7] But there was nothing to be done about it then. They would have to uncover and examine the entire foundation to figure out the full extent of the problem and what it would take to fix it.

Knowing they would have to fix any part of it was a frustrating prospect, but the delay would give them time to address some other challenges. They still hadn't solved the transportation problems inherent in moving the granite—the canal was unfinished and the road to the southern canyons would need improvement if they had to keep hauling the stone by wagon. Several times the territorial and county governments had tried to harden that road, but the soil south of Salt Lake City near the base of the mountains was porous in places and resisted all efforts at firming up the surface. Winter snowmelt and spring rains usually made it impassable until summer approached and dried it up.

They also needed to set up shop in Little Cottonwood Canyon. They'd harvested granite from Big Cottonwood Canyon for the foundation and first courses of the basement walls, but the masons decided that the granite from Little Cottonwood Canyon farther south was superior. That would add time and miles onto the trip for the teamsters, but they thought the higher quality rock of Little Cottonwood justified the effort. Brigham concurred and issued a contract to John Sharp, owner of the Red Butte Quarry, to establish the camp and extract and deliver five hundred cords of granite.[8]

In truth, *extracting* wasn't precisely what Sharp's men would be doing. The canyon floor was strewn with enormous granite boulders of all sizes, some as large as fifty feet in diameter, the remnants of some seismic disturbance eons before that had broken off whole chunks of the mountain and sent them tumbling down where the Saints could get at them.[9] Unless those ran out, all the men would have to do was crack them apart on the spot. What came next would be challenging—they would have to cut each block to size by hand with hammers and chisels; drag them to a loading dock, yet to be built, where they would be lifted into wagons using nothing more than ropes, pulleys, and muscle; then haul them twenty miles over four days. At least the Lord had saved them a bit of labor by laying the rocks out on the ground for them instead of making the workers climb the mountainside to carve out what they needed. But, given the temple's planned dimensions, they would need *thousands* of granite blocks, one to three tons each, from Little Cottonwood to finish the building.

In 1860, John Sharp told a team of his best stonecutters to pack up their tools, make their way down to Little Cottonwood Canyon, and set up camp.[10] For some of them, it would be home for almost three decades to come.

The early months of 1860 passed by uneventfully, with the army at Camp Floyd having almost nothing to do. The Saints were keeping to themselves as much as the soldiers and their hangers-on would allow, so there were no breaches of the peace requiring military force to restore order. Johnston did his best to keep his men occupied through drills, parades, and manual labor. He authorized some smaller expeditions to survey and build roads throughout the territory. He also allowed them to establish a theater and a Military Dramatic Association to stage plays for the men's amusement. As there were no women in uniform available to fill female roles, they invited actresses who were Latter-day Saints from the surrounding settlements to join the stage productions.[11] But there were limits to how much such diversions could sustain morale, and alcohol and prostitution were common alternatives. "The army is inactive," Secretary of War Floyd reported, and it was costly to maintain such a large force so far from home while it was just sitting idle. With no evidence at hand that the Saints had ever really been in rebellion against the country, there was simply no justification for keeping Johnston's army where it was. Floyd offered no concession that the entire Utah Expedition had been ill-advised from the start, and instead claimed that the Saints were "a conquered and sullen people." But in the next breath he admitted that "there is in the present attitude of affairs scarcely any necessity for the presence of troops in Utah, and they will be otherwise disposed of in the coming season."[12]

The "coming season" arrived more rapidly for General Johnston than he could have hoped. He received orders in late February to return east, with an extended leave granted before reporting to his next assignment. He'd never been one to disobey orders even if he considered them distasteful, but these were the most gratifying orders he'd received in years. He reviewed his troops for the last time the next day, March 1, and addressed them from the saddle. He complimented their patriotism and devotion to duty despite the great hardships they'd endured together. Johnston then rode his horse out of camp and onto the southern trail for California. He had never visited Great Salt Lake City again since passing through some twenty months before in 1858, nor had he ever actually met Brigham Young in person. That was no quirk of circumstance. Johnston held the Saints in contempt and Brigham most of all. Johnston had no desire to see the man who had been the primary source of all the frustrations and discomforts the general had endured for more than two years.

It would not be long before the rest of the army followed Johnston. The news coming from the East—which could now arrive from Kansas in just six days, courtesy of the Pony Express—was all turmoil and strife. Congress was quarrelling more or less incessantly about slavery in the states, pausing only enough to argue about polygamy in the territories. The Democratic Party held a convention in Charleston, South Carolina, in April to nominate a presidential candidate and failed. The Southern delegates insisted on a pro-slavery plank that called on the federal government to actively protect their "peculiar institution," which set off two days of bitter debate. The Northerners won, and fifty Southern delegates walked out. When the convention moved on to vote for nominees, the remaining members were so bitterly divided that they couldn't manage the feat. The convention adjourned without choosing anyone. They tried again six weeks later in Baltimore, but the scene was a repeat of the first convention. The Southerners refused to compromise on their pro-slavery demands and walked out again, this time a full third of the delegates marching out the doors. They arranged their own convention and nominated a separate candidate—John C. Breckinridge of Kentucky, Buchanan's own vice president. The Northerners finally nominated Stephen A. Douglas, but the Democratic Party had split itself in half.

The Republican convention in Chicago in May was much less spirited. The only nominee they could finally agree on was the Illinois lawyer who had sparred with Stephen Douglas in a series of debates a few years before, Abraham Lincoln, but he was almost no one's first choice. Some newspapers had not even included him on their lists of contenders most likely to win the Republican candidacy. Many delegates and reporters were nonplussed when he took the nomination on the third ballot. The Party had come together around a single candidate without anyone walking off the convention floor in protest, but no one was convinced that they had chosen the right man.[13]

The political divisions on display only hardened the growing belief among many that the Union's dissolution was inevitable. It was a conclusion that Brigham shared. A civil war was coming, he decided, and he saw it as a just punishment for the country's persecution of the Saints.

> The North and South [are] gathering large armies and preparing for war. The banks and capitalists throughout the whole country are concentrating capital, to sustain the war. The nation has persecuted the saints of God and made them confiscate their all and flee from place to place to save their lives and now it is their turn. The Lord has said, "He would vex the nation," and he will surely do it. Civil war has begun in earnest and it will go on until the will of God is done. All that they have sought to bring on us, will come to pass on them.[14]

Lincoln won the election that November. Douglas and Breckinridge split the Democratic vote, allowing Lincoln to win an electoral college majority with less than forty percent of the popular vote. The national reaction was immediate and divisive. It was apparent to the slaveholding states that their ability to influence the federal government to protect the institution of slavery had been crippled. South Carolina, Mississippi, Florida, Alabama, Georgia, Louisiana, and Texas passed ordinances of secession from the Union, which set off several desperate attempts in Congress to approve legislation to protect slavery, including a constitutional amendment that would have guaranteed the institution wherever it existed and admitted New Mexico as a slave state. Still deeply divided, Congress was unable to pass any of it.

In a final effort to avert a war, a peace conference convened at the Willard Hotel in Washington in February 1861. Delegates included former President John Tyler, retired governors and senators, representatives, federal cabinet heads, and a parade of senior state justices. It came to nothing. The Republicans wanted slavery's expansion stopped; Democrats were still divided over whether and how to protect it anywhere that it already existed. The final proposed legislation that emerged satisfied no one and failed to pass Congress. At the same time, 600 miles away, delegates from the seceding states were meeting in their own convention in Montgomery, Alabama. In a matter of days, they established themselves as a provisional legislature and elected a president—Jefferson Davis, former Secretary of War and recently resigned senator from Mississippi. To establish the legal foundation for their new country, on March 11, they adopted a Provisional Constitution—a revision of the US Constitution with added language and provisions to firmly protect slavery and states' rights. With that act completed, the Confederate States of America was born.

Lincoln assumed the presidency of the United States on March 5, and the dithering Buchanan hurried off the political stage, to no one's disappointment. The new president had promised in his inaugural speech that the United States would "hold, occupy and possess" all federal property. His first effort to do that was a creative stroke that put the South on the horns of a dilemma. A few months previous, US troops had pulled out of bases in Charleston, South Carolina, to Fort Sumter, which sat on an island in Charleston Bay. On April 6, Lincoln sent a messenger to Charleston to tell the governor that the United States would be sending only provisions to the men occupying Sumter. If South Carolina would not interfere with the humanitarian shipment, the US would not try to send in additional men or weapons. This was an ugly choice, not just for the governor but for Confederate President Jefferson Davis also.

The confederates wanted Sumter, but if they fired on the supply ships, they would stand convicted of having taken the first violent step toward war. If they allowed the supply ships to go through, they would be admitting that they lacked the power or nerve, or both, to defy the military power of the United States. The Confederacy might come apart, with individual states going their own way rather than lashing their fates to a weak-kneed government too timid to oppose the Union.

Facing those choices, and with his fellow Southerners howling for action, Davis made his choice. Through his secretary of war, he ordered General Pierre Gustave Toutant-Beauregard, commanding the South Carolinian militia, to "at once demand [Sumter's] evacuation, and if this is refused proceed, in such manner as you may determine, to reduce it" before the supply ships arrived.[15]

The nation had almost split once before. In 1832, South Carolina had defied the federal government by declaring null and void tariffs imposed by the United States government. The federal response had been a proclamation that such defiance of national authority amounted to rebellion. The argument had escalated nearly to bloodshed. Joseph Smith had been following the events through the newspapers and, on Christmas Day that year, felt a powerful impression through the Spirit about the direction of future events. He recorded the following:

> Verily, thus saith the Lord concerning the wars that will shortly come to pass, beginning at the rebellion of South Carolina, which will eventually terminate in the death and misery of many souls;
>
> And the time will come that war will be poured out upon all nations, beginning at this place.
>
> For behold, the Southern States shall be divided against the Northern States, and the Southern States will call on other nations, even the nation of Great Britain, as it is called, and they shall

also call upon other nations, in order to defend themselves against other nations; and then war shall be poured out upon all nations.

And it shall come to pass, after many days, slaves shall rise up against their masters, who shall be marshaled and disciplined for war.[16]

Joseph was not some doomsday preacher. He was an optimistic man by nature, but the revelation predicted a violent conflict and was detailed as to where it would start and what would follow. With a sure conviction that the revelation would be fulfilled, he declared that "not many years shall pass away before the United States shall present such a scene of bloodshed as has not a parallel in the history of our nation."[17]

He received another prophecy just a few days later. This one also contained some dark apocalyptic warnings, given as signs that God's work was in progress, but the revelation also offered counsel and commandments to prepare the people for coming events. Among them was the first direction for the Saints to build a temple, which would be a spiritual refuge for them in the midst of a world roiled by conflict. "Organize yourselves; prepare every needful thing; and establish a house, even a house of prayer, a house of fasting, a house of faith, a house of learning, a house of glory, a house of order, a house of God."[18]

But the war didn't come. A few weeks later, in February 1833, the federal government reached a compromise with South Carolina that averted the violent conflict that had seemed so unavoidable. Perplexed and unsure how to reconcile the peaceful resolution with the revelation that had predicted a civil war between the states, Joseph refrained from talking much about it. He did not discuss it in his sermons or include it in any of the compiled editions of his revelations published in his lifetime, and he never lived to see the prophecy fulfilled. He just filed it away and focused his attention instead on the revelation to build a temple, setting to work on establishing a house of the Lord in Kirtland.

The literal fulfillment of Joseph's prophecy of civil war began thirty years later, on April 12, 1861, at 4:30 a.m., when General Beauregard opened fire on Fort Sumter with forty-seven howitzers and mortars. Major Anderson, the Union officer commanding the Sumter garrison, had refused the demand to evacuate, and the Confederates' bombardment continued all that day and into the night. Anderson must have suffered through the attack feeling a sense of deep personal irony—he had been Beauregard's artillery instructor at West Point, and now his former student was demonstrating his mastery of the subject the major had taught him. The South Carolinians fired more than four thousand rounds in all into the bastion. The massive outer walls held, but the troops' quarters and other buildings on the interior burned when the Confederates started lobbing red-hot incendiaries into the fort. Anderson and his men returned fire with their forty cannons, but Sumter had been engineered for use against naval vessels, not the land forts on the nearby coast. Anderson and his troops were fighting not to win but to satisfy honor, and the Confederates knew it. At one point the Union troops paused firing briefly, and Beauregard wondered whether his old teacher was about to surrender. When Sumter's cannons resumed their attack a minute later, the Confederates stood up and cheered their opponents' fortitude and devotion to duty, then resumed their attack on the fortress.[19]

Seeing no relief possible, Anderson ran up the white flag and surrendered the fort to Beauregard unconditionally. The genteel Southern officer allowed his opponent the privilege of a ceremony to lower the United States flag and then retire with his men to one of the Union vessels waiting outside the bay. No one on either side was killed in the attack. The first official casualty of the Civil War occurred during Anderson's fifty-gun salute to the flag. A burning ember from one of the cannons landed in gunpowder and set off an explosion that killed Private Daniel Hough and injured five others. Anderson completed the ceremony, collected the charred flag, and retired his men from the island. Their

Confederate opponents stood on the beach, their hats over their hearts in a display of respect, with no cheers or other expressions of victory.

The Saints learned the following week of the fall of Sumter. Despite the torments that their country had inflicted on them over the years, they took no pleasure in seeing the nation fall into civil war—but it did strengthen their faith that they were led by prophets. They interpreted the attack on Sumter specifically as "the commencement of the war at South Carolina in fulfillment of the revelation given through Joseph Smith the Prophet in 1832."[20] And with the war's beginning, Brigham declared that they should now see the Lord's wisdom in allowing the mobs to push the Saints westward from Ohio, Missouri, and Illinois.

> We are infinitely more blessed by the persecutions and injustice we have suffered, than we could have been if we had remained in our habitations from which we have been driven—than if we had been suffered to occupy our farms, gardens, stores, mills, machinery and everything we had in our former possessions. Had we not been persecuted, we would now be in the midst of the wars and bloodshed that are desolating the nation, instead of where we are, comfortably located in our peaceful dwellings in these silent, far off mountains and valleys. Instead of seeing my brethren comfortably seated around me today, many of them would be found in the front ranks on the battle field. I realize the blessings of God in our present safety. We are greatly blessed, greatly favored and greatly exalted, while our enemies who sought to destroy us, are being humbled.[21]

Years of persecution and wandering as refugees from state to state had not been pointless. As much as they had suffered, the Lord had allowed their persecutions to save them from a greater calamity. There, too, was a lesson in faith.

———•··•———

Charleston Bay was sixteen hundred miles from the valley, but the fall of Sumter was quickly felt in Great Salt Lake City. Many Southerners in federal service had abandoned their posts or resigned to support the Confederacy. Cumming was not one of these. His home state of Georgia had seceded from the Union, but he personally had not. That hardly mattered. The loyalty of all Southerners still in federal service would be suspect for a time, and the new president would want to name appointees who had his full confidence. Governor Cumming resigned his office and left quietly for the States with his wife on the seventeenth of May. The Saints lamented his departure. Cumming had arrived bearing some of the same prejudices toward them that most Americans held, but he had become a friend, and the Saints had precious few of those. They also worried about whom the president might send in his place. The Republican Party considered slavery and polygamy to be barbaric institutions cut from the same cloth, and that put both the South and the Saints in the sights of the administration. Lincoln was now leading a war against slavery, and the question was whether he could take on polygamy at the same time. Brigham did not think so. The Civil War would have to run its course first before Lincoln could turn his attention to the Saints, he thought. "Old 'Abe' the President of the U.S. has it in his mind to pitch into us when he had got through with the South," he told Heber C. Kimball.[22]

The war's start also meant the federal troops would be leaving and dismantling Camp Floyd, which had been renamed Fort Crittenden after Senator John J. Crittenden of Kentucky, who had labored at the peace conference to forge a compromise and avert the war. The outpost's original namesake, John Floyd, Buchanan's secretary of war and one of the Utah Expedition's most vocal supporters, had resigned his office and thrown his support to the Confederacy. Reviewing his tenure, investigators realized that Floyd had "scattered the army so that much of it could be captured when hostilities should commence, and distributed the cannon and small arms from Northern arsenals throughout the South so as to be on hand when treason wanted them."[23] Some wondered whether Floyd hadn't supported the Utah Expedition from the beginning as part of that very scheme, sending thousands of US soldiers across the continent so they wouldn't be available for months after a war began.

If so, it had been a smart gambit. A significant fraction of the federal army was sitting idle in Utah, doing nothing useful for the war effort while draining the federal treasury at a ferocious rate. It was expensive to keep the garrison supplied, and the money and resources going to Fort Crittenden were needed to defeat the Confederacy. So the government sent orders for the troops to dismantle their base of operations, auction off the buildings and equipment, and march east as quickly as possible. The resulting fire sale transferred some $4,000,000 of military gear into the Saints' hands, for which they paid the army a grand total of about $100,000. Wagons that had cost the government $150 to $175 each were sold for $6.50 apiece. Tents, tools, mules and livestock, stock feed, clothing, and huge quantities of food changed hands at prices far below cost. One buyer purchased the fort headquarters for $75.[24] After all of the distress that Johnston's army had caused, the thought of "the great Buchanan Utah Expedition, costing the Government millions, and accomplishing nothing, except making many of the Saints comparatively rich" was immensely satisfying to Brigham.[25]

As the blue columns marched out of the valley, he must have finally felt some relief, if nothing else, but the reason for their departure was not a cause for celebration. Brigham and the Saints followed the war through the papers, the mail, and later through the transcontinental telegraph, which was completed in October. The Union and Confederate armies had fought a number of battles since Sumter's fall. The largest clash had been the decisive Southern victory over the Union army at Manassas Junction in Northern Virginia. Each side engaged about 18,000 troops, and the total casualties numbered about 4,700, with the North suffering about one-third more than the South. Spectators who had come out from Washington expecting to be entertained by the sight of the US Army whipping some disorganized rebels had found themselves fleeing in a panic when the Confederates drove their opponents from the field like frightened cattle in a humiliating rout. But that and the other battles thus far had been relatively small compared to the ones to come.

———————• • • •———————

Isolated from the enduring hostilities in the East, the Saints had passed much of the year of 1861 digging out the temple foundation, repeating the feat they had accomplished once before in 1853. There was no deadline pressing down on them this time, no specific day by which they had to have the trenches emptied. Brigham did not push them to hurry. He was usually blunt about what he wanted to see happen, but perhaps he thought a light touch might be appropriate this time, given that the men were being asked to remove the immense amount of dirt from the same site for a second time. Or maybe he saw that the job was simply going to take however long it was going to take, and the workers didn't need an anxious prophet standing over them.

While the tithing hands had been hauling dirt away from the foundation, stonecutters had been taking care of business in Little Cottonwood Canyon, breaking down massive boulders into squared chunks weighing two or three tons and getting them into the teamsters' wagons. To see a group of teamsters and their ox teams bringing in a rock of such size was an impressive moment. Annie Wells Cannon, famed suffragist and one of the first women to serve in Utah's legislature, was a little girl during those first years when the wagons carried the granite up to the city. Thirty years later, she noted how "as a little child I remember the sight of the great stones one at a time being hauled along the streets by two yoke of oxen." She added, perhaps with a bit of adoring exaggeration, that "we would all stand for them to pass with a feeling of awe and reverence."[26] The twenty-mile trip from the quarry to the temple site often did take four full days, as estimated, but thus far they'd managed to keep the wagons moving. The teamsters had been hauling stones and dropping them at the temple site, where the craftsmen had been cutting them to shape. When the foundation and basement walls were fully revealed and construction again started in a few months, there would be any number of stones ready to be laid down. One of the Church historians reported:

> The foundation walls of the Temple, which were temporarily covered up . . . have recently been uncovered and the rubbish cleared away preparatory to the commencement of the work of building early in the coming spring.
>
> There has been a large quantity of granite blocks hauled from the Little Cottonwood Quarry during the last two months [November and December], most of which has been squared and fitted for the places they are to occupy in the walls. The continual noise made by the many stonecutters with their hammers and chisels, for many weeks, has been pleasing to the ears of all who desire to see the work progress as fast as circumstances will permit, of which no doubts are entertained, and at no very distant day the announcement that the temple of the Lord at Great Salt Lake City in the tops of the mountains, has been erected and completed may be expected to be heralded to the ends of the earth.[27]

Hopes were high that the work would go quickly enough to make up for lost time. The Saints had been without a proper temple for fifteen years now, and they'd been laboring on this one for nine—the Kirtland and Nauvoo Temples *combined* had taken less time to build. They had the Endowment House, but that was always meant to be a temporary facility. It was suitable for the purpose and nothing more, but it was not, in anyone's estimation, a true house of the Lord.

Brigham's own hopes for rapid progress were tempered somewhat that year by several issues, Truman Angell's health being among them. The architect's constitution had always been fragile, but of late he had been suffering worse than usual. A few years before, during the troubles with the army, he had told Brigham that he was looking for a change of surroundings. "If I was back in some of the newer settlements . . . I could start anew and perhaps make out something," he said. "My health being poor persuades me to try some method that will count to feed [and] clothe my family."[28] But the difficulties of the times prevented him from "starting anew" as he had hoped. He took up his old trade of carpentry, but he found that his health made that job harder than he'd remembered it being. "I am satisfied that most kinds of carpenter work racks my body more than farming," he told his brother-in-law in early 1860, "for I stood a good deal of hard toil at that last year, but there was too much hard labor in getting wood that seemed to use me up, and all this winter I have felt a setback." So Truman asked about Brigham's plans for the coming year so the architect might schedule affairs to allow a sabbatical for the sake of his health. "I wish to know . . . if you have any buildings that you want me to arrange for this spring, or if there is anything to be done on the temple, would it not be well to arrange the plans before they are wanted, if so or not as it may please you. . . . If not, I want to make such other arrangements for spring as may open for me."[29] He did not get his sabbatical. With no assistant at hand, Truman was the only qualified architect at Brigham's disposal, and there were indeed projects that required his unique skills that year.

Truman's relief came to Salt Lake late in 1860 in the form of William Harrison Folsom. Folsom was also a New Englander, born on March 25, 1815, in New Hampshire to a father who owned a contracting company. The elder Folsom raised his son in the family business, and young William excelled enough at carpentry, joinery, and architecture to become a foreman over many of his father's projects while still a teenager. He and his wife, Zerviah, first heard of the gospel while they were living in Buffalo, New York, and they joined the Church in February 1842. The nearby Niagara River was frozen over, which required William and the missionaries to cut a very large hole through twenty-eight inches of ice to perform the baptisms. The Folsoms relocated to Nauvoo in the fall of the following year, where William developed friendships with Joseph and Hyrum Smith. William also developed a friendship with the superintendent of joiners, Truman Angell, when the new convert volunteered his construction skills for the building of the Nauvoo Temple. William's relationship with Joseph would last only a few months, until the prophet met his death at Carthage Jail. His relationship with Truman would endure for more than four decades.

The Saints began evacuating Nauvoo in February 1846, but William remained behind to finish the interior of the temple. He was one of the very few present when they finished the building three months later in May. Fifteen hundred mobbers besieged the city the following September, and William joined a small group of 150 who held the anti-Mormons at bay while the remaining Saints crossed the Mississippi to the safety of the Iowa side of the shoreline. As the Saints were outnumbered ten to one, the outcome of the protracted Battle of Nauvoo was never in doubt. William and his family were among the last to go, and they were forced to flee without any provisions. They waited in Montrose, Iowa, with a large contingent of refugee Saints for relief wagons from Winter Quarters, but the Folsoms, for reasons unknown, did not remain with the relief party. Instead, they went to Farmington, twenty miles northwest, where they occupied a vacant home. It was very nearly a fatal decision. In 1847, while William was in Farmington, a group of drunkards identified him as a Latter-day Saint, surrounded him, and tried to hang him. They left him dangling three feet off the ground and went into a nearby store, but an acquaintance came by and released him before he strangled. The near-death experience persuaded William that it was time for his family to move on from Farmington.

The Folsoms eventually settled in Keokuk, Iowa. William left his family there while he went to California seeking work, and in two years' time he made a small fortune in mining and construction. In 1851 he returned home by way of Hawaii and Cape Horn; Buffalo, New York, where he visited his father; Philadelphia; and then Ohio, where he reunited with his wife and five children. After finally reaching their homestead back in Keokuk, they settled in and remained in Iowa for nine more years. The Folsoms didn't make their way to Utah until October 1860, which was none too soon for Truman's taste.[30] With the exception

One of Truman Angell's sketches for the temple's rounded windows. Note the labels to the left marking the stone "courses" ("X, Y, Z, A, B, C"). Beginning at the lowest level, each layer of stones in the temple walls was assigned a successive letter of the alphabet A–Z, with the pattern starting over each time the end of the alphabet was reached, until the tops of the spires were reached.

of William Weeks, who had fallen far out of Brigham's circle of trust, Folsom was the first man to reach the valley who was truly qualified to take over as Church architect. In fact, within days of his arrival, Folsom had opened an architecture business on Main Street in downtown Salt Lake, and he was bringing unique experience to the table. His travels since leaving Nauvoo and his extended stay in the Midwest had exposed him to newer building styles and construction methods that had not yet reached Utah. He was almost certainly a superior architect to Truman at that point.[31]

With a suitable replacement finally at hand, Brigham determined to give Truman the relief that his brother-in-law had been seeking. He called William Folsom to be the assistant Church architect within a few months, the first man to hold the position since William Ward had abandoned the post almost five years before. Folsom's first assignment was a pet project of Brigham's—the new Salt Lake Theatre that would stand on the corner of State and First South Streets. Under Brigham's personal

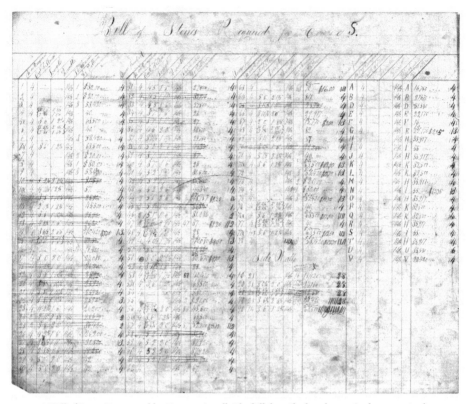

A "Bill of Stones" prepared by Truman Angell. The bill described each stone's placement in the "course" or level, the dimensions of the stone, and the total number of that type of stone required.

supervision, Folsom designed an enormous building in a Greek Revival style that was unlike any other in the valley—or the rest of the territory, for that matter.[32] The finished product was later described by visitors to Salt Lake as "a rare triumph of art and enterprise . . . alike in capacity and elegance of structure and finish, along with the opera-houses and academies of music of Boston, New York, Philadelphia, Chicago and Cincinnati."[33] If there had been any public doubts about Folsom's qualifications to take over for Truman, the Salt Lake Theatre crushed them.

Even with his old friend's assistance and energy taking much of the load, Truman was, quite simply, burned out. He soldiered on through most of 1861, but his health continued to decline until, with Brigham's approval, Truman resigned his position in the fall. On October 7, 1861, during the morning session of the second day of the fall general conference, William Harrison Folsom was sustained as architect for the Church.[34] If Truman felt any pangs of conscience over giving his friend the very job that had broken his own health, they weren't enough to change his mind. Truman walked away from architecture and construction, retired to a parcel of land apart from the city, and took up sugarcane farming.

In his new position, Folsom's first duty was to oversee the excavation of the temple foundation and cached stones. Truman had settled the design for the temple exterior under Brigham's guidance years before, so there was nothing for Folsom to do on that score. But it was now his responsibility to oversee the precise dimensions and placement for each granite stone to be laid down in the temple. It was tedious work, to say the least. Each stone required a hand-drawn "bill" containing its design and measurements, with copies made in triplicate—one for the architect, one for James Livingston at the quarry, and one for the stonemasons on the temple block. The collected Bills of Stones ran 169 handwritten pages of numerical tables,[40] and the Diagrams of Courses showing the position of every stone in the building totaled 344 pages.[41] The "Truman System," as the paperwork was known, kept Folsom busy that winter.

The other issue that must have worried Brigham was his knowledge that there were problems with the temple's foundation. He'd already told Wilford Woodruff that they would have to take up at least one tier of the foundation stones, and he had discussed the problem with Alonzo Raleigh as well. "Had an interview with Pres. B[righam] Young at his office [and] Pres. D[aniel] H. Wells at his residence. It is thought that a part of the wall above the foundation is not sufficiently solid [and] will have to be taken up," Raleigh wrote in his diary, without offering any reason as to the cause.[35] It must have been a source of some embarrassment to Raleigh. In his autobiography, he reduced all of his involvement in temple building down to a single sentence without any details except for his length of service in that "special duty or labor of the Holy Priesthood."[36] And nowhere did he record any of the questions that Brigham surely must have put to him, but there were a number that the prophet might have asked. Was there only one course of mislaid stones that needed to be leveled? How many courses of stone might they have to rework? How far down might they have to go to correct the problem? Could the masons just lift the stones out intact, make the necessary adjustments, and lay them back down? Would they need to cut new stones from the Red Butte Quarry? Now that the foundation finally was uncovered, they could get answers. On May 28, the workmen were able to go down into the trenches and look over the courses of rock already laid down.

The reality was about as bad as anyone might have imagined. There were fissures in the ashlars underneath the flagging stones on which the first basement walls were sitting. In some places, the stones were so askew that workers had left the wooden rollers in place to keep things level. That would practically have guaranteed a structural failure of the building, as moisture in the ground would have rotted out the wood over time, leaving gaping holes in the temple footings. So there was no way that the foundation could possibly support the massive weight of numerous courses of granite blocks yet to be laid. At some point, sooner rather than later and certainly long before the temple was fully raised, one or more of the walls would collapse and probably kill someone in the process. It was a dangerous situation, and the peril would only increase with every stone they laid.

Brigham asked Truman, Daniel Wells, William Folsom, and others to give him their evaluation of the foundation and suggestions for how deep the repairs needed to go. "I can truly say I consider it a bad job," Folsom wrote to the prophet. "As it was found on raising some of the stones they were not brought to a bed. They were also filled in the joints with cobble rock and spalls and some of them were never bedded in mortar. Holes were left large enough to run my hand in. The mortar that was used seemed to be of very poor quality."[37] Wells agreed that "the mason work and mortar are both bad, and . . . the work [should be] taken up down to the flagging."[38] As the first architect under whom the work had been done, Truman came back to examine the foundation and give his own assessment. In his letter, Truman simply assumed that Brigham understood the foundation was shoddy and went straight to his proposed solution. "I would remove from that footing to the under side of the flagging, and then . . . would take it to the level from end to end, repairing any places that might require it. This would bring you to the line of earth in the cellar," he suggested.[39]

If Brigham had harbored any hopes that the poor engineering performed on the foundation could be easily repaired, they were surely blasted now. There would be no quick fix. The construction of the Salt Lake Temple was now halted dead in its tracks. There was no point in laying down another single stone until the foundation was repaired. To do that, they would have to take up much, if not all, of the basement walls and set those stones aside; then take out the level flagging stones; then remove the top layer of ashlars. At that point they could extract all of the stone shims, rubble, wood, and other junk added in that crude attempt to straighten up that top layer. Only then could they put down a firm, level layer of ashlars, but to get to that point they would have undone years of work, and that was painful to accept. If Brigham had ever entertained a thought about quitting work on the temple, this was the moment it would have felt most justified.

———— • · • ————

One unconfirmed anecdote recounted through the years claims that, upon learning the magnitude of the problem, Brigham sat down on one of the foundation stones and vowed not to move until the Lord revealed to him what he should do. Within a short time, Bishop Archibald Gardner came walking past the temple site and found Brigham sitting on a rock, pondering the problem. According to the story, Brigham waved him over. "Bishop, sit down," he said. Gardner did as Brigham asked, and the prophet proceeded to use him as a sounding board. They discussed the problem, examined the foundation, the materials, and the manner in which it had been put together. Then Brigham said, "Bishop, can you tell me what to do?" Bishop Gardner told the prophet that he saw no other option but to take the foundation out and start over. According to the story, Brigham put his arm on Gardner's shoulder and said, "Brother Gardner, you are right. That is my revelation."[40]

Whatever Brigham may have done to work through his thoughts and feelings about the problem, by June 1 he was settled on the course to take. He took to the pulpit in the Adobe Tabernacle that day and "spoke upon the laying of the foundation of the Temple," explaining the reasons why the foundation had to be taken up. Wilford heard the speech and personally was mortified as Brigham spoke. "[President Young] had some of the stones taken up and they were not laid solid but were laid on chinking, small stones and I am ashamed that I have had anything to do with it," he wrote. "The men who have bossed the laying of those stones are fools or consummate rascals." Brigham apparently felt the same way. He let his feelings be known in plain terms, but Wilford chose not to preserve any more of the prophet's hard words for posterity. Instead, the younger Apostle simply noted that "many other remarks were made upon the subject," and left the matter there.[41]

There is no evidence that Brigham ever considered, for even a moment, calling off the work. The temple had to be finished because the Endowment House simply was not an appropriate edifice in which to perform all of the holy rites the Saints needed to undergo. "There are some of the sealing ordinances that cannot be administered in the house that we are now using," Brigham explained. "We can only administer in it some of the first ordinances of the Priesthood pertaining to the endowment. There are more advanced ordinances that cannot be administered there; we would, therefore, like a temple, but I am willing to wait a few years for it."[42] This was not going to be some temporary building. This would be a permanent structure as enduring as the mountains that surrounded it, where generations of Saints down to the end of the world would enter in and receive those ordinances, the same as this generation. "I expect this Temple will stand through the Millennium," he said.[43]

Nor would the Salt Lake Temple be the only house of the Lord. Thus far, the Saints had only ever had one temple at a time, when they'd had one at all. That would not always be so. The prophet tried to expand the people's minds, to help them understand the scope of the work yet to be done.

> This is not the only temple we shall build. There will be hundreds of them built and dedicated to the Lord. This temple will be known as the first temple built in the mountains by the Latter-day Saints. And when the Millennium is over, and all the sons and daughters of Adam and Eve, down to the last of their posterity, who come within the reach of the clemency of the gospel, have been redeemed in hundreds of temples through the administration of their children as proxies for them, I want that temple still to stand as a proud monument of the faith, perseverance and industry of the Saints of God in the mountains in the nineteenth century.[44]

They determined how much of the basement walls, flagging, and footings needed to come out, and Brigham sent the formal request to begin the repairs to Daniel Wells, who was still the superintendent of public works. "I wish you, as speedily as possible, to have all the rock and flagging in the Temple wall taken down to the top course of the foundation, and have that course hewn level to commence laying the Temple wall upon," Brigham wrote.[45] Wells received the written letter detailing the prophet's wishes, and the masons were taking up the foundation by the end of the week.[46] A week later, they had reached the record stone in which Brigham, Wilford, and the others had placed Church documents, books, and samples of currency as a time capsule just prior to the confrontation with Johnston's army. Seeing that taken up was a melancholy moment for the men who had sealed the materials up five years earlier. "The workmen are taking off the large top stones today and they have

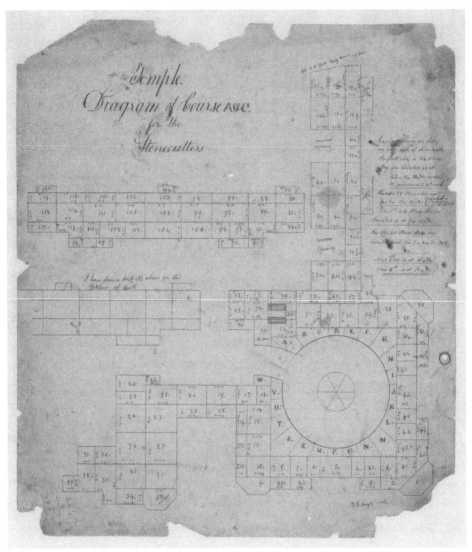

A "course diagram" showing the placement of each stone in a single level of the temple walls. This course diagram is for one of the temple's corner towers.

taken out our deposit of records [and] coin . . . which we deposited in the foundation, which I never expected to live to see taken out when I saw it deposited," Wilford noted.[47]

Repairing the foundation was no easy process, but it proceeded at a surprisingly rapid pace, with visible progress made quickly. The basement courses were taken out and set aside; then the flagging was removed. Lifting an ashlar out of the trench to get at the shims, spawls, and rubble was no easier than laying it down had been, requiring the same equipment and muscle. They were undoing the work of years, but the repaired footings were soon ready to bear the granite loads that would be coming. "The Temple foundation [i.e., the flagging layer and top ashlar course] has been taken up in part [and] re-laid [and] many improvements have been made," Wilford recorded, ending his journal for the year on a happier note.[48]

———— •——•——• ————

The first year of the Civil War had seen mostly small engagements that produced relatively light casualties. The second year was a blood-bath. The western theater of the war saw several horrific battles in 1862, but the worst was the Battle of Shiloh, so named for a nearby church. The armies fought for two days at Pittsburgh Landing in south-western Tennessee. The Union forces were led by a cigar-smoking, hard-drinking major general named Ulysses S. Grant; the Confederates were commanded by the man once entrusted to lead the Utah Expedition—General Albert Sidney Johnston. After Sumter's fall, Johnston had re-signed from the US Army and offered himself to the Confederate military. Jefferson Davis assigned him to command the Confederacy's Western Military Department. He personally led a force of 40,000 men against Grant's 63,000 and caught his Union counterpart by surprise on the morning of April 6. Johnston drove the Union forces toward the Tennessee River throughout the day. Around two-thirty in the after-noon, Johnston was personally leading a brigade attack when an enemy round struck him behind his right knee. He felt the bullet penetrate but decided the wound was not severe and remained on the field instead of retiring behind the line and seeking out a surgeon. It was a fatal mis-take. The general didn't realize that he was bleeding profusely into his boot—the lead ball had torn open the popliteal artery in his leg. Within minutes, the effects of blood loss became apparent. Johnston slumped in his saddle. Tennessee governor Isham Harris was nearby and asked the general if he was wounded. "Yes, and I fear seriously," Johnston replied. He was helped from his horse and laid down under a tree—but, not knowing where he was wounded, his staff did not apply a tourniquet. Before a surgeon could be found, Albert Sidney Johnston bled to death on the field at Shiloh. Believing that the general's demise would be too demoralizing to the Confederate troops, Johnston's second-in-command, General P. G. T. Beauregard, the hero of Sumter, kept the senior officer's fate from the men that day. But Beauregard was so sure of the battle's outcome that he sent a telegram to President Jefferson Davis declaring victory.

A hard rainstorm opened up around ten o'clock in the evening and poured on both armies all night. Adding insult to injury, the Confederates who had overrun the Union camps during the day now took shelter from the downpour in their enemies' tents. Grant's army had no shelters and spent the night exposed to the weather. One of Grant's subordinates and good friends, General William Tecumseh Sherman, found his commander sheltering under a tree and smoking a cigar.

"Well, Grant, we've had the devil's own day, haven't we?" Sherman asked.

"Yes," Grant replied. "Yes. Lick 'em tomorrow, though."

And he did. Grant received 20,000 reinforcements during the night, and the following day, April 7, he counterattacked. The Union Army drove Beauregard's forces back, retaking all the ground lost the day before. The Battle of Shiloh had been the bloodiest battle of the war to date and would prove to be the bloodiest of the western theater throughout the conflict.

Most of the Confederate soldiers did not learn of Albert Sidney Johnston's death for days, until Beauregard sent out a statement of consolation.

HEADQUARTERS ARMY OF THE MISSISSIPPI,
Corinth, Miss., April 10, 1862

SOLDIERS: Your late commander-in-chief, General A. S. Johnston, is dead.

A fearless soldier, a sagacious captain, a reproachless man, has fallen; one who in his devotion to our cause shrank from no sacrifice; one who animated by a sense of duty and sustained by a sublime courage, challenged danger and perished gallantly for his country whilst leading forward his brave columns to victory. His signal example of heroism and patriotism, if imitated, would make this army invincible. A grateful country will mourn his loss, revere his name, and cherish his manly virtues.

G. T. BEAUREGARD,
General, Commanding.[49]

In the eastern theater, the Union Army under the command of General George McClellan tried to end the war quickly by landing more than 100,000 men at Fort Monroe on the Chesapeake Bay and marching up the Virginia peninsula to take Richmond, the Confederate capital. The Northern troops were just five miles outside the city when the Confederates met them at the Battle of Seven Pines. The Confederates' senior general, Joseph E. Johnston, was wounded, and President Jefferson Davis gave command of the army to his military advisor, General Robert E. Lee. What followed was a series of clashes, the Seven Days Battles, in which Lee drove McClellan's army back off the peninsula while inflicting 35,000 casualties combined, including 4,200 men killed in just a week. Eight weeks later, Lee defeated the Union Army at the Battle of Second Manassas, fought on the same ground as the largest battle of the previous year. Emboldened by that victory, Lee invaded the North with 55,000 men, crossing the Potomac River into Maryland. McClellan pursued with 87,000, moving cautiously, but eventually meeting Lee and his forces at the town of Sharpsburg. The Battle of Antietam, named for the creek that ran through the battlefield, was and still remains the single bloodiest day in United States history. The two armies suffered 22,000 casualties in twelve hours, an average of one man killed, wounded, or captured every two seconds throughout the day.

Lee retreated into Virginia, and Lincoln fired McClellan for failing to stop the Confederate escape. The president gave command of the Union Army to General Ambrose Burnside, who truly didn't want the post and warned that he was not fit for it. He proved that his self-assessment was correct when both forces met again at Fredericksburg, Virginia, in mid-December. Burnside launched feckless attacks against heavily fortified positions, including Marye's Heights, where the Confederates fired from behind a stone wall at the lines of blue-clad soldiers marching in neat rows across the open field. Watching from his command post, Lee turned to James Longstreet, his second in command, and said, "It is well that war is so terrible—we should grow too fond of it!"[50] He had reason to feel satisfied with the day's work that his men had wrought. In one day of fighting, the Union's casualties totaled about 12,600 men, more than the army had lost at Antietam. The Confederates' losses were less than half that number. When the sun went down, the temperatures plunged, and many of the wounded, unable to move themselves off the field, froze to death. For some, their last sight was a rare aurora borealis that shimmered overhead in the cold air. The Union Army withdrew back across the Rappahannock River, leaving behind the pillaged and battered town of Fredericksburg.

Within days, President Lincoln relieved Burnside of command. "We are now on the brink of destruction," the president told a friend. "It appears to me that the Almighty is against us, and I can hardly see a ray of hope."[51]

———— ◆ · · ◆ ————

It was probably for the best that Brigham Young wasn't in Washington to hear the president say that. The prophet surely would have agreed with Lincoln. It was not that Brigham wanted to see the country split in two—the very first telegram that he'd sent east had included a declaration that "Utah has not seceded, but is firm for the

Constitution and laws of our once happy country."[52] It was, to him, a simple matter of divine justice. It would have been tempting to take some satisfaction in the suffering of their fellow citizens as the war dragged on, but Brigham reminded the people that "Joseph said many and many a time to us—'Never be anxious for the Lord to pour out his judgments upon the nation; many of you will see the distress and evils poured out upon this nation till you will weep like children.' Many of us have felt to do so already, and it seems to be coming upon us more and more."[53]

Brigham's refusal to gloat was wise, because the country being vexed was not yet finished vexing the Saints. The department of the army decided to reestablish a military presence in Utah, ostensibly to protect the mail and telegraph routes from attacks by native tribes, though the Saints were still a suspect population and the US government wanted them watched. To that end, the army dispatched 700 volunteers from Nevada and California under the command of Colonel Patrick Edward Connor to the Salt Lake Valley. Connor was as hostile to the Saints as anyone the federal government had sent yet, declaring them all "a community of traitors, murderers, fanatics, and whores."[54] It was his considered opinion that "the sooner we are rid of the evil, and the nation of the stigma [of the Latter-day Saints], the better it will be for us." Indeed, it was a great irony that whereas the Saints thought the Civil War was the Lord's punishment on the nation for past persecutions, Connor believed that "if the present rebellion is a punishment for any national sin, I believe it is for permitting this unholy, blasphemous, and unnatural institution [The Church of Jesus Christ of Latter-day Saints] to exist almost in the heart of the nation."[55]

Albert Sidney Johnston had tried to keep some distance between his troops and the Saints, but Connor decided to station his men as close to Great Salt Lake City as he could manage. That decision was not made entirely for provocative reasons. Connor had considered Fort Crittenden but found it was no longer an option. Most of the buildings there had been taken apart for their construction materials, the few that remained were in poor shape, and the owner demanded $15,000 from the army to retake possession of them. Connor refused and settled on a new site. He reported:

> It is on a plateau about three miles from Salt Lake City, which commands the city, and where 1,000 troops would be more efficient than 3,000 on the other side of the Jordan [River]. If the general decides that I shall locate there, I intend to quietly intrench my position, and then say to the Saints of Utah, enough of your treason; but if it is intended that I shall merely protect the overland mail and permit the Mormons to act and utter treason, then I had as well locate at Crittenden. The Federal officers desire and beg that I will locate near the city. The Governor especially is very urgent in the matter. [56]

Connor's superiors did so decide, and Camp Douglas—named for Senator Stephen A. Douglas of Illinois—was established in the Wasatch foothills three miles east of Great Salt Lake City, near the mouth of Red Butte Canyon. The location was provocative. Albert Sidney Johnston had kept his command more than a day's ride to the south to keep the peace and avoid unnecessary clashes with the local population. Planting a unit just three miles from the largest city in the territory on an elevated ridge—desirable in case artillery was needed—made it feel like Colonel Patrick Edward Connor and the United States Army were trying to pick a fight.

———— · · · ————

That year of 1862 also saw another development that would cause the Saints great distress. On April 9, just three days after Albert Sidney Johnston bled out on the field at Shiloh, Congressman Justin Smith Morrill of Vermont submitted a bill to the US House of Representatives that received little attention at the moment. A single notice in the *Congressional Globe* recorded the event.

> Mr. MORRILL, of Vermont, by unanimous consent, introduced a bill to punish and prevent the practice of polygamy in the Territories of the United States, and for other purposes, and to disapprove and annul certain acts of the Legislative Assembly of the Territory of Utah. . . . [57]

Morrill was fifty-three years old and had almost no formal education. He was the son of a country blacksmith who had hired him out as a shopkeeper for the salary of thirty dollars a year to help support the family. Young Justin's labor there had led to a career in business, in which he made a modest fortune by the time he was thirty-five. He retired to become a gentleman farmer, married well, and was revered by his fellow citizens as a man of "absolute and unvarying integrity." When the representative of his congressional district chose not to stand for election in 1854, his neighbors pressed him to run. Morrill, standing as a Whig candidate, won the open seat by fifty-nine votes out of 16,701 cast.[58] After the Whig Party dissolved that same year, Morrill joined such other notables as Salmon P. Chase, William H. Seward, and John C. Frémont to found the Republican Party. Being a Party founder, he supported its declared opposition to the "twin relics of barbarism, slavery and polygamy," but the Party was in no position to act on that opposition until Lincoln ascended to the presidency.[59] Unlike the president, Morrill believed that the US government could indeed take on both institutions at once, and so proposed his anti-polygamy law.

Under the terms of Morrill's bill, anyone found guilty of plural marriage could be fined not more than five hundred dollars and sent to prison for a term of not more than five years for each offense. The "certain acts of the Legislative Assembly of the Territory of Utah" that the bill targeted included the ordinance approved by the Utah territorial legislature in 1851 to incorporate The Church of Jesus Christ of Latter-day Saints. Morrill was seeking to undo that and any other Utah laws that the congressman believed were designed to "establish, support, maintain, shield, or countenance polygamy."[60] To that end, the bill also proposed that no "corporation or association for religious or charitable purposes" in any US territory could own real estate holdings over the aggregate value of $50,000. All property so owned beyond that limit would be escheated—forfeited—to the United States government. Morrill didn't just want the Church disincorporated as a legal entity, he also wanted it stripped of nearly all of its financial resources. Money was power, after all.

Morrill made no speech when he introduced his bill, and there was no debate about it on the floor of the House after the bill's introduction. The clerk read the proposed law twice; it was accepted without objection and forwarded to the Committee on Territories for further consideration. The Committee approved the bill and returned it a few weeks later for the full House to vote. It passed on April 28 with virtually no debate and by an overwhelming margin. It was not a controversial bill. The Saints had virtually no defenders in Congress, and polygamy, it turned out, was far less divisive than slavery. So when the Senate took up the bill shortly thereafter, it continued to move quickly through and was passed almost unanimously on June 3. After a few minor amendments were ironed out, the final bill went to Lincoln's desk, whereon he signed the Morrill Anti-Bigamy Act into law on July 8, 1862. He could hardly do otherwise. Had Lincoln failed to approve the law, he would have created dissension in his own party's ranks at the very time he needed their united support to continue fighting the war. But Lincoln also had no desire to provoke the Latter-day Saints. They had declared their loyalty to the Union, and he didn't want to give them a reason to change their minds. Lincoln certainly didn't want to be put in a position where he would be pressured by his own party to stage a repeat of "Buchanan's Blunder," especially now, when the nation could spare neither men nor resources. Simply put, Lincoln disagreed with Morrill that the US government should try to wipe out both peculiar institutions at the same time. So the Morrill Anti-Bigamy Act may have been the law of the land, but Lincoln considered it to be a dead letter from the moment he signed it. Some time after

Lincoln signed the bill into law, a *Deseret News* editor asked the president what his intentions were toward the Saints. Lincoln, as he often did, explained his thinking on the matter through an allegory.

> When I was a boy on the farm in Illinois there was a great deal of timber on the farms which we had to clear away. Occasionally we would come to a log which had fallen down. It was too hard to split, too wet to burn and too heavy to move, so we plowed around it. That's what I intend to do with the Mormons. You go back and tell Brigham Young that if he will let me alone, I will let him alone.[61]

That was a policy that Brigham was quite happy to support. It was exactly what he and the Saints had wanted all along.

There was, however, the matter of the Morrill Act's provisions that would allow the government to seize Church property in excess of $50,000. It was hardly unthinkable that some hostile federal officer in Utah, acting on his own accord, could try to enforce that part of the law. Brigham decided to preempt any trouble by transferring ownership of Church assets to individual members who could be trusted with their stewardship. On paper, the Church divested itself of a significant number of assets, but in practice all of those assets were still available for Church programs and projects. Brigham himself transacted business under his own name that, though not openly declared, was for the Church's benefit. This strategy protected Church property from seizure under the Morrill Act, but it did have the unfortunate side effect of making Brigham and other Church leaders appear to be enriching themselves personally off the labors of the members. The prophet was not concerned. The members knew and trusted him; the accusations of enemies and critics, who would never be persuaded of his honesty no matter what he said or did, bothered him not at all.

The stonecutters, masons, teamsters, and tithing hands had carried on throughout the seasons and made considerable progress on fixing the temple footings by May of 1863. The resulting foundation was sound enough to earn Brigham's approval. After one of their regular inspections of the site, Wilford recorded the prophet's opinion of the work performed since the previous year's unhappy discovery. "I took a walk with Presidents Brigham Young & D. H. Wells & W. H. Folsom through the Temple Block," he wrote. "President Young expressed his satisfaction with the present work on the Temple. Was much better than it was before the foundation was taken up."[62] The fears of an unstable base were gone now, replaced by confidence that the footings could now support whatever load would be laid on them soon.

Still, one could hardly fault any of the Saints who might be feeling impatient. The ten-year anniversary of the cornerstone ceremony had come and gone, and the basement walls still could not be seen above ground. As inspiring as the sight of teamsters and oxen hauling granite stones may have been, their slow travel must have seemed like a metaphor for the slow progress of the entire effort. But for anyone who felt to complain about the rate of progress, a visit to the stone quarry of Little Cottonwood Canyon would have been in order. Some time spent with James Livingston and his quarrymen might have instilled a new appreciation for the "faith, perseverance, and industry" behind the entire project, no matter how things looked at the temple site.

CHAPTER 7

MAKE THE EVERLASTING HILLS TO TREMBLE BEFORE THEM

I n the year 1860 I was called to take a few men and start getting granite for the Temple from the mouth of Little Cottonwood Canyon."[1] James Campbell Livingston was either a man of deep humility or simply one of few words, for his autobiography contains only four sentences about his work as a stonecutter. Given the results of his labor, he could hardly have been faulted if he'd filled page after page with descriptions of his labors in the granite quarry south of Salt Lake City. But he never played up his part in the story, and thus he rendered his greatest service to the Church very nearly anonymously.

The eight years since James had arrived in the Salt Lake Valley in 1853 had not been quiet. He married the year after his arrival in the valley and was able to earn enough through his job at Red Butte to help his siblings, his grandmother, and an aunt and uncle emigrate from Scotland to Utah. The Livingstons had been present at the celebration in Big Cottonwood Canyon in July 1857, which was interrupted when the Saints had all learned of the coming of Johnston's army. The quarry had closed, and James had deployed with the Nauvoo Legion to the canyons until winter had set in and put an end to any worries of an invasion that year. During the "Move South" of the following spring, James had worked under John Sharp, his employer at the quarry, to relocate Church property south to Provo. Brigham's delay in restarting temple construction after the Saints returned to their homes meant there was little work for the Red Butte Quarry, which left James looking for other employment to provide for his family for a time. He took a number of odd jobs, including working on road construction in Provo Canyon and American Fork Canyon and delivering firewood for the soldiers at Camp Floyd. He also joined the Salt Lake Police Department as a "special policeman," which apparently meant he was deputized to serve without remuneration whenever the department needed some extra muscle to keep the peace or chase down criminals and fugitives. James served in law enforcement for thirty-five years and rode out with the militia more than a few times to settle trouble with the Indian tribes. But those jobs were all ancillary to stonecutting. When the work on the temple resumed, James went back to his regular job. If he expected to return to Red Butte, however, that thought was quickly turned aside. John Sharp had picked a group of men to go south to set up the new granite quarry, and James was the man who would lead them.

There was no question that this assignment would be for the long term. Cutting granite is no quick process. Reducing a single boulder to the needed size and shape of the blocks in Truman Angell's bills and diagrams could take weeks, and the temple would need blocks by the hundreds. Before he had even laid eyes on Little Cottonwood Canyon, Livingston would have known going in that men would be working out of this quarry for years. They would need more than tents for shelter and a campfire for a kitchen—and not just for themselves. Church wards would be sending volunteer workers from around the valley, and that temporary help would need housing and a place to eat. The teamsters would need accommodations for themselves and their animals for the duration, and that wouldn't change once the canal was completed—they would still need those men and animals to get the blocks out of the canyon to the closest dock. That might reduce the distance the teamsters traveled from twenty miles down to a few, but even one mile was a hard trip when the cargo they pulled weighed some two or three tons (though a few would reach four and a half). Nor could the stonecutters work without blacksmiths forging, repairing, and sharpening the tools that would be blunted and broken by daily pounding against the rocks; so there would be buildings to house the forges and bellows. They would need cooks to feed the men, carpenters to repair the wagons, a shopkeeper or two to provide incidentals, certainly a doctor or at least someone with enough training to bandage up cut hands and splint broken bones. They would need an entire community around them. The quarry would have to become a settlement all its own.

They picked a spot near the canyon's mouth in a small hollow on the north side of Little Cottonwood Creek, which ran westward down from its source eleven miles back up in the mountains. It was convenient to the north-south road in the valley, offering easy access to the teamsters and volunteers, and to families and Church leaders coming to visit. The creek offered water for drinking, sanitation, and laundry, as well as for watering cattle and oxen. Also, perhaps as important a resource as any other, there was accessible timber not far distant, which they would need to build cabins and other buildings, to keep fires stoked for warmth and cooking, and for any other reason that men needed fire in the backcountry. There was also a sawmill in Big Cottonwood Canyon, a few miles to the north, where the men could process trees into lumber for the buildings that would eventually go up. Demand in the area for that particular resource would be so great over the next decade that John M. Woolley would eventually build a creek-powered sawmill near the quarry, but for the moment they would either have to use rough-cut logs or make trips to Big Cottonwood. Compared to the difficulty involved in moving rock, hauling trees and lumber a few miles would feel like child's play.

As it turned out, they stayed at that location only briefly because the "granite was understood to be of a texture unsuited for quarrying."[2]

So the men packed up their tents, and Livingston relocated the camp another mile and a half up the canyon to a new site close to large granite deposits in the form of the boulders on the canyon floor and striations that ran along both canyon walls. They did not know it at the time, but the camp they were setting up would make the quarry one of the area's most important hubs for another reason beyond its contribution to the temple. Prospectors would establish the town of Alta six miles or so farther up the canyon when the discovery of silver there would lead to the opening of the Emma and Flagstaff mines and draw workers and investors from all directions. The quarry settlement would become a waypoint for miners hauling their ore down the canyon for smelting or going back up after a trip into Salt Lake or another town for supplies. At its height, still more than a decade in the future, the stonecutters' little camp in the hollow on the east shore of Little Cottonwood Creek would grow to more than fifty buildings, including stores, cabins, industrial shops, and boarding homes.[3] Eventually, they would call it Granite City. For the moment, it was just a small camp of tents and a cookhouse.

They were now much farther from the mouth of the canyon, which would add more time onto the teamsters' journey to the city with each stone, but there was no help for it, and for the first five years, they only "worked a few months every fall" anyway.[4] Until the temple foundation was repaired, the stonecutters on the temple block needed only enough granite to replace some of the cracked sandstone ashlars being pulled out; other projects like the canal would siphon away some of the manpower and resources available to work on the temple. The light schedule kept at the quarry gave Livingston time during the summer to take on other tasks, including an unusual mission in 1863 that called for the young Scot to discover some skills well outside his usual field of labor.

Colonel Patrick Connor's hostile posture toward the Saints from his outpost above the city led Brigham to conclude that he needed a man inside the army's camp.[5] "It was deemed advisable to have a man that could go into [Camp Douglas] at any time night or day and become acquainted with the officers and men that we might know of their plans, etc., for at that time there was bitter feeling manifested by both officers and privates against [the Church's leadership] and a great many threats were made against them."[6] The prophet asked the local bishops and a "leading number of the city" to nominate men they thought fit for the job. "There were quite a number of names presented," James recalled, though he didn't record the total. Brigham interviewed the assembled candidates and explained that whoever the chosen man was, "if you are caught, it will mean the firing squad." Then he added, "I don't think the Lord will allow you to be caught if you will act in wisdom, and if the right man volunteers." The group recommended several men as the top candidates, but Brigham did not feel impressed to choose any of them. "Brethren, I do not think you have mentioned the right man," he announced. The prophet stood, walked over to James, and put his hand on the stonecutter's shoulder.

"Will you volunteer?" Brigham asked.

"Gladly," James replied, but he added that he thought several men present were better suited. The prophet persisted, and James announced that he would "give his life willingly if he could be of service to the presiding officers. The brethren then took him up and gave him a wonderful blessing in which he was told no hair of his head would be harmed if he obeyed."[7]

Thus charged with his duty, James came up with a plan to infiltrate the army's outpost. He drove a wagon up toward Camp Douglas, which was not far from the mouth of Red Butte Canyon. When stopped by the sentries, he informed them that he was a stonecutter—which had the virtue of being true—and, being intimately familiar with the canyon and quarry where he'd spent years working, he was well prepared to answer any questions along those lines. Satisfied with his answers, they gave him a pass that would allow him to come through the guard post as he pleased. Having thus established his bona fides, James went back up a few days later under the same pretense, this time with a keg of whiskey in the back of his wagon. He arranged for the barrel of booze to roll off onto the ground at an appropriate moment near the soldiers, but continued on as though oblivious to the loss of his liquid cargo. After a short time, he returned as though looking for the whiskey. The soldiers had recovered it, of course, and James agreed to share some of the liquor as a finder's fee. The guards talked freely as they imbibed, and one of them admitted that he'd been assigned as an aide to an officer in the camp. James "got one of the men to go to the city with him while they were all kind of fuzzy," and James and some compatriots relieved the drunken soldier of his uniform. When the guard sobered up, his kindly abductors gave him an undisclosed sum of money and told him "not to be seen" in that part of the country. The soldier apparently was amenable to the arrangement, and he possibly used his new slush fund to return home because he wasn't seen in Utah again. James took up the man's identity and replaced him in Camp Douglas. How he went unrecognized is not entirely clear. Perhaps the soldier had been a recent arrival and was still largely unknown to the general for whom he was acting as an aide. But however he managed the feat, James was never caught. For weeks, he recorded every important message that came into the camp via the telegraph during the day, slipped out of the camp and reported to Brigham each night, then returned in time to answer roll call.[8]

For all of Colonel Connor's vitriol, he and his men kept themselves busy for the most part by fighting native tribes suspected of raids along the mail route. The soldiers were spending most of their time in the field far from Camp Douglas, and that suited Brigham just fine. But Connor's campaign to suppress the native population culminated in the "Battle of Bear River," which occurred 120 miles north of Salt Lake, in January of 1863. Connor's troops massacred an entire tribe, killing 224 Shoshones. That earned their commanding officer a promotion to brigadier general, which reward demonstrated just how little regard Connor and the army had at the time for the lives of Native Americans.

Whenever the soldiers were back in camp, the tensions between them and the Saints ran high. In March, a rumor began that Connor was going to arrest Brigham for "uttering treasonable language," and a large number of Saints rallied around Brigham's house. Connor denied that he had any intention of arresting the prophet. "There has been nothing in my conduct or language which could be construed so as to induce that belief further than what I said when I first entered the Territory, to the effect that 'any person, whosoever he might be, who was guilty of using treasonable language would be arrested and sent to Alcatraz Island,'" he protested.[9] But he interpreted the gathering as a display of hostile defiance and a bid to provoke him into attacking civilians. Connor requested, unless he could be reinforced, that his troops be withdrawn from the territory and put to better use elsewhere until the United States could spare enough soldiers to return and "forever put a stop to [the Saints'] outrageous, unnatural, and treasonable institutions."[10]

◆ ◦ ◦ ◦ ◆

Lincoln could not spare such troops. If the Lord was truly "[vexing] the Gentiles"[11] as Joseph's prophecy on war had declared, then 1863 was the beginning of some of the worst vexation the nation would see. After the disaster at Fredericksburg, Lincoln had replaced General Burnside with General Joseph Hooker, an arrogant officer who declared, "My plans are perfect, and when I start to carry them out, may God have mercy on Bobby Lee, for I shall have none." Hooker marched his men south from Washington and found General Lee and the Army of Northern Virginia waiting for them across the Rappahannock just as they had met Burnside the previous December. The armies clashed at Chancellorsville, fighting for a week with Hooker's forces outnumbering Lee's by more than two to one. It was a rout in Lee's favor, but he lost his principal lieutenant, General Thomas "Stonewall" Jackson, when Rebel pickets mistook him and his officers for Union troops and opened fire, hitting Jackson three times and knocking him from his horse. In a bid to save the renowned general's life, a surgeon at a nearby field hospital amputated his left arm, after which Jackson was carried to a nearby plantation to rest. For several days he appeared to be recovering, but he developed pneumonia and died eight days after he was shot. When told that his death was imminent, Jackson, a deeply religious man, took comfort knowing he would expire on the Sabbath. "It is the Lord's Day; my wish is fulfilled. I have always desired to die on Sunday," he said.

Lee turned north again. He marched his army of soldiers clad in butternut yellow and light gray through Maryland and into Pennsylvania. Lee moved quickly, and for a month he thought that the Union's Army of the Potomac was far behind him—on the south side of the Potomac River, in fact. He was quite surprised to learn from a spy hired by one of his senior officers that the enemy was, in fact, only hours behind him. Lee's chief cavalry officer, General Jeb Stuart, had been off seeking fame and glory near Washington, D.C., and had failed to report to his commander on the enemy's movements. Thus blind, Lee stumbled in early July into the bloodiest battle of the Civil War at a small town called Gettysburg. Lee's 75,000 men fought for three days in early July against 105,000 commanded by General George Meade, Lincoln's replacement for Hooker. Some of the men engaged there had been part of Johnston's army. Union General John Buford, Johnston's quartermaster at Camp Floyd, fought a desperate holding action northwest of the town on the first day against another of Johnston's former subordinates, Confederate General Harry Heth, to hold the rebels back until the rest of the Union Army arrived. On the second day, Lee's Army of Northern Virginia made bloody assaults on parts of the battlefield later remembered as the Peach Orchard, the Wheatfield, Devil's Den, Little Round Top, and Culp's Hill. On the third day, Lee ordered a massive infantry assault against the center of Meade's line, an attack forever after called "Pickett's Charge." It was a slaughter. Of the 12,500 men who had made the attack, barely half returned.

Eight thousand men on both sides had been killed, with another 42,000 wounded, captured, or gone missing in three days of fighting. Lee began his retreat to Virginia late the next day, July 4th, Independence Day. That same day, far to the west, Union General Ulysses S. Grant captured the Confederate city of Vicksburg after an almost-two-month siege. The victory gave the United States unfettered control of the Mississippi River and cut the Confederacy in half. The war had finally turned in favor of the Union, and no one saw it more clearly than the Confederates themselves. One Rebel officer recorded in his diary:

> Events have succeeded one another with disastrous rapidity. One brief month ago we were apparently at the point of success. Lee was in Pennsylvania . . . Vicksburg seemed to laugh all Grant's efforts to scorn. . . . Now the picture is just as somber as it was bright then. . . . It seems incredible that human power could effect such a change in so brief a space. Yesterday, we rode on the pinnacle of success—today absolute ruin seems to be our portion. The Confederacy totters to its destruction.[12]

It would totter on for almost two more years filled with blood and horror.

———•··•———

With no troops coming from the East to help him, fears that General Connor would attack the city eventually waned, and James Livingston was able to leave his assignment as Brigham's mole in the army and return south to the quarry when the weather was favorable. The repairs on the temple foundation were going well, and it would soon be time to resume building up the basement walls. The Little Cottonwood Quarry would need to deliver granite blocks in greater quantities than ever before.

The challenge was that they still had no choice but to haul the stone by wagon. The canal that Brigham had hoped to complete years earlier was still unfinished. Some sections had been dug out by contractors, others by volunteer tithing labor. Each ward had received an assignment to excavate a particular section, but the sections were sufficiently long that men were having to donate one to two days per week instead of one in every ten, as the "tithing" term would have suggested. Obstructions of terrain had prevented them from carving a perfectly straight line from Great Salt Lake City to the quarry—in places they'd had to open up curves, and in at least one location the workers had been forced to cut a "V" in the ground to avoid a ravine. But they had finished the sections from a little south of Big Cottonwood Creek to "Kanyon [sic] Creek," twenty feet wide and four feet deep, and they had used that much of the canal to transport water for irrigation even before Johnston's army had entered the territory. But as they now tried to resume their work on the canal, they made a discovery, almost as unpleasant in its own way as finding the cracks in the temple foundation had been.

Some planned sections of the canal weren't going to hold water. In some places, the soil was too sandy and porous; in others, as they dug down, they found the subsurface terrain filled with large rocks. They would have needed oxen to pull those out, but there were precious few of those to spare. Between the farms and the granite quarry, most of the oxen in the Salt Lake Valley were already spoken for. So, after some consideration, Brigham and his advisors were forced to admit that the amount of labor, money, and other resources required to overcome those problems would be prohibitive. The Church had already spent $169,000 on the effort—almost $3,000,000 in modern prices when adjusted for inflation—and there was no telling how much more it would cost now. The money just wasn't there unless Brigham wanted to divert it from the temple or other projects, and he wasn't willing to make that sacrifice. So Brigham called a halt to the program.

> The canal that we started from Big Cottonwood Creek to this city was for the purpose of transporting material for building the Temple. . . . We have learned some thing in relation to the nature of the soil in which the bed of the canal is made that we did not know before. We pretty much completed that canal, or, in other words, we hewed out the cistern, but, behold it would not hold water.

We have not the time now to make that canal carry water, so we will continue to haul rock with cattle, and when an opportunity presents, we will finish the canal.[13]

They considered digging out other canals at various points, both for irrigation and for transporting temple granite, but the projected costs of even the shortest canal were estimated at almost $300,000. The Saints in areas that would have benefited showed a distinct reluctance to commit themselves to any undertaking that expensive, and the territorial governor likewise refused to dedicate public resources without much more study by civil engineers to firmly fix the design and control costs. To do just that, a few entrepreneurs started companies dedicated to canal construction. Some of them won some contracts, including the Deseret Irrigation and Navigation Canal Company, which proposed to finish the waterway needed to boat temple granite for an estimated $365,500. The company worked on the project until 1870, but it was finally abandoned. No granite block in the Salt Lake Temple was ever carried to the temple site by water.

———•·•·•———

So Livingston and his men did the best with what they had. They established their second camp on the south side of Little Cottonwood Creek, living out of their tents set up over planked floors and constructing the other buildings they would need as time and available labor allowed. The teamsters, most of whom were volunteers from local wards, slept nearby in tents that looked very much like wickiups—domed houses made of brush and timber—near the makeshift cattle pen built to contain their animals.[14]

They built a cookhouse next to the quarry proper, which doubled as the dining hall and a rest area when men needed a few minutes off their feet to recover their strength. It was forty by sixty feet, two stories, with four windows and a single door. The lower story housed the kitchen and the dining room, which was large enough for two rows of tables kept "scrupulously clean" with soap and water. The upper story was home to the camp cook and became a bunkhouse in the winter. Livingston also kept his office in the upper floor of the cookhouse, storing the account books and Bills of Stone he received from Truman Angell and William Folsom. The cook, at least in the early years, was a crusty man named Sandy Glenn, described as being "somewhat irritable" and known to threaten the stove with an axe when he could not get it hot enough to cook the day's meals.[15] He and his successors received wages of $2.00 per day, with assistant cooks and dishwashers drawing $1.50.[16] Glenn was often assisted in his kitchen by some of the laborers' wives, which served the dual purpose of providing help and raising the morale of the camp by increasing the quality of the food served.[17]

Uncooked meat, vegetables, and fruits were stored in cellars behind the building, and the men built a trough to bring water from the creek directly to the cookhouse.[18] The wood-burning oven was kept outside; in it Glenn and his female line cooks baked bread, pies, and other treats for the men. Food deliveries came weekly, and there was no shortage of bread, beef, pastries, and dried fruits for the men to consume at all hours. Breakfasts were hearty, featuring eggs, biscuits, mutton chops, potatoes, and fruit. Stables for horses and mules were also set up by the creek near the cookhouse, which may have added some interesting aromas to the meals beyond what Glenn and his helpers produced in the kitchen on any given day.[19]

Livingston established a schedule for the camp by which it ran for decades, until the last temple stone was cut. It was practically military in its precision. The stonecutters worked ten-hour days, six days a week.[20] Each workday started at six o'clock, with breakfast served a half hour later. Men were expected to report to their stations by seven and work until noon, when lunch gave them an hour's break. They resumed their labors at one and worked until six, when Livingston would call for the workday's end. Supper began at six-thirty and finished an hour later, when the entire camp would assemble under a bowery for group prayer. The men were free to engage in whatever recreation they chose afterward. Board games were favored pastimes, and especially check-ers, at which some of the men became "real experts at the game." Two croquet grounds were staked out for summer matches. Many of the men were avid readers and spent their free time in study and self-education. Few men played cards, as gambling and alcohol were forbidden at all times. That was no issue for the quarrymen, who were all Latter-day Saints, but the restrictions may have chafed some of the Alta miners passing through Granite City who were not. Some of the men sang as a hobby, though there is no reliable record of the vocalists' talent or lack thereof. The workforce took only the Sabbath to rest, and some left the quarry Saturday evening to return home and attend church with their families. Those men who were single or whose families lived too far away to visit and return in a single day would walk down to the mouth of the canyon to attend the local ward there.[21]

Volunteers from the various wards worked rotations of seven to ten days and often lived together, clustering their tents apart from those of Livingston and the full-time stonecutters, for whom the quarry was both a permanent home and a full-time job. These men were expected to bring their own equipment and provisions—an expectation that was not always communicated, causing many to arrive with no supplies or food of their own, and so creating headaches and bad moods all around.[22] Many of those temporary laborers were recent European emigrants, con-verts from Scotland, England, Wales, and Scandinavia.[23] Many were in debt to the Church's Perpetual Emigration Fund Company, which had paid for their Atlantic passage. Lacking other marketable skills—includ-ing, in many cases, a command of the English language—they were sent to the quarry to work off what they owed and earn money to fund the same trip for wives, children, and other relatives still waiting in their home countries.[24]

The total population of their small labor force hovered on average between thirty and forty men plus a few women.[25] That too would grow over the years, but the total number of semipermanent workers seems

*A studio portrait of eleven men who were construction workers on the
Salt Lake Temple. James Moyle, head stonecutter and later the superintendent
of the temple block, is seated in the front row, third from the left.*

to have remained less than a hundred. The number always dropped
off sharply during the winter, when the quarry closed and fewer than
a dozen men would stay behind.[26] Trying to break granite was not the
safest occupation during warmer weather, but when snow and ice descended on the canyon, even moving around the rocks became a haz-
ardous exercise. Death by avalanche was a real concern well into the
spring, when the sun and warm air began loosening the snowpack along
higher elevations. Four men learned that particular lesson when they
were caught in a snowslide in Mill Creek Canyon to the north on April 1,
1864. John Bowen escaped by catching hold of a tree limb before the
slide could move him, and Edmund Ellsworth Jr. survived when the avalanche swept him into another tree branch across his path; he suffered
nothing worse than getting the wind knocked out of him. Thomas Pierce
was far less fortunate. The snow smashed him into a tree *trunk* at high

speed, causing internal injuries that proved fatal within forty-five minutes. He was awake and aware of his condition until he died. The fourth man, Robert Spurgeon, disappeared beneath the white powder, and his body was not located until a month later, when the snow melted in early May.[27]

The men never had to cut granite directly from the canyon walls, which was surely a relief even when the cliffs weren't covered in ice and snow. There was enough and plenty to spare in the boulders lying about the canyon floor, but cutting the granite itself was a tedious process.[28] As each course of the temple progressed, the Church architect would send Livingston order sheets and Bills of Stone detailing the dimensions for specific blocks, as well as scaled drawings to help the workers see where more intricate cuts were required. Livingston would assign granite blocks to men based on each worker's demonstrated skill and the difficulty of the stone's planned design, with less skilled apprentice cutters working on rough-cut stones planned for an inner course of the temple. The more challenging stones destined for the outside courses that would be visible to the public went to master stonecutters. The final precision cutting was reserved for men working on the temple block using smaller tools designed for such detailed, intricate work.[29] There was no shortage of men there who could take on the assignments. Some were donating their labor as tithing, others were getting paid, and some were working for free to demonstrate their skill in a kind of audition that they hoped would lead to a paid job.

Once a team of quarrymen had received an assignment, they would start the process by attacking the top of a granite boulder with an eight-pound sledgehammer and a stone point drill sixteen inches long with a $\frac{3}{8}$- or $\frac{5}{8}$-inch bit. One man would hold the drill against the rock while his partner swung the hammer, with the lower man rotating the drill a quarter turn with each blow to keep the wear on the bit even. The man wielding the sledge clearly had the harder job, so they would switch off as necessary to let each man rest his muscles throughout the day. As the drills were dulled or even broken from the repeated pounding, men, and sometimes younger boys, would collect and carry them to the blacksmith shop and then return with newly sharpened drills.[30] The smiths were kept busy more or less constantly; there were at least six men qualified to do that work.[31]

The stonecutters would drill each hole until it measured three and a half inches deep, and holes were spaced between four and seven inches apart across the rock face. Once the men had a line of holes drilled across the top of the boulder, they would insert two slips—four-inch-long convex rods that were flat on one side—into each hole, followed by a wedge, a longer rod that tapered down to a flat end ⅝-inch in diameter. At that point, the call went out for everyone below the rock to clear out of the way. Once the area was clear, men standing behind the "line of break" would drive the wedges down into the holes in sequence with their sledgehammers, cracking the boulder along the line. To make a horizontal split along a boulder's face, the same process was also used with the line of holes drilled level across the rock, the men standing on wooden scaffolding. Using this method, boulders the size of large houses were broken down into much smaller stones, with the same steps repeated each time to cut the rock into ever-smaller and smaller pieces.[32] For all this labor, each man was paid a wage of $2.50 per day plus room and board, unless the weather prevented them from working outside. The men generally were paid in credit at the tithing office for whatever goods were available there, though they did receive small amounts of cash when possible.[33]

Watching granite boulders broken down by the use of nothing more than muscle and metal tools was awe-inspiring to quarry visitors. One guest, Robert Campbell, described such a rock: "There it stood like a great castle, seemingly bidding defiance to any set of competitors who should undertake to handle it." But all around the quarry was evidence that boulders like that one could and would be taken apart. "There is great cause for alarm when forty and fifty men can thus handle the mountains as a very little thing and make the everlasting hills to tremble before them."[34]

Once a stone was broken loose, the men would make further rough cuts to get the block nearly to the dimensions on the architect's specification chart. Livingston would then assign someone to make any finishing cuts to get it down to size. Not all of the stones were rectangular; some required tapered or oblique sides, which shapes were achieved through the use of heavy chisels or a "bull set," a heavy wedge nearly the same size as the head of a sledgehammer. The stonecutters made smaller adjustments using a single-jack hammer that a man could wield in one hand—it weighed only a few pounds and was a foot long—while he held a small drill with the other. If the length to be cut was truly small, a chipping hammer came into play, which would remove only fractions of an inch of material. But the stonecutters still had to be careful at all times. Granite splits along one of three possible grains readily recognizable to experienced stonecutters, but a less experienced man might misread the grain and split the rock badly, taking off more material than required, ruining the stone and therefore wasting the work that his fellows had expended on it previously.[35]

When that last stonecutter reported that he had finished, Livingston or another experienced man would inspect his work. If the block matched the required dimensions and its grain did not turn to create a potential fault line to weaken it, it was numbered according to the architect's order sheet and flagged for loading. Even the smallest stones weighed tons, which forced the use of log rollers to move them any significant distance. The men felled trees of roughly equal size, stripped them of branches, and laid them in parallel lines in front of the blocks. Once a group of men had muscled the stone onto the rollers, they used metal pry bars to push and steer it across the rolling logs toward the loading dock. Transporting a single stone by this method could take hours or longer, depending on the distance it had to travel from the site where it was cut to the dock—a misnomer, for the "dock" was actually a ditch. The teamsters would lead the oxen down the embankment into a trench sufficiently deep to put the wagon bed at ground level. With the bed touching the trench wall, the quarrymen could slide the rock off the rollers directly onto the wagon, where they tied it down with chains or ropes. Then the teamsters led the oxen out of the ditch, which was challenging, as the animals had to move the loaded wagon from a dead stop up an incline. Four days later, if all went well, that team would arrive at the temple site, where they would unload the granite block and then start the long march south back to the quarry.[36]

To keep the granite moving at a steady rate from the quarry to the temple site, Livingston and Sharp deployed sixty wagons organized into four companies of fifteen wagons each. One company would always be at the quarry loading dock; one on the road to Great Salt Lake City; one at the temple block unloading; and one on the road back. Within companies, the wagons were staggered to arrive at either end of the journey, each having one hour to load or unload its cargo. To keep to that schedule, the wagons were spaced a little more than a mile apart on the road, assuming no delays due to weather or breakdowns. To manage the latter problem, Sharp's men kept two crews moving along the route to repair the road, bridges, or wagons as necessary.[37] It was an elegant system in theory, probably as efficient a plan as anyone could have devised, but keeping the wagon trains running on time was a challenge in practice. Livingston himself reported in 1877 that the quarry was shipping only three or four wagons of granite per day.[38] Wagons weighed down by their granite cargo often could not be pulled from the mire after a hard rain, which could disrupt the system; nor could they be repaired on a schedule—maybe not repaired at all if the body and axles shattered under the load of a three-ton block. It was not uncommon for travelers to see shattered wagons and fallen blocks pulled off to the side of the road between Salt Lake and Little Cottonwood Canyon. But even when the wagons were cooperating, the oxen sometimes did not. Decades after the temple was finished, one anonymous former quarry worker recalled a day when some of Joseph Sharp's animals were reluctant to keep to the schedule.

Never saw such a big cart nor such big, fat oxen as those that pulled the cart around. They must have weighed over a ton each. A Swede drove them. When a rock was chained to the cart, he would sort of chirp to them, then whistle, and finally say, 'Ve is ready, Yonny an' Yake. Move along an' take anudder rock for the House of the Lord.'

'Yonny' and 'Yake' soon got so used to hearing him whistle and chirp that they paid little attention to him and finally when they did move it was slower than a snail's pace.

Brigham [Young] was standing there one day watching those slow-moving oxen when a man walked up to him and said, "If you don't get these finished rock [sic] out of the way faster than you're doing now, then I'll have to pull some of my teams off, for there's not much space left to pile the rough stones."

Brigham turned and said, "Brother Joseph, you're in charge of transportation. You're the one we hold responsible for not just getting the rocks to the yard but also for getting the finished stones to the temple."

. . . Well, Joe didn't say one word but walked over to a bull-whacker who was unloading, and when he came back he was carrying a long bull whip. The oxen were coming back empty at a snail's pace; they only had to go about one hundred yards. He and Brigham stood in silence while the next stone was chained to the cart. Then Joe told the Swede to step aside and he spoke to the oxen. They went on chewing their cud as usual. Now this span of oxen belonged to Joe, but they didn't recognize their master's voice. He spoke again, and still they stood there. Then he whirled the bull whip around his head and brought it down across the back of both oxen.

You should have seen what happened. Those oxen went right through their ox staples as if they were matches. Well, it took us about an hour to get them back and some new staples made, but say, when Joe spoke to them again they stepped right out and, to use an expression of today, went into high gear.

What did Brigham say? Not one durned word. Went away holding his sides and laughing.[39]

Many of the wagons used were the army surplus sold off at auction when the soldiers had marched out of Camp Crittenden for the East to fight in the Civil War. They were freight wagons with heavy beds made of thick timber to bear heavy loads, and broad tires built to handle rougher terrain, which was helpful given the road between the quarry and Great Salt Lake City. Despite efforts by both the local government and the Church to improve it, the soil was always sandy and loose, a far cry from the hard ground to the north that had broken the first settlers' plows in 1847. The only solution was to make sure there were enough yokes of oxen to pull the heavier loads and hope that the wagons wouldn't buckle. Necessity spurs invention, and so the men began to experiment with changes to wagon designs to reinforce them. Heavy timbers were attached to strengthen the undercarriages and sideboards, and nonessential parts were stripped to reduce the weight as much as possible. In a fit of creativity, the men designed an entirely new class of wagon that carried the granite blocks in a kind of suspension harness. The unnamed quarry worker who related the incident with Joseph Sharp's oxen also gave a description of the new vehicle:

> You see, we used to load the smaller stones on wagons, but the big ones we hung under them. We'd been having a terrible time. The rocks were heavier than most men thought, and many a wagon broke down. Then one day a brother of Bishop Sharp drove up there with a whole string of heavy freight wagons. . . . On those high-wheeled wagons they put two long red pine logs and chained them to the front and back bolsters. Then when the men had a rock ready the loaders would put some red pine rollers, about six inches through and five feet long, under this rock, and with smaller poles as levers, they would roll it to where the wagons could be loaded.

226

They would get a wagon astraddle [sic] this rock, dig some holes for the wheels, and sink it till the top of the rock touched the bottom of the logs. Then they would chain it in place and when the oxen started, the poles under the rock would roll a little, and as soon as the wheel is got out of these holes the rock was swinging free under the logs. And that is how it was done.[40]

At least two men loaded each wagon, which, fully loaded, carried one larger or two smaller stones and typically required at least six oxen to pull it. The entire operation needed at least 120 teamsters and 360 head of oxen working when all of the wagon trains were running, but oxen and men need to eat and rest, and some loads were heavy enough to require eight oxen. So more teamsters and animals were required to keep things moving, which drove up the transportation costs of the already expensive operation. The daily pay for a teamster was four to six dollars, depending on whether the teamster was providing his own animals and wagons; so hiring a pair of teamsters to make the four-day trip to the temple site meant that the Church was paying up to forty-eight dollars per block in transportation alone, assuming no injury or damage to man, beast, or wagon.[41] The public works delivered hay and forage to keep the animals fed, and the local wards who sent volunteer teamsters to bulk up Livingston's labor pool provided the grain. The Church owned herds of oxen and provided most of the animals, wagons, and gear, but some volunteer teamsters provided their own.[42] Livingston had the men construct a livestock pen able to contain 300 oxen, and they rotated animals in and out of the herd as necessary to give them some rest.[43]

There was another project Brigham was contemplating that promised to be large and expensive, but by 1863 he was perfectly willing to call upon the Saints to devote the time, money, and labor. Immigration into Utah by the Saints had been fairly steady over the last fifteen years, and now the population of Great Salt Lake City and its environs was approaching 20,000 people. The Church was, quite simply, outgrowing its existing facilities—the Adobe Tabernacle in particular. That building was only a decade old, but it was somewhat primitive in its design and construction, and it could hold only 2,500 people—and then only when they packed themselves in. A large majority of the city's population belonged to the Church, so fewer than one in ten could fit into the existing tabernacle to hear the prophet or the Apostles preach on any given day. Nor was Brigham planning on immigration slowing or stopping anytime soon. Missionaries were still going out, and new converts to the faith were coming in, and the more, the better. The math was clear to Brigham and had been for several years. They needed a larger meeting hall—much larger. A general lack of resources and the coming of Johnston's army had prevented the construction of such a large building, but now the need for it was too great to ignore.

The request for a new, larger meeting hall would not have seemed especially problematic, except for some design requirements that Brigham imposed, which obviously were going to require some complicated engineering. The building needed to seat several thousand more people than the existing Adobe Tabernacle, possibly as many as ten thousand; it should have no interior columns to block the audience's view of the rostrum from any point in the hall; and it should have excellent interior acoustics so the larger audience could hear a speaker clearly anywhere inside. It was that last demand that led Brigham himself to conceive that the new building should be generally rounded in shape. The prophet had both addressed the Saints and listened to other speakers many times under the curved plaster ceiling of the Old Adobe Tabernacle, so he understood perfectly well how the shape of the ceiling and walls carried the sound of a human voice.

Brigham turned to William Folsom, the Church architect, to work up the initial plans. The foundation and walls would not be difficult to construct, but Brigham's vision of a domed ceiling was another matter entirely. Creating a curved roof that large would require some innovative structural engineering that was beyond anything Folsom had ever created. So Brigham turned to another man, and a most unlikely one, for the solution: Henry Grow, a bridge builder. In 1849, the Saints had constructed a single-lane bridge across the Jordan River in the Salt Lake Valley, which, by 1860, was coming apart. The bridge was an "ill-shaped, ill-contrived and ponderous concern"[44] that required constant, expensive maintenance, and the territorial legislature decided to replace it. Brigham hired Grow to handle the job, and he was perhaps the most highly qualified man in the territory for it. Before he'd joined the Church in 1842, Grow had worked in Philadelphia for the Remington Company, which business had constructed bridges, among other things. The company also owned the rights on an innovative lattice truss design that used diagonal timbers to distribute the weight load on a bridge. Remington had granted Grow permission to use the design in Utah, and he applied it to the new Jordan River bridge. The resulting structure was the most advanced bridge in the territory and would last for almost fifty years before it would finally need replacing.

Impressed by Grow's work on the bridge, Brigham approached him for a solution to the problem of the new tabernacle roof. Brigham's daughter Clarissa later claimed that her father had used the analogy of a hard-boiled egg, cut in half lengthwise and set up on toothpicks, to illustrate one possible approach.[45] If Brigham did indeed use his breakfast as a model, Grow was not put off by the strange suggestion. Grow's ceiling lattice eventually rested on forty-four stone supports that ran around the building's perimeter, each measuring three feet wide and nine feet deep, all made of sandstone set in a lime-and-sand mortar.

The lattice itself was composed of a three-layered grill of timbers, each nine feet deep and made of two parallel top and bottom ribs with two more sets of intermediate ribs set between. Additional braces and trusses would be affixed to reinforce the roof against high winds. The difficulty of Grow's design was increased by the fact that building materials were in short supply—in particular, metal nails and bolts.[46] Building a structure to enclose almost more than 1.25 million cubic feet would

The Salt Lake Tabernacle under construction, c. 1865.

have required vastly more nails that the Saints could spare, and getting a sufficient supply would have required bringing in several shipments from more than a thousand miles back East. That would have been problematic in peacetime, but with the War Between the States still raging, the US government was consuming mass quantities of iron and steel to keep the Union Army supplied with matériel. As a result, the available supply of nails was low and the prices high. Grow, Folsom, and their crews would have to improvise, and the solutions they developed were both clever and durable. To manufacture their own nails, they pilfered iron from the dozens of Army wagons that Lot Smith and his men had burned and from other carriages since broken and rendered unusable. The iron hoops that armored the wheels, chains, bolts, brake levers, and axles all became raw material to be stripped, melted down, and reworked into the needed bolts and nails.

Grow also applied another method that he had tested and proven while building the Jordan River bridge—wooden dowels. The carpenters would drill or burn holes through the wood, through which they would push the dowels until a few inches extended on either side. They would then drive wedges into the dowels to split the ends apart to lock them into place. It was a method that would require very precise fittings between the dowel and the hole; ill-fitting dowels that moved in overly large holes would let the superstructure flex, diminishing its ability to bear weight and resist the shearing force of winds bearing down against the rounded roof. On the bridge, that method was successfully holding trusses and braces as tightly as a metal bolt and nut could have managed. And here, where any timbers began to crack from the stress, the workers could bind the wood with wet rawhide strips that would dry tight in place. Once the superstructure was constructed and locked in position, they would cover the whole with shingles and seal the entire framework against moisture with a combination of lime, tallow, lamp-black, and salt.

Such was the plan.[47] How it would work out in practice was something they would learn only by doing. The Remington lattice system was a tested design, but there was, at the time, no actual mathematical formula worked out for Grow to use in calculating the lengths and angles of the trusses. That was something he would have to figure out as he went through no small bit of trial and error. Brigham could only hope that Grow's past practice would be experience enough for the bridge builder to work out the measurements for the complex tabernacle roof as he went. Otherwise, the Saints might find themselves in the same unpleasant situation they'd endured with the temple foundation, having to waste years of work by tearing it out to rebuild it.

<hr />

The fourth year of the Civil War, 1864, would prove to be the bloodiest yet. President Lincoln had finally found the soldier he wanted to lead the Union army in General Ulysses S. Grant, the victor at Shiloh and Vicksburg. Lincoln promoted Grant to lieutenant general in March and gave him command of all the Union armies, making him answerable only to the president himself. Grant's strategy was simple but promised to be gory. Where his predecessors had tried to end the war by capturing the Confederate capital of Richmond, Grant looked to win simply by attacking Confederate armies wherever and whenever he could. The United States Army had more men and matériel at its disposal than the South, so Grant would bleed the Confederacy to death.

Grant took direct control of the Army of the Potomac in Virginia while his closest friend, General William Tecumseh Sherman, took command of the Union Army in the deep South. Sherman marched out of Mississippi into Georgia, beginning his "march to the sea." Sherman was even more hard-nosed than Grant. He intended not merely to destroy the enemy in his front or deprive the Confederacy of the supplies it needed to continue the war; he was determined to break the Southern will to fight at all. His troops burned houses and farms as they went, destroying virtually everything in their path. They tore up railroads, burning the wooden ties in bonfires over which they heated the metal rails until they glowed hot; they then wrapped those rails around trees and left them to cool, rendering them useless as anything but symbols of Union power. The soldiers called them "Sherman neckties" in tribute to their commanding officer.

Sherman's armies reached Atlanta in late August, and the city fell a few days later. The general ordered all civilians out and then had all government and military facilities burned to the ground. The fires spread, torching homes and shops, laying waste to the city, and the destruction had the effect on the people that Sherman desired—it not only crushed their hopes of victory but made them despair for their very survival. "The end has come. No doubt of the fact. . . . We are going to be wiped off the face of the earth," wrote Mary Chesnutt in her diary.[48]

In Virginia, Grant pushed south from Washington and clashed with Robert E. Lee for three days in May in the tangled forest of the Wilderness, then for almost two weeks at Spotsylvania Courthouse, and another thirteen days at Cold Harbor. Each battle was uglier than the last, and Grant racked up about as many casualties in one year as his predecessors had in three. Critics called him a butcher and demanded Lincoln replace him, but the president ignored them. Grant continued pushing south until Lee's army was finally trapped in the trenches around Petersburg, just ten miles south of Richmond. The siege lasted for nine months, from June of 1864 to March of 1865. To ensure that Lee could not easily get more supplies for his men, Grant sent Generals David Hunter and Phillip Sheridan to the Shenandoah Valley, the "breadbasket of the Confederacy." When asked why he was detaching those forces, Grant explained to Washington that their mission was to convert the valley into "a barren waste . . . so that crows flying over it for the balance of the season will have to carry their provender with them."[49] Sheridan and Hunter took six months to finish the operation, not because they were slow or incompetent but because they were exceedingly thorough. As his mission drew to its close in October 1864, Sheridan reported to Grant:

> I have destroyed over 2,000 barns filled with wheat, hay, and farming implements; over seventy mills filled with flour and wheat; have driven in front of the army over 4,000 head of stock, and have killed and issued to the troops not less than 3,000 sheep. . . . A large number of horses have been obtained, a proper estimate of which I cannot now make. . . . My engineer officer was murdered beyond Harrisonburg, near Dayton. For this atrocious act all the houses within an area of five miles were burned. . . . When this is completed the Valley, from Winchester up to Staunton, ninety-two miles, will have but little in it for man or beast.[50]

In years to come, the residents of the Shenandoah would refer to Sheridan's campaign through their countryside simply as "the Burning."

After the South's defeat at Gettysburg, most of the Confederate leaders had pinned their hopes for independence on Lincoln losing reelection in November of 1864. The war had lasted far longer—and the cost in blood and treasure had been far higher—than anyone had imagined, and the election would certainly be a referendum on Lincoln's leadership. All the signs had pointed to his defeat at the ballot box, and his opponent,

William McClellan, the general whom Lincoln had fired after Antietam, had promised that he would halt the fighting and negotiate. Of course, once the fighting had stopped, the South was sure that no one in the North would be willing to let it start again. The United States might not agree to sign a peace treaty for years, but the Confederacy would be a separate nation in every real way. But with Atlanta's fall to Sherman and Lee's being bottled up in Petersburg, it was finally apparent that the North was winning the war. Lincoln crushed McClellan at the ballot box, claiming 212 electoral votes to McClellan's 12 and carrying every state except Kentucky, Delaware, and New Jersey. The Confederacy's hope for an armistice disappeared in an instant.

The Saints followed all of this from afar, concerned for a country that they loved more than it loved them—but the distance left them free to continue building their cities, the temple, and the Tabernacle throughout 1864 and into the next year. With the exception of General Patrick Connor's abrasive dealings—he posted a provost guard station directly across the street south of the Tabernacle construction site—events in the Salt Lake Valley were about as tranquil as they'd been at any point in recent years. The Tabernacle was rising much faster than the temple across the way, but that was to be expected, given its design and construction materials. William Folsom estimated that the new meeting hall would seat almost nine thousand people when it was finished, not quite so many as Brigham had hoped, but a significant increase over the older Adobe Tabernacle.[51] Progress on the temple was indeed slower, but the footings had been repaired and improved, and the level of flagging stone was going down. In fact, to ensure the flagging would be perfectly level, they had decided to lay down a second level of flat stones on top of the first. The workmen could compensate for variations and irregularities in the top surface of the lower layer by varying the amount of mortar laid on it, thinning or thickening it as needed, or taking any other steps necessary to ensure the new upper layer would be perfectly flat and horizontal. Once that was done, the basement walls could again be laid down. On August 15, 1864, Brigham directed John Sharp to arrange contracts "to have the flagging and cut stone laid in the west wall of the Temple, between now and the rough weather of next fall or winter."[52]

—•·•·•—

In early March of 1865, the people of Salt Lake held "a grand celebration on the occasion of the second inauguration of President Abraham Lincoln."[53] General Connor had received a promotion to a higher command outside of the territory but had not yet left for his new assignment. He was likely surprised to be invited to the festival, which was "more imposing than anything that had yet been witnessed in the city of the saints."[54] He did not come down from his post above the city—though whether out of personal pique or an honest lack of time imposed by the need to prepare for his departure is unknown—but he really had no choice but to send down a contingent of troops from Camp Douglas to march along with the Nauvoo Legion in the mile-long parade. The day featured speeches, fireworks, the firing of cannons, and the "flying [of] national flags upon numerous public and private buildings."[55] Afterward, the Legion's cavalry unit escorted the troops back to camp and extended another invitation to General Connor and his staff to dine with federal officials from Washington at a banquet at City Hall. Connor again begged off, but a group of officers attended in his stead. They ended the evening by watching a show at the Salt Lake Theater and then a display of fireworks under the dark night sky. "The federal officials [were] well pleased, and perhaps a little surprised at the exuberant loyalty of the Mormons."[56]

Of course, none of them knew that President Lincoln would be dead in a little more than a month. In late March, General Grant successfully cut the last of four rail lines still supplying Robert E. Lee's beleaguered men in the Petersburg trenches. Lee ordered a retreat from the city, hoping that he could turn the Army of Northern Virginia south and combine with Confederate forces in North Carolina, but Lee's men were tired and starving and could not march with much vigor. For days they moved west but were unable to put any real distance between themselves and Grant's forces, which were never more than a few hours behind. A week later, finally trapped near Appomattox Station, Lee agreed to surrender. On April 9, at the same time the Saints were sitting through a session of their annual general conference, Generals Lee and Grant met near the Appomattox Court House in a sizable home owned by Wilmer McLean. McLean had owned a farm in Manassas, Virginia, years before and fled south when part of the First Battle of Bull Run had been fought across his property. In a real way, the war that had started in his front yard would now end in McLean's parlor.

Lee and Grant exchanged pleasantries, and then the Union general sat and scribbled out the terms of surrender in pencil on a single sheet. Lee was surprised at the generosity offered. His entire army would surrender its weapons and flags, and then all of his men would be paroled and sent home, to be disturbed no more so long as they obeyed the law. Lee signed the paper, and, with his signature, the hopes and dreams of a Confederate nation were put to rest forever. The war didn't end in that moment. It took a few months for the word of Lee's surrender to reach the other Confederate forces, but the news reached Washington by nightfall. At nine o'clock that evening, Secretary of War Edwin M. Stanton ordered a salute of 200 cannon be fired "at the headquarters of every army and department, and at every post and arsenal in the United States" in celebration.[57]

The national celebration that followed went on virtually unabated until the following Friday evening. Lincoln went to Ford's Theater to see a performance of *Our American Cousin,* a three-act comedy by an English playwright that had become popular in recent years. He had invited General Grant and his wife, Julia, to accompany him and the First Lady, but Grant had declined, and another military officer, Major Henry Rathbone, went in his place. During the second scene of the final act, an actor named John Wilkes Booth quietly made his way to the unprotected door of Lincoln's box, opened it, and shot the president in the back of the head with a .41-caliber Philadelphia Derringer pistol. Major Rathbone leaped at Booth and tried to wrestle him down until the killer pulled a knife and stabbed him in the left forearm. Booth then leaped from the box railing onto the stage, but his boot spur caught one of the flags decorating the box and he landed off balance, breaking his left leg. In the pandemonium he managed to hobble out the back of the theater to a waiting horse and escape the city. Lincoln was carried across the street to a private house, where the wounded president lingered all night before he finally passed away at 7:22 a.m.

The news that Lincoln had been killed reached Salt Lake City by telegram during the early-morning hours of Saturday, April 15.[58] The mood in the city turned melancholy. Despite their difficult relations with the US government, the Saints still considered themselves loyal citizens, and none wished the president ill. In fact, Abraham Lincoln had earned the Saints' respect, not by doing anything special for them, but merely by leaving them alone to practice their religion and by encouraging the federal officials he appointed over the Utah Territory to do the same. That was more than most presidents had ever done for them and more than some would do in years to come. They mourned his passing in ways that might have surprised federal officials back East. "All the stores and places of business were closed, flags [were] all flying at half mast." Even Brigham's home was decorated with flag crepes in the president's honor. Most telling, some of the leaders of the Church eulogized Lincoln during the following day's services in the Adobe Tabernacle. Wilford Woodruff "preached a highly instructive and edifying discourse upon the uncertainty of human life and the present mournful condition of our country, occasioned by the assassination of our Chief Magistrate."[59] Elders Franklin D. Richards and George Q. Cannon offered similar remarks in the afternoon. The US government declared April 19 a day of general mourning, and thousands assembled in the Adobe Tabernacle to take part in the services, including many who were not Latter-day Saints. The death of a president had allowed the Saints and federal and military officers in Salt Lake to finally close ranks to some degree and find a common cause together, at least for a time.

• • •

It didn't last, of course. Lincoln's death hadn't erased the old divisions, and the tensions returned. The Saints had made an impression with their patriotic display, but it didn't change the key fact that they were promoting an institution the rest of the country would not abide. That point was made clearly in mid-June with the arrival in Great Salt Lake City of the Honorable Schuyler Colfax, the Speaker of the United States House of Representatives. His traveling companions were Lieutenant Governor of Illinois William Bross; Samuel Bowles, editor of the *Springfield* (Massachusetts) *Republican*; and Albert Richardson, war correspondent for the *New York Tribune*. Colfax inferred that he'd been sent west by Lincoln before the assassination to "thoroughly investigate the affairs and interest of the Pacific States and Territories" because the now-dead president had believed the area would become the "treasure-house" of the nation. That may have been true, but Colfax may have had a secondary mission. Lincoln's hands-off policy toward the Saints had never been popular among the Republican Party faithful who regarded plural marriage as no better than slavery. They had been content—barely, in some cases—to follow Lincoln and leave polygamy for another day while the nation grappled with the rebellion of the Southern states. But the war was ended, slavery's destiny as an institution was settled, and Lincoln was gone, albeit too soon. So those Republicans naturally wanted to take care of the other half of the promise. Andrew Johnson had assumed the presidency, and the Republican hard-liners in Congress and elsewhere would pressure him to "adjust the affairs of Utah simultaneously with those of the 'conquered South.'"[60] Ending polygamy was unfinished business.

Perhaps not knowing where Colfax stood, the Saints tried to make a good impression and gave the Speaker of the House and his party an exuberant welcome. The federal officials assigned to Utah joined in, and Colfax was practically besieged by the well-wishers. "There was an element of rivalry between Mormon and Gentile in it, adding earnestness and energy to enthusiasm and hospitality," one of the journalists noted.[61] The Saints and the federal officers were trying to outdo each other. On that score, the Saints had the advantage. The three things any weary traveler wants are a clean bed, a hot shower, and a good meal, and the Saints provided them all. They escorted their visitors to one of the city's finest hotels and then to a natural hot spring within the city limits to wash off the dust of the trail. ("Bless their Mormon hearts," Bowles recorded in his memoir of the trip. "We washed out all . . . the accumulated grime and fatigue of the journey, and came out baptized in freshness and self-respect.")[62] Receptions with political, military, and ecclesiastical leaders followed over the coming days; they took in shows at the Salt Lake Theater, including a performance with one of Brigham's daughters in a starring role; and the dinners were downright lavish—"as rich a variety of fish, meats, vegetables, pastry and fruit as I ever saw on any private table in the East," Bowles observed with surprise. "And the quality and the cooking and the serving were unimpeachable."[63]

Brigham, Wilford, and several other Church leaders were on a tour of Utah Valley when Colfax first arrived, but they reached Great Salt Lake City soon after and called on Colfax. Brigham was no refined gentleman by Eastern standards. He was "cool and quiet in manner . . . rather formal, but courteous . . ."[64] His grammar was occasionally imperfect, and his opinions on political topics of the day were offered in strong and sharp-edged, though not hostile, terms. So it was probably with some trepidation that Colfax broached the one topic that must have been unavoidable. As it turned out, the Speaker and his party were pleased to find the prophet willing to engage in an extended and open discussion of plural marriage. But as the conversation progressed, they were surprised—perhaps completely shocked—to hear Brigham's thoughts on the subject.

> The conversation . . . on this subject of polygamy, was introduced by his inquiring of Mr. Colfax what the government and people of the East proposed to do with it and them, now that they had got rid of the slavery question. The Speaker replied that he had no authority to speak for the government; but for himself, if he might be permitted to make the suggestion, he hoped the prophets of the church would have a new revelation on the subject, which should put a stop to the practice. . . . Mr. Young responded quickly and frankly that he should readily welcome such a revelation . . . that it was not an essential practice in the church, but only a privilege and a duty, under special command of God.[65]

To hear the prophet declare that plural marriage was not an "essential practice" and that he would welcome a revelation bringing it to a close must have given Colfax some hope that the US government and the Church could find some mutually agreeable way to end the practice. But the Speaker's hope was apparently grounded on the assumption that any "revelations" were just Brigham's personal dictates presented to the gullible Saints as divine communications. By suggesting that it would be helpful for Brigham to receive such a convenient directive ending polygamy, Colfax was practically giving him a wink and a nod as he spoke. So when Brigham said he would welcome such a revelation, Colfax might well have thought the prophet was confirming the Speaker's beliefs. If so, he was mistaken. Brigham was not confirming Colfax's cynical suggestion, he was simply being honest—and he was not going to perpetrate a fraud on the Saints by presenting his own wishes as divine commands when he knew better.

Samuel Bowles, the *Tribune* correspondent, noted that the conversation between Colfax and Brigham "was said to be the freest and frankest ever known on that subject in that presence, ended pleasantly, but with the full expression, on the part of Mr. Colfax and his friends, of their hope that the polygamy question might be removed from existence, and thus all objection to the admission of Utah as a State be taken away; but that, until it was, no such admission was possible."[66] Brigham gave them no such assurance, but Colfax and his party had clearly latched onto Brigham's statement that it was "only a privilege and a duty, under special command of God." That seemed to have had a powerful effect on their opinions regarding how the government might deal with the Saints going forward. After leaving the Salt Lake Valley, Bowles proposed to his readers a policy for dealing with the Saints that seemed grounded in Brigham's explanation.

> I find that Mormonism is not necessarily polygamy; that the one began and existed for many years without the other; . . . and that the Nation and its government may oppose it and punish it, without at all interfering with the existence of the Mormon church, or justly being held as interfering with the religious liberty that is the basis of all our institutions.[67]

Not everyone would agree with Bowles's claim that the government could move to eliminate plural marriage without trying to destroy The Church of Jesus Christ of Latter-day Saints. The Saints themselves would, in coming years, put up a fierce resistance to government enforcement of anti-polygamy laws that would lead many to conclude the opposite. But Brigham had proposed that one could go on without the other if the Lord so commanded. That command never came in his lifetime. In the end, it would be another prophet called to shoulder that load.

<hr />

The year 1866 passed by without incident, the quietest period the Saints had enjoyed for some time. In Washington, Lincoln's vice president, Andrew Johnson, had assumed presidency after his predecessor's murder. Johnson was a Democrat from Tennessee, the only Southern senator who had not resigned his seat when his home state had seceded from the Union. He had remained loyal to the United States, and Lincoln had chosen him as a running mate in the 1864 election. Now the new chief executive was showing no desire to deviate from Lincoln's policy toward Utah. Johnson made no move to enforce the Morrill Act and made no federal appointments to territorial offices calculated to antagonize the Saints. Just as Lincoln had wanted to stay focused on fighting the Civil War, Johnson was focused on the reconstruction of the South. The Republicans in Congress had found that hard enough to swallow from Lincoln, a fellow party member, while the war was ongoing. Now that it was over, they found it intolerable from Johnson, a Democrat. The clash became so bitter that all discussion of asserting more federal control over Utah and other western territories was mostly lost in the din. For their part, the Saints largely kept their heads down and went on with their economic and religious pursuits for the few years that the temporary reprieve granted them. During that window, several events happened that would prove to be hinge points in the building of the temple.

One of these proved not to be very memorable, passing by almost unnoticed because it was achieved so gradually. The teamsters making the round trips to and from Little Cottonwood Canyon had been dropping off their cargo at a rate that was constant but not fast enough to keep up with the demand at the temple site. The *Millennial Star* reported that the temple was "rising from its foundations as fast as the rock can be obtained for the workmen."[68] The teamsters and their four-day journey from the quarry were the bottleneck; one hard rainstorm could bog down the roads and slow down everything. At the temple site, there was manpower enough to keep things moving. Between fifty and eighty stonecutters were at work most days, squaring off and finishing the stones wherever the teamsters dropped them. The men would raise the stone onto blocks to make the working height suitable, and then attack it as necessary. If a stone was especially rough, a stonecutter would go after it with a "bull set" of very large chisels that could take off a considerable amount of granite with each strike of the hammer. Once it was suitably squared off, they drew a chalk outline to show the necessary

Workmen in front of the Salt Lake Temple.

dimensions, and the stonecutters would chisel it to size. For stones set in the walls above ground level in later years, the men would then use smaller chisels to take off less granite until the stone face was as smooth as they could make it. If the stone needed a design inscribed on it—stars or other visual elements—the stonecutters would use a heavy-point drill to cut the deeper parts and again take up the small chisel to smooth out the decoration.[69] But stonecutting was more art than science, and the men who practiced the craft were free to work their stones in whatever way they thought necessary, using whichever tools they thought proper, so long as the final stone was the right size and shape and of acceptable quality. It could take a month to prepare a stone, but the results justified the time required. The stones in the temple walls today feel as smooth as if cut by a saw in most places.[70]

Folsom oversaw the marking of each finished block with numbers or letters in paint to indicate its position in the course.[71] The masons had built a series of derricks equipped with blocks and tackle to move the marked stones into position down the line of the course, one after another. Altogether, they had organized the entire process in a system that was really quite simple and would enable constant, if slow, progress.

The vagaries of the weather notwithstanding, they finally arrived at a point that no one present at the groundbreaking in 1853 had imagined would require a decade of work and reversals to reach. There were no parades this time, no gatherings, no speeches when the day came, but sometime near the close of the year, the walls of the temple *finally* reached ground level. That was no small accomplishment, given that the trenches were sixteen feet deep. A passerby standing at a distance on the street, looking through the openings in the wall around the block, could finally see granite stones rising up from the foundation trenches.

—————•••—————

Besides marking the finished blocks for placement and drawing up Bills of Stone, Folsom really had little to do on the temple project—Truman had finished the architectural designs for the most part before retiring to pursue a career in sugarcane farming. That was fortunate, as Folsom was then able to spend time working with Henry Grow on the new Tabernacle. What was unfortunate was the two men's partnership, or rather their lack of one. Folsom had overseen the initial construction of the Tabernacle's foundation and pilasters, but the men had some kind of falling-out between 1864 and 1865. Construction ground to a halt, due at least in part to their inability to cooperate, with the result that Brigham replaced Folsom with Grow as the construction supervisor. Grow's daughter, Nellie, wrote years later that Folsom couldn't leave the project alone; he stood around the site making derogatory comments and predicting the building's inevitable collapse. Grow finally asked Brigham to order Folsom to stay away, and the prophet apparently complied with the request.[72]

With the field clear of interference, Grow finished the new Tabernacle in three years at a final cost of $300,000. The intricate latticed roof had required 1.6 million board feet of lumber to assemble and was covered by 350,000 shingles. Assembling that had required the services of many tradesmen and teamsters and a significant amount of the Church's available funds. Brigham had not wanted the Tabernacle to draw away resources from the temple construction, but whether they were able to manage that is hard to judge. With both skilled laborers and money in short supply, devoting both to the new Tabernacle could easily have siphoned away some resources from the temple's construction effort. But even if it did, the temple was proceeding so slowly that an observer hardly could have noticed any impact.

When it was finished, the new facility was impressive. It was a unique structure, an innovation in architecture and engineering and far more striking than the old Adobe Tabernacle. It was also the largest meeting hall in the territory and would remain so for decades. After pews were installed, the new Tabernacle could seat 7,500 people, three times the capacity of its predecessor—and, as desired, it had no interior supports or columns to block the view of the rostrum.

The building met all of Brigham's initial design criteria except one: its acoustics were terrible. Brigham himself tested them, standing at the pulpit and speaking with his face turned toward various sections of the hall to see whether an audience would be able to hear him clearly. The results were not promising. In some areas the audience could hardly hear anything; in others it was an echo chamber where any noise—from the speaker's voice to the shuffling of feet—was magnified and muddled with other sounds in the building. The acoustics improved as the number of people in the building rose; the bodies of the audience members deadened the echoes. But even then, the congregation had to sit entirely still so the speaker's voice would be the loudest noise in the entire cavernous hall. That was a difficult task, especially on hot days when speakers might drone on for hours at a time, as was the norm during the era. It was a disappointing performance for the edifice. However, in his desire to accommodate as many people as possible inside the Tabernacle, Brigham had requested balcony seating around the interior perimeter, starting and ending on either side of the rostrum. Those went up and, when the first public meeting was held after the gallery's completion, the Saints filled the hall. And to everyone's delight, the acoustics were vastly improved. The echoes had been virtually eliminated but the speaker could still be clearly heard throughout the building.

Brigham's design demands had finally been met in every particular but one—the new Tabernacle was not large enough to seat every Saint in the city who wanted to attend a session of general conference to hear the prophet. That goal was too ambitious from the start for any architect to have achieved it, but what they had constructed was a masterpiece that would became nearly as iconic a fixture on the Salt Lake City skyline over the years as the temple itself.

Folsom's frustration with his removal from the Tabernacle project led to another of the turning points in 1867. The two largest building efforts in the Church—and in the territory, for that matter—were taking place within a hundred yards of each other, and there was nothing creative for him to do on either one. He'd been banished outright from the Tabernacle site, and he was more of an overseer on the temple than an architect, just marking stones for placement according to Truman's design. He was also a member of the Salt Lake City Stake high council, an ecclesiastical position, and he was a partner in a separate business. In short, he felt underutilized by the Church, and there were considerable demands on his time elsewhere. So Folsom asked to be released from his duties as Church architect, the task at which he was making the least difference.

Brigham had removed Folsom from the Tabernacle's construction to keep the peace, but he didn't want to lose the man's talents. The number of skilled architects to which the Church had access was not large, and Folsom was the most skilled of the lot—almost certainly the most highly trained architect the Church had ever had, in fact. He was easily as talented as either William Weeks or Truman Angell had ever been, and Henry Grow was a bridge builder, not an architect. It was unproven whether Grow could build anything that wasn't based on a Remington lattice. But Brigham couldn't ask Folsom to just swallow his grievances and stay on in his present job without alienating him further.

After some thought and discussion, Brigham hit on a two-part solution. The first step was to ask Truman Angell to come back and take over as the Church architect again. Truman's career as a sugarcane farmer had been short-lived. He'd found it enjoyable for a couple of years, but then his physical health had given out on him again. "My health so left me that I resigned to W[illiam] H. Folsom and went out on my farm and here the parts of my body that was not called into use in the designing room was put into use on the farm and for one or [two] years it seemed to do me good but alas I found I must stop," he recorded.[73] The cold weather always knocked him down, it seemed, and he considered relocating farther south. He decided against it and, after a period of recuperation and pondering, "came to the conclusion [he] would try joiner work on the new Tabernacle."[74] He was hired and joined the carpenters laboring under Henry Grow.

Truman's old trade agreed with him, and by the end of the project he was responsible for preparing the Tabernacle's interior. But exactly why he thought carpentry might be any easier on his health than farming is a mystery, and the result was predictable. "The cold day[s] of late fall sent me from this back to the farm here. I stayed till spring or April conference some [five] months and did not do a day's work."[75] It was at that point that Brigham approached Truman and asked him to take on his old job as the Church architect. It was logical, in retrospect. If Brigham was going to let William Folsom walk away, he would need another skilled architect to take the job, and he wanted one willing to defer to the prophet's judgment when necessary, especially when it came to the temple. Brigham could count on one finger the number of men in the territory who met both those criteria.

Truman did not immediately say yes. He'd left the job once for good reason and had no obvious expectation that it would be any less a burden on him and his health than it had been the first time. But Brigham's

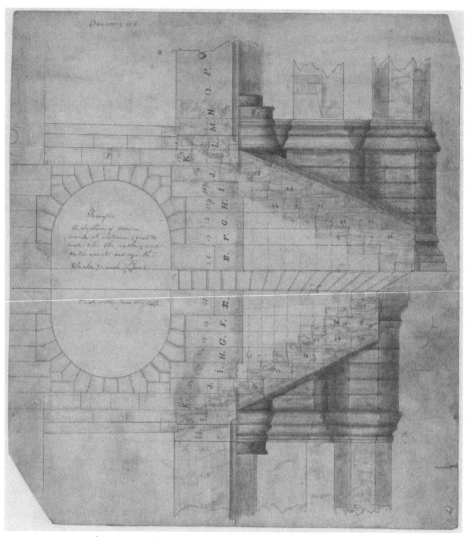

One of Truman Angell's sketches for the temple's east and west entrance stairs.
The alphabetical labels to the left mark each of the stone "courses."

requests always carried great weight with him. Truman's esteem and deeply held respect for the prophet was second to none. So, after a brief period of consideration, he told Brigham, "If you do wish me to apply myself again to the Architect's calling I will do so with all my might. You said to me at that time you would let me do about as I pleased; I shall make it my duty to always give heed to your will and sound counsel, and therefore let it rest as you please."[76] The calling thus accepted, Truman was sustained as the Church architect at the next general conference in April, and he was again responsible for managing the temple's construction. Truman's own son, Truman Angell Jr., was sustained as an assistant architect as well. Despite appearances, that calling was no act of mere nepotism. Truman Jr. was an able draftsman and promising architect in his own right and would be able to shoulder his fair share of the work.

The second step in Brigham's solution was to keep Folsom on as another assistant architect. The prophet probably made the request in part to keep Folsom's talents available to the Church and in part to lighten Truman's load and thus prevent his health from breaking under the strain as it had before. Folsom agreed. It was, perhaps, not an entirely unselfish act. In accepting the demotion, Folsom surely recognized that Truman had an emotional investment in completing the temple and so would readily take on the responsibilities there. Also, with Truman back in charge, Folsom would not have to interact with Henry Grow in any way on the Tabernacle project. With those off his plate, Folsom would be free to take on other projects. None of them would garner anything like the same level of attention as the two projects on the temple block, but that was the very reason he could have more creative freedom with less oversight from Brigham and other Church leaders. He would trade prestige for autonomy, and that was apparently worth the exchange. Folsom was sustained at the same general conference in April as Truman's assistant.

———— ◆ · · ◆ ————

The most significant development of 1868 was one that came from the outside and for which the Saints, including Brigham, had been clamoring almost since they'd first entered the valley. For twenty years, everything and everyone that moved in, through, and out of the Utah territory did so by pure muscle power. Every wagon and handcart was pulled by men, horses, mules, or oxen, and things moved no faster than man or beast could walk or run. That placed a limit on how quickly cities, settlements, and the temple itself could grow, and how much commerce the Saints could carry on with each other and the rest of the country. Their first serious attempt to build an alternate transportation system—the wooden railroad to Red Butte Quarry—had proven both dangerous and ultimately unnecessary for its primary purpose of hauling stone to the city. Their second attempt—the canal—had fallen far short of expectations when the entire effort had far exceeded the costs in time, money, and labor that Brigham had first calculated.

But in 1868, two companies were converging on Utah, bringing another mode of transportation that promised to render oxen and canal barges obsolete for transporting heavy cargo. Those two companies were the Union Pacific and Central Pacific Railroads.

CHAPTER 8

THE WHISTLE
AND THE PUFFING OF
THE IRON HORSE

The United States had already laid some 31,000 miles of railroad track by the time the Civil War began, more than all the railroad lines in the rest of the world's nations combined. Trains could carry cargo for fifteen cents per ton-mile regardless of weather or season, which caused the prices of some commodities to drop by an order of magnitude during the 1850s as the amount of track laid down in the Eastern states tripled. The cost of a passenger's ticket depended on distance, but averaged less than three cents a mile. Those fares made longer trips too expensive for the average person, but those who could afford the ticket could travel thirty miles an hour and reach Chicago from New York City in two days.[1] For anyone looking farther west, a train could carry a traveler as far as Iowa or Texas. As the steel ribbons of the railways spread out in that direction, access to the train network became the key to economic survival for towns on the frontier. Those near a rail line prospered, and those far away withered. The benefits were so apparent that even the War Between the States had not stopped the growth of the railroad, at least in the North—Union troops destroyed a significant amount of the Confederacy's rail capacity. The Union held a two-to-one advantage in railway mileage over its opponent, and the ability to quickly move men and supplies to more places in larger quantities helped carry the nation to victory in a very real way.

Abraham Lincoln had foreseen other purposes for the railroad beyond military movement and economic growth. The railroad, he thought, could connect the nation not just physically but also politically. The Confederacy hoped that some of the Western states might join its cause—including, perhaps, Utah. Indeed, given the Saints' past clashes with federal officials, many in Washington feared that Brigham would gladly seize the opportunity to throw off the federal yoke and either join the rebellion or outright declare Utah an independent nation of its own. Brigham's telegram stating that "Utah has not seceded, but is firm for the Constitution and laws of our once happy country"[2] did not entirely dispel those worries. In the midst of the Civil War, where North and South were divided, the sixteenth president had thought that starting a project to connect East and West by rail might be a "means of keeping the Pacific coast in the Union," as well as Utah, Nevada, and other territories, and of healing the divides once the war ended.[3] So on July 5, 1862, Lincoln had signed the Pacific Railroad Act and initiated the great enterprise to connect the two coasts of the United States by train.

That act, and four subsequent public laws, authorized the creation of two companies specially empowered by the government to build a single rail line across the continent. Before the war, the Northern and Southern States each obviously favored a transcontinental route through their own regions, but secession had settled that question.[4] The Union Pacific Railroad Company would start at Omaha, Nebraska, and lay track westward, while the Central Pacific Railroad Company would start at Sacramento, California, and work eastward. Money was no object. Each company would receive a thirty-year government loan to fund its operations, with the amounts calculated according to terrain—$16,000 per mile across the plains, $48,000 per mile through mountainous regions, and $32,000 per mile through the Great Basin between the Sierra Nevadas and the Wasatch Range. The companies could issue first-mortgage bonds at 6 percent interest to generate the funds, and the government would honor them up to the total amount of the final loan. In essence, the US government gave the Union Pacific and the Central Pacific the right to print their own money.[5] And the two companies would race each other to accrue the rewards promised by the act, which were enormous. Each company was promised 500 feet of public land extending out from both sides of the rail line, and an additional ten square miles of land for every mile of track they laid. The final amount they received together was in excess of 175 *million* acres, only slightly less than the area covered by Utah, Idaho, and Nevada combined.

The Central Pacific, led by Theodore Judah, a railroad engineer, started work on January 8, 1863, just a little more than six months after Lincoln signed the Pacific Railroad Act. Judah was from Connecticut, the son of an Episcopal pastor, and an exceptional student who enrolled at age twelve in the Troy School of Technology, the forerunner of the Rensselaer Polytechnic Institute (which would later give the Saints another architect to direct the work on the Lord's house). He was there for only eighteen months before the death of his father forced him to return home to help support his family, but while at the school he learned the basic principles of engineering railroads. He made them his life's work and helped build many in New England before the proposal to build the first transcontinental railroad was made.

The Union Pacific effort was managed largely by Dr. Thomas C. Durant, the company's largest shareholder. His ownership stake enabled him to act as a Union Pacific vice president, chief executive, financial agent, and business manager all at the same time. Durant had been born into a wealthy Massachusetts family in 1820 and had graduated cum laude from Albany Medical College at the age of twenty, but he left the field of medicine quite early on after finding the pursuit of profit to be far more satisfying. At the time Lincoln signed the Pacific Railroad Act, Durant was forty-two and had morphed into "a lean and reckless engulf-and-devour shark of a speculator"[6] with a taste for extravagant living and a willingness to cheat anyone, including his friends. His unethical methodology garnered him considerable wealth and power—the *Omaha Herald* once called him the "Napoleon of railways"[7]—but much of it caught up with him in time. By the time the transcontinental railroad was finished, Durant was accused of multiple counts of fraud and bribery, most of which were true, and he was ultimately fired from the Union Pacific by then-president Ulysses S. Grant. He didn't go to jail, but he lost most of his wealth in the financial panic of 1873 and spent the rest of his life defending his interests from lawsuits brought by creditors and investors.

The Union Pacific did not start laying track until July 1865, three months after Robert E. Lee's surrender to Grant at Appomattox. However, the Union Pacific was able to work at a faster pace than its rival, courtesy of the flatter terrain of the Midwest and the ability to bring supplies quickly from the East by way of the very rail line that its workers were laying down. The Central Pacific was starting from the West Coast, which lacked the industrial capacity to manufacture all of the necessary supplies in quantity. The rails, ties, and other materials had to be shipped by sea from the East Coast and either carried around Tierra del Fuego or laid ashore at the Isthmus of Panama and moved overland and reloaded on another vessel to continue the journey. Either way, the cargo had to be unloaded at the San Francisco dockyards and moved to Sacramento before it could be loaded onto trains and shipped ahead to the end of the line. The Tierra del Fuego route took almost a year, the Panama route somewhat but not much less, and no matter which route the company chose, any delays in the shipping were not easily remedied. So Durant and the Union Pacific working westward outpaced the Central Pacific eastward effort by a significant rate. By the end of 1866, eighteen months after it had finally broken ground, the Union Pacific line had laid 300 miles of track, reaching as far as North Platte, Nebraska. In the coming year they would reach Cheyenne, Wyoming. After that, the Utah Territory and the Wasatch Range sat waiting. The work crews would be slowed down almost to a halt very nearly at the same time the Central Pacific was getting ready to break out of the Sierra Nevadas, when it would accelerate its efforts and move quickly across Utah to reach Promontory Summit, or perhaps Salt Lake or Ogden, before its rival. If Thomas Durant and his partners didn't want work crews to slow down almost to a halt, they would need more men to throw into the canyons there. There was, of course, only one person in Utah who could mobilize so many workers. The Union Pacific needed Brigham Young.

— · · · —

The Church's enemies were quite certain that the arrival of the railroad in Utah would be a disaster for the Saints' religion generally and Brigham in particular. Opening up a rail line to the East, they thought, would weaken Brigham's influence over the Saints by freeing them from any dependence on the Church for news or resources. That belief was so common that George Q. Cannon, a member of the Quorum of the Twelve, addressed it in general conference. "We are told—openly and without disguise, that when the railroad is completed there will be such a flood of so-called 'civilization' brought in here that every vestige of us, our church and institutions shall be completely obliterated," he said.[8] Cannon was not putting words in the critics' mouth. Quoting one of the newspapers of the day verbatim, he read an editorial that declared:

> The Salt Lake basin is a rich oasis in which nature has lavishly congregated all that is needed at the Halfway Point on the great National highway, the Pacific Railroad, and it all belongs to the citizens of the United States, and not to Brigham and his crew. . . . Hitherto this Territory has only been of interest to the people of the United States because of the infamous establishment [The Church of Jesus Christ of Latter-day Saints] sought to be up in it in the sacred name of religion, and the motor of warfare against the gross outrage has been alone the moral sense of the country, but now . . . a commercial interest is added, and the two together

will as surely as truth is truth, and right is right, crush out the vile thing and rid the country of the foul blot, peaceably if possible, but with a besom of destruction if that is inevitable. . . . This force only awaits the opportunity that the railroad will give it.[9]

Whoever wrote the editorial did not know Brigham's mind. He is reputed to have dismissed the notion that the railroad would destroy the Church with the retort that "[ours] must, indeed, be a . . . poor religion, if it cannot stand one railroad."[10] No one disputed that the railroad would bring negative influences to the territory that would challenge the religious society the Saints had been trying to establish, but even Brigham thought the benefits outweighed the cost. So he and the rest of the Saints had been anxiously awaiting the day when the railroad would reach deep into the West, and it couldn't arrive too soon, so far as they were concerned.

It was simply a given that a railroad would build the economy. The ability to ship goods and raw materials quickly and in quantity to and from the East would bring labor, raw materials, and luxury goods to the territory at rates and prices that were simply impossible by wagon train; plus, the Saints and others would earn more profit from their own goods and materials sold far away. But commerce was not the reason Brigham wanted to see the railroad come. Quite the contrary: he had been calling on the Saints for years to become entirely self-sufficient. He wanted the kingdom of God to be completely independent, not needing outsiders for anything, whether food, clothing, or anything else. He certainly didn't want to see the Saints enriching outsiders instead of each other. He'd also discouraged the Saints from engaging in mining and other speculative activities that might have been very profitable in favor of building up manufacturing and industries that would produce needed goods, even if they were less profitable. So Brigham's reasons for wanting the railroad had little, if anything, to do with money. Instead, he saw it as a tool for expanding the Church in Utah and beyond in three ways.

The first was missionary work and Church administration. For years, missionaries called to serve anywhere outside Utah faced months of travel to reach their fields of labor. Those destined for the Eastern States could reach their mission areas in a few months by wagon; those trying to reach Europe or the Pacific faced that much travel just to get to an ocean port where they could board a ship. General Authorities of the Church visiting congregations and missions outside the territory faced the same difficulty. But the railroad would reduce those travel times to days. Missionaries and Church leaders could spend more time preaching and ministering and less time traveling, to say nothing of reducing the long separations away from their families. And once the railroad connected the East and the West, the Saints could run spurs north and south, connecting their own settlements. They would be able to travel from Great Salt Lake City to St. George and anywhere in between in a few hours any time of year, regardless of weather. Brigham and the rest of the leadership could visit with congregations far removed more often to strengthen their faith and help them feel united with the rest of the Church, despite their isolation.

Brigham's second reason for embracing the railroad was immigration. Converts from the Eastern United States and foreign countries were still coming to Utah in large numbers every year despite the time, cost, difficulties, and dangers of the journey. Travel costs for poor members and the Church's Perpetual Emigration Fund would be greatly reduced, as would the dangers of the trail. The railroad would put an end to wagon trains and eliminate the need to gather months' worth of rations and supplies for each person before setting out across the plains. There would be no more need to drive herds of cattle, which were always inviting targets for raids. Suffering and death from exposure would be over. The elderly and the infirm could come west, no longer blocked by the rigors of a journey that was a challenge for the young and healthy. And those Saints who did come could bring more of their own supplies and possessions to help them get established in the territory after they arrived, instead of having to depend on the Church to assist them. Anyone coming by wagon had faced weight and space restrictions on personal items; a train could haul any amount of personal luggage and equipment, limited only by what the passenger could pay.

The third motivation was one that Brigham had talked about on many occasions, perhaps more than the others. The prophet had been thinking about hauling stone for the temple by rail before Saints had turned the first spade of dirt for the Lord's house. "We cannot get the stone for the foundation without the railroad from this place to the quarry,"[11] he had told them in 1853 at the groundbreaking. As it turned out, that assessment had been overly pessimistic. John Sharp's Red Butte Quarry had been close enough, and the downward sloping road into the city sound enough, that wagons had been entirely sufficient to do the job. Brigham's claim was closer to the mark, though still not accurate, regarding the granite coming from Little Cottonwood Canyon. But his essential point was not lost on anyone, especially not on James Livingston, his stonecutters, or the teamsters. They were never going to move two-ton blocks quickly without trains, and no more explanation than that was needed. The railroad's superiority over wagons and oxen for moving heavy cargo like granite boulders was so obvious that no one was going to argue Brigham's essential point even though the teamsters had done well to move as much stone as they had.

When the Central Pacific and the Union Pacific finally reached out to Brigham, anyone who had been paying attention to the prophet's sermons over the previous fifteen years could hardly have been surprised when he readily talked with both companies about hiring the Saints to build the railroad. Only the Church's critics could have been flummoxed by that news, but they had never really paid honest attention to what Brigham had to say anyway.

—— ◆ · · ◆ ——

Both companies had been eyeing Utah for some time, and both knew that whichever one secured Brigham's cooperation would gain a major advantage over the other. The Saints in the Salt Lake Valley were the single largest reserve of manpower anywhere in the West, and whichever side they joined would be able to accelerate construction through the mountains. So each company maneuvered to win Brigham's support for its side. Charles Crocker, one of the Central Pacific's principal investors, dispatched a colleague to Great Salt Lake City to conduct some "quiet political reconnaissance" on the Union Pacific's attempts to woo the prophet, and what kind of reception Brigham was giving their representative, Grenville Dodge. The report came back that Dodge had been delayed in Wyoming and had not met with Brigham.[12]

What the Central Pacific did not know was that its rival was moving on more than one front to secure Brigham's support, and they had an ally in one of the prophet's sons. That same month of July, Brigham Young Jr. was traveling through Chicago on his way home to the Salt Lake Valley when he learned that several officers of the Union Pacific were in the city and preparing to ride the line under construction to its current terminus in North Platte. Acting on that intelligence, Brigham Jr. made the acquaintance of Sidney Dillon, "one of the chief directors" of the group. Dillon recognized the opportunity that had presented itself and invited Brigham Jr. to ride with his party, which included US Senator John Sherman and Ohio Governor Jacob Cox. The prophet's son accepted the offer and soon found himself and his family traveling by rail in a train car that was "most elegantly fitted up." Neither man gave up the chance to talk business. "They were anxious to awaken a real interest in the minds of our people to push this railroad through our Territory," Brigham Jr. reported.[13] They must have been pleased to hear that the interest was already there, and Dillon moved the business courtship forward another step, asking whether the Saints might be willing to partner with the Union Pacific "in laying out the U.P.R.R. and building the road."[14] The young man was equally interested and was sure his father would be also. "We shall be able to make contracts which will enable our emigration to make the entire journey from New York to Cheyenne without changing cars more than once or twice."[15] That may have been true at the time, but eventually he would be wrong on that point. Saints emigrating from Europe eventually would be able to get off the boat at New York City and make the entire journey straight to the Salt Lake Valley by rail. Many would still need the help of the Perpetual Emigration Fund to buy their tickets, but paying to ride a few days on a train was still far cheaper than outfitting a wagon with supplies for a few months on the trail.

However, there was one problem as far as Brigham Sr. was concerned. The planned route for the Union Pacific line ran westward into Echo Canyon for thirty winding miles, and then could take one of two forks. The northwestern path would run the line through Weber Canyon, exit the mountains at Ogden, thirty-seven miles north of Great Salt Lake City, and curve around the northern end of the Great Salt Lake. The southern path would take the track down Emigration Canyon and enter Great Salt Lake City itself, then pass around the southern end of the lake. Brigham much preferred the latter course, and he said so publicly in no uncertain terms. He wanted to see the line come right into Utah's largest city, and, he noted, it would be far easier to lay track in Emigration Canyon. Weber Canyon was a narrow passage full of "endless tumbled boulders" and hard-to-navigate rock formations such as Devil's Gate, a large split gorge through which ran the Weber River. Despite those challenges, both the Union Pacific and the Central Pacific rejected the Emigration Canyon route. On that point, both companies and their engineers and surveyors were united. All of the terrain east of Great Salt Lake City and south of the lake itself was "a morass of sinkholes and mudflats."[16] Shoring up the ground to make it solid enough to support a railroad would have required even more labor and resources than the work crews would need to cut their way through Weber Canyon. So whichever company reached the area first was going to take the path of least resistance—the northern Echo Canyon-to-Weber Canyon route to Ogden—and all of Brigham's attempts to persuade the builders of the railroad otherwise would come to naught.

That disagreement alone did not put Brigham off the enterprise. The benefits were too great for him to ignore, no matter what route the train took through the Wasatch Mountains. So when Durant extended the offer of a contract to Brigham the following year in May, he took the deal. Under the terms, the Saints would be responsible for "all the grading and masonry on that part of the Union Pacific Rail Road between the heavy work at the head of Echo Canyon and the Salt Lake Valley at or near the mouth of the canyon in the valley of the Weber river, being a distance of about fifty-four miles."[17] The fee that the Union Pacific would pay depended on the types of earth excavated and removed—plain earth was worth only fifty cents per cubic yard, granite was eight times that amount, and anytime they had to cut a tunnel, the price rose to an astonishing fifteen dollars for the same volume of material. Durant's company would also be responsible for providing the Saints with "teams and tools for the work; also, to furnish . . . powder and fuse, steel for drills, shovels, picks, sledges, wheelbarrows, scrapers, crow bars, derrick irons, and such other tools" at cost.[18] Laborers would earn the daily wage of three dollars. To further sweeten the deal, Durant agreed to let members of the Church designated by Brigham travel the Union Pacific railroad at the same reduced price that construction contractors were paying. The cost to European Saints emigrating to the Salt Lake Valley for the duration would be cheaper than for a regular US citizen traveling west on the same train for any reason.

Work preparing the road for the track laying had to begin within ten days of the contract's signing and be completed by November 1, 1868, a little less than six months. Thomas Durant wanted the Union Pacific crews and subcontractors to lay a backbreaking total of 700 miles of track by August—to essentially do in four months what had previously required eight—and push on to the eastern slopes of the Sierra Nevadas. The goal was a site called Humboldt Wells, in today's northeastern Nevada. The Central Pacific was moving at a snail's pace through the mountains, so if the Union Pacific could achieve its goal, it would rob its rival of the chance to break out into open territory, accelerate toward the Salt Lake Valley, and seize easy rewards. Grenville Dodge warned Durant that pushing that hard would cost the Union Pacific an additional ten million dollars just to reach Ogden. Durant told him to ignore the expense. The value of the land the company would receive in return would easily be worth that amount.[19]

Brigham signed the contract on May 21, with Samuel B. Reed, the Union Pacific superintendent of construction, signing for the company. The prophet was delighted by the opportunity. The entire nation had been suffering an economic recession since the Civil War's conclusion, and many of the Saints were struggling to support themselves. The US government had been a free spender during the war but had tightened its belt after, and now serious deflation had set in. The Saints and everyone else in the territory were now short on cash, but they had a surplus of available labor. So to have the Union Pacific come in with its near-bottomless pockets, ready to hire every man who could wield a shovel and pay almost unlimited amounts of money for as much earth and rock as the Saints could move, was as much a divine blessing as Brigham could have hoped for.

> This contract is viewed by the brethren of understanding as a God-send. There is much indebtedness among the people, and the Territory is drained of money, but labor here and coming we have in large amount, and this contract affords opportunity for turning that labor into money, with which those here can pay each other and import needed machinery, and such useful articles as we cannot yet produce, and those coming can pay their indebtedness, and have ready means with which to begin to gather around them the comforts of life in their new homes.[20]

To complete the contract on time, Brigham would need all the workers he could get. A group of civic leaders proposed a mass meeting to unify the public behind the effort, and Brigham agreed. As the new Tabernacle was the largest meeting hall in the valley, he offered it up for the assembly, which took place on June 10. Thousands came, "representing every class of . . . citizens; and the most prominent names in the Territory were among the audience or on the Stand."[21] A committee planned to submit resolutions to the audience for a vote whether to support the project, but that seemed to be a mere formality. Enthusiasm was high, and the people needed no convincing. Brigham was speaking for the crowd when he told them he wanted "to hear the whistle, and the puffing of the iron horse every evening and through the night, in the morning and through the day."[22] Agreeing with the prophet, several of the Apostles, including Elders John Taylor and George A. Smith, addressed the public notion that the Saints did not want the railroad to come. "It has been thought and charged by some that we are averse to improvements, and that we disliked the approach of the railroad. Never was a greater mistake [made]," Taylor announced. "We have always been the advocates of improvement, of the arts, science, literature, and general progress . . . we are always first and foremost in everything that tends to ennoble and exalt mankind."[23]

Daniel H. Wells, who was the mayor of Great Salt Lake City among his many other occupations, presented the resolutions, asking those present to declare that "Utah welcomes to her borders the coming Railroad, and hails with pleasure closer contact and more intimate relations with her friends east and west," and "that every advancement in civilization and enterprise will always and at all times receive a helping and friendly hand from the people of Utah."[24] The vote in favor was unanimous.

——— • · • ———

Heber C. Kimball attended the meeting but did not speak. He was feeling ill and complained of "dizziness, and torpidity of his right side; he attributed the feeling to rheumatism, with which he was sometimes affected."[25] His health declined rapidly, and within two days he was confined to his bed, unable to move the right side of his body. He soon could not speak despite being conscious of everyone and everything around him. "When his particular friends called upon him, especially Presidents Young and Wells, he seemed to arouse himself to speak, and by the pressure of their hands and the beaming of his countenance, would signify his pleasure at seeing them," an observer wrote.[26] But he continued to fail until, on June 22, he fell unconscious as though going to sleep, and soon passed away. Brigham's oldest and closest friend, his counselor in the First Presidency for twenty-four years, and the man who had joined him in their conversion to the faith when they were still young men, was gone.

Flags flew in the city at half-mast and the Salt Lake Theater went dark in respect for Kimball's passing. Mayor Wells directed that all businesses in the city should close on the day of the funeral, which was held in the Tabernacle. Looking down at his friend's casket from the podium, Brigham struggled to speak. "What can we say to one another?" he asked the audience. "Live as he [Heber C. Kimball] has lived; be as faithful as he has been; be as full of good works as his life has manifested to us. If we do so, our end will be peace and joy, and we will fall asleep as peacefully."[27]

———•——•——•———

After Heber was laid to rest, Brigham renewed the call for every available man to come forward to work on the railroad. That included the men laboring at the temple site. The greatest contribution they could make would be to the north. That would halt construction on the house of the Lord, but once they were done, the railroad would allow them to make up for lost time and then some. When all of Utah's major settlements were connected by the "iron horse," and the Little Cottonwood Canyon quarry connected to the temple site by its own spur, the days of hauling stone by wagon and oxen would be over. On that day, the stonecutters would start receiving temple granite faster than they could handle it.

Four thousand men responded to the prophet's call. They were organized and sent north . . . where many of them sat waiting with nothing to do—or, more specifically, nothing with which to do their labor. The Union Pacific had stockpiled immense quantities of tools, rails, wooden ties, and other supplies at Cheyenne, but was slow in delivering any of it to the men waiting in Utah. When August came, many of the men were still waiting for equipment, and some finally went home in frustration. Infighting among the company's senior personnel had snarled up the shipments of supplies, and it took some personal intervention by retired General Ulysses S. Grant, by then the Republican candidate for president and favorite to win, and William Tecumseh Sherman, soon to be the commanding general of the US Army, to quash the bickering and untie the logistical knot. Even Durant, corrupt and scheming, had to back down in the face of Grant's thinly veiled orders. The problem now solved, the tools and supplies finally reached the end of the line, and the Saints went to work laying rail.

The process of building a railroad track was deceptively simple. Surveyors led the way to locate the most desirable routes, which they marked on maps and on the ground with stakes. Following behind came the grading crew. These were men armed mostly with shovels, pickaxes, and wheelbarrows whose job was to create a raised, level bed of earth on a straight line, filling in swales and leveling ridges as needed. If the grade of the earth was too steep, they made a cut through it. Where a river or a deep valley cut across the path, they constructed a bridge or viaduct over it. If they came to a forest, the men became lumberjacks, felling and hauling trees and using black powder to blow the stumps out of the ground. During the winter, many of them just shoveled snow so others could get to the frozen ground with their tools. It was as hard a job as any in building a railroad.

The track-laying crew followed behind, with supplies carried forward on cars riding the newly laid rail line itself. Wooden ties that had been "burnetized"—weatherproofed with zinc chloride—were laid perpendicular to the direction of the rail bed. Each tie was eight feet long, eight inches wide, and six inches deep, and each cost about two dollars and fifty cents when there was no shortage of supply. As those were being placed, a team of four men used metal "nippers" to retrieve a rail from the supply car. Each rail weighed 560 pounds and was twenty-six feet long. Once the new rail was set in place, men would connect it with the previous beam with a "fishplate" fastener, which was a metal bar bolted to the sides of the rails at the ends to fix them together. Then the new rail was spiked down to the tie. The process was repeated simultaneously on the other side, with a man responsible to make sure the two ties met the "standard gauge" spacing of precisely four feet, eight and one-half inches apart. On average, laying a single mile of track required about 400 rails, 2,500 ties, and 4,000 spikes.[28]

The men could finish between one and three miles of track each day, and averaged two—but they could lay more if the materials arrived in a timely fashion and the weather cooperated. And following behind the entire army of railroad workers were government inspectors. The federal officers checked every single mile to ensure that, in the race for profit, neither company was engaged in engineering malpractice that might endanger some future train filled with passengers. When the inspectors confirmed that each section met the required specifications, they "accepted" it on behalf of the government and certified that the company was due its reward.

By the time the Union Pacific reached Utah, its crews had practiced the processes of grading and track laying until the men functioned as a single machine. As one reporter described it:

> The track laying on the Union Pacific was a science. . . . A light car, drawn by a single horse, gallops up to the front with its load of rails. Two men seize the end of a rail and start forward, the rest of the gang taking hold by twos, until it is clear of the car. They come forward at a run. At the word of command the rail is dropped in its place, right side up with care, while the same process goes on at the other side of the car. Less than thirty seconds to a rail, and so four rails go down to the minute. The moment the car is empty it

is tipped over on the side of the track to let the next loaded car pass it, and then it is tipped back again, and it is a sight to see it go flying back for another load, propelled by a horse at full gallop at the end of sixty or eighty feet of rope. Close behind the first gang come the gaugers, spikers and bolters, and a lively time they make of it. It is a grand 'Anvil Chorus' that those sturdy sledges are playing across the plains. It is in triple time, three strokes to the spike . . . ten spikes to a rail, four hundred rails to a mile. . . . Twenty-one million times are those sledges to be swung . . . before the great work of modern America is complete.[29]

The Saints worked on both the grading and track-laying crews and themselves mastered the basic processes of building railways. It was experience that they would soon put to use building their own north-south line from Ogden all the way to the southern settlements, with spurs running off east and west as needed. It was grueling labor, but the Saints had never shied away from hard work, and once they saw what they were to do, they were able to keep pace with the gentile crews. The Union Pacific's own teams were accustomed to working seven days a week, often as much as sixteen hours a day. The company demanded that the Saints keep the same schedule, which meant working on the Sabbath— taking an entire day off was unacceptable in this race. The Saints resisted, then finally agreed, but demanded that the Union Pacific pay them double for doing so.[30] To keep their morale up, the Union Pacific's Irish crews would sing chanteys whose lyrics were not always fit to print. But as company officials entered Echo Canyon, they found the Saints singing their own work songs, which carried a very different message.

> *At the head of great Echo the railway's begun,*
> *The Mormons are cutting and grading like fun;*
> *They say they'll stick to it until it's complete—*
> *When friends and relations they're hoping to meet.*
>
> *Hurrah, hurrah, the railroad's begun,*
> *Three cheers for the contractor; his name's Brigham Young.*

Hurrah, hurrah, we're honest and true,
And if we stick to it, it's bound to go through.

Now there's Mr. Reed, he's a gentleman too—
He knows very well what the Mormons can do.
He knows they will earn every cent of their pay,
And are just the right boys to construct a railway.[31]

Aside from the work of the grading and track-laying teams, there were some stretches of the surveyed passage through Echo and Weber Canyons that required a more specific set of skills to prepare. The chosen route passed through some narrow passes with steep cliffs, and the only way to get a train through the mountains in those places would be to drive it, quite literally, *through* the mountains. The Saints needed to cut some tunnels through the Wasatch Range. It was fortunate, then, that Brigham had a group of men possessed of the specific skills to carve up mountains.

＋　·　·　＋

"In the year 1868, I went with about one hundred men and started grading for the Union Pacific Railroad at Devil Gate in Weber Canyon," James Livingston wrote in his autobiography in his usual terse style. He set up the quarrymen in four camps of twenty men each to work on several sections of the rail bed simultaneously, and then took the remainder to Lost Creek, where a pair of tunnels needed to be cut.[32] It was, by far, the most dangerous part of building any railroad. The days of men hollowing out a path through a mountain with nothing more than hammers, chisels, and pickaxes were gone. Using nothing but tools and human effort, the workers could barely move forward a foot per day, depending on the kind of stone they had to auger out of the mountainside. At that rate, cutting a tunnel could take years. The method James Livingston and his stonecutters had employed of splitting stone with slips and wedge offered no improvement in speed, assuming it could even work in places where the "boulders" they were splitting were the mountains themselves. This was a race between two companies for unfathomable financial profits, and the men in charge wanted a faster way. Explosives were the order of the day.

Black powder was the first choice. The workers would cut foot-deep holes in the rock—which could take a day by itself—then fill them with the black powder and set them off. But the powder wasn't terribly powerful, and progress remained slow, so the railroad companies turned to a newer explosive with more destructive power. An Italian chemist had invented nitroglycerin twenty years before, but it was such a dangerous compound to handle that a number of countries had banned its transport through their territories, much less its use for any constructive purpose. Alfred Nobel had experimented with ways to stabilize the notoriously touchy explosive after an accident with it killed his younger brother and several other men. He had finally developed a stable version called "dynamite" in 1867, but it wasn't yet in wide use in the United States. So nitroglycerin was still the only real option for the two companies building the railroad across America.

The Central Pacific Railroad experimented with the explosive while trying to cut its tunnels through the Sierra Nevadas. It proved to be a far more effective tool for cutting through mountains than a pickaxe or a sledge, even if using the chemical virtually guaranteed that some workers would be lost in the process. That was not considered a showstopper. Most of the Central Pacific's labor force were Chinese immigrants, 10,000 brought over from their homeland through the port of San Francisco, and their lives were held cheap, so the company pushed ahead using the explosive for a time. The Union Pacific couldn't allow its competitor to have any edge in the race and so had also taken up the use of nitroglycerin. It too would surely lose some workers, but its workforce was composed mostly of Irish immigrants and some former slaves, neither of which were held in any higher regard than the Central Pacific's Chinese workers. The company still had not abandoned the explosive when it hired the Saints to work, so the chemical was brought to the end of the line to help carve out the tunnels through Weber Canyon.

Livingston never recorded whether he'd favored its use or not. He had split enough sandstone and granite by hand over the previous fifteen years that he would have appreciated an easier way. He and his men certainly didn't go on strike to protest the nitroglycerin's use. But whether he was enthusiastic about using the chemical or not, Livingston was not the kind of man who left subordinates to do dangerous work that he wasn't willing to do himself. So he took charge of handling the explosive personally. "I used about eight tons of nitroglycerine, handled and exploded it myself individually," he recalled later.[33] For months he managed to use it safely, with no casualties, but the day finally arrived when Livingston's good fortune came to an abrupt end.

With the Central Pacific nearing the eastern side of the Sierra Nevadas, the Union Pacific was determined to work on through the winter to lay as much track as possible and maximize the government rewards. Money was no object, and so Livingston's team worked on through the cold winter months until they reached the mouth of Weber Canyon in February 1868. Livingston did not record exactly when or how it happened, but sometime after that February, the head of the temple quarry suffered a terrible accident. A container of nitroglycerin that Livingston was handling exploded, mangling one of the quarry foreman's limbs and driving shards from some nearby wood into his body.[34] "I had the misfortune to have my right hand and arm badly shattered by a blast," he said.[35] Without more detail, it is impossible to say how close Livingston was to the explosion, only that it either wasn't large enough or close enough to kill him. But any blast large enough to cripple his arm would have inflicted at least some of the kinds of injuries common to such events—burns, concussion, bone fractures, and damage to the eardrums from overpressure, leading to hearing loss and tinnitus.

Livingston's days working on the transcontinental railroad were over. His men evacuated him from Weber Canyon, and he was eventually carried home by wagon—there was no other way to transport an injured man—to his home to begin an extended convalescence. Livingston was not the most docile patient. His injuries were quite painful, and with no effective painkillers on hand, the crusty Scot resorted to some unsaintly profanity to relieve his suffering. Such cursing was unusual for him and out of place in the Livingston home, enough so that the salty language upset his grandmother, Christina.

"Oh Jimmy, I dinna like to hear you swear like that," she said, rebuking him.

The injured man replied, "Gran, don't you know that I can pray to God and He will give me five minutes to swear any time?"[36] Livingston replied. Given his injuries and the fact that he'd acquired them in response to the prophet's call, the quarry foreman apparently was sure that the Lord would forgive a little salty language.

Livingston's condition improved throughout 1869, but his arm did not, and he eventually decided that it needed amputation. The deed was done—whether he had access to a stronger painkiller than harsh language for the operation, he did not say—and Livingston was left without his right arm. There had been major advances in artificial limbs in recent years, given the number of soldiers who had lost limbs in the Civil War, so when it became known that the temple quarry foreman was now short one limb, well-wishers began sending him information about manmade replacements. "He was receiving so much literature setting forth the advantages of artificial limbs, that it almost made him feel that it ought to be an advantage to lose a limb in order to get one of the artificial ones," his nephew wrote. "I think he bought a hand and arm, but I do not recall that he ever used the hand. He had a hook on the end of the arm and it was a much more formidable means of defense than the hand would have been."[37] Livingston continued to act as an occasional lawman for years to come, and the hook would indeed have been useful in that line of work. The sight of Livingston, muscled from years of cutting stone, holding a revolver in one hand and wielding a metal hook for the other, might well have given rowdy criminals a reason to reconsider their careers.

The work on the railroad continued through the year while Livingston was recuperating at home. Progress was steady, but the greatest challenge turned out to be entirely man-made. The Union Pacific, whether through incompetence or Thomas Durant's chicanery, was slow to pay the Saints and others working to extend the end of the line. In fact, Brigham was paying many of them out of his own pocket so as to keep the work going. "A number of the men who have finished their jobs are anxious to get pay for their day's work. I should be pleased if in your next assessment you could include these items in your payment," Brigham wrote to one of the Union Pacific representatives on September 7. Two weeks later he was having to plead with the same executive for funds to pay salaries. Listing off several men by name who'd received no payment for services rendered for the last several months, Brigham noted that "the men are exceedingly anxious to get their pay for day work performed last June and since."[38] It was a constant refrain. As of October, the Union Pacific was $46,860 in arrears to Brigham alone for wages that the prophet had had to cover from his accounts so the Saints could continue laying the track.

As the year turned over and 1869 dawned, the financial situation only worsened. The Union Pacific sent no money in either January or February to pay the men, and Brigham pushed hard to get it. But the Union Pacific was behind in its payments, not just to Brigham but also to a number of other subcontractors, some of whom would file lawsuits that would take years to settle. In the end, Brigham sent Bishop John Sharp to Boston to negotiate with Durant and the Union Pacific's leadership for a settlement. The prophet never was paid the full amount he thought he was owed, which was $198,942.68, the amount that Sharp presented to the Union Pacific board. The number drew an open laugh from the executives, but Sharp was not amused.[39] He settled in, pushed back, and the negotiations went on for two months. In the end, Sharp settled for $70,000, half in cash, half in notes payable over three months.

As the financial troubles mounted, Brigham exhorted the Saints to stay at work. Finishing the railroad was worth any sacrifice. The crews stayed on the job, progress was relatively steady, and the railhead reached Ogden on March 7, 1869. With flags waving, a large crowd gathered to watch the first steam engine come into town, arriving around 2:30 in the afternoon. Elder Franklin D. Richards and Ogden's mayor, Lorin Farr, addressed the crowd. A band played "The Star-Spangled Banner." Utah was, for the first time, officially connected to the Eastern United States by rail.

From there, the Union Pacific work crews turned north, arcing the line slowly westward past the bays and inlets of the Great Salt Lake. Durant's goal of reaching the Sierra Nevadas before the Central Pacific could exit the mountains had been a failure. The rival company had passed Humboldt Wells some time before and was now in the Utah Territory. The race was almost over, and the rewards left to be seized were fast approaching zero. Both companies pushed as hard as they ever had to lay every last rail they could to grab what little territory was left. But having both come so far in opposite directions, it was ironic that the two rival companies struggled to decide where, precisely, to meet in the middle. While they had been separated by such a vast distance, the Union Pacific and the Central Pacific had been largely free to adjust the route as necessary every day to overcome whatever obstacles were in the way, so long as they didn't vary too far from the surveyed course. Now they had to come together at some point with, literally, no inches to spare—but no such point had ever been chosen, and they had graded a hundred miles of road *past* each other in parallel lines. That was unacceptable, but the decision of where to connect the rails would mean the gain or loss of hundreds of thousands of dollars.

Durant and his Central Pacific counterpart, Collis P. Huntington, were called to meet in Washington and negotiate a connecting point.

The two could hardly say no, and, surrounded by interested politicians and with now-President Ulysses S. Grant nearby, the failure to reach a compromise would be unacceptable. With all of that political attention and pressure brought to bear, Durant and Huntington settled on the place. Congress ratified their decision on April 10 with a joint resolution mandating that "the common terminus of the Union Pacific and the Central Pacific Railroads shall be at or near Ogden; and the Union Pacific Railroad Company shall build, and the Central Pacific Railroad Company shall pay for and own, the railroad from the terminus aforesaid to Promontory Point, at which point the rails shall meet and connect and form one continuous line."[40]

Both sides pushed ahead, and by the end of April, the Union Pacific was within fifteen miles of the meeting place. Durant's crews had laid more miles of track, courtesy of the flatlands it had enjoyed, as opposed to the Sierra Nevadas through which its rival had navigated. But the Central Pacific was determined to make one more stab at glory. Durant's men held the record for the most miles of track laid in a single day—eight. The Central Pacific announced on April 29 that the following day, it would lay ten—and so it did, with another 1,800 feet tacked on just to silence any naysayers. In one day, between the rails, the spikes, and the bolts and nuts, the crew laid down some two million pounds of iron. They took twelve hours to complete the job, but at their peak, the Central Pacific team was laying down one mile of track per hour.[41]

Both sides each had only a few more miles to go, and together they finished what was left on another day. They all reached Promontory Summit on May 1, but they didn't connect the rails for more than a week. Delegations of senior railroad company officers, journalists, and officials from distant states wanted to come out aboard the newly constructed railroad to witness the fusing of the continent together. So the two companies stopped short of the final point, short one pair of rails each. The transcontinental railroad—1,776 miles long—sat unfinished by a mere fifty-eight feet. To the east, it stretched back 1,086 miles to

Missouri. To the west, it covered 690 miles to Sacramento. When those last ties were laid down, a person would be able to travel from one coast to the other in just five days.

For the first time in months, the workers on both sides rested.

———— · · · ————

The ceremony finally took place on May 10, 1869, two days later than planned. While Durant was en route to Promontory Summit, 400 unpaid workers had unhooked his travel car and moved it onto a side track, effectively kidnapping the Union Pacific vice president. The angry mob threatened to kill Durant unless they were immediately given their back pay—five months' worth. Durant wired for $80,000, which arrived the following day, and he was set free to journey on, setting back the completion of the railroad by only a few days.

Promontory was a plateau in the mountains, and the connection site was located at the highest point along the road in the area. It was a level, grassy place, through which the track ran along east to west. The day was bright and temperate, with almost no clouds and a slight wind. Each company brought invited guests on the trains that would become famous as participants in their own right. The Central Pacific's Jupiter-60 and the Union Pacific's Rogers-199 were parked facing each other only a short distance apart. The senior officials of both the Union Pacific and the Central Pacific had come, as had the governors of California and Nevada, and reporters from more than twenty newspapers. The total number of spectators estimated from the photographs taken was five or six hundred.[42] The Saints were well represented in that number, but Brigham was absent. He was surely expected, given his contribution and modest ownership stake in the Union Pacific, but the prophet had decided to visit with Saints in southern Utah instead. He recognized the blessing that the railroad would be to the Saints, but the event marking the end of the project did not hold enough of a fascination for him to travel north.

Crowds began to gather at the site by seven o'clock in the morning, and the proceedings began five hours later, at noon. Various speakers addressed the audience until 12:45, when the final spikes and a silver-headed mallet were brought forward to finish the work. The Nevada delegation produced a silver spike made of metal extracted from the Comstock lodes. Arizona's governor, A. P. K. Safford, presented a spike made of a gold, silver, and iron alloy. Representatives from Idaho and Montana gifted their own gold-and-silver spikes, and from California came two golden spikes. The now-famous "last spike" was $5\frac{5}{8}$ inches long and just shy of fourteen ounces of pure gold. On the four sides, the makers had inscribed the start and end dates of the Central Pacific's effort; the names of Central Pacific's directors and corporate officers; and the phrase, "May God continue the unity of our Country, as this Railroad unites the two great Oceans of the world." On the top, the words "The Last Spike" were stamped in capital serif letters. But it was not the last spike driven—gold is a soft metal, and to hit it with regular force would have marred it. There may have been some ceremonial taps given, but none hard enough to leave a mark.

The true last spike was iron, like all the rest. Both it and the mallet given to Central Pacific President Leland Stanford were wrapped with wires connected to a telegraph line that had been strung to the site to signal the rest of the country that the final spike had been put in place. Each blow would connect a circuit and thus send out one of the three Morse Code dots that would mark the completion of the project. Nervous, Stanford swung . . . and missed the spike, striking only the rail. The telegraph operator chose to tap out the dots signaling completion of the railroad to the rest of the country. In Washington, New York, Philadelphia, Sacramento, San Francisco, Omaha, and other major cities, cannons were fired and celebrations began. In Salt Lake City, the Saints and their gentile neighbors filled the new Tabernacle and, when the signal came, let out cheers of jubilation.

At Promontory Summit, surrounded by the mob of spectators, Stanford was too embarrassed to try again and handed the mallet over to

Durant. The Union Pacific vice president took the hammer, raised it, and swung it down . . . and the ring of silver striking against iron rang out as Durant also missed the spike. He and Stanford pondered what to do for a moment. In the end, they simply tapped the spike with light blows, then let James Strobridge and Samuel Reed, both superintendents for their respective companies, do the actual work of driving the nail down. No one ever recorded which man struck the final spike for the last time.[43]

Durant and Stanford shook hands across the rails, and other dignitaries were afforded a chance to strike light ceremonial blows on the gold and silver spikes. When all who wanted a turn had taken one, the Jupiter-60 engine backed up so the Rogers-199 could ease forward over the connection point; then the Rogers returned the courtesy so the Jupiter engine could do the same. There was now not a single inch of iron track from Omaha to Sacramento over which no train had not run both east and west.

The transcontinental railroad was complete.

CHAPTER 9

EDUCATION AND AGITATION ARE OUR BEST WEAPONS

For Brigham, the end of that monumental project was simply the launch point for another. He'd been unable to convince the Union Pacific to run the transcontinental line through Salt Lake City. Had that turned out differently, the Saints could have run a line from the city south past the mouth of Little Cottonwood Canyon and the temple quarry in a matter of a few weeks. Now getting a spur south to the quarry meant the Saints would have to build their own line from Ogden to Salt Lake first. So they would have to lay not twenty miles of track but fifty-seven, which would take far more time and effort and was not without its risks. They would not have to use explosives and risk suffering more casualties like James Livingston, but four other Saints had died in Weber Canyon working for the Union Pacific—David Fisher, Christian Jergensen, James Read, and Richard Gibbs had all been killed within five months while working on the railroad. There was no stretch between Ogden and Little Cottonwood Canyon that promised to be as dangerous as Weber Canyon, but accidents would happen, and the more track they had to lay, the more accidents they would suffer.

Brigham was not a procrastinator. Exactly one week after the ceremony at Promontory Summit, he broke ground on May 17 for the newly chartered Utah Central Railroad, a line that would run south from Ogden. The short two-week vacation that the Saints had enjoyed from grading and track laying was over.

There was no question that the railroad would accelerate the building of the temple, and given that the Union Pacific had been able to lay two or three miles of track per day on average, it seemed reasonable that the Saints might be able to get that fifty-seven miles of track laid down before the year's end, so long as supplies like the rails, ties, and spikes were on hand. After that, the temple would start rising at a rate that would feel miraculous.

Even so, there had always been some Saints who were pessimistic about temple building. Their worries were not grounded in doubts about whether they had the ability to build a house of the Lord, but in fears about the opposition that always seemed to rise up when they tried. Brigham had always tried to dispel such worries. Some years before, in 1861, the prophet had given a sermon in the old Adobe Tabernacle in which he'd told the Saints not to be afraid and to devote themselves to building the temple. "Some say, 'I do not like to do it, for we never began to build a Temple without the bells of hell beginning to ring.' I want to hear them ring again," he said.[1]

If the bells started to ring in 1869, they did so quietly at first. Predictions that the coming of the railroad would bring about the end of the Saints as a people and a religion were overblown (as events would prove), but the Church's enemies had been right about one thing—distance alone no longer provided isolation. Ever since the Civil War had ended, the US government had been working to expand its control over the Western territories; now the railroad, a primary tool to accomplish that goal, ran right through the Saints' home. It was unavoidable that a stream of US government officials would end up transiting Utah and see for themselves firsthand what most had only heard about through rumors, newspaper editorials, and affidavits, many of which had proven to be completely false.

The first set of officials to ride the rails to Utah came in August when a joint congressional delegation disembarked at Ogden. The party included, among others, congressional representatives from Pennsylvania, Ohio, and New Hampshire, and senators from those latter two states as well as New Jersey and Vermont. In fact, the senator from Vermont was Justin Morrill, the man responsible for the Morrill Act of 1862, which had outlawed plural marriage, tried to disincorporate the Church, and declared that no religious entity could own more than $50,000 in assets. Now he would see up close the society whose culture he had tried to change years before.

The group boarded coaches for the territorial capital of Salt Lake City—the name had been shortened the year before, with the "Great" dropped from its moniker—and the federal visitors attended services the following day in the new Tabernacle across the way from the unfinished temple.[2] Inside the new meeting hall, Elder George Q. Cannon spoke on the subject of plural marriage at length, and he clearly aimed some of his comments to the elected officials as a group, if not to Morrill specifically. "Do they, who seek by every means in their power to break us up and destroy our organization because of our belief, have an idea of the sacrifice of feeling and reputation it cost the first Elders of the Church to introduce, sustain and declare this principle?" Cannon asked. "When I look back to that time and think of the men who entered into that order and advocated it conscientiously, because they knew the command to practice it was given by God Almighty to them, a feeling of admiration for them fills my heart, and I thank God that I live in a day when men are so valiant as they were."[3] Cannon clearly was not trying to build bridges with the senator from Vermont.

After the services and a tour of the city, Brigham received the entire delegation into his own home for a personal meeting. He didn't record the subjects they discussed with him, but, given Cannon's lengthy sermon and the wives and children they would have met in Brigham's house, the subject certainly must have been on their minds.

Morrill and his compatriots left town later that week and were barely gone before Senator Richard Yates of Illinois and Senators Kellogg and Harris of Louisiana came for their own brief stay on their way to California.[4] That brought the count of federal legislators visiting in August alone to three representatives and seven senators, the latter being almost one-tenth of the entire Senate. The *Deseret Evening News* reported that no other city in the United States "had been visited this season by more Senators, Representatives, and leading citizens than Salt Lake City."[5] This increased flow of important visitors was a development that they hoped would work in their favor. They thought that government officials would see the growth and prosperity of Salt Lake City and realize for themselves that the Saints were neither ignorant, indolent, nor rebellious toward their country, as their enemies had claimed. "The stale falsehoods of our enemies, which have been their stock of trade for so many years, and which but for our isolation they could not have used, are exposed, and they will have to resort to the manufacture of others to keep up their warfare," claimed Elder George Q. Cannon.[6]

As for plural marriage, the Saints wanted to prove to visitors that it was a blessing and not a curse to the people who practiced it in accordance with God's command. On the whole, the Saints' efforts were proving to be a mixed bag. At the same time the railroad was helping to dispel lies and slanders, it was also giving the outside world a better look into the Saints' practice of plural marriage—and the visitors, not sharing the Saints' belief in Joseph Smith's revelations, came away unpersuaded that the institution was divinely inspired, to say the least.

Schuyler Colfax was the case in point two months later. The former US Speaker of the House had been Ulysses S. Grant's running mate in the previous November's election, which Grant had won handily as expected. Now the nation's vice president, Colfax returned to Salt Lake City on his way east from California, his second visit in five years. He stayed in the newly built Townsend House at the corner of West Temple and First South Streets, which had become the finest hotel in the city upon completion and was located within sight of the temple block. In the evening of his first day in the city, a crowd gathered outside the hotel, and Colfax walked out onto the portico to say a few words to the assembled audience. He "praised the industries of the Mormon people" and all the developments of the city that had been completed since his prior visit. "I have enjoyed the opportunity, also, of visiting your Tabernacle," he shared, "erected since I was here before, the largest building in which religious services are held on the continent. . . . Nor did I feel any the less interest on my present than on my former visit, in listening to your leading men in their places of worship, as they expounded and defended their faith and practice, because that faith and practice differed so widely from my own." It was at that point that Colfax could not refrain from calling out the obvious practice that seemed to differ the most from his own. Plural marriage he condemned on both religious and civil grounds, citing both the Book of Mormon and US law.[7] "Our land is a land of civil and religious liberty, and the faith of every man is a matter between himself and God alone," he declared. " . . . But our country is governed by law, and no assumed revelation justifies any one in trampling on the law."[8] The Morrill Act was the law of the land, he argued, and the Saints were obligated to obey it. He may not have been aware of the fact that, not a half mile from where he stood, plural marriages were performed in the Endowment House on the temple block—and the Saints fully planned on performing them in the true house of the Lord once it was completed. They were building a temple in which they planned to continue doing precisely what Vice President Colfax was telling them they could not do.

The devil's bells, as Brigham would have called such opposition, were ringing for those who had ears to hear them. Now that the railroad connected the Saints with the East, another serious collision with the United States government was inevitable. With the telegraph and the railroad in place, Utah's isolation was no longer a barrier to federal officials looking to finally end the institution of plural marriage. This clash, more than any before, would threaten to destroy the Church and end the building of the temple for good.

—— • • • ——

The tracks of the Utah Central Railroad reached Salt Lake just after the New Year began, on January 10. The Union Pacific had provided the iron rails as partial compensation for the unpaid labor debt it still owed; the Saints had made the wooden ties and performed all the grading work themselves. Amidst a crowd of 15,000 people, Brigham himself drove the last spike in celebration, an iron nail with the words "Holiness to the Lord" stamped into the head.[9] The entire First Presidency of the Church and Quorum of the Twelve were there, as were officers of the Central and Union Pacific companies and senior military officers from Camp Douglas. All of them stood to benefit from the new connection of the Utah territorial capital to the transcontinental railroad running through the north, but the Saints most of all. No more immigrants would be coming in or missionaries going out on foot or by wagon. As for using the railroad to haul temple granite, they had only to lay another twenty miles of track before they could run a spur up into Little Cottonwood Canyon. They'd laid the thirty-seven miles from Ogden in less than eight months and now needed to cover only a little more than half that distance. They were clearly not threatening to break any of the Union or Central Pacific speed records, but surely they could finish the job this year. Then they would be able to move granite to the temple block as fast as James Livingston and his stonecutters could break it down. With that goal in sight, the prophet asked the quarry foreman—now recovered from his injuries and outfitted with his artificial limb—to return to his old labors.

Undeterred by the loss of his right arm, Livingston accepted the call and went back to the temple quarry. He would not leave the job again until his crew of men had quarried the last stone for the Salt Lake Temple. "In the year 1870 I was again called by Pres. Young to take a few men and start getting rock for the Temple, and from that time until the capstone was quarried I was in full control of the Salt Lake Temple Quarry," he later wrote. And this time, he and his men were determined to enjoy a bit more luxury than they had before. They were going to be on the job for years, and there was no reason they should be living out of tents. So "while quarrying rock for the Temple we had a beautiful camp made by the workmen at the quarry." They built permanent structures to make the quarry a true home for themselves and for any family members who would come to join them. Granite City became a sufficiently large settlement, and the weather in the canyon moderate enough during the high summer months, that a "great many of the leading brethren of the Church had summer quarters built and their families occupied them in the hot season. Thus I had the privilege of becoming intimately acquainted with these brethren and their families and enjoying their society, which I appreciated very much."[10]

Given the events that would shortly follow, the Church's leaders could hardly be blamed for wanting to escape Salt Lake City. The first sign that the recent visits of federal officials had not changed hearts or minds regarding the Saints was the introduction of several new anti-polygamy bills in Congress. The most extreme of these was the Cullom Bill, named for its author, Republican Shelby Cullom of Illinois, chairman of the Committee on the Territories. In addition to all of the terms of the Morrill Act, Cullom's bill proposed to eliminate the statute of limitations barring prosecution of plural marriage, and any man convicted of the crime could be fined up to $1,000 and imprisoned for up to twenty years. Cullom must have been expecting his proposed law to pack the prisons because he included a provision to authorize convicted Saints to serve their terms in a military prison if there was no room available in any local penitentiary. The US marshal could call on military troops to assist in capturing suspects wanted for arrest on such warrants. No one practicing plural marriage could vote, hold public office, or serve on a jury, and no foreign-born Latter-day Saint could become a US citizen.

Election officials could make anyone wanting to vote sign a legal oath that they were not practicing plural marriage and never would.[11] The list went on.

A copy of the bill reached Salt Lake City on January 3, 1870, and the response was predictable—but this time, it was not Brigham and the Apostles who protested the bills.

This time, it was the women of the Church.

———— • • • ————

In their speeches in Congress, Morrill, Cullom, and others who had submitted bills over the years to abolish plural marriage had always denounced the institution, in the most strenuous terms, as oppressive to women. Sarah Melissa Granger Kimball, president of the Salt Lake Fifteenth Ward Relief Society, begged to differ. Sarah was one of the most experienced members of the Church still living, having joined in 1833 when it was centered at Kirtland, Ohio. She had been fifteen then; she was fifty-one now. She'd known the Prophet Joseph in her youth and had made her way through the fierce persecutions inflicted on the Saints in those earlier days. Sarah had also been the first impetus that had led to the formation of the Relief Society. Noting that the men working construction on the Nauvoo Temple needed replacement clothing, she and seamstress Margaret Cook had decided in 1842 to make shirts. The project quickly drew in help from their friends, and Sarah decided they should form a Ladies' Society. Such charitable organizations were common in early nineteenth-century America, and Sarah thought Nauvoo should have its own. She asked her friend Eliza R. Snow to draft a constitution and bylaws and present them to Joseph for review. He read them over and felt impressed to organize the sisters of the Church in a different way, and thus was born the Relief Society.

Sarah was as prominent among the Church members as any woman, and she could command attention to a cause when she wanted—and now she wanted. She was not shy about speaking her mind, and she thought women had every bit as much right to involve themselves in politics as men. "Just and equitable government is essential to happy homes and refined society," she said. Therefore it was "an important part of woman's work to help to establish purity in politics and to establish an equal code for men and women." Her philosophy was that "education and agitation are our best weapons of warfare" in pursuing that or any other good cause.[12] She would eventually become a noted advocate for women's suffrage and a good friend of Susan B. Anthony, the great crusader for the right of women to vote.

Strong-willed woman that she was, when the *Deseret News* published the contents of the Cullom Bill that early January, Sarah decided that she and all of her sisters in the Church needed no man in Congress to tell them whether or not they were being oppressed. They were perfectly capable of speaking for themselves about their own experience, and Sarah decided to do precisely that. She convened a "Ladies Mass Meeting" on January 6, which drafted two proposals. The first was a demand to the territorial governor that women in the Utah territory be given the vote. It was a bold maneuver in one sense, as no other state or territory had yet extended the electoral franchise to women. But Congress had considered approving that very request a few years prior, believing that women would use their newfound suffrage to vote against laws enabling plural marriage. The second proposal called for two female representatives to be sent to Washington, D.C., ostensibly to lobby against the Cullom Bill. The two proposals passed.[13]

Eliza Snow suggested that the "mass meeting" should be only the first of many, and the women present agreed. The word spread through Salt Lake City, and many other sisters of the Church wanted in. Another meeting was scheduled for the following Thursday, this time in a much larger venue.

January 13 was an ugly day weather-wise, "cold and frosty,"[14] but the temperature did nothing to deter women across the city from gathering in the Tabernacle, and they overfilled the building beyond its seating capacity. "As it will comfortably seat five thousand persons, there could not have been fewer than between five and six thousand present on the occasion," noted an observer.[15] It was standing room only for an assembly that was "densely packed with ladies of all ages, old, young, and middle aged."[16] There had never been a meeting of the Relief Society quite like this one, and certainly not one in which the women were standing up to defend the men of the Church.

The meeting began at four o'clock in the afternoon. On the stand were, among others, Sarah Kimball; Eliza R. Snow, General President of the Relief Society; Bathsheba Smith, wife of Apostle George A. Smith and future General President of the Relief Society; Harriet Cooke Young, one of Brigham Young's wives and a member of the original vanguard pioneer company of 1847; and Phoebe Woodruff, wife of Apostle Wilford Woodruff. Without exception, through marriage, friendship, or both, every woman in that group had enjoyed close associations with several prophets and numerous Apostles and were as devoted to the gospel as any of those men.

The meeting began, and Eliza, deferring to her friend as the prime mover behind the convocation, nominated Sarah to be sustained as the president of the meeting. It was done, and Sarah wasted no time in making clear why they were all here. "We are not here to advocate woman's rights, but man's rights," she declared. "[The Cullom Bill] would not only deprive our fathers, husbands, and brothers of enjoying the privileges bequeathed to citizens of the United States, but it would also deprive us, as women, of the privilege of selecting our husbands, and against this we most unqualifiedly protest."[17]

She asked the other Relief Society leaders to speak in turn. One woman after another stood and denounced the Cullom Bill in terms no less adamant than Sarah's had been. Eliza Snow went straight after the assumption that women in Utah were in a state of bondage. "Are not our interests one with our brethren?" she asked.

> Ladies, this subject as deeply interests us as them. In the kingdom of God woman has no interests separate from those of man;

all are mutual. Our enemies pretend that in Utah woman is held in a state of vassalage; that she does not act from choice but by coercion. That we would even prefer life elsewhere were it possible for us to make our escape. What nonsense! . . . They must be very dull in estimating the energy of female character who can persuade themselves that women, who for the sake of their religion left their homes, crossed the plains with hand-carts, or, as many had previously done, drove ox, mule, and horse teams from Nauvoo and from other points. . . . To suppose that we should not be aroused when our brethren are threatened with fines and imprisonment for their faith in and obedience to the laws of God is an insult to our womanly natures.[18]

By then, the great poetess of the Saints was in high dudgeon. If education and agitation truly were the best weapons of political warfare, then Eliza Snow was at that moment the best prepared soldier in this army of sister Saints, and she marshaled her considerable oratorical and literary powers to call her fellow women to arms.

I wish to say to my sisters, to the mothers in Israel, and to the daughters, cultivate in your bosom the spirit of freedom and liberty which has been bequeathed unto us by our fathers. . . . If fortitude and nobility of soul be cultivated in your own bosoms you will transmit them to your children, your sons will grow up noble defenders of truth and righteousness and heralds of salvation to the nations of the earth. . . . I consider it most important, my sisters, that we should struggle to preserve the sacred Constitution of our country, one of the blessings of the Almighty; for the same spirit that inspired the prophet Joseph Smith inspired the framers of the Constitution, and should ever hold it sacred and bear it off triumphantly.[19]

Phoebe Woodruff answered Eliza's call. Woodruff's wife was not a woman of so many words and not so eloquent as Eliza. In fact, Phoebe was plain and direct in her comments. When she took to the pulpit, she declared in explicit terms that it was the politicians in Washington and not the Saints who were trampling on the laws of the land. "I . . . had the privilege of living in the days of the Prophet Joseph, and heard his teachings for many years. He ever counseled us to honor, obey, and maintain the principles of our noble Constitution, for which our fathers fought, and many of them sacrificed their lives to establish. President Brigham Young has always taught the same principle," she explained. "Cullom's bill is in direct violation of this declaration of the Constitution . . . [it] commits a violent outrage upon our rights and the rights of our fathers, husbands, and sons." Then she warned the federal legislators on Capitol Hill that if they passed their bills, instead of seeing women rejoice, the government would instead be treated to the spectacle of wives standing by their husbands, even if it meant following them into a life of incarceration. "If the rulers of our nation will so far depart from the spirit and the letter of our glorious Constitution as to deprive our prophets, apostles, and elders of citizenship, and imprison them for obeying this law [plural marriage], let them grant us this our last request, to make their prisons large enough to hold their wives, for where they go we will go also."[20]

———— • · · • ————

The meeting adjourned, but it was only the first of many throughout the territory. By March, similar smaller meetings had convened in virtually every major city and town in Utah—the *Deseret News* listed fifty-two—attended by an estimated 25,000 women.[21] Assuming that half of Utah's reported 1870 population of 86,000 people were women, then more than half of all the women in the territory attended one of Sarah Kimball's "indignation meetings," if the *Deseret News* estimate was roughly correct. Indeed, if the Tabernacle really was filled past its seating capacity, then something like two-thirds of the roughly 9,000 women living in Salt Lake County had attended the convocation that cold mid-January afternoon.[22]

Congress and the Church's critics apparently took little notice, if any, of the mass meetings. In fact, they continued to speculate that extending suffrage to women would encourage them to vote to ban plural marriage and support policies and politicians who would undermine Brigham's influence among the Utah population. Anyone paying attention and doing the math would have realized that extending suffrage to women likely would produce the opposite effect. Indeed, Brigham and the Church leaders supported giving women the vote, and on February 10, the territorial legislature did exactly that. The governor signed the bill two days later, making Utah the second territory to extend the franchise to women. (Wyoming had done so first on December 10, 1869, the year before, but had not yet held an election.) So when Saray Young, one of Brigham's grandnieces, cast a ballot in the February 14 election a few days later, she became the first woman to exercise the right to vote under the new law.

Cullom's bill did not pass Congress that session, and neither did any of the spate of legislative proposals designed to quash plural marriage. The Saints had earned another reprieve, but, like the ones before, it would not last. Cullom's bill was dead, but the provisions it contained would return in another form in a few years. The United States government was determined to put the institution down sooner or later.

———— • • • ————

Why Brigham did not push for the immediate extension of the railroad south that year is unclear, but it was not until January 17, 1871, that he and the same body that had chartered the Utah Central Railroad gathered to do the same for the Utah Southern. The new line would run from Salt Lake City south to the Point of the Mountain, then on to American Fork, Provo, and Payson. Rather than asking the workers to start trying to grade the frozen ground along the route in the winter, the prophet mercifully postponed any push to start that task until May 1. The work proceeded much more slowly than Thomas Durant and the Union Pacific ever would have tolerated. The slow pace may have been due to the persistently poor road south from Salt Lake City. That particular stretch of highway had always been rough and rutted, swamping easily with the rain. No amount of effort or money had ever seemed to improve it much, to the dismay of the teamsters hauling temple granite. But to lay track along that route, the road had to be fixed and leveled once and for all. It took three months to grade twenty miles, a little more than one mile of road per week on average, whereas the Union Pacific had averaged more than that per day.

It was not until September 23 that the line finally reached Sandy, where the spur—to be called the Wasatch and Jordan Valley Railroad— would turn off and enter the mouth of Little Cottonwood Canyon.[23] It was late in the season, and the route into the canyon was still mostly ungraded, so the tracks would not reach the quarry that year. Still, that was no cause for complaint. The teamsters now needed to haul granite only seven miles down the well-worn canyon road, and gravity would be working for them all the way. Even with foul weather or a broken wagon, the trip would still take one full day or so, but that was a significant improvement over the previous average of four. Workers, tools, and other supplies could be brought in more quickly and cheaply now. Perhaps best of all, the stonecutters could finish work on a Saturday evening, ride the rail north to Salt Lake to be with their families on the Sabbath, then ride it back late Sunday or early Monday morning to return to work. No man or woman had to live in the quarry for weeks or months at a time without seeing family.

Livingston and his men put the railroad to work, and the results were gratifying. Granite started arriving at the temple block much faster than ever before. The stonecutters there were dressing and laying the stones at a more rapid pace than had been possible previously, and the temple walls began rising at a noticeably faster rate.

But no happy moment for the Saints ever seemed to last. On October 2, just nine days after the Utah Southern line reached Sandy Station, the US marshal appeared at Brigham's house about four o'clock in the afternoon and declared that the prophet was under arrest. The lawman produced a writ confirming that the court had indicted Brigham for "lascivious behavior"—the favored legal charge for prosecuting any man practicing plural marriage. Brigham was in poor health; his physical condition had been declining noticeably in recent years, courtesy of his advancing age. He was now seventy years old, he had grown portly, and his resistance to cold weather had weakened. His lawyer asked the presiding judge, Chief Justice James McKean of the Superior Court of the Utah Territory, to grant bail so that Brigham would not have to appear in court on account of his illness.[24] The prosecution objected, stating, "The people demanded that Brigham Young should appear in court, the same as anybody else." If by "the people" the prosecutor meant the actual residents of Salt Lake City, overwhelmingly Latter-day Saints, they were demanding no such thing. That led a reporter for the *Salt Lake Herald* to note wryly that the objection was "the first time we were given to understand that said deputy was of such monstrous girth that he embodied 'the people.'"[25] Judge McKean declined to grant bail, but he did allow a week's extension for Brigham to enter a plea in the case. McKean was not one to waste the time, however. The marshal arrested Daniel H. Wells the following day, and George Q. Cannon four days after that, after the Saturday sessions of general conference. Both were indicted on the same charge. When Wells appeared in court, McKean granted bail, set at the hefty sum of $5,000.

Brigham appeared in court on October 9 as scheduled and pleaded not guilty to the charge. McKean granted him bail, also set at $5,000, and postponed the trial, as the prosecutor apparently was not prepared that morning to try the case. The prophet left Salt Lake City for St. George a little more than two weeks later. His health declining, he intended to spend the winter in the southern city to escape the cold as much as he could before he had to return to stand trial. The railroad could take him little farther than Sandy Station, and so he made the rest of the 290-mile journey by horse and buggy.

Brigham's mind appears to have been focused on the future. He was an old man now, his health precarious, and at some point it must have occurred to him that he would not live to see the Salt Lake Temple completed. He felt he had a commitment to fulfill to the Prophet Joseph to make the temple endowment, in complete and accurate form, available to the Saints in a true house of the Lord. But after eighteen years of labor, the temple's granite walls were still not far above ground level, just to the first set of semicircular windows, not even to the height of an average person. Even with the increased rate of construction that the railroad now allowed, it was obvious that at least another decade of work lay before the Saints to finish the building, perhaps more—and that was just the exterior. To finish the interior of an edifice that large would be another enormous undertaking. Did he have another ten years, perhaps fifteen, left in him? His health at the moment did not give him much reason for optimism.

At some point during the trip down to St. George or shortly after his arrival there, Brigham settled on the decision that the Saints needed to start work on a second temple before they had finished the first that they'd been laboring on for so long. Joseph Smith had taught the Saints that the salvation of the dead "is necessary and essential to our salvation . . . that they without us cannot be made perfect—neither can we without our dead be made perfect."[26] The Saints had a divinely ordained duty to redeem those who had died without a knowledge of the gospel or a chance for baptism, and for that work they needed a temple. The ordinances performed in the Endowment House were for the living only, not for those who had passed on. Neither Brigham nor anyone else could have expected that building the temple in Salt Lake City would have taken so long. But there was no reason that they had to finish one temple before they could start another, assuming such dual construction would not divert labor or resources away from the effort in Salt Lake.

How long Brigham had been pondering the subject is a mystery, but he had settled it in his mind by the time he reached St. George. On the second day of the conference there, November 4, he had the issue presented to the Saints. They responded unanimously and "resolved to use their utmost endeavors to build a temple."[27] To begin that work, on November 9, Brigham assembled a group of Saints at a six-acre plot in St. George that he had chosen as the site for a temple. At the prophet's request, Elder George A. Smith offered the dedicatory prayer, which was quite fitting—the settlement of St. George itself had been named after the Apostle. "Bless this ground on which the Temple is to be erected, that it may be held sacred for this purpose," he pleaded to God. "And do thou bless the people who shall be engaged in building a Temple upon this ground. Grant that the walls of that Temple may be laid in truth and the top stone be laid with shouts of Hosanna to God and the Lamb. Cause that thy power may be in the house; that angels may enter therein and minister to thy servants."

When Elder Smith finished, Brigham stepped forward to speak to the assembly. "The idea may arise that this is a hard land in which to get a living. Now I am very thankful for the land just as it is. It is a splendid country to rear saints in," he said. He promised that if the Saints would "undertake to do this work with one heart and mind," the Lord would prosper them. Then he asked those present for a show of hands whether they would "prosecute the labor of building this Temple by faith, prayer, and good works." All hands went up. They sang a hymn, and then Brigham took up a shovel, declared, "I now commence by moving this dirt in the name of Israel's God," and moved a spade of dirt. All those in attendance came forward and did the same.[28]

For the first time in the Church's history, the Saints were building more than one house of the Lord simultaneously. Truman Angell, as the Church architect, was called to design the new temple, and the project would endure its own set of severe construction challenges that the Saints' brothers and sisters to the North could appreciate. But as Brigham turned that first shovel of dirt, he might well have wondered whether he would live to see this or any other temple finished before the end of his life.

Judge McKean called Brigham back in the dead of winter, setting his trial date for December 4. It was impossible for Brigham to reach Salt Lake City in time for that date, but he was compelled to leave St. George and travel north anyway. He arrived home on December 26, having spent the Christmas holiday on the road. He appeared in court just after the new year on January 2, 1872, only to see Judge McKean set a new trial date in March and refuse to grant bail even when Brigham's lawyer offered the eye-watering amount of $500,000—the modern equivalent of more than $10,000,000. So Brigham was forced to remain in his own house under guard by US deputy marshals until the court was ready to try him. He and his fellow defendants could hardly have been expecting anything like a fair trial. In a previous polygamy case, Judge McKean had expressly told the jury:

> You have your duties, gentlemen, and I have mine. My duty is to pick you out and pack you in; to fix the trial at such a time as will be least convenient to the defendant; to exclude all evidence that may help him and to admit all evidence that may hurt him; to rule all points of law against him; to pick out from acts of Congress and acts of the Utah Assembly those laws which, combined, may convict him; in short, gentlemen, my duty is to secure a conviction.[29]

McKean clearly was no paragon of judicial neutrality, but he was, if nothing else, a man of his word. Thus far, he had certainly made good on his "duty" to fix Brigham's trial at the most inconvenient time, calling the ill prophet back to Salt Lake from St. George in December. If he intended to follow through on his other so-called duties, Brigham, Wells, Cannon, and the rest hardly stood a chance in court to be found not guilty.

Their deliverance came through the grace of the US Supreme Court. To facilitate indictments and convictions for plural marriage, McKean and US Marshal M. T. Patrick had ignored territorial statutes governing jury selection in favor of federal rules that allowed the marshal to oversee jury selection. For cases going back more than a year, Patrick had picked which citizens would serve—and ensured that no Saints who might be sympathetic to the defendants were ever chosen. The high court ruled that McKean and Patrick had no legal justification to ignore the territorial rules and vacated every judicial proceeding and indictment that had involved one of Patrick's hand-picked, stacked-deck juries.[30] McKean took the decision badly. Upon hearing the news, he "indulged in some contemptuous expressions concerning the Supreme Court, and still maintained that he himself was right." "The poor creature is evidently crazy," one witness observed.[31]

His case thus dismissed, Brigham walked away a free man.

———···———

Within six months of the construction of the Utah Southern reaching Sandy, the railroad's effect on the construction of the house of the Lord was unmistakable. All hopes that the "iron horse" would accelerate the building of the temple were being fulfilled. There was as yet no way to transport stone the entire distance solely by rail; teamsters still had to haul the blocks down the canyon to Sandy on wagons, which could take a day or more if the weather was uncooperative. Once the stones were loaded onto the flatcars, they could ride as far as the Utah Central depot, which was one-half mile east of the temple block. Stones had to be unloaded there and hauled that short distance by other means.

Still, it was a vast improvement over the wagon-only system the Saints had been employing over the past years. The progress it enabled was obvious enough that Elder George A. Smith of the Quorum of the Twelve took note of it in his discourse in general conference the following April.

> Our brethren can observe that a very handsome addition has been made to the foundation [i.e., the basement walls] of the Temple here since the last Annual Conference and they can now begin to form some idea of how the work is going to look. When you

realize that all the granite that is in that immense foundation has been hauled some seventeen miles with oxen, mules and horses, you must realize that a very great job has been accomplished. But at the present time we have a railroad almost into the quarry, and the result is that the labor has been greatly lessened, and the rock and the sand and other building material can be brought here at vastly less expense than formerly, and consequently we will be able to push the work forward more rapidly.[32]

But they could do better. Tracks were being laid through Salt Lake to allow rail transport through the city itself, and the construction of a spur that would run directly to the temple block was approved. One of these internal city lines ran up South Temple Street, and the proposed temple block spur would turn from that track just past First West Street and run through the temple block gates right onto the grounds in front of the Tabernacle. Work crews began setting track on July 9 and were done within weeks. On August 21, the first load of temple granite pulled by engine arrived at the site.[33]

All that remained was to connect the temple quarry with the Utah Southern line at Sandy, and the Saints would be able to haul every bit of granite by flatcar without the need for a single wagon or yoke of oxen.

———•··•———

George Q. Cannon observed that the prophet's "health was very poor and he was quite feeble" when the following winter arrived. So Brigham again left for St. George for the same reason he had gone the previous year. He began his trip south on December 12 and arrived at his destination two days before Christmas, and this time there was no legal summons to call him back halfway through the season.

While there, he visited the St. George temple block to take in the progress on this second house of the Lord. Truman's design for it was modeled after both the Kirtland and Nauvoo Temples, with the lower assembly room able to be partitioned for use in creating ordinance rooms. But construction here had run into problems almost from the very beginning. As it turned out, the area Brigham had chosen for the building was quite swampy, with subsurface streams running under the site. The ground had to be fortified before the foundation could be laid. No temple was going to come easy, it seemed. Undeterred, the Saints were packing crushed basaltic volcanic rock harvested from a long-since-cooled lava field northwest of St. George into the excavated site to solidify it enough to support the building. They had no pile driver, so, with some creative determination, they'd used an old cannon that a member of the Mormon Battalion had acquired in California and brought overland. The workers used a pulley system to hoist the cannon and then drop it, letting gravity do the work of breaking the stone and packing it into the swampy earth. When the cannon bounced three times on the crushed stone, they knew that section of the foundation was ready to support the weight of a building. It was a clever solution and effective, but it was not by any means quick. It would take them two years to pack the ground full enough to start construction. With that kind of a start to the project, Brigham could have been forgiven if he'd thought he might not live to see this temple finished, either.

———•··•———

Brigham returned home to Salt Lake in late February of 1873. It was a little more than a month later when the news came from Sandy that the Wasatch and Jordan Valley Line being laid in the Little Cottonwood Canyon would reach the temple quarry in early April. The exact date, as it turned out, was April 4, the day before the start of the Church's annual general conference.

Brigham traveled to Little Cottonwood Canyon to mark the occasion on that same April day the rails reached Granite City. Traveling in the company of George Q. Cannon, John Sharp, and several others, Brigham left Salt Lake at one o'clock riding the Utah Southern as far as the Sandy Station. There they switched to a train on the Wasatch and Jordan Valley Line, which was a narrow-gauge railroad, so built because the challenges of building a line up the canyon demanded it. Once aboard their new transport, they rode six and a half miles east to the quarry. "It was of a very exhilarating character, the road being a continual ascent until you are fairly in the mountains," one of the travelers wrote. "The little steamer did her work gallantly, running along at about twelve or fifteen miles an hour."[34] They arrived at the quarry sometime around two-thirty or shortly thereafter. A granite block was loaded onto the flatcar attached to their steam engine, "an arch stone 5½ feet long, 3 feet wide and 2 feet thick, weighing approximately 7,500 pounds." After the loading was complete and the prophet and others had said their good-byes, their "little steamer left the quarry at 4:00 p.m."[35] They rode the rail the six and a half miles back down the canyon to the station at Sandy, where they pulled the narrow-gauge flatcar alongside a standard-gauge flatcar on the Utah Southern track, close enough that they almost touched. The workers set up a series of rollers between the two and transferred the stone to the latter car by moving it across the rollers with a pinch bar. The whole process took only a few minutes. Once the granite block was secured, Brigham, his companions, and the stone were steaming their way north.[36] When Brigham's train arrived in the city, the flatcar was shunted onto the South Temple Street line to cover that final stretch. Brigham's party arrived in Salt Lake City at 5:15 p.m., one hour and fifteen minutes after they'd left the quarry, "having had a very pleasant journey."[37]

Twenty years after Brigham had told the Saints that the temple could not be completed until they had a railroad in place to haul stone, they finally had a complete set of lines connecting the Little Cottonwood Quarry with the temple site. The task of hauling a single granite block had been reduced from four days by wagon to a little more than an hour by train, which could transport tens of thousands of pounds of stones in a single load. No doubt, it was a pleasant journey indeed.

CHAPTER 10

JOSEPH!
JOSEPH! JOSEPH!

Brigham Young must have had a fine sense of the dramatic. His train ride to and from the temple quarry took place on a Friday, the day before the Church's annual conference convened in the new Tabernacle. The *Deseret News* did not record how many witnesses saw the prophet dismount from the train on the temple block, but the news of the event must have spread through all of Salt Lake City to all those who had not been present. Anyone attending the conference that weekend, going to or coming from the Tabernacle, would have seen the rails on the ground entering the temple block, the many stones that had been delivered previously, and the stone that Brigham and his company had ferried back on the fourth. Seeing that granite would now be arriving fast and furious from the quarry, Elder George Q. Cannon suggested from the conference pulpit that "about two hundred boys should learn the business of stone cutting."

And not content to leave out the young women, the Apostle urged "the employment of girls and women in type setting" and learning other trades. "The employment of ladies would not injure any business in the least," Elder Cannon assured the men in the audience, and "he advocated very strongly the necessity of teaching not only boys but also girls how they could make a living without being dependent on others."[1] The sisters of the Church were fully capable of making contributions in the workplace as well as in the home, the meetinghouse, and the temple.

But whatever enthusiasm Brigham's train ride had ginned up, he dampened it himself with an announcement delivered during the conference. His seventy-second birthday was only two months away, and he was almost thirty years past the average man's life expectancy at the time. He was now a heavy man and had to leave Salt Lake for months at a time in the winter to escape the cold for the sake of his health. Age and the exertions of a hard life were truly taking their toll on Brigham now, and he could not keep up with the heavy workload that his position imposed on him. He had no choice but to divest himself of some of his responsibilities and accept more help to work through what remained on his desk. To that end, he proposed during the general conference in April that he give up some of his Church duties. In a letter to the Saints, he explained:

> The time has arrived when I feel it to be right and proper for me to request this Conference, that they appoint some person, other than myself, to be Trustee in Trust for the Church.
>
> I will state that my object in this, is to be relieved, so far as possible, from all secular business, and, accordingly, I have resigned (or will resign) all offices of that character which I have heretofore held.[2]

He'd asked to be released as Trustee-in-Trust before, which job gave him control over all Church properties, including the temple, "and the people were then averse to it." Cannon suggested that the people would "defer to his desire now, with the understanding that President Young should still retain supervisory power over the trusteeship." In other words, he could appoint someone to manage the Church's properties, but the members wanted him to retain overall control. For that, the vote was unanimous, and the congregation sustained Elders Lorenzo Snow, Brigham Young Jr., Albert Carrington, John W. Young, and George Q.

Brigham Young.

Cannon as counselors to the prophet in addition to Elders George A. Smith and Daniel H. Wells, already members of the First Presidency. Brigham now had these seven men plus a number of others to help him manage the responsibilities that he'd been shouldering since Joseph Smith's death almost twenty-nine years before. But there was no denying that Brigham was an old man and his physical stamina was in decline. It was a matter of faith that he would be the prophet so long as the Lord wanted, but he would not be there forever.

⸺ • ⸱ • ⸺

George Q. Cannon's call for 200 boys to learn the craft of stone-cutting may have been overly optimistic, but it was grounded in a real need. During the first year after they started using the railroad to move stone, James Livingston's men would dispatch 8,706,000 pounds of granite to the temple block at the going rate of $9.00 per carload.[3] That was enough to provide full-time work for any number of skilled stonecutters that could be found. They were now the bottleneck in the system. Even a handful of masons could lay the granite faster than the available stonecutters could finish it. So Cannon's plea would not be the last time the leaders of the Church would urge the membership to deliver more skilled laborers or, if they had none to spare, to train more.

The rise of the walls, heartening as that was to see, was also creating another problem. As each new course of stones was placed, lifting the finished granite pieces with pulleys, block and tackle, and muscle was becoming more challenging. It had been doable enough—though never truly easy—when they had been lowering stones down below ground level into the foundation trenches. Gravity had been working for them then. Once the walls rose above ground level, gravity had started working against them. Now the walls were above head height, with enough finished granite on hand to build up three more courses, and Truman Angell's blueprints called for the temple spires to reach over two hundred feet into the air.[4] Over the summer of 1873, the need for a different system for moving and lifting stone was becoming acute.

Truman himself provided the solution. He designed what the *Deseret Evening News* called "a most ingenious arrangement by which the huge blocks of granite are to be raised upon the walls and adjusted in their places."[5] His "ingenious arrangement" was a construction derrick. The machine was composed principally of a tall mast, like that used aboard a ship, with a long job arm affixed at a right angle. On the mast some distance below the arm was a platform where men would stand to turn a crank wheel to wind or unwind a rope that ran up to the arm, through the pulleys there, and down to the ground. The arm could be swung around the mast by means of men pulling ropes from the ground, until it reached over the waiting block. The workers would tie up the block with the rope, whereupon the men on the derrick platform would turn the wheel to raise the stone off the ground into the air. Once it was elevated to the needed height, the men on the ground would turn the jib arm, swinging the stone over its intended position. The men on the derrick would then reverse the direction of the wheel's turn and lower the granite onto the wall.

To show the feasibility of the machine, Truman built a working scale model "by which its practicability was . . . roughly demonstrated."[6] With the basic design thus proven, plans were made to construct four derricks, all inside the temple walls, with one near each corner. The old method of rope, pulleys, and muscle hadn't been completely replaced, but it had been scaled up and mechanized with improved efficiency. The first working derrick was in place by September 13. Within short order, three courses of stone were laid and the temple walls were completed up to the arches of the lowest tier of windows, about eight feet above the base rock. "The walls there are now sufficiently high to give some idea of the magnificent character of the work," the *Deseret News* reported. "It will be one of the most solid and altogether one of the finest pieces of masonry in the world."[7]

—•••—

Brigham left for St. George again in late November, as had now become his annual habit, and he was able to travel as far as Provo on the Utah Southern Line before having to switch over to a carriage.[8] The railroad was taking him farther and farther south each year, shortening his trip a little each time, though delays in his travel occurred for other reasons. One year as he rode the rails south—the date is uncertain—he was slowed up as his train met another coming up the line in the opposite direction, forcing both to halt near the Point of the Mountain.

> The engineers dropped from their diamond-shaped smokestack locomotives and were soon joined by their respective crews in heated argument. Someone would have to back down the hill to the passing track at the bottom. Finally, one conductor, a little more level-headed than the rest, said: "I've got Brigham Young in my hind car. Let's send for him." Brigham . . . came and patiently listened and then asked: "Which one of you engineers have paid your tithing?" One engineer hung his head, while the other fished in his coat pocket and came up with a greasy receipt. "That settles it," Brigham Young announced. "The engineer without the receipt backs down. Come on, let's be going. I've got a conference in the next town."[9]

The year 1873 had ended in relative quiet, and the prophet's winter sojourn passed by much the same way. Construction on the St. George Temple had progressed well. The southern Saints had finished stabilizing the site with the lava rock and their cannon-as-pile-driver contraption and now had laid the foundation. Just before his departure for home, Brigham attended a ceremony to deposit a box of records in the southeast corner, much as they had done in Salt Lake before the coming of Johnston's army. Among the works placed in the box were copies of the

Church's standard works; a hymnal and various tracts written by members of the Quorum of the Twelve Apostles; Church periodicals, including the *Millennial Star* and the *Women's Exponent*; a collection of poems by Eliza R. Snow; and a "Synopsis of Description of the Temple at Salt Lake City" written by Truman Angell. At noon exactly, Brigham placed the box in the foundation and offered the dedicatory prayer.[10]

The house of the Lord in St. George had come further in two years than its counterpart in Salt Lake had come in ten. The southern temple was not so large and ambitious as the one being built in the north, but the Saints' accomplishments were still impressive. In Salt Lake, the rise of the temple there had been positively glacial; now with the railroad and Truman's derrick in full operation, it was merely slow, but it was an improvement and cause for hope. In a letter Brigham wrote to his son John Willard in October, he cheerfully reported, "The temple is looming up fine and we may expect the rock work to be pushed another season as it has never been. Our increased facility for laying rock . . . [bodes] fair to complete both temples at an early date."[11]

———•—•—•———

That "increased facility" was accompanied by a change in the actual rock that James Livingston was shipping out of the quarry in Little Cottonwood Canyon. After the winter season ended and quarry operations resumed in the spring of 1874, Livingston's men found another granite deposit a mile and a half farther up the canyon, this one of noticeably higher quality than the one they'd been cutting on for over a decade. Wanting to use only the finest materials to build the house of the Lord, they chose to use the new deposit, which meant moving the quarry. They named the new site Wasatch.

The move imposed some hardship on the stonecutters. The Wasatch and Jordan Valley Railroad crews had continued laying track in that direction since Brigham's ride the year before, but it appears the line had not reached the new site. So Livingston and the men had to return to hauling stone with wagons some distance until they could reach the rails

The Salt Lake Temple under construction, c. 1875.

where they could load it onto the flatcars. A visitor to the new Wasatch site observed the following year, "All the rock had to be brought by teams which was very arduous work as the wagons were constantly breaking down and squares of granite had to be left by the roadside."[12] After a year of moving rock purely by rail, having to go back to using wagons and oxen, even if only for a short time until the railroad reached that far into the canyon, must have felt like an unpleasant step backward.

———•·•———

Around the time Livingston and his crew were moving from Granite City to Wasatch, Brigham returned to Salt Lake City from the south. Whether he stopped by the quarry on his way home is unknown, but once he arrived home, he soon found his attention turned toward legal matters. The federal government was making another push to resolve what the country was calling the "Mormon Question"—whether the institution of plural marriage would be allowed in Utah. Anti-Mormons in Washington and elsewhere had never stopped pushing Congress to empower federal officials to take hard measures against the Saints, and several hostile bills had been submitted to do precisely that. The Cullom Bill and others had been defeated in Congress, but one passed this year that caused significant problems for Brigham and his closest associates. Congressman Luke Poland of Vermont submitted a bill in April that proposed to ease the enforcement of the Morrill Act of 1862 by restructuring the Utah courts and empowering judges and prosecutors to disallow potential jurors if they practiced plural marriage or even believed that plural marriage was moral.[13] The Poland Bill passed the House of Representatives handily on June 2, the Senate narrowly almost three weeks later, and President Grant signed it into law on the twenty-third.

With his newfound powers, US Attorney William Carey immediately set out to indict as many of the Church's senior leaders as he could manage, but his plans were upset by numerous legalities. He could not prosecute anyone for any marriage performed prior to the Morrill Act's passage in 1862, nor could he compel new plural wives to testify against their husbands under spousal privilege. Thus frustrated, Carey proposed a bargain—he would stop trying to indict the Church's leadership en masse if they would provide a defendant for a test case to settle the constitutionality of the law. Brigham and other Church leaders were still confident that the courts would strike down the Morrill Act as unconstitutional under the free exercise clause of the First Amendment, but to accept Carey's proposal, someone would have to submit to arrest and conviction, and then appeal his case as far as the Supreme Court, if possible. That person might very well spend the entire time in prison if the courts did not choose to stay the sentence while the appeals were being heard. In modern parlance, someone was going to have to "take one for the team."

After some discussion, Elder George A. Reynolds agreed to be the defendant. Reynolds had joined the Church twenty-one years before when he was just fourteen years old. He had been Brigham's private secretary for a time before accepting a mission call to England, from which he'd returned the summer of the previous year. He was now a member of the University of Deseret Board of Regents and was "somewhat widely known and . . . extensively respected." Carey secured the grand jury indictment on the October 23, and Reynolds surrendered himself to the court three days later. He was granted bail in the amount of $2,500, which Daniel H. Wells and several others posted on his behalf. There was no chance whatsoever that Reynolds was going to jump bail and run. Brigham and the other leaders wanted this case to be heard. "Should Brother Reynold be convicted in the District Court and the verdict be sustained by the Supreme Court of the Territory, it is probable that the case will be carried to the Supreme Court of the United States, when the constitutionality of the anti-polygamy law of 1862 and other points will be tested," the *Deseret News* explained. That was the hope, anyway.[14]

<hr />

Brigham had arrived in St. George for his annual sabbatical just the day before. He'd been feeling very poorly before he left, and the trip down had been very unpleasant "in consequence of the rough roads." He was also suffering from severe rheumatism now, and the jostling of the carriage had caused his joints to ache terribly as it rolled along the rough trail south. The weather had already turned cold enough for snow to fall, and at points his carriage had to push through five inches of powder. Brigham stopped with his party at settlements along the way, staying with friends and preaching to the Saints despite his weakened condition, teaching them about the importance of performing ordinances for the dead and building temples.[15]

He kept to his room for a few days after arriving at St. George to rest and recuperate. His health started to improve again, and by December 12, he was well enough to go on an inspection tour of the temple site and the nearby quarry.[16] Getting a temple completed before he ran out of life, whenever that might be, was clearly a pressing matter for Brigham, for, during the next three months, he visited both sites as often as his health allowed. But he was hardly walking some days, as his joints ached considerably. On days when he was confined to his room, Elder George A. Smith, one of his counselors in the First Presidency, went in his stead. Either the prophet or his Apostle surrogate went to the construction site or the quarry almost daily to give direction and oversee the work for the duration of their stay.

The workers had laid 300 tons of rock down on the temple walls in the previous week before Brigham's arrival on November 12,[17] and Elder Smith found that the quarry had 120 men cutting stone there.[18] The Apostle thought that number was too low, and he exhorted the southern Saints to do more. "I invited some of the Brethren that had come down . . . to volunteer to learn stonecutting as we had not enough of that class of workmen. . . . I told them they could learn to cut stone well enough for our purposes in a week if they had faith," he wrote in his journal.[19] They may have been lacking in stonecutters, but support for the project was coming in healthy amounts in other ways. Members from nearby settlements were sending supplies, including money, tools, and other needed items, as well as tithing labor in the form of blacksmiths and other craftsmen. One donation came in the form of a herd of beef cattle driven down to feed the workers.[20]

The temple was rising quickly. If the Lord would preserve Brigham's health for just a few years more, there was a good chance that he would see a house of the Lord finished before he took his last breath—but there was no question by now that it would not be the temple in Salt Lake. The St. George Temple would be the first completed since Nauvoo. The only question was whether the prophet would live to see it finished.

If he hadn't understood the feeling before, by now Brigham must have known how Joseph had felt thirty years before, watching the Nauvoo Temple being constructed and wondering whether he would live long enough to dedicate it.

The new year arrived, with the date for the trial of Elder George Reynolds fast approaching. It was scheduled to begin in late March, and a surprising development occurred thirteen days before the trial. With no warning, President Ulysses S. Grant removed Judge McKean from the bench. The Saints had no complaints about that. McKean had demonstrated a serious "want of discretion and his non-judicial temperament," and the Saints believed that his replacement, whoever it was, had to be an improvement. "We know nothing of the judicial qualifications of his successor," the *Deseret News* reported, "but it is to be hoped that he will be able to exercise that discretion, moderation and insight which have long been wanting in Utah."[21] But that hope was tempered when the announcement of the Chief Justice's ouster came with an express statement that "the government, in the removal of Judge McKean, does not intend to abandon its policy in regard to polygamy."[22]

George Reynolds's trial finally convened on the thirty-first of March, and the arguments lasted precisely one day. The jury began deliberations on April 1 at ten o'clock in the morning and took just thirty minutes to return a verdict of guilty. Elder Reynolds was sentenced to one year's imprisonment and a $300 fine, but pending an appeal of the verdict, he was allowed to remain free on a $5,000 bond.[23]

Then came a surprising development—Elder Reynolds's exoneration at the hands of the Territorial Supreme Court a little more than two months later. In a unanimous decision that would have appalled the now-departed Justice McKean, the court ruled on June 15 that the grand jury that had indicted Elder Reynolds had been improperly assembled. McKean's successor, Justice David P. Lowe, concurred in the decision, no doubt to US Attorney Carey's consternation. The indictment was quashed, Reynolds's conviction was overturned, and now there would be no case to appeal to the United States Supreme Court.[24]

———— • • • ————

Brigham had returned from the south in February in plenty of time for the hearings. What his reaction was to the Reynolds conviction and exoneration is unknown. He could not have been unhappy to see his friend stay out of jail, but without a test case, the political and legal fight over the "Mormon Question" would drag on. But an opportunity to shift the balance of forces a bit appeared soon after, when the news came that President Ulysses S. Grant himself would be coming to Salt Lake City in

October. The Saints' attempts to change the hearts and minds of other senior US officials passing through their city had largely failed. Tours of the city, visits to the Salt Lake Theater, the Tabernacle, the temple construction site—these had all impressed their guests, but not enough for the visitors to pick up the torch on the Saints' behalf when they returned to Washington. If they could succeed this one time and win over Ulysses S. Grant, they would gain one of the most powerful friends possible.

President Grant and his wife, Julia, arrived in Ogden on Sunday, October 3. As he stepped down from the Pullman car onto the platform at twelve-thirty in the afternoon, the Saints present would have seen a brown-haired, bearded man of medium height, whose once-lean frame had expanded noticeably in the years since the end of the Civil War. Grant looked somewhat older than his fifty-three years, the premature aging probably stemming from his love of cigars, a weakness for alcohol, and the physical stress of war. His public manner was restrained by military training, but he could be jovial and even bawdy in the company of friends. "Grant was full of humor [and] full of the appreciation of it," his friend Sherman would later say of him. "Grant was no namby-pamby fool; he was a man—all over—rounded [and] complete."[25]

His true name was Hiram Ulysses Grant—the US Army had given him the "S" by mistake. After arriving at the US Military Academy at West Point to begin his education, he tried to register under his given name, only to find that the congressman who had nominated him for admission had erroneously written "Ulysses S. Grant" on the letter of nomination. The army could not change the registered name, so Grant accepted the new moniker.[26] His fellow cadets, including William Tecumseh Sherman, promptly began to tease the new cadet over his new initials, "U. S." They decided it was short for "Uncle Sam," and Grant was thereafter called "Sam" by his friends.

After Grant's string of victories during the Civil War, the Northern public had decided that the initials stood for "Unconditional Surrender." They cheered his elevation by Lincoln to commanding general of the army in March of 1864, but he was labeled a butcher by year's end, as his drive to end the war resulted in a string of costly battles that incurred tens of thousands of casualties in a matter of months. That perception was wiped away for the most part when he accepted General Robert E. Lee's surrender at Appomattox Courthouse on April 9 of the following year. Grant was the man who had won the War Between the States, and the prestige that came with that accomplishment was unequaled. Only Lincoln would have exceeded him in public respect after the war, had the president not been murdered. The Republicans essentially drafted Grant by unanimous ballot at their 1868 convention to run for the presidency, despite his protests that he preferred to remain in the army. Grant did not even campaign for office, instead taking advantage of the now-finished transcontinental railroad to escape on a tour of the western part of the country with his old friend General William Tecumseh Sherman. Grant won the election handily anyway, becoming, at age forty-six, the youngest US president ever elected to date; he defeated Horace Greeley in 1872 by an even larger margin to win reelection. He was the president who oversaw the troubled reconstruction of the South, and now he was determined to ensure federal control of the Western territories.

Now he had come to Utah. Brigham made the journey on the Utah Northern Line to greet the chief executive, an effort that he rarely made for anyone these days, given his health. The prophet and the nation's president enjoyed a "hearty and cordial" meeting of a half hour before they all departed for Salt Lake City. They arrived an hour later, and the president and his wife, Julia, boarded a carriage for a ride through the city with the current territorial governor, George W. Emery. Julia Grant was quite surprised at the reception. Thousands of children were lined up along South Temple Street between the train depot and the temple block. "The street was lined up with rows of children, I should say three deep . . . all singing songs of welcome and literally strewing the President's roadway with flowers," Mrs. Grant recorded.[27]

President and Mrs. Grant stayed at the Walker House overnight and took their tour of the city the following morning. Temple Square was the first stop, and their guides showed them the temple under construction. Whether its purpose was explained to the president and his wife, no one recorded, but Julia Grant, who was a keen observer of events and a diarist in her own right, was deeply impressed by the new Tabernacle. In her own memoirs, she recalled:

> Our visit here was most interesting. I went with two of the elders . . . to the Temple. These gentlemen conducted me through [the] great [Tabernacle], had the magnificent organ play for me, and, as the great volume of solemn sacred music filled the [Tabernacle], I could not help kneeling with bowed head and my heart, always so susceptible to the power of music, full of tenderness, to ask God's blessing to these people. The gentlemen asked if I had offered a prayer for them. "Yes," I answered, "a good Methodist one."[28]

The Grants left for Denver later that afternoon. "The universal expression of the members of the party, the President included, was one of unmixed pleasure with their visit to Salt Lake City, and the ladies especially regretted that their stay had been necessarily so short," the *Deseret News* reported.[29] Whether the Grants' short visit had been enough to sway them in favor of the Saints and against the hostile current of public opinion against them back East was unknown, but the Saints hoped for the best. The Deseret News editor theorized:

> [Grant's] party, one and all, will be sure to entertain an increased interest in Utah affairs, resulting from their visit and the acquaintanceship which they formed during the limited time of their stay. One always feels a sort of personal interest in a place which one has once visited . . . and therefore the inference is legitimate that the President and his family . . . will hereafter entertain something like a personal interest in Utah, and in all that affects the welfare, progress, and prosperity of her citizens.[30]

Even publishing such an optimistic editorial was itself a triumph of hope over experience.

———•··•———

A month after the president's visit, US Attorney Carey decided it was time to take a second swing at enforcing the Morrill Act. On November 1, he indicted Elder George Reynolds for polygamy yet again. Elder Reynolds was arrested and then released on a $2,500 bond, as before—and, as before, he was convicted in short order when his trial convened the following month. His sentence this time, handed down just a few days before Christmas, was for two years' imprisonment and a $500 fine. As he, Brigham, and other Church leaders had originally planned, Reynolds appealed the conviction. Pending the hearing of his case by the Supreme Court of the United States, he was again released on bail, but this time the amount required was $10,000.[31] The test case was back on track. Brigham hoped that the Supreme Court would settle the constitutionality of plural marriage once and for all, strike down the Morrill Act, and leave the Saints able to follow the dictates of their religious principles free from government interference.

———•··•———

Brigham was detained in Salt Lake City that winter with his own domestic and legal concerns and so was unable to make his annual pilgrimage to St. George. He was fortunate that the weather that season was not unusually harsh, so although he did not enjoy his usual recuperation period, neither did he suffer too much. He continued to manage Church affairs as much as his declining health allowed, but his mind was still caught up in the need to finish the temple. Twenty-three years was a long time to have labored on it, given what they had to show for all of their work. The walls were not a dozen feet above ground level.

Then a unique event occurred in April, the day before the scheduled start of general conference, which turned everyone's attention firmly away from any thoughts of temple construction or anything else.

For reasons unknown, at 4:48 p.m. on April 5, the day before the conference convened, a massive cache of gunpowder stored at Arsenal Hill, where the Utah Capitol Building now sits, exploded. The cause was never conclusively determined, though it was later believed that some boys had been firing guns in the vicinity, a burning paper wad from a shotgun had landed among some loose gunpowder, and, in quick succession, had set off the magazines where the rest was stored. Tens of thousands of pounds of charcoal, niter, and sulphur erupted in a series of blasts that shook the entire city below.

> An immense mass of flames shot heavenward at each succeeding report, and rising above the fire, then shot a great shower of debris, which seemed to vanish with lightning rapidity, when the air was filled with missiles which whistled and tore through the atmosphere, scattering all around within a radius of over two miles, and a vast cloud of smoke which arisen floated to the southeast. The concussion was so powerful that all around in a circuit of the extent already named houses tottered and shook, roofs, walls and ceiling were rent, windows innumerable were smashed, and hundreds of people were suddenly prostrated upon the ground.[32]

The arsenal building itself was reduced to a crater in the ground, and four people were killed instantly, three of them children. Panic rolled through the city as rocks, wood, and metal rained down from the sky, tearing into buildings, people, and animals. "The immense shower of missiles from the size of small boulders to rocks weighing a couple of hundred pounds, pieces of iron, concrete &c, it is marvelous that there were not a larger number of persons killed . . ."[33] the *Deseret Evening News* reported. Dozens of people were wounded by flying debris, some more than a mile away from the epicenter, and the property damage was immense. The shock wave tore into homes, businesses, and church buildings for a considerable distance, utterly destroying some and leaving others badly damaged, practically beyond repair. A 115-pound boulder was thrown as far as First South Street, smashing its way into the

Theatre Saloon there. "Nearly every building of any size, for a mile and a half or two miles around [was] damaged to a greater or less extent."[34]

The temple block was well inside the radius of the shock wave and the falling missiles propelled by the blasts. The temple itself, having the advantage of being solid granite, was entirely undamaged. Temples were considered places of spiritual refuge, but for those working inside the stone walls that day, the temple might well have been the safest location in all of Salt Lake City.

———·—··—·———

General conference convened the next day as scheduled. The explosion had understandably "been almost the sole topic of conversation" among the residents of Salt Lake City,[35] and the Saints certainly would still have been talking about it as they made their way into the Tabernacle, the north windows of which had been smashed by the eruption. Many of them would have come nursing their own minor injuries from the explosion or knowing friends and family who had fallen victim to it. Others would have suffered damage to homes and businesses, in some cases catastrophic, and would have come preoccupied by questions of how they would repair or rebuild, how long that would take, and how much it would cost.

Brigham had not been in Salt Lake the day before—he'd been in Ogden inspecting a new iron bridge under construction there—and so had missed the pyrotechnics, but he'd been touched by the disaster too. His flour mill on City Creek, just a half mile away from Arsenal Hill, had been destroyed, and his home and other buildings he owned were within the blast radius. One of his daughters had been cut by broken glass when the shock wave shattered a window near where she was sitting. The prophet understood perfectly well what was on the minds and in the hearts of the Saints that morning.

But he chose not to talk about the explosion, nor did any of the Apostles mention it who spoke that day. Brigham called the conference to order, but he left it to others to address the Saints. To a man, every Apostle that morning talked about the need to finish the Salt Lake Temple. "I consider that the building of Temples is one of the important things required by the Lord of the Latter-day Saints in the dispensation of the fullness of times, that we may go into those Temples and not only redeem the living but redeem our dead." Wilford Woodruff said.

> We have been a good many years here in the valleys of the mountains, and we have not yet got a Temple finished to the name of the Lord. We have one pretty well forward in St. George, and I am very glad of it; but we want one here. We have got the foundation laid; it has been standing a good many years, and I think that we should go to and finish it, and do what we can to redeem our dead.[36]

Elder John Taylor followed Wilford, and his discourse consumed the entire afternoon session of the conference. Taylor was the only Apostle senior to Wilford in the Quorum of the Twelve, and he was not an American by birth. He'd been born in 1808 in Milnthorpe, Westmorland, England, and had joined the Methodist church when he was a teenager. His parents immigrated to Canada when he was twenty-two, and Taylor followed a few years later. Though active in their Protestant faith, he and his wife had identified what they perceived as doctrinal problems with its teachings. Taylor's theological questions remained until he encountered Elder Parley P. Pratt in Toronto in 1836. Pratt taught the Taylors the gospel, and they were baptized shortly thereafter. They moved to Far West, Missouri, the following year, in time to share in the persecutions of the Saints there and in the years to come. Joseph Smith ordained Taylor an Apostle in 1838, just two years after the British Saint had first learned of the restored gospel. But his faith was solid, and Taylor was with the Prophet Joseph the day he was killed in Carthage Jail. Taylor himself had been wounded in the attack, shot four times, in the left hand, the right thigh, and the left knee. The first two balls were extracted without the use of anesthesia; the bullet in his knee could not be removed, and so there it remained until Taylor died decades later. Taylor was, in 1876, the last living witness to Joseph Smith's martyrdom.[37]

This man, greatly respected among the membership of the Church, declared that the building of temples "ought to rest with force upon the minds of all good Saints." Their intentions were good, he said, but they had to be truly willing to do all within their power to accomplish God's purposes, including finishing the temple. "A great many are doing the best they know how, and are desirous, with their whole soul and spirit, with their intellect and their substance and everything they have, to dedicate themselves and all they have for God and for his cause and kingdom, and for building up Temples, and for accomplishing everything that God requires at their hands," he assured them.[38] The Lord expected His people to contribute their time, talents, and skills, and those unwilling to do so would not share in the eternal rewards waiting for those who did all they could. To make his point, Taylor quoted from memory, and not quite verbatim, the Lord's warning that "not every one that saith Lord, Lord, that shall enter into my kingdom, but it is he who does the will of my Father who is in heaven."[39] Now was the time to show their faith by their works.

—————•··•—————

The conference ended after four days of sermons, and Brigham was finally able to make his annual trip to St. George on May 1. He went this time not to escape the cold for the sake of his health. Spring was far advanced, and the weather was warm—in fact, snowmelt from the canyons in the Salt Lake Valley was flooding the city, causing significant damage and complicating the effort to repair the damage from the previous month's Arsenal Hill explosion. This trip south for the prophet was to strengthen the Church members and to evaluate the progress on the other house of the Lord. The journey turned out to be quite pleasant. Brigham and his party were able to travel by rail as far as Nephi that year before having to switch over to wagons and carriages. They reached St. George on the ninth, the fastest time Brigham had ever covered the

320-mile distance.[40] Arriving in good spirits, as he approached the city he was greeted with a sight in the distance that he must have found inspiring. "The Temple [looked] magnificent in contrast with the surrounding country."[41]

The day after he arrived, Brigham went up to the temple site to see for himself exactly how far advanced the work was on the building. The exterior of the building was near to being finished, and, despite his advanced age and rheumatism, he was able to ascend the tower and look out over the city.[42] The roof needed finishing, but that would happen in a matter of months, given the rate at which the carpenters and masons were working. The interior work would surely be done not very long after that. The day was fast approaching when Brigham would be able to dedicate this house of the Lord and the Saints would again be able to perform all the ordinances for both the living and the dead necessary for salvation.

Brigham was able to stay only a month in St. George this time, but he had seen what he needed to see, and it had left him "feeling first rate."[43] Brigham departed the city on June 12 for Salt Lake—the day before Elder Reynolds's conviction for plural marriage was argued before the Territorial Supreme Court—and he took his time making the return journey. He didn't arrive until July 1, tired, but having enough time to rest up so he could enjoy the national centennial celebration three days later on the Fourth of July.

The good feelings of that day must have dissipated when, two days later, the court handed down its decision in the Reynolds case. It must have come as a disappointment, though not a surprise, when the court upheld the guilty verdict. The plaintiff remained free on bail for the time being, and, as expected, Reynolds's lawyers immediately filed an appeal to the Supreme Court of the United States.

———— • · · • ————

The recent push from the pulpit by the Apostles to draw more help in finishing the temple was bearing some fruit. The *Deseret Evening News* reported that Temple Square now presented "a very lively scene, there being in the vicinity of a hundred hands busily engaged cutting stone and otherwise employed."[44] And not only were there more hands at work, the laborers were getting creative in finding ways to speed up the construction and reduce their own load at the same time. Truman's four derricks had been a help in moving the granite stones, but they were still driven by muscle power, with workmen having to crank the spindle on the masts to raise and lower the heavy blocks. Someone thought that ought to be rectified, and by August, they had brought in an eight-horse-power steam engine to take over that job. They placed the engine inside the temple walls, where it could be moved from corner to corner depending on which derrick would be handling the stone. Moving the engine would take up a half day, but once it was connected to a derrick, they would be able to raise and lower stone much faster than muscle power alone could manage—three times as fast, as it turned out. With Truman Angell and John Sharp, the superintendent of construction, looking on, the workers used the engine for the first time to move a block at eleven o'clock in the morning on August 16. The engine performed its job as hoped. That happy news brought Brigham and Elder John Taylor to the temple site later that afternoon, doubtless to see the engine at work and watch as the masons lifted and laid stones mechanically. Truman and Sharp calculated that with the engine in place, the masons would be able to lay five full courses of stone by winter on the quadrant of the temple covered by that derrick. Then they would move the engine to another corner and repeat the process, laying five courses, until they'd gone around the wall. That would "make quite a marked difference in the appearance of the building" before the year's end. [45]

It was also decided that the workers could push the temple forward more efficiently if they had some kind of protection from the elements. Given that squaring, carving, and finishing a single stone could take a month of work, anything that could keep the stonecutters shielded from sun during clear, hot summer days and dry from the rain during any season was worth the investment. So Superintendent Sharp approved the construction of five large sheds to be erected south of the temple and north of the railroad spur. The sheds were open to the north and south, had thatched roofs—much like the old bowery had used—and covered more than one hundred workers when placed end to end. Once they were in place, the stonecutters would be able to work all day regardless of the weather.

With the need to accelerate temple building having weighed on his mind of late, this was all a cause for optimism and "glad tidings"[46] for Brigham. The day after the derrick engine went to work, Brigham sat and penned a letter to his son Alfales, who was studying law at the University of Michigan. During his teenage years, the boy spent some time laboring for the public works on the temple block, so he would have had a personal interest in the temple's progress. Brigham apparently had been keeping his son informed on it, and this bit of news was delightful. "For the first time in the history of building temples to the Lord, so far as I am acquainted," Brigham wrote, "we are now laying the rock by the help of the steam engine, and the speed and ease with which it does its work is very encouraging." Then, almost as an afterthought, he noted that "our news from the St. George temple is also very pleasing[.] The work is being pushed ahead there with much energy and success."[47]

Brigham's optimism was not misplaced. On November 29, Elder George Reynolds informed Brigham that Truman and Sharp's estimate that the masons could use the new steam engine to lay five courses of granite before winter had indeed been met. "Bishop Sharp wished me to tell you that the five courses of rock were in place on the Temple wall and rock laying was finished about a week ago," he told the prophet. "He considers the walls are made safe for the winter, the joints between the rock have been raised and the top of the wall sanded. The sheds for the workmen are nearly completed, and the engine is being put under cover."

In his letter to Brigham, Reynolds also included "a circular issued to-day to the quorums relative to work on the Temple during the winter."[48]

The increased number of stonecutters, the steam engine, and the sheds were all welcome advances, but the Church leadership still felt it necessary to call for more help. James Livingston and his crew were still delivering granite faster than the stonecutters at Temple Square could process it. They had a fair number of men who could do the rough cuts, but there was a particular need for men who could handle the fine cuts required to perfectly square the stones, and especially to do the decorative work on the artistic parts. The result was that granite blocks were stacking up inside the temple walls, numbered according to the order in which the masons would lay them as they were ready. So on November 10, the First Presidency issued the circular to the Saints in the area, calling for more workers to come.

> Dear Brethren—It is expected in accordance with a circular issued some time ago, "that the labor upon the Temple here will continue to be pushed forward by those now engaged in it," viz.: the Seventies', Elders' and High Priests' Quorums.
>
> The Presidents of Seventies have issued a circular calling upon their Quorums to continue in their present labors on the Temple and in the quarry. It is desirable that the High Priests' and Elders' Quorums should continue their labors as heretofore, that the work upon the Temple may progress as fast as practicable during the winter, and that preparations may be made for the accomplishment of a good work the next summer. If any of the Quorums can provide for the payment of competent workmen to do the fine cutting for the outside courses, it should be attended to, as there is a large amount of common stone now cut, and being cut, and it requires a stronger force of workmen for the outside finish, that all portions may progress equally and with celerity and dispatch. There are a number of such workmen in the city, and perhaps elsewhere, who stand ready to do this face work when called upon.[49]

The announcement went out over the signatures of John W. Young[50] and Daniel H. Wells, Brigham's first and second counselors in the presidency, and Elder John Taylor, the President of the Quorum of the Twelve Apostles. To ensure that the maximum number of people read it, the *Deseret News* published the circular on the front page of the December 6 edition. To reinforce the urgency of the request, members of the First Presidency and the Twelve went out to visit congregations as far north as Kaysville and Brigham City, with plans to hold frequent meetings with wards throughout the region to urge the members there to "keep up their quota of labor on the Temple and do what further lay in their power in accomplishing the work."[51]

By then, Brigham was in St. George again. He, Wilford Woodruff, George Q. Cannon, Truman Angell, and others had left for the south on November 1, and, as with his previous trip in May, not merely for the sake of escaping a cold winter. The temple in St. George was far enough advanced that Brigham felt it was ready for dedication to the Lord.

The building was not quite finished. In recent weeks, workers there had been laying canvas to create a temporary roof, and the carpenters had been trying to finish the domed tower and window frames. The masons had been finishing up the parapet and the baptismal font in the lower level. Daniel H. Wells had traveled south in September to see whether the interior could be finished "sufficient for baptisms and endowments." After touring the building, he'd written to Brigham and reported that he thought the job could be "easily accomplished in a few months." That had been enough for Brigham to travel south to dedicate the building at the earliest possible date.[52]

The prophet and his party arrived on November 9 and went through the temple the following day. They "went through every part of it from the baptismal font in the basement to the top of the roof," and Wilford considered it a "glorious sight." The finished building, he said, was "as white as snow both inside and out and is a beautiful contrast with the red appearance of the surrounding country."[53]

A myth developed over the years that there was one part of the temple with which Brigham was unhappy—the tower. According to the tale, Truman had designed it shorter than Brigham wanted, and the prophet thought it was too squat and out of proportion with the rest of the structure. But whether he was unhappy with it or not, the prophet did not order any change to it that would have delayed the end of construction. He wanted to see the temple dedicated as soon as possible, and the tower was merely a decorative part of the building and not required for the performance of any ordinances. They could always fix it later.

When they weren't preaching to the Saints in St. George and nearby settlements, Wilford and Truman spent much of their time working on the temple interior, giving instructions on how the rooms were to be arranged and organized to allow for the performance of ordinances. Brigham was unable to help much of the time. His health, always tenuous by that point, took a turn for the worse as his rheumatism flared up. It left him laid up in bed, with pain in his extremities so severe that he could "not hardly touch [his feet] to the floor."[54] So the work of directing the temple preparations fell to his counselors, the other Apostles in his party, and Truman. They took no holidays, and they did not consider themselves above doing any of the manual labor themselves. On Christmas Day, Brigham was finally recovered enough from his aches and pains to ride out to the temple, and there he found Wilford working with forty women from the local wards who were sewing and laying carpets.[55] Despite their best efforts, the interior was not completed by year's end, but Brigham decided that the work was far enough along to justify going ahead and dedicating a section of the building that was finished.

On January 1, 1877, Brigham, Wilford, and Elders Erastus Snow and Brigham Young Jr. joined an assembly of 2,000 Saints in the lower level of the temple and conducted the first temple dedication since that of the Nauvoo Temple almost thirty years before. Brigham presided over the ceremony but was still too infirm to conduct—he was in such pain that he could not walk and had been carried in a chair into the building by three men—so he asked Wilford to lead the meeting. At twelve-thirty in the afternoon, Wilford stood on the upper step of the baptismal font and addressed the congregation. "We are this day blessed," he said, "with a privilege that but few since the day of Adam have ever enjoyed. Few . . . have ever had the privilege of entering into a temple built by the commandment of God in which to administer ordinances for both the living and the dead. We have now assembled to dedicate portions of this temple unto God." Recognizing that the packed crowd could not kneel down, he asked them to "bow [their] heads and [their] hearts" and silently repeat the words of the dedicatory prayer in their minds, "that our prayers may ascend into the ears of the Lord . . . that they may be answered upon our heads." This he asked them to do because, as he explained, "the Saints do not prize as they should the blessings they enjoy."

Wilford concluded his remarks, and the congregation sang, "The Spirit of God Like a Fire is Burning," which had become a traditional hymn to sing at public events related to the building of any temple. Wilford then offered a lengthy prayer of dedication. He named the parts of the building and all it contained and asked for blessings on them and on the "servants and handmaidens" who would serve in the Lord's house. He also prayed that the Lord would grant Brigham a "renewal of his body and the healing of his infirmities and the lengthening out of his days and years" so that he might "live to behold other temple[s] built and dedicated."

More hymns were sung and more prayers offered by the other Apostles present. When all were finished, Brigham forced himself onto his feet and addressed the crowd before him. He could not consent to leave the temple without speaking to the Saints, he told them. Then he repeated the words Wilford had spoken, that the people assembled were enjoying a privilege few had enjoyed since the days of Adam. "Brethren and Sisters, do you understand this?" he asked. "It seems a great many of the people know nothing about it." He spoke a minute about the biblical history of temples and the Saints' own painful experiences in building and losing them. He spoke about the dead waiting in the spirit world for someone to perform saving ordinances on their behalf. "We enjoy privileges that are enjoyed by no one else on the face of the Earth," he told them, and so the responsibility was on them to stop chasing after wealth and the cares of the world and take care of the work entrusted to them. His language was blunt, and he did nothing to soften his warning. "You may think this is plain talk," he admitted. "It is not as plain as you will find by and by. You will go to the gates of Heaven and Jesus will say I never knew you," if they did not carry out this responsibility.

Thus finished, he looked out and told the Saints there: "I do not know whether the people are satisfied with the services of the dedication of the Temple or not. I am not half satisfied and I never expect to be satisfied until the devil is whipped and driven from off the face of the Earth." He drove home his feelings on that matter in literal fashion, striking the pulpit with his hickory cane. Old man though he was, and weakened by illness, he hit the stand hard enough that he "buried three of the knots into the solid wood."[56]

With the house of the Lord partially dedicated, the Saints commenced to perform baptisms for the dead on January 9 at twelve o'clock in the afternoon, the first such ordinances carried out in a proper temple since the Saints had fled Nauvoo in 1846, thirty-one years before. Brigham, Wilford, and the other Apostles conducted the ceremonies. Baptisms were performed for 224 people. The first endowments were performed two days later, with the ordinance being performed on behalf of seventy-three people. Wilford, who would soon be called as the first temple president over the St. George Temple, practically lived in the building, spending virtually all of his time doing vicarious work for hundreds upon hundreds of deceased persons. "What is gold or silver in comparison to the redemption of our dead?" he asked in his own journal. He answered his own question with a terse response—"Nothing."[57]

Brigham chose to remain in St. George throughout the winter and into the spring, attending the temple as often as his health and energy

St. George Temple.

permitted. At the same time, laborers continued working on the exterior and interior of the building, and by April it was finished. The prophet decided that, for the first time since the Saints had arrived in the Rocky Mountains, the general conference of the Church would convene somewhere other than in Salt Lake City. This time, the conference opened in the St. George Temple at ten o'clock in the morning on April 6, with Brigham using the occasion to dedicate the house of the Lord in its entirety. Elder Daniel H. Wells offered the prayer at the start of the meeting, after which the conference proceeded as usual.

Brigham spoke for a few minutes during the conference, but he said nothing about his own feelings about the occasion. Instead, he called on the people to be selfless in sharing their time, talents, and energy in the cause of building up the Lord's kingdom. As for himself, he was tired. "I feel many times that I could not live an hour longer, but I mean to live just as long as I can," he assured the Saints. "I know not how soon the messenger will call for me, but I calculate to die in the harness."[58] With that, Brigham sat down, and the first session of the conference adjourned.

———— ◆ · ◆ ————

Brigham left for Salt Lake City ten days later, on the sixteenth of April. He'd been in St. George now for almost six months, and he'd spent more of the last year there, or on the road traveling to or from the southern settlement, than he had in Salt Lake City. But there was no question now that he would not live to see the Salt Lake Temple completed, so there'd been no other alternative but to focus on the one temple that would be finished during his lifetime.

It would be surprising if he hadn't looked back at the now-finished temple as he rode away north in his carriage. He surely felt some kind of relief that there was, finally, a finished house of the Lord on the earth again—and, more than that, the contents of the endowment ceremony and other ordinances had been recorded and were now preserved in a temple. A few months before the temple's dedication, Brigham had built a small office next to his home in St. George, and he spent much of his time there with Wilford and other leaders, writing out the text for the ordinances so they could be presented to the Saints without error. Until then, the script for each one had been preserved in the memories of those who performed them and taught to new temple workers through oral training. That practice risked the introduction of variations in the ceremonies, depending on how sharp an individual temple worker's memory actually was. Brigham wanted to ensure that the ordinances would always be performed correctly and accurately, and that no changes, no matter how innocently they arose, would creep in over time. That worry even had a doctrinal foundation, he believed. In the Old Testament,

Isaiah had prophesied of that very problem and its consequences, writing, "The earth also is defiled under the inhabitants thereof; because they have transgressed the laws, changed the ordinance, broken the everlasting covenant."[59] The Saints believed that Isaiah's prophecy had been fulfilled after the deaths of the ancient Apostles. Without the inspired guidance of the Lord's chosen servants to ensure that doctrine and ordinances remained free from error, changes had been introduced periodically. Small and incremental, and often made by well-meaning individuals trying to do right, those minor alterations over time had added up to large variations that produced churches, doctrines, and ordinances very different from the original. Far from the "One Lord, one faith, one baptism" that Paul had written about to the Ephesians, Christianity itself had fractured into countless denominations over those changes.[60] The Saints believed it was for that reason the Lord had had to restore His Church to the earth again.

To prevent that from happening now, Brigham worked with Wilford Woodruff and others to transcribe the temple ordinances and ceremonies and create a permanent and accurate record that depended on no one's memory alone. Now, with that labor completed, all of the work could be performed in exactly the same way, using exactly the same wording, in all temples everywhere. And in future years, that record would facilitate the accurate translation of those ceremonies into different languages as temples spread across the earth.

—— · · · ——

Brigham stopped over in Manti on his return journey from St. George. The settlement there was a little more than halfway to Salt Lake, and Brigham was still traveling by carriage—the railroad terminus was somewhere between Santaquin and Nephi to the northeast. Brigham had sent a group of Saints to the area back in 1849, and the settlers had arrived in November of that year, too late to construct cabins. They had survived their first winter by digging into a hillside to create temporary shelters from the snow, and they'd fought an army of rattlesnakes to establish their new city when the spring came.

Now the prophet was here to dedicate a site for another temple, one that he surely knew he would not live to see finished. During the general conference in October of 1876, the year before, Brigham had told the Saints in Manti and the surrounding areas to start work on a temple. "As soon as you are ready to commence, I will provide the plan," he assured them. "The ground is already selected." Now they were ready, and on April 25 Brigham rode to the top of the hill and offered up a prayer to consecrate the site. When his appeal to heaven was finished, he then turned to the assembled crowd and gave them some prophetic instruction on the proper way to build a house of the Lord. First and foremost, he said, their motives had to be pure.

> We want to rear this Temple with clean hands and pure hearts, that we, with our children, may enter into it to receive our washing and anointings; the keys and ordinances of the holy Priesthood; and also to officiate in the same for our fathers and mothers and our forefathers who lived and died without the Gospel, that they with us may be made partakers of the fruits of the tree of life, and live and rejoice in our Father's kingdom.

Laborers should not come motivated primarily by money because "it is not in keeping with the character of Saints to make the building of Temples a matter of merchandise." They should support each other and give what they had freely to those dedicating their time and talents, so the workmen could eat, drink, and be clothed. That call was extended to the sisters of the Church as well. "They can do a great deal by way of encouraging their husbands and sons, and also by making clothing of various kinds for them, and in otherwise providing for them while they are working here," Brigham told the women nearby. And the work needed to begin as soon as possible—they would not be able to work during the winter as their fellow Saints had done in St. George, so they needed to finish everything they could "in the milder portions of the season."

Then, finished with his duty there, he bid farewell to the Saints of Manti. "God bless you, brethren and sisters; we hope and pray that you will be inspired to perform this work with honor to yourselves and glory to God," he said in parting. "This is the work of the latter days that we are engaged in, and . . . the good work of redemption and salvation will continue until all is completed, and Jesus presents the kingdom to the Father. Amen."[61]

◆ · · ◆

Brigham reached home two days later. The Utah Southern Railroad would have carried his party from at least Santaquin all the way to Salt Lake City in a matter of a few hours, and after disembarking and riding up South Temple, he would have seen his own house for the first time in six months. There he rested for a few weeks, but there was one more temple site to dedicate, this one in Logan, in Cache Valley to the north. Truman Angell wanted to keep his focus on the Salt Lake Temple, so he lobbied for another man to supervise the construction of this new build-ing—Truman Angell Jr., the Church architect's son. Truman Jr. was still young, just twenty-five years old, but he'd studied building and architec-ture under his father and showed promise; overseeing the construction of a major project such as the Logan Temple would teach him much and give his career a boost. The job would also be made easier for him be-cause he was already familiar with his father's designs. The exterior of the Logan Temple would resemble the St. George Temple in many re-spects, but the interior would be patterned after the Salt Lake Temple's floor plan. Given the favorable site chosen and the learning gained from building the St. George Temple, Brigham was hopeful that they could erect this one faster than any that had come before.

He boarded the train again and rode north, with Truman Sr. and Elders John Taylor and Orson Pratt of the Quorum of the Twelve joining him for the dedication of the temple site. The ceremony took place on May 18, 1877, and this time Brigham left it to Elder Pratt to officiate. When the prophet finally rose to speak, he called on the Saints to finish the temple there within three years. They could do it, he promised, if all were united in "our interests, our faith and labors, that our hopes and the results of our labors may be concentrated in the salvation of the human family."[62]

Thus finished, Brigham returned home.

———•··•———

The walls of the Salt Lake Temple were a little higher than twenty feet now—a bit less than one foot above the ground for every year the Saints had been working—and just above the level of the first full set of windows. If Brigham was disappointed that twenty-four years of labor had only gotten the building that far, he didn't say so. Still, it would be understandable if he'd felt any sorrow that he would never see the granite temple completed. He'd had every reason to think he would see it finished on that long-ago day when he'd stamped his cane into the ground of this once-empty valley and declared it the place for a temple. He'd seen it through the Spirit—"I have never looked upon that ground, but the vision of it was there"[63]—and for years he'd kept William Ward's hand-drawn picture of the planned building on his wall, where he would have looked at it often. But thirty years had come and gone, and he could not have hoped now that he would ever see the finished product.

———•··•———

On the evening of August 23, 1877, Brigham suddenly began to feel very sick. His intestines were cramping, he became nauseated, and he began to vomit. The discomfort persisted through the night. His nephew Seymour, a physician, he came to his home the following morning and diagnosed the prophet with "cholera morbus," a general term for stomach flu. The doctor later decided that the true cause was appendicitis, but diverticulitis or several other ailments could have produced the same symptoms.[64]

Brigham suffered for several days, attended by several physicians, but none could relieve his discomfort, which had become intense. His family and Church leaders stayed near him, and his counselors administered priesthood blessings to him throughout the week. Everyone was hoping for his recovery, but soon it must have become apparent that his time on earth was short.

In St. George, Wilford Woodruff received a telegram on August 27 reporting Brigham's failing condition. He had known the prophet as long as anyone had. The two men had ridden into the Salt Lake Valley together in July of 1847, Wilford driving the wagon, Brigham stretched out sick in the back. Now his old friend and spiritual leader was failing, and all Wilford could do for him was pray. "I notified all the people that I could to join in prayer which we did throughout the city as far as we could," he wrote. He returned to the temple the next day and prayed all day for the prophet. "I gathered together some 100 elders [and] 30 women [and] we went into the temple . . . and prayed through the day and night until 2 o'clock in the morning."[65]

On August 28, Brigham began to fade. He developed a fever and soon was no longer fully lucid. The following day, August 29, his strength failed him at last. His fever spiked to 105 degrees and his breathing stopped. "It was but a gasp or two, a slight and almost imperceptible tremor—the rush of a thimble of blood to his lips—when his pulse ceased to denote the vibrations of his heart—his countenance assumed the blanched pallor of death, and all was quiet in that room."[66] He was gone.

Brigham's last words before he died were "Joseph! Joseph! Joseph!"[67]

Wilford left St. George the day after Brigham passed and arrived in Salt Lake City after two and a half days of travel. Brigham's body was lying in state in the Tabernacle, with 10,000 Saints passing through daily to view their deceased prophet. "The Tabernacle was handsomely decorated," Wilford saw. "Each column with the organ, the stands and the whole front of the platform tastefully draped in black."[68] Brigham was laid to rest on September 2, four days after he passed. An estimated 25,000 Saints came to pay their respects. When the funeral program was completed, Brigham's coffin was removed to the burial site. Wilford dedicated "the ground, the vault, and the body unto the Lord."[69]

On the fourth, two days later, the Quorum of the Twelve met as a body and assumed the leadership of the Church, just as they had done thirty years before when Joseph Smith had been killed. The ten Apostles present—Orson Pratt and Joseph F. Smith were both in England—sustained Elder John Taylor, the Quorum's senior member, as the President of the Quorum, which made him the Church's highest leader. The Saints sustained their new leadership on October 6 in a solemn assembly during the general conference of the Church.

———•••———

Out of respect for the prophet, there was no work performed on the Salt Lake Temple during the days between Brigham's death and his funeral. But as the crowds came to the temple block and waited to enter the Tabernacle, they would have all seen the temple walls and the granite stones, the derricks and the railroad spur, the sheds and the stonecutters' tools, all reminders that Brigham had been urging them to come and help finish the building. The Saints' desire to build this temple in particular had never really slackened despite their setbacks, but now they had another reason to finish it. This house of the Lord would also be a kind of monument to the prophet who had pushed it forward more than anyone.

For his part, Truman thought it an opportune time to see whether President Taylor wanted to make a change in affairs on the temple construction. The job was as stressful for him now as it ever had been, and his advancing age—he was sixty-seven—was leaving him less and less able to shoulder his responsibilities. So he offered his resignation to the Church's new leader if Taylor wanted it. "My plans [for the temple] have received the sanction of our late President, I think, as I have placed them before him at sundry times," Truman wrote to Taylor and the Twelve. "I wish to say to you, Brethren, you can continue me in the Architect's Office or not as you see fit, I am at your service."[70] With the plans for the house of the Lord settled, there was no reason they had to keep him on; if they wanted to bring in someone younger and stronger, he would take no offense. Quite the contrary, he'd always found it a relief when he could walk away from architecture, even if only for a time. But John Taylor saw no reason to change that particular horse in midstream, and the Brethren asked Truman to stay on.

So the work went on without fanfare. Winter was fast approaching, with only a few weeks remaining before the cold would hinder the construction efforts. With the engine-powered cranes helping the workers lift the stones, the temple walls rose a bit more that year. They laid as many stones onto the courses as they could while the weather allowed, and then they covered the steam engine for the season.

———•·•———

The work resumed in 1878, and they added another twelve feet onto the walls, a noticeable amount. At that rate, it would still take several more years to bring the walls up to the square and then construct the planned spires at the corners and the midpoints of the ends. But if nothing happened to disrupt the work, they could finish the building's exterior in a few years. Once that was done, they could remove the derricks and go to work on the interior. If the Saints in St. George could build their temple in six years, surely the Saints in Salt Lake could now finish theirs just as quickly.

As it turned out, the Saints in the south were not quite so finished building that temple as they had thought. During the early hours of August 16, just shy of one year after Brigham's death, a furious storm arose over the city, and a single bolt of lightning struck the St. George Temple's spire. After the sun came up and the Saints there could evaluate the damage, Stake President John D. T. McAllister dispatched a telegram to John Taylor and Wilford Woodruff, which read:

The bolt first struck the dome on the east face, near the top, breaking it in and shattering the wood of all the section on the east front, then down to the first rise above the square of the octagon of the dome, then followed down to the foot of [the] top flight of steps and ran quartering north east to [the] floor of [the] parapet, down through the floor, then divided running North and South through the lath and plastering above the square of the rock foundation of the tower. Striking both of the circle window frames on the south east corner marring the plastering on the outside, and leaving the smoky black mark of fire in its course. No damage done to any other part of the Temple below the timbers of the roof.[71]

McAllister asked for instructions. "Shall we repair the damage done or not? Until we hear from you, we shall use a wagon cover etc., to prevent damage by rain. . . . It has not in the least interfered with our ordinance work."[72]

Of course, the temple would be repaired, and that direction was given. And when the spire was reconstructed, it was built significantly taller, this time to a height that Brigham surely would have found satisfactory.

CHAPTER 11

PREPARED TO ABIDE
THE PENALTY

As the fall season of 1878 arrived, the walls of the Salt Lake Temple had climbed another twelve feet, which was a cause for celebration. The pace of the construction was as fast as it had ever been. To make sure there were no repeats of the foundation fiasco, Truman was daily taking measurements with his level and being generally obsessive about ensuring that all of the stones were perfectly horizontal, no shims or spawls allowed. To achieve that, every stone had to be cut to a high level of precision, which kept the stonecutters working eight hours a day, six days a week. Truman reported to John Sharp that the craftsmen "during the [eight] hours' work are going beyond their natural strength, and many are shortening their natural lives by working so very hard." At the going wages, they were earning an average of $75 each day. The architect projected that if they started working ten-hour days—which Truman thought was likely impossible, given the energy the men were already expending—their daily earnings would climb to $93.75.[1] With ninety-two stonecutters at work "when there is a sufficiency of stone on hand," it was costing an average of $6,900 per day just to shape and dress the granite for the walls.[2] That total did not include any wages paid to other workers on the temple site, the salaries paid to Truman and his assistants, the cost of freighting the granite from Little Cottonwood Canyon, or any of the other multitudinous expenses incurred daily. But the numbers were adding up. The temple was proving to be an extremely costly endeavor.

———•··•———

The human cost to building the temple climbed again that year. Men had been hurt working on the temple throughout the years, suffering the usual kinds of injuries that any construction crew incurs when putting up a large building—strained and sore muscles, cuts, bruises, the occasional broken bone. A decade before, when Brigham had redirected the workers to help build the transcontinental railroad, in part to accelerate the temple's construction, James Livingston had suffered one of the worst injuries courtesy of that accidental blast of a vial of nitroglycerin. He'd been fortunate to escape with only bad memories and the loss of his arm, while a few other Saints had died in accidents while building the railroad. One man, Archibald Bowman, had died in 1855 in an accident quarrying stone for the building.[3] But 1878 was the year when the first workman died at the temple site.

The temple walls were high enough that the workmen had to change their system for lifting the stones into place. Instead of using the derricks to lift the stones from the ground, they hauled the blocks inside the temple walls and lifted them up to the height of the wall on a steam lift. Then the men could use a derrick to raise the stone from the lift and position it for placement. On September 27, a workman named Sam Kaealoi was working up on one of the wooden walkways suspended along the upper levels of the building. Kaealoi was a native of the Marquesas Islands in the South Pacific, a convert who had arrived in Salt Lake the previous spring. He'd taken a job working on the temple, and that had been his only employment during his months in the valley. His job that day was to guide the boom arm of the derrick used to move finished granite blocks to the designated places on the stone course where the masons would lay them down. Around two o'clock in the afternoon,

Kaealoi was swinging the derrick arm, and it carried the heavy stone over the edge of the platform. There were no safety rails on the walkway, Kaealoi did not let go of the guy rope as he should have, and he was pulled over. He fell more than thirty feet from the top course of stones to the ground. A doctor was nearby and rushed over to render any help he could, but he quickly saw that Kaealoi was bleeding from his nose and ears, a sign of serious head trauma. Kaealoi's injuries were mortal—his skull was fractured at the base. There was nothing that could be done for the suffering man, and Kaealoi expired within a few minutes.[4]

⎯⎯•••⎯⎯

Six weeks after Sam Kaealoi's fatal tumble off the temple wall, the case of *Reynolds v. United States* finally reached the Supreme Court of the United States. Reynolds's lawyer, George W. Biddle, argued that the lower court had made several mistakes in deciding the case, but the major one was its answer as to "whether the United States Congress has a constitutional right to prohibit polygamous marriage in the territories." Biddle claimed that it did not, because, he said, the government was "not the custodian of morals of the country" and could "no more prescribe a certain form of marriage than it can instruct parents in their duties and relations to their children." US Attorney General Charles Devens countered that "an interpretation of the Constitution which would restrain Congress from attaching a penalty to the crime of polygamy on account of its being an article of religious faith, would also restrain it from attaching a penalty to any other crime which might be sanctioned by religion."[5] That would open the door to all kinds of mischief and wrongdoing.

The day after the arguments before the high court finished, the women of Salt Lake City convened another mass meeting, this one in the Salt Lake Theater, to protest the "misrepresentations" of the Church's antagonists regarding plural marriage. If the critics' argument hinged on the assumption that plural marriage was detrimental to the well-being of women, then the testimony of the sisters of the Church was the best evidence in the Saints' defense. So, Eliza R. Snow and many of the same sisters as before took to the stand and declared that they had been "misjudged and misrepresented to the nation, by those in [their] midst of [their] own sex, in regard to [their] most sacred rights, the rights which pertain to the holy relations of wifehood and motherhood."[6] They were loyal US citizens, the women argued, but the government had no right to tell them whom they could marry or the kinds of families they could enjoy.

The theater was filled and the women were energetic, to a degree that left the men of the city somewhat amazed. In a letter to the editor of the *Salt Lake Herald*, one citizen observed, "A man with a grievance is an individual not desirable to encounter, but a woman with a grievance, who wishes to be button-holed by her? Yet here are a band of 100 or 200 women with a grievance." Many who attended the public meetings came away with the belief that the sisters of the Church, when aroused in their ire, were not to be trifled with.[7]

———— • • ————

The justices on the high court did not deliberate the case of *Reynolds v. United States* very long. On January 5, 1879, less than two months after oral arguments, they issued a unanimous decision. The US government had the power to outlaw plural marriage, they declared. Writing for the court, Chief Justice Morrison Waite quoted Thomas Jefferson, the revered Founding Father who had authored the Virginia Statute on Religious Freedom and had been a passionate advocate for freedom of worship. In a letter to a committee of Baptists in Danbury, Connecticut, in 1802, then-US President Jefferson had explained that government had no right to police a person's beliefs, but a person's beliefs gave him no right to defy the law.

Religion is a matter which lies solely between man and his God; that he owes account to none other for his faith or his worship; that *the legislative powers of the government reach actions only, and not opinions,* . . . [the] legislature should 'make no law respecting an establishment of religion or prohibiting the free exercise thereof,' thus building a wall of separation between church and state.[8] (emphasis added)

Thus, Justice Waite explained, the Constitution deprived "Congress . . . of all legislative power over mere opinion, but [it] was left free to reach actions which were in violation of social duties or subversive of good order."[9] So allowing the Church to practice plural marriage in defiance of the law "would be to make the professed doctrines of religious belief superior to the law of the land, and in effect to permit every citizen to become a law unto himself. Government could exist only in name under such circumstances."[10]

George Reynolds's conviction was upheld, and the Morrill Act remained the law of the land. Reynolds was resentenced that June in the Third District Court of Utah to two years' imprisonment and the maximum fine that the law could impose—$500. Back in Washington, D.C., George Q. Cannon, still the Utah delegate to Congress, immediately submitted a petition for pardon on Elder Reynolds's behalf to the president, Rutherford B. Hayes. The entire Reynolds case had been a test case, in agreement with the prosecutor, to test the constitutionality of the Morrill Act, and Reynolds was a volunteer "put forward to represent the Mormon people." Thus, Cannon argued, "owing to this peculiar condition of facts, Reynolds, representing the whole people, should be pardoned." President Hayes discussed the matter with his cabinet, which was divided over the request. Hayes, wanting "to do what he can to uproot the institution of polygamy," decided against clemency.[11] The US government had just breached its gentleman's agreement with the Church, and George Reynolds would have to serve his sentence.

John Taylor visited Reynolds the day before he was to be taken into custody. The senior Apostle gave the convicted man a priesthood blessing in which he declared that Reynolds was "a sacrifice in behalf of Israel" for having volunteered to stand before the courts. The Apostle promised that "as thou hast been adjudged guilty in this case, and the laws of the country apportion thee to imprisonment for obeying the law of God," the Spirit of God would accompany him so that he would "ever feel consoled and comforted," and he would be well treated by his jailers. Elder Taylor also promised that "the time of thy punishment may be short, thou mayest be speedily delivered therefrom, and speedily return (if thou shouldst leave) to the bosom of thy family and friends and rejoice again among the people of God."[12]

Reynolds was indeed leaving—the court had assigned him to serve his time in a penitentiary in Lincoln, Nebraska, almost 900 miles to the east. Two days after sentencing, on June 16, he boarded the seven a.m. train for Lincoln in the company of two deputy marshals. The journey, Reynolds said, "was a pleasant one," but it was a wasted trip.[13] A telegram went out the same day that he left for Nebraska stating that if he "was not yet removed from Utah to retain [him] in the Territorial Penitentiary," but it arrived after Reynolds had already left.[14] For some reason, it took the prison bureaucracies a month to straighten out the issue, but on July 17, Reynolds arrived in Salt Lake City again to serve his sentence near his home, family, and friends.

———•··•———

A few weeks after the high court sustained Reynolds's conviction, the US marshal traveled to southern Utah looking for polygamists generally and for Wilford Woodruff specifically. As a senior Apostle and the president of the St. George Temple, Wilford was the most visible Church leader in the region and therefore the marshal's highest-priority target. Forewarned of the marshal's coming, the Apostle left St. George to go into hiding in Arizona. He would spend a year in exile, including a cold winter in the San Francisco Peaks near modern-day Flagstaff, and he was able to stay in contact with family and friends through letters. He spent much of his time reading and had to hunt for his supper on many an occasion. It was a lonely life.

In January of 1880, after a year in isolation, Wilford retired to his bed one evening. He slept a bit, but awakened at midnight and found himself wrapped in a vision.

> The Lord poured out his spirit upon me and opened the vision of my mind so I could . . . comprehend in a good measure the mind and will of God and his purposes concerning our nation and the inhabitants of Zion . . . and when I comprehended the great and mighty responsibility which rested upon the Quorum of the Apostles in the sight of God and the heavenly hosts, my head became a fountain of tears and my pillow was wet as with the dews of heaven and sleep departed from me and the Lord revealed unto me our duty.[15]

The revelation included the Lord's assurance that the United States was in the wrong for trying to prevent the Saints from living the institution of plural marriage. The Saints' prayers were heard and the Lord would sustain them in their trials, the worst of which were yet to come.

President Taylor would call Wilford back to Salt Lake City in a few months, where the Apostle would share his vision with the First Presidency and the Twelve, who would accept it as the word of the Lord. And in future years, when the responsibility to deal with the government over plural marriage would fall on him and Wilford would find himself wrestling to save the Church, his thoughts would be influenced by a vision received from the Lord in the dead of night on the snow-swept side of an Arizona mountain.

———— • • • ————

By the end of that season, the walls of the Salt Lake Temple had reached a height of forty-five feet, almost as tall as the Tabernacle just across the way. The workers had added another twelve feet of granite that year, doubling the temple's height from the ground in the few years since Brigham's death. It was a noticeable and heartening advancement, and powerful evidence that the combination of the railroad, increased numbers of stonecutters working under sheds on the temple block, and

The Salt Lake Temple under construction, c. 1880. Note the construction derricks erected inside the temple walls for raising stone.

steam-engine powered derricks had sped up the work considerably. Truman's plans called for the building's main body (not counting the six spires) to reach a height of 167 feet. At their present rate of twelve feet of stonework per year, they would still need another decade to reach the roof level. So they were not close to the end, but the rate of progress at least now could inspire hope and not despair that the current generation of Saints might live to see the finished edifice.

They worked until the growing cold called an end to the construction that year, and the Saints on the temple block and in Little Cottonwood Canyon shuttered their operations for the season. The holidays came, 1880 rolled in clear and cold, and the work resumed in the spring. Several more courses of granite blocks went on the walls that season as the summer rolled by. It was an uneventful year, and the workmen on the temple block made the most of it.

The time for the Church's general conference arrived. Three years had passed since Brigham had died, which was the same amount of time that the Saints had waited after Joseph's death to sustain Brigham as their prophet. Following Brigham's precedent, John Taylor, the President of the Quorum of the Twelve, had led the Church through an apostolic interregnum, but now he felt it was time to reorganize the First Presidency.[16] On October 10, a Sunday, the Saints gathered in the Tabernacle and sustained President Taylor as the prophet and third President of the Church. He had not sought the position, he asserted, but it had fallen on him only by virtue of his seniority, as it had on Brigham before him. "Had it not been our duty to have the Church organized fully and completely in all its departments, I should have much preferred to have continued with the brethren of the Twelve," he explained. "I would have said, things are going on very pleasantly, smoothly and agreeably . . . let things remain as they are."[17]

<hr />

The following year, 1881, did not pass by quite so "pleasantly, smoothly and agreeably" as President Taylor might have hoped. The trouble started little more than a week after the year had begun. In the race for territorial delegate to Congress, Elder George Q. Cannon received 18,567 votes, 93 percent of all the ballots cast, soundly thrashing Liberal Party candidate Allen G. Campbell. But Governor Eli Murray, the latest in the long line of hostile administrators, decided to certify the defeated Campbell as the winner despite his paltry 7 percent showing at the ballot box. Murray justified his decision by claiming, falsely, that there was no record of Cannon becoming a naturalized US citizen—he was British by birth and so was disqualified from holding Congressional office. The excuse was so flimsy and transparent that newspapers across the country that previously had shown no editorial sympathy for the Saints called Murray out for exceeding his authority.[18] The governor was openly trying to disenfranchise all of the Saints in the territory. Cannon filed a protest with the House of Representatives and was seated as the provisional delegate pending resolution of the dispute. After a year, Congress would decide that neither Cannon nor Campbell was entitled to the seat and declared it vacant.

But for the moment, the Saints' ire was soothed a bit ten days later when one of the happier events of the year came to pass. George Reynolds completed his prison sentence minus five months for good behavior, and was released from the territorial penitentiary on the twentieth of January. He'd been productive during his incarceration, having spent his days organizing a Book of Mormon concordance, and he had "tabulated more than 25,000 passages" during his seventeen-month stint.[19] Reynolds clearly had nothing but time on his hands during those seventeen months in jail.

———— · · ————

The usual half dozen or so courses of granite were added to the temple walls that year, raising them now to a height of sixty feet. The increase in the height of the walls over the last several years had caught the public's notice, enough so that the *Deseret Evening News* reported on the "constant stream of visitors to view the Temple." There was much for them to see now that "rock setting for the season [had] resumed." The curious public had also been taking in the construction cranes, now in operation for several years, that had made the progress possible. "The hoisting derricks have been raised," the paper reported, "and the cables which hold them securely anchored to two massive granite pillars. . . . Rock [can now be] hoisted a distance of about 85 feet. The work is progressing steadily."[20]

The work did indeed go forward for the next several months as predicted, steady and without interruption, until October, when the workers were nearing the end of the "rock setting season." On the third of that month, another accident occurred that was very nearly an exact repetition of Sam Kaealoi's fatal fall three years earlier. Sometime between one and two o'clock in the afternoon, William Pullen was handling the guide ropes for the derrick on the temple's southwest corner when a hard wind gust swung the derrick's arm around in an arc. Whether the arm struck Pullen or he simply repeated Kaealoi's mistake in not letting go of the rope is unclear, but Pullen fell off the walkway. He plunged some sixty feet into the open basement and landed on the stonework below. His fellow laborers rushed to help the injured man, but there was nothing they could do for him there. They transported him "into a house on the Temple Block"—whether it was the Endowment House, the as-yet unfinished Assembly Hall that they'd recently started building, or just one of the sheds is also unclear. Wherever he ended up, he was attended by a doctor, but his injuries were internal, severe, and mortal. Pullen lingered for a short time, then died at three-forty p.m.

———•··•———

The Saints had, for the most part, enjoyed a period of calm since Brigham's death almost four years ago. The deaths of two workers to accidents were melancholy events to be mourned, but the temple's rapid rise during the same period was a cause for rejoicing. The Saints had lost their appeal to the Supreme Court, but the government had not resumed its previous attempts to prosecute the Morrill Act. It was as close to the Saints' longed-for peaceful life as they had enjoyed since the coming of Johnston's army twenty-four years prior. But President Chester A. Arthur put a stop to that on December 6, 1881, the day that he delivered his First Annual Message to Congress.

Arthur, the son of an Irish Baptist preacher, was a lawyer and a Republican. He'd climbed the party ranks in New York by learning the dark arts of patronage politics—he was, if not outright corrupt, at the very least a complicit crony in some legally dubious political activities. He'd landed on the 1880 Republican presidential ticket under James Garfield only as a compromise tolerated to unite some warring factions and win the election. No one had actually wanted Arthur to ever become the nation's chief executive, but a disappointed office seeker shot Garfield just a few months into his term. He lingered in great pain for weeks, with the nation dreading Arthur's possible promotion as a disaster in the making. The *Chicago Tribune* declared that "if anything could add to the universal grief of the American people over the attempted assassination of President Garfield, the anticipation of three and a half weary years' government under Mr. Arthur, and all which that implies, will be by the American people generally accepted as a pending national calamity of the utmost magnitude."[21]

In time, Arthur would disprove all of his critics. As Garfield declined, Arthur went through an intense period of soul-searching. Then Garfield expired on September 19, and gaining the presidency because of another man's murder seems to have finished the reset of Arthur's moral compass. In a display of stunning political repentance, he governed the country for the next three years with honesty and integrity—a complete reversal of the behavior observers had come to expect.

But in December of 1881, as Arthur journeyed to Capitol Hill, he had been president not quite three months. Congress still didn't know what to expect from him, and what it got that day was a lengthy speech of 13,000 words that addressed a wide array of subjects. The section that would augur one of the most painful periods in Latter-day Saint history came seventy-five minutes into Arthur's almost-two-hour speech. Speaking of the nation's interests in the West, Arthur addressed the issue of plural marriage.

> The existing statute for the punishment of this odious crime, so revolting to the moral and religious sense of Christendom, has been persistently and contemptuously violated [in Utah] ever since its enactment. Indeed, in spite of commendable efforts on the part of the authorities who represent the United States in that Territory, the law has in very rare instances been enforced, and, for a cause to which reference will presently be made, is practically a dead letter. . . . It imposes upon Congress and the Executive the duty of arraying against this barbarous system [polygamy] all the power which under the Constitution and the law they can wield for its destruction.

He then offered Congress a few suggestions for how to go about that task and invited its members to come up with a few of their own. He was amenable to almost any measures they might conceive. "I assure you of my determined purpose to cooperate with you in any lawful and discreet measures which may be proposed to that end," he told them.[22]

Arthur's invitation would gain him a devoted ally in the person of Senator George F. Edmunds of Vermont. Hearing Arthur's call for Congress to "devise other practicable measures," Edmunds took five days to put his ideas down on paper. On the sixth day, December 12, he submitted a bill to the Senate that would soon be known as the Edmunds Anti-Polygamy Act. It was only two pages long, but it contained provisions that would nearly cause the destruction of the Church and the loss of all its assets, including its temples, finished and unfinished.

One of Edmunds's provisions made "unlawful cohabitation" a crime, obviating the need for prosecutors to prove that a plural marriage had occurred—a man could be jailed simply for sharing a home with more than one woman. Another section barred anyone who even *professed* belief in plural marriage from serving on a jury. Anyone convicted of unlawful cohabitation became ineligible to vote or hold political office. All existing elected offices would be immediately declared vacant and elections placed under the supervision of a five-man "Utah Commission" whose members would be presidential nominees. President Arthur and Governor Murray would thus have a clean slate to make new federal and territorial appointments, and Saints practicing plural marriage—a number later estimated to be as high as 10,000—would be disqualified from holding any of them.[23] The entire territorial legislature would have to be reconstituted in a new election, and a significant number of Saints would be ineligible to stand as candidates or to vote for those who could. And virtually no Church member would be able to sit as a juror in any criminal case. In a stroke, Edmunds's proposed law would drastically diminish Latter-day Saint influence in Utah's political and judicial affairs.

The bill moved through Congress with stunning speed, narrowly

The Salt Lake Temple under construction, c. 1883.

passing the Senate in mid-February 1882 and comfortably passing the House a month later, in March. The Saints had virtually no time to mount any kind of organized opposition to its passage. President Arthur signed the Edmunds bill a week after its passage, and on March 22, it became law.

———————

By the fall of 1883, the Salt Lake Temple's walls had reached eighty-five feet—a total of sixty feet added since Brigham's passing, and a tripling of the total height in just six years. The stonecutters had finished, and the masons laid down, some 2,500 *tons* of granite that year alone.[24] The arches over the uppermost line of oval windows were in place, and the workmen were looking to start setting timbers the following year for the roof. If they were able to continue the work at the same rate, they could expect to finish the walls in the next year or two.

The good spirits of the Saints regarding temple construction were given another boost in May 1884, when the Logan Temple was finished and dedicated. President Taylor made the trip north to conduct the ceremonies that would open a second house of the Lord for ordinance work. It was another Truman Angell design with two spires, one each at the east and west ends, and surprisingly gothic compared to the other temple plans that he'd drawn up. Now the Church had two working temples, and the Saints in the northern settlements faced a much shorter journey to attend a temple than they had when traveling to St. George.

———•••———

With the Logan Temple essentially completed and ready for dedication, Truman Angell Jr. was free to return to Salt Lake City and lend his talents to the temple there. His time working in Cache Valley on the house of the Lord had given him some ideas for changes that he hoped would improve on his father's designs for the Salt Lake Temple. The first change he wanted to see was to the temple's six spires. His father's plan called for spires to be constructed of a wooden framework covered with metal plating. Truman Jr., apparently thought that the change of materials between granite walls and metallic spires would be too jarring to the eye. He wanted to see the spires, like the walls, made of granite all the way to the top. That change would unify the appearance of the building.

The second change Truman Jr. favored would be more extensive. His father had based his original floor plan for the Salt Lake Temple on the Nauvoo Temple's design. That temple's interior had consisted of a basement baptistry and, above it, two large assembly halls. The Salt Lake floor plan used that model, as did the now-finished temple in St. George. But as the Saints gained experience conducting ordinances in those buildings, they were learning how to better organize a temple inside and make better use of the space. Brigham had "said that it was not required that temples be alike, neither in the interior or exterior design and construction."[25] So Truman Jr., apparently unbidden, had redesigned the Logan floor plan and submitted it to President Taylor. The prophet had agreed with his predecessor that temples did not have to be identical, and he approved the new arrangement.

With that success under his belt, Truman Jr. thought they should make similar changes in Salt Lake. He drafted a new design that kept the baptistry in the lowest level, but the lower assembly hall was replaced with a series of smaller rooms for temple ceremonies, and a new level was devoted to meeting rooms for the First Presidency and Quorum of the Twelve, and for other priesthood quorums. All of the space above that was dedicated to a single, multistory assembly hall complete with side balconies to maximize the number of people who could fit into the cavernous room. The design had a number of advantages that the young architect laid out in his proposal. His suggestion that they use steel for some of the interior supports, instead of the all-wood construction his father had designed, would allow them to remove interior columns that would block the views of temple patrons during the various ceremonies. The new design would double the number of people who could attend the ceremonies in a single day, up to three hundred, and the interior lighting would be improved.

The younger Truman submitted his ideas to President Taylor on April 28, hopeful that the prophet would give his consent just as he had done with the Logan alterations, but the young architect made it clear that he knew his place and would willingly change anything and everything as Taylor required. "I have the building planned for greater convenience," Truman Jr. explained, "but can easily change the location of said rooms if you see fit to order it so."[26]

Truman Sr. learned of the proposed changes and was not happy—especially as his son had included the senior architect's name on the new designs. To ensure his own views on the matter were heard, Truman Sr. wrote a letter to President Taylor. He recounted his own long personal history building temples and pointed out that Brigham had approved the previous plans. He urged the prophet not to change anything. "It seems to me to alter the plans now would make a bad thing of the house; but

I should think the plans as approved all along till now better continue." Then, acknowledging it wasn't his decision to make, he ended the letter with the humble declaration that "not my will, but the will of the Presidency of the Church be done."[27]

President Taylor reviewed the proposals, considered the senior architect's opposition, and in the end rendered a split decision. He agreed to consider the proposed changes to the interior, but he disallowed the changes to the spires—as planned, they would be a wooden lattice covered with metal plating. Building them out of granite would have added several years to the construction; after thirty-three years of labor, the prophet may not have favored any change that would lengthen the time any further. The architects could change the interior around without adding any delays, as they hadn't yet reached that stage of the project, but given the weight, cost, and time involved in carving granite, making that change would have demanded far more time, money, and labor. Given the trouble that the new Edmunds Act promised to heap upon the Saints, those were three elements that John Taylor may have thought were soon going to become much more scarce.

April 24, four days before Truman Jr. offered up his proposal to President Taylor, would mark the start of the most tumultuous time in the Church's half-century existence since the Prophet Joseph's martyrdom or perhaps even the Missouri persecutions. That morning, a grand jury of the Third District Court handed down an indictment against twenty-seven-year-old Rudger Clawson on the charge of polygamy.

Clawson was born in Salt Lake City in 1857, the same year that the US government had dispatched Johnston's army to the territory, and was still a teenager when he was called to be Elder John W. Young's secretary. With that calling already under his belt, it was simply a given that he would be called as a missionary to preach the gospel when he was of age. That expectation was fulfilled when he was called from the Tabernacle pulpit in April 1879 to serve in the Southern States Mission.[28] Living far from home for years at a time to teach the gospel among people hostile to the Church had been a common crucible for missionaries since the Church was founded, but three months into his service, young Rudger crossed paths with true murderous opposition.

That summer, he and his companion, Joseph Standing, were returning to their residence near Varnall's Station in Whitfield County, Georgia, when three horsemen rode up and ordered them to stop. Nine other men approached on foot, all "armed to the teeth with clubs, pistols and guns." The mob told the young missionaries that they were under arrest. Clawson and Standing demanded to see the warrant and to know by what authority they were being detained. They were told that they would find out soon enough, and the missionaries were marched into the woods.

As they walked, the mob demanded to know the whereabouts of other Church members, to which Clawson replied "that he was under the impression that the United States was a country of religious liberty." "There is no law in Georgia for Mormons," his captors advised. They cursed the young Saints and threatened them with execution by hanging if they didn't leave the country. At some point during the twenty-minute march, Standing decided that if they were going to die, he would not go meekly. He seized one of the mobber's pistols, pointed it at one of the horsemen, and ordered him to surrender. Another gunman drew his own weapon and shot Standing in the face at point-blank range, killing the twenty-five-year-old missionary instantly. The rest of the mob turned on Clawson and, thinking he might try to escape, one of his captors ordered the others to "shoot that man."

After a moment's thought, Clawson just folded his arms. "Shoot," he said.

Surprised, the men lowered their weapons. Clawson knelt down to examine his dead companion. One of the mobbers, perhaps trying to assuage his own conscience, said, "well, he shot himself, didn't he?" The others agreed and "took up the ingenious subterfuge and endeavored to persuade [Clawson] that his brother had accidentally killed himself while bringing his weapons into position." Clawson, having seen everything, knew better, but he said nothing. Instead, he walked away to get help so his companion's body could be returned home. When he returned, the lynch mob was gone and Standing's body had been mutilated. Clawson helped identify the murderers, who were indicted. The missionary then returned home to Salt Lake City with his deceased companion.[29] He later returned to Georgia to testify in the trial of four of the assassins. The jury returned a verdict of not guilty.

Now, five years later, Clawson again found himself under arrest, this time for real. The US marshal took him to court, where he was processed and released on a $3,000 bond. Not a single member of the Church had been empaneled on the jury, as "no one who admitted belief in the Book of Doctrine and Covenants, containing the tenets of the 'Mormon' Church, was allowed to serve as a grand juror."[30]

The trial took place in October, with Judge Charles S. Zane presiding at the bench. Zane was a New Jersey transplant to Illinois, where he had become a law partner at Abraham Lincoln's firm when he was elected sixteenth president of the United States. Zane had also been an associate of Senator Shelby Cullom, the author of the Cullom Bill that had gone down in defeat after Eliza R. Snow and the other women of the Church had staged their public meetings a decade before. Knowing Zane's anti-polygamy convictions, Cullom had nominated him for a judgeship. President Arthur had granted the appointment earlier that year, and Zane had arrived in Utah in late August, less than two months prior to Clawson's trial.

Seating the jury took a day and a half, after which the prosecution began to call witnesses to the stand. It was a long list that included, among others, President John Taylor, George Q. Cannon, Joseph F. Smith, several other Church leaders, and numerous members of Clawson's own family.[31] The first witnesses were family members, and none of them were very cooperative, but US Attorney W. H. Dickson

soldiered on, trying to build his case. Turning from Clawson's kin to ecclesiastical leaders, Dickson summoned John Taylor to the stand around
three-fifteen in the afternoon on October 17. The President of the
Church took the stand as required and was placed under oath. What followed was a master class in giving truthful answers that offered nothing
useful to the prosecution. President Taylor refused to answer a question
only once, when he was asked to describe the marriage ceremony performed in temples, and Dickson demurred from pressing further on that
point. But the rest of the time, Taylor deployed a cheeky British wit that
left his interrogator frustrated.[32]

> Q.—Do you know whether a record of marriages [performed in the
>   Endowment House] is kept?
> A.—It is very probable there is. . . .
> Q.—If you wanted to see it is there any means of ascertaining
>   where it is?
> A.—I could find out by inquiry. . . .
> Q.—I understand you to say you could inquire as to their where-
>   abouts. Will you be good enough to do so and give us the in-
>   formation?
> A.—I do not think I am good enough.
> Q.—Is it not a fact, Mr. Taylor, that plural marriage is a secret rite,
>   a secret ceremony?
> A.—It is a secret to some and not to others.[33]

The five-day trial resulted in a hung jury, but Dickson refused to
give up. Clawson had been neither convicted nor exonerated, so Dickson
could take a second bite at the apple if he so chose. He did so choose,
and the second trial started on October 21, just three days after the first
one ended. This time, instead of trying to patiently build a detailed case,
Dickson employed a new strategy that went straight for the defendant's
emotional jugular. Because the US government refused to recognize
any marriages other than the first, any other wife did not enjoy spousal
privilege—the right not to testify against one's husband or wife. Dickson

called one of Clawson's plural wives, Lydia Spencer, to the stand. She refused to testify against her husband, so Zane committed her to the penitentiary for contempt of court until she was prepared to answer Dickson's questions under oath. Unwilling to let his wife languish in jail for an indefinite period, Clawson consented to let Lydia testify against him. The following day she returned to court and confirmed that she was, indeed, one of the defendant's plural wives. That was all the evidence that Dickson needed. Judge Zane sent the jury out to begin deliberations, and the twelve jurors took only seventeen minutes to return a verdict of guilty.

One week later, on November 3, Judge Zane sentenced Rudger Clawson to the maximum penalty allowed under the law. On the charge of polygamy, he imposed a sentence of three years and six months in prison, and a $500 fine. For the crime of unlawful cohabitation, another six months in prison to be served consecutively and a $300 fine.

———•••———

The first member of the Church had been successfully convicted under the Edmunds Act, and, with that done, the legal floodgates could open. The second trial of a Latter-day Saint for plural marriage, that of Joseph Evans, started just two days after Rudger Clawson was sentenced. From that point forward for the next five years, hardly a day passed when a Latter-day Saint wasn't indicted, arrested, tried, convicted, sentenced, or remanded to the penitentiary under the Edmunds Act. Trials were short, often just a few hours long, and many days saw more than one person convicted and sentenced in the same courtroom. Men went to prison by the score, and women who refused to testify against their husbands were not spared. Convictions and sentences appealed to the Utah Supreme Court were almost universally upheld. Prisoners were often sent outside of Utah, far from family and friends, to serve their terms of incarceration, with convicted Saints being shipped off to places like Yuma, Arizona, and Detroit, Michigan.

Members of the Church's leading councils were obvious targets, and they resolved to resist what they believed was an unconstitutional crusade against their faith. So on February 1, 1885, three months after Rudger Clawson was convicted and sentenced, the President of the Church stood in the Tabernacle and gave the final public sermon of his life to the Saints. The US marshal and his deputies had covered the street-level exits to arrest the prophet once the meeting was finished. If that worried President Taylor, he didn't show it. He spoke for two hours, denouncing the Edmunds law and proclaiming his absolute unwillingness to forsake the commandments of God. Then he counseled the Saints to bear up under this trial with fortitude and patience. "This storm will blow past as others have done. . . . Let these men have their day and pursue their own course; we will protect ourselves from them as well as we can," he said.[34] But he urged the Saints to be loyal citizens in every other respect. "We will obey every institution of man for the Lord's sake so far as we can without violating our consciences and doing things that are wrong and improper."[35] Thus finished, the prophet walked off the stand and down a flight of stairs to the Tabernacle basement. When the meeting ended, he was nowhere to be found. The marshals realized too late that their quarry had left the building by another exit they hadn't known about.

John Taylor, along with George Q. Cannon, a driver, a secretary, and an aide, had gone into hiding. He would change hideouts eighteen times during his first year in exile, staying in any one place for only a few weeks at most, and each new hideout was usually close to the last one to minimize the amount of time that he would be out in the open. He returned to the Gardo House only once during his exile, a month after he went into hiding, and it nearly resulted in his arrest. He was physically sick and thought it not overly dangerous to go home so his wife could tend to his ailment—but federal officers raided the house shortly after his arrival. His bodyguard whistled a prepared signal, giving President Taylor a few moments to conceal himself in a closet specially constructed for the very purpose of hiding him. He heard the marshals walking about the house, searching methodically through the rooms. They looked briefly in the room where the prophet was hidden, but his son had told them it was used only for storage, and they left without making a thorough search. President Taylor never returned to his home again after that night. He remained separated from his family until his death, communicating with them only through letters.

Despite the prophet's escape, the legal crusade continued, picking up steam as it went, and not just in Utah. Two days after President Taylor's final sermon, Governor William Bunn of Idaho signed a bill into law that banned any Latter-day Saint from voting in elections. US marshals would soon launch raids in Idaho, Nevada, and Wyoming, looking for anyone practicing plural marriage. No home, building, business, chapel, or tabernacle was off-limits. US marshals even raided the unfinished temple at Manti at one point looking for a "cohab," as men suspected of plural marriage came to be called by the lawmen who searched for them.[36]

The raids finally reached the temple block in Salt Lake City on April 24. About three o'clock in the afternoon, four deputy marshals and a fifth man in their company entered the construction site to arrest Joseph Dean, a carpenter, for unlawful cohabitation. When told he wasn't present, they proceeded to go through the carpenter's shop in search of their quarry. One lawman thought he saw a man run for the Tabernacle, and they gave chase, but found no one.[37] Dean escaped capture that afternoon, but every day thereafter, any man working at the temple site who practiced plural marriage had to look over his shoulder to see whether the marshals might be coming for him that day. Just showing up to work became an act of faith that God would not see them dragged away while they tried to build the house of the Lord.

Another fatal accident on the temple block added to the workers' woes a month later. Samuel Ensign was an eighty-year-old man described as "one of the oldest and most trusty and respected of the Church employees."[38] He had joined the Church in 1838 and was one of the dwindling few who had also worked to build the Nauvoo Temple. Now that he had the chance to assist in building another, he could hardly be kept away from the site despite his advanced age and Henry Grow's protests that he shouldn't place himself in danger. "He was never satisfied while the carpenters were engaged in the Temple walls without being with them," the *Deseret Evening News* later reported, "and on account of his extreme age he was humored and allowed to do pretty much as he liked. . . . [He] was a general favorite with the Temple Block employees, who revered him almost as a father and studied his comfort in every way they could." He had been at work on the Temple for almost the entire life of the project, since the Saints had first broken ground for the foundation back in 1852.

On the morning of June 24, Ensign was one member of a team of four assigned to haul the derrick "cage"—the framework that surrounded the crane—up into position. By ten o'clock in the morning, Ensign was sitting atop the temple wall on a wooden plank three inches thick and twenty inches wide, taking in the slack of the rope as the other three lifted the cage. He had done this before, sitting on the makeshift ledge, and no one thought it was particularly dangerous. But the cage swung in his direction, and Ensign shifted on his seat to avoid it. The cage "struck him lightly on the side—not sufficiently hard to hurt him, nor to unseat him had he not moved." But he *had* moved, and when the cage bumped him, Ensign lost his balance and fell. He plunged ninety feet to the ground, striking wooden planks and scaffolding as he went. He landed on his feet and immediately pitched forward onto his face. Workers on the ground saw his fall and reached him in moments, but he was already dead, "life extinct," having suffered severe head trauma and two broken legs.

The sudden loss of the father figure of the temple block was a deeply depressing moment for the workers. In addition to his family, "a great host of friends will mourn the sudden death of Brother Ensign," the

Deseret Evening News told its readers, "but will be consoled and reconciled with the assurance that he has been true to his covenants, fought the good fight, kept the faith and has now gone to reap the reward in store for the righteous."[39]

The temple construction suffered more setbacks that year, all of them the result of the Edmunds Act. Truman Angell Jr., assistant architect under his father, was arrested, as were John Sharp, Henry Grow, and James Moyle, the chief stonecutter on the temple block.

Moyle was British, born in Cornwall, England, on All Hallow's Eve in 1835 and raised in Plymouth, where he learned the stonecutter's craft from his father, John Rowe Moyle. The elder Moyle had become curious about the new religion when he came across an anti-Mormon article so virulent that he determined to investigate the Church and see for himself whether such wild claims could possibly be true. The Moyles heard the missionaries, accepted their message, and were baptized into the faith in 1851. They wanted to join the Saints in Utah, but money was scarce for the family, so they followed the practice of many emigrant families and sent one person ahead to earn funds in Salt Lake City and prepare a place for the rest of the family that would follow. James, being the eldest son, was the logical choice to go. At the age of eighteen, James sailed to the United States by himself early in 1854, with the Perpetual Emigration Fund paying for his passage. He joined a wagon company departing from Missouri and arrived in the valley in September of that year. James found employment as a mason building Brigham Young's home, the Lion House, for which the teenager earned three dollars a day. He saved his money, paid back his seventy-dollar debt to the Fund, and then proceeded to build a life for himself in Salt Lake City. The rest of the family arrived two years later, having crossed the plains as members of one of the first handcart companies.

Moyle's father, John, relocated most of the family to a homestead in Alpine, twenty-two miles from the city, while his son stayed in Salt

Lake City. Both men found work as stonecutters on the temple block, with John commuting from his farm to the city very early on Monday mornings, staying in James's home during the week, and then walking home Friday evenings after his shift ended. The elder Moyle did his farm chores on Saturdays, attended church on Sundays, and then repeated his commute, doing this for a number of years. His long walk to and from the temple block became somewhat more difficult in later years when he lost a leg. Family stories claim that he lost the limb when an ill-tempered milk cow kicked him and shattered his tibia; the *Deseret News* reported that his leg was crushed by a log.[40] However the injury occurred, the leg had to be amputated. Given his advanced age at the time—the elder Moyle was in his seventies—it's surprising that the shock didn't kill him, but Moyle recovered. He carved himself a wooden leg, complete with a then-ingenious ankle hinge, taught himself to walk on it, and eventually returned to his labors on the temple block.[41] He was also the man who carved the inscription "Holiness to the Lord" into the main dedication plaque—actually composed of five stones—that sits on the temple's eastern wall.

The younger Moyle was "five feet ten inches in height, square shouldered and muscular. His features were rugged and strong . . . his eyes were dark and deep set, characterized by a thoughtful expression."[42] Brigham was familiar with Moyle's character and his skill at his craft, and had personally chosen him to become the chief stonecutter on the temple block in 1875. He had accepted the post, which gave him authority over his own father, and he'd reported to Daniel H. Wells in that position for the last ten years. Now Moyle was in jail, and Wells was living in another hemisphere. Truman Jr. avoided incarceration when he appeared in court and promised to obey the law, whereon Judge Zane let him off with a fine and no jail time. John Sharp chose to do the same, for which he drew a rebuke from the Church's leadership. Moyle and Grow did not, and they were convicted and shipped off to the penitentiary.

For ten months, Judge Zane had been throwing the book at Saints appearing in his courtroom. He'd often imposed the largest fines and longest sentences that the Edmunds Act allowed, but the Saints' resolve to "abide the penalty" remained unbroken. Men showed no remorse and women proved to be as recalcitrant as their husbands—the judge had sent more than one woman to prison for contempt of court when they refused to testify. Seeing the sisters of the Church being marched off to the prison was only hardening the Saints' perception that the federal campaign was not a pursuit of justice and anyone convicted was a prisoner of conscience.

Judge Zane decided that more pressure had to be brought to bear, and that called for some legal innovation. His creative solution was called the "segregation policy." Zane decided that every single year a man spent in "unlawful cohabitation" with a plural wife could be "segregated"—or carved out—as a separate criminal offense. Delighted by Zane's new interpretation of the Edmunds Act, US Attorney Dickson exclaimed, "Well, if that don't stop it [plural marriage], I don't know what will. . . . By that ruling, the thing can now be made almost a life matter."[43]

Soon there was no "almost" about it. One of Zane's fellow justices, Orlando Powers, went further and decided that every single day a man lived with a plural wife was a separate offense—365 possible crimes every year, each punishable by the maximum fine and prison term allowed by the law. Under Judge Powers's interpretation, one year spent living with a plural wife could earn a man a fine of $109,500—the modern equivalent of more than $3,000,000 dollars—and a total of 1,825 years in prison. It was a far cry from the penalties of $500 and five years called for in the plain text of the Edmunds Act.

———— • · • ————

To overturn Judge Zane's segregation policy, the Saints needed another defendant willing to endure prison while his case went through the appeals process, as George Reynolds had done. The man who finally shouldered that particular burden was Elder Lorenzo Snow of the Quorum of the Twelve.

At six-thirty in the morning on November 20, seven deputy marshals descended on Elder Snow's home in Brigham City and took him into custody. Word spread throughout the town quickly when the officers appeared, and a considerable crowd had gathered outside the Apostle's residence by the time the marshals emerged with their prisoner. The lawmen feared that the bystanders might overwhelm the officers to free Elder Snow, but the Apostle "told [the crowd] he wanted no demonstration and no violence used." The officers trundled him into a carriage for the ride to Ogden, where he would be processed by the court. He rode surrounded by three deputies, with the remaining four trailing behind in a second carriage, ready to race after Elder Snow if he somehow overpowered his captors and tried to run. The show of force from beginning to end seemed like overkill to the local residents, especially after Snow's request for calm. The papers could not quite restrain their sarcasm about the number of men sent "to accomplish the dangerous feat." "It is to be hoped that those zealous officers are now taking a much-needed rest, and that they will not expose themselves so recklessly hereafter," the *Deseret Evening News* drily advised.[44]

Elder Snow was granted bail and did not have to spend Christmas and New Year's Day in jail, but those days with his family ended when his trial began on January 4. Jury selection took up the first day, and the legal cases were presented on the second. After being sent out to deliberate, the jury returned, quite literally, two minutes later and announced their verdict of guilty. Elder Snow stood convicted of having engaged in unlawful cohabitation for three years. Fortunately for Elder Snow, his judge did not use the Powers interpretation and declare that every day of cohabitation was a separate crime. Instead, he followed Judge Zane's lead and said that each year with a plural wife was a separate crime, resulting in a sentence of just eighteen months in jail and a $900 fine.

Bail was set at $15,000—an excessively high amount, given that unlawful cohabitation was a misdemeanor offense—but Elder Snow wanted to expedite his appeal to the US Supreme Court, so he chose to go to prison instead. On March 12, he reported to the penitentiary to begin his sentence. The wheels of justice turned about as quickly as they could, and his case reached the high court seven weeks later, in late April.

The court gave its verdict in the case of *Snow v. United States* two weeks later. It was the worst possible outcome that the Apostle could have expected. "We conclude . . . that we have no jurisdiction of these writs of error, and that they must be dismissed for that reason," the court announced.[45] The Supreme Court declared that it had no authority to decide whether Judge Zane's "segregation" theory should stand, and now Elder Lorenzo Snow had no choice but to sit in prison for the duration of his sentence.

Any urge that Judge Zane might have had to celebrate was being tempered by public opinion about what his segregation theory had wrought. The raw numbers of defendants, the harsh sentences being handed down, and the apparent zeal with which all of this was going on was finally starting to look heavy-handed even to some Church opponents. Nor did it help that the sisters of the Church had been staging more mass protest meetings to raise awareness that wives were being forced to either testify against their husbands or go to jail themselves.

Zane and Governor Caleb Walton West decided together that they needed to counter the accusation that they were acting out of malice. So West made a trip to the penitentiary a few days after the Supreme Court declined to rule on Lorenzo Snow's appeal. The governor met with the Apostle there and made him an offer that he thought the convicted Saints would surely accept.

> I conceived that it would be a very opportune time to call and submit to you a proposition, which, in conjunction with Judge Zane and Mr. Dickson, we have thought advisable to make, in order to

show you and the people of the Territory that they are mistaken in believing that those charged with the execution of the laws in the Territories are animated by any spirit of malice or vindictiveness towards [the Saints]; that on the contrary their only wish and only desire, one which is nearest to their hearts, is to have the people of the Territory obey and respect the law. . . . I have come to say to you and your people here that we would unite in a petition to the Executive to issue his pardon in these cases upon a promise, in good faith, that you will obey and respect the laws, and that you will not continue to live in violation of them.

Elder Snow made it clear that the Saints would not be accepting the offer. Indeed, the Apostle all but accused the governor of acting in bad faith when he made it.

"It seems to me you cannot say that you have no confidence in the protection of the courts and the officials here—" West began to protest.

"I have no confidence whatever," Elder Snow assured him.

"That Judge Zane and Mr. Dickson, who have concurred with me, are not doing it in good faith; that is the only way you can say that, because you must have confidence in us or you must believe we are not acting in good faith . . ."

"I certainly believe in your sincerity, but you are not the court," Elder Snow explained. "As to Dickson and as to Zane, I have no confidence in them at all."

"Mr. Snow, I think you are very unjust in that opinion, because I know that this suggestion that I make—"

Elder Snow cut him off. "If you had suffered, you would think differently."[46]

The governor left the prison empty-handed, and the incarcerated Saints put their refusal in writing. "Dearly as we prize the great boon of liberty, we cannot afford to obtain it by proving untrue to our conscience, our religion and our God," they wrote in a letter published ten days later in the *Deseret Evening News*. Forty-eight men signed it, including Lorenzo Snow; Rudger Clawson, who was still serving time on his original sentence; and James Moyle, the chief stonecutter for the temple.[47]

An unexpected visitor came to the prison on September 14, four months to the day after Governor West had come with his amnesty proposal; this visitor was even more senior than the territory's chief executive. Chief Justice of the Supreme Court Morrison Waite had stopped in Salt Lake City while on a tour of the western parts of the country. Waite was a charismatic person, described as "exceedingly affable, cheerful and informal" with his hosts, and his manner "set everyone present at perfect ease."[48] While he was visiting with the governor in the city, someone had asked the Chief Justice whether he had "ever looked into the Mormon question," to which Waite replied no, only as cases had arisen before the high court. "I had intended to look into [it] while here, but my stay being so short, I am afraid I will have but little opportunity."[49]

Justice Waite took a tour of the city, which included a visit to the unfinished temple, an organ recital in the Tabernacle, and a reception at Fort Douglas. At some point thereafter, he apparently took the opportunity to "look into the Mormon question" by conversing with some of the men who had been convicted for it. He visited the penitentiary and, while there, he encountered Lorenzo Snow, the man whom the high court's recent non-decision had condemned to eighteen months in prison.[50] How long exactly Chief Justice Waite conversed with Elder Snow is unclear, and any questions about plural marriage that the judge asked were likely of the same strain that other visitors had offered; the Apostle likely would have given Waite the same polite explanations that he gave other curiosity seekers.[51] After they were finished, Justice Waite took his leave of Elder Snow and left for the East Coast the following day.

Elder Snow and his companions spent Christmas and New Year's in prison, waiting for the day of their release. Then another of the Apostle's legal appeals reached the Supreme Court in mid-January of 1887. This time, the court tackled Judge Zane's "segregation policy" head-on. Citing US and British legal cases going back more than a hundred years, the high court unanimously ruled that no court could "divide a single continuous offense running through a past period of time into such parts as it may please, and call each part a separate offense." Accordingly, Judge Zane's segregation theory was unconstitutional, and any prisoner sentenced under it who had served a sentence longer than six months for a single offense had to be released.[52]

Whether Justice Waite's visit with Elder Snow had influenced his thinking about the "Mormon question," the former did not say. The court's written opinion in the case makes no mention of it. But on February 8, the day after the court released its opinion, Elder Lorenzo Snow walked out of the Utah State Penitentiary a free man.

———— • • ————

It had been apparent for some time that, for all the pain that the Edmunds Act was heaping upon the Saints, they were still willing to "abide the penalty." Now the Supreme Court had relieved a small bit of that pressure by shutting down Judge Zane's attempt to turn the misdemeanor of unlawful cohabitation into a crime worthy of a life sentence. Still, before it was all over, more than a thousand men would go to prison under the Edmunds Act. The Utah Commission, by its own estimation, had disenfranchised at least 15,000 in its first year of operation alone.[53] With their owners in jail, some businesses had closed, leaving women and children destitute, and the Church's role in the territorial economy was greatly reduced. The result was a serious and widespread decline in economic activity, producing suffering and misery for many, not just those who practiced plural marriage. But the Saints were soldiering on.

That was unacceptable to Senator George Edmunds of Vermont. If the Saints were not breaking, the government would have to apply even more pressure. To that end, he partnered with Congressman John Randolph Tucker of Virginia to submit a second bill bearing their names. The Edmunds-Tucker Act passed both houses of Congress and went to President Cleveland's desk for his signature in February of 1887. Cleveland opposed the bill—it was overly harsh, he thought—but the Saints had no real friends in the federal government, and Edmunds was a powerful figure in Washington politics. To veto the bill would have cost Cleveland political capital for nothing in return. So he let the bill sit on his desk unsigned for ten days, after which it automatically became law.

The Edmunds-Tucker Act contained provisions similar to some that had been contained in the Morrill Act of twenty-five years before (but that had been effectively ignored), as well as some significant new ones. It dissolved The Church of Jesus Christ of Latter-day Saints as a corporation and declared that all Church property held in violation of the Morrill Act's $50,000 limit was escheated—forfeited—to the United States government. The Perpetual Emigration Company was dissolved, its assets likewise seized. The court was empowered to seize any Church records. Granting suffrage to women in Utah had not produced an electoral groundswell against plural marriage, so the women were disenfranchised, losing the right to vote that they had enjoyed for more than a decade. Children of plural marriages were legally disinherited. The territorial courts were to take control of the schools. A "test oath" was imposed on prospective voters, jurors, and government office holders. The Nauvoo Legion was disbanded.

Taken as a whole, the new law was, arguably, a bid to completely destroy the Church's ability to wield any economic or political influence whatsoever, if not to outright destroy the Church itself.[54] Some legislators had denounced the bill on those very grounds. "It cannot be denied that this is not a bill to suppress polygamy," Senator Wilkinson Call of Florida declared.

> And the methods by which it proposes to suppress this sect, this teaching of polygamy, is the confiscation of its property, the seizure of the contributions of its followers, and then arbitrary appropriation by Congress to such purposes as it thinks proper,

the trial of its followers by partial juries on evidence forced from the lawful wife. . . . These unlawful methods are not the proper means for [the Church's] overthrow and can never accomplish the purpose.[55]

But it was all for nothing. On March 7, The Church of Jesus Christ of Latter-day Saints was dissolved as a legal entity, and its assets—including the Salt Lake Temple itself—were laid open to seizure by the US government.

—————•—•—•—————

John Taylor had been leading the Church while in exile for two years by then, mostly through correspondence as he moved from home to home. But by July of 1887, he was a seventy-eight-year-old man at a time when the average life expectancy in the United States was less than fifty years, and his current fugitive lifestyle was not conducive to rest and good health. He was, in fact, visibly declining. Elder George Q. Cannon was handling most of the Church's administration as he tried to lift as much of the load from President Taylor as he could. The prophet's other counselor, Joseph F. Smith, had gone to Hawaii, where he had served two missions. Between his mastery of the native language and the many friends he had there, Elder Smith could live on the islands indefinitely until he was called back.

That time was now. Cannon felt impressed to write to his fellow counselor and ask him to return, and he also summoned the prophet's family to come be with him. Cannon was growing concerned about the President's health, and he was not the only one. Down in St. George, Wilford Woodruff was having dreams that the prophet's time was short and the Apostle needed to return to the Salt Lake Valley. He wrote a letter to Cannon, explaining his premonitions and intentions. "The dreams, as he described them, were true," Cannon wrote in his journal, "and President Taylor's condition was seen by Brother Woodruff in them. He said that he knew President Taylor would not live and remarked, his death 'is sure to come.' He speaks of coming north."[56]

Joseph F. Smith arrived a few days after Wilford's letter reached Cannon. The *F* of his middle initial stood for *Fielding*, which was his mother's maiden name. If the Latter-day Saints had had any conception of royalty, Joseph Fielding would have been a member of the nobility. He was the son of Hyrum Smith and the namesake of his uncle, the Prophet Joseph. He had been born while his father and uncle languished in Liberty Jail, and his mother had fled the mobs of Missouri carrying the infant in her arms. He'd spent his earliest years playing in the streets of Nauvoo, but his childhood had ended abruptly when he was only five years old. One of his earliest memories was that of his father and his uncle sitting on horseback in June of 1844, and Hyrum leaning down to lift young Joseph Fielding up for a last hug before he and his prophet-brother rode off to Carthage and martyrdom. His mother, Mary Fielding Smith, now a widow, chose to follow Brigham and the Twelve to the Salt Lake Valley, unlike his aunt Emma, the Prophet's wife, who chose to remain behind in Nauvoo with her children. Mary was determined to make the journey even without a husband to help, and young Joseph Fielding was pressed into service. When the family entered the valley on September 23, 1848, nine-year-old Joseph was driving one of the ox teams. But his mother died only four years later, leaving the young teenager an orphan.

Joseph was called to serve a mission to the Hawaiian Islands at the age of fifteen, and he spent three years on Maui and Molokai, learning the native language with such fluency that he spoke it as well as he could English. Brigham recalled him home to Utah in October 1857, and Joseph arrived the following February, while Johnston's army was spending its unpleasant winter in the burned-out remains of Fort Bridger. After a few months' service in the Nauvoo Legion, Joseph married Levira Annette Clark Smith and began to settle into domestic life, but it was short-lived. Brigham called the twenty-one-year-old newlywed to serve another mission, this one in England. Dutifully he went, and there he stayed for another three years, leaving for home again in June 1863, the same time that General Robert E. Lee was marching his Confederate Army north into Pennsylvania toward a small town called Gettysburg.

Joseph Fielding's time at home was even more brief this time before he was again asked to serve. He was to return to Hawaii, acting as an interpreter for Elders Ezra T. Benson and Lorenzo Snow, who were being dispatched to set the Church's affairs in order in the wake of a dishonest leader's malfeasance. He was gone only a year this time, and then, his mission service finished, Joseph Fielding was finally able to put down solid roots for the first time in his life.

Now an Apostle and a member of the First Presidency, he was handsome, tall and thin, with a full head of dark hair that was only now starting to gray. He had long worn a mustache and was starting to grow the iconic beard that would one day reach a length to make a Civil War general proud. No longer young at forty-eight, he was still vigorous enough to withstand the rigors of clandestine travel that had taken such a toll on President Taylor. He rode up to the safe house hidden in a covered wagon and went inside to meet with the prophet, but Taylor was only barely lucid. "I tried to convey to President Taylor who it was," Cannon recalled. "He was barely conscious and, I think, recognized Bro. Smith. I said to him, among other things, 'This is the first time the First Presidency have been together for two years and eight months; how do you feel?' The response came back, in a scarcely distinguishable whisper: 'I feel to thank the Lord.'"[57]

— • — • —

Within a week, President Taylor was generally unconscious. His only sign of life most of the time was his heavy breathing, and on Monday, July 25, even that began to fail. The family summoned the President's counselors to the bedroom, where they "found him in a dying condition, almost breathing his last," Cannon later wrote.

> He lay without any movement and his breath was very short and faint. Once or twice it stopped, and it was thought that he had gone; but he breathed again and continued to breathe quite gently

until five minutes to eight o'clock, when his breath ceased. This was so gentle and so like a babe falling asleep that for a brief period we stood around and watched, not certain whether his spirit had taken its flight or not. It was gratifying to see his death so peaceful and so easy.[58]

President John Taylor passed away exactly forty years and one day after Brigham Young and Wilford Woodruff had first entered the Salt Lake Valley.

Upon the prophet's death, George Q. Cannon and Joseph F. Smith summoned as many of the Twelve Apostles to Salt Lake City as might be able to safely come. Wilford was on his way north from St. George, but he was making slow progress—he was traveling by carriage because he considered the Utah Central Railroad, with its single line between Salt Lake and all points south, too easy for the marshals to watch. Erastus Snow was in Mexico and George Teasdale in England, far beyond the reach of the marshal. No one was quite sure where Brigham Young Jr., Francis Lyman, and John H. Smith were, and Elder Cannon sent dispatches to "two or three different points in Arizona, for the purpose of getting word" to the three men.[59] Lorenzo Snow was in no danger of arrest, having served his sentence, and there were no warrants out for Franklin D. Richards, Heber J. Grant, or John W. Taylor at the moment. All the rest were at risk, but they came anyway. In the end, only George Teasdale and Brigham Young Jr. were absent.

After the group had assembled, as many as could, they set to work regulating the Church's affairs and giving instructions on a number of projects, including the house of the Lord just a few miles away. Early work was now under way on the battlements and the towers, and the rate of progress on the walls had been encouraging. If nothing else interfered, the walls would reach their planned height of 167 feet in just a few years, at which point the construction would enter a new phase. All the energy had been focused on the walls for almost thirty-three years now, and thoughts of the interior work had been far enough off in the distance to be a dream—but no longer. The quorum discussed "the question of finishing the interior and roof of the Temple at Salt Lake City. . . . Most of the brethren were in favor of making the building fireproof, and using iron or steel for the roof and cement, tiles and iron for the joists, girders, floors, [and so on]."[60] Talking about the interior design work must have felt surreal to Wilford and the others after more than three decades of watching the walls rise in fits and starts. It may also have been daunting. The building was an enormous and empty granite cube, the operative word being *enormous*. The plans—which had been revised several times before and would be again—called for the temple to have more than a quarter-million square feet of floor space. But they were close enough that Wilford might have held out hope that he would live to see it finished.

Any such hope rested on the assumption that the Saints would be allowed to continue the construction undisturbed. That was a shaky supposition. Whether by intention or coincidence, the US government had given the Saints just time enough to lay the Church's third president to rest and not one day longer before moving against the Church's assets. On July 30, federal officers acting under orders from the US attorney general filed a lawsuit with the Supreme Court of the Utah Territory to recover all Church property in excess of the $50,000 allowed by law. By his best estimation, the attorney general believed the Church was holding some $2,000,000 in real estate and another $1,000,000 in personal property.[61]

The truth was that the Church was holding very little, at least on paper. John Taylor had seen this day coming long before he died and, anticipating that the Edmunds-Tucker Act or some other bill like it would become law, he had expanded the practice of transferring ownership of the Church's assets to trusted parties to keep those assets safe from legal seizure. The Tithing Office, the Church Historian's Office, the Gardo House, the quarry in Little Cottonwood Canyon, and other properties were already held in the names of individual men. President Taylor had extended the strategy to cover virtually everything the Church owned— office buildings, meeting halls, farms, and businesses. Nonprofit associations were established to hold titles to the St. George, Logan, and Manti Temples. Tithing held in the forms of animal herds and other physical property was signed over to the individual stakes in which those properties were located. When all was said and done, the only real estate that the Church technically still owned was the Office of the President; the Church farm in Salt Lake City and a few other farms around the territory run for the benefit of local tribes; and the temple block, including the Tabernacle, the Assembly Hall, and the unfinished temple. In the case of the temple block, Church leaders had hoped that the government receiver would have to bypass those buildings under the Edmunds-Tucker provision that any building used solely for religious worship would be exempt from seizure.

Now there was little for Wilford and the Apostles to do but prepare their response to the lawsuit and then wait. The fate of the Church's assets, including the Salt Lake Temple, was in the hands of lawyers, judges, and the Lord.

——— · · · ———

That was all beyond the control of the architects, stonecutters, and masons, so they went about their business as best they could and trusted that higher powers would ensure that the troubles beyond the walls of the temple block stayed outside. The time to start installing the roof and building the spires was approaching, and once that process was under way, any further changes to their design would become more difficult by the day.

Truman Angell Jr. was growing increasingly anxious about that impending deadline, as his father's design for the spires still rankled him. He'd tried to convince President Taylor to approve a radical change in their construction and have them built of granite instead of metal covering a wood lattice. The elder Truman had opposed that idea, and Taylor

375

One of Truman Angell's elevation sketches for the Salt Lake Temple, lacking the spires.

had sided with the older architect. But now Taylor had passed on, and Truman Jr. hoped that President Woodruff might take a different view from his predecessor. So he wrote to Wilford explaining his proposal. To his credit, he did give an honest history of his idea and President Taylor's rejection of it, but said that he felt pressed to go forward anyway.

Three years ago last June [1884] I suggest to our late President Taylor the propriety of completing the temple towers of stone instead of topping them with wood, after holding the matter under advisement for several months he concluded to favor wood according to the original designs, but the question since has almost ever been on my mind, and I feel impelled to bring the matter up again for consideration. I am very enthusiastic in favor of stone instead of wood and very respectfully beg to submit the question.[62]

Wilford and the Twelve considered the proposal and, as Truman Jr. had hoped, ultimately decided in favor of it. The prophet put his decision in writing on October 4 and sent the letter to the assistant architect.

Learning of the senior Apostle's change of course, Truman Sr. begged him to reconsider, but his attempt suffered from a bit of familial sabotage. His health had never been good, as his weak constitution had left him frequently sick, often to the point of incapacitation. For some time now, he'd been afflicted by dropsy—swelling of the tissues from an accumulation of fluids—and the effects of age were stealing what little strength he'd ever had. So Truman Sr. physically could not write a letter for himself. He asked Truman Jr. to act as his scribe, which he did—but as he took his father's dictation, he also took the opportunity to include his own counterarguments to his father's claims.

Wilford declined to reverse his decision. Truman Sr. was disappointed, but he did not have to stew over Wilford's decision very long. He was now an old man of seventy-seven years, frail, and unable to resist the effects of the changing seasons on his lungs. The summer passed, the fall arrived, and with it the cold temperatures that have ever invaded the Wasatch Front. By the middle of October, Truman had developed a severe cold, and it aggravated his other health conditions to the point that he was finally overcome. He passed away a little before noon on October 16 at his home in Salt Lake City. His death came as "a great shock to his relatives and friends," who had thought he might live several more years despite his ailments.[63]

He was hailed as "an old veteran in the Church," a "modest, unassuming man, of genial disposition," and "a staunch and true Latter-day Saint . . . respected for his sterling worth."[64] He had been the Church architect for thirty-five years, except for his short reprieve during the Civil War, and, in one capacity or another, he had helped to build every temple from Kirtland on. Now the man who had designed the Salt Lake Temple had died, as had Brigham and growing numbers of others, without living to see it finished. "The Temple now in process of completion in this city will serve to perpetuate his memory," the *Deseret Evening News* promised.[65]

The Church again found itself in need of an official architect, and in Wilford's mind, the qualifications required were more than mere schooling in the discipline. The person called to that office needed to know and understand the ceremonies thoroughly and design the building around them. "No architect in building a Temple who is not thoroughly acquainted with giving Endowments should go to work to build a Temple according to his own ideas without consulting with the Building Committee and the Presidency of the Church and those who do understand what is necessary for the work of the Endowments," Wilford had decided.[66] He had learned that lesson through hard experience. Truman Angell Jr. had made some critical mistakes while working on designs for the Logan Temple, and some of the construction work had to be redone as a result. Wilford was anxious to avoid repeating that error.

That requirement kept the list of possible replacements very short. Truman Jr. had successfully managed the construction of the Logan Temple, though not without some troubles, and he was intimately familiar with the Salt Lake project. He was a skilled draftsman and a competent architect, good enough that Presidents Taylor and Woodruff had adopted changes he favored over his father's objections. He was confident in his own abilities, though perhaps a bit too much. He wasn't insubordinate when he promoted his ideas, but he certainly didn't wilt even when a prophet looked over his proposals with a critical eye.

William Folsom had proven many times over that he had the necessary skill. He had overseen the Salt Lake Temple construction for a time; he had also designed the house of the Lord being erected in Manti and was overseeing its construction. But when he'd held the position of Church architect twenty-five years earlier, he had chafed under the oversight and clashed with Henry Grow and others. Whether he could oversee the architect's office without causing contention was an open question.

Joseph Don Carlos Young.

Henry Grow was a possibility. He'd designed the Tabernacle roof and several other buildings, but he was more of a civil engineer, a builder, and less a designer. His candidacy also would have suffered from the same drawback as Folsom's—if the two men couldn't work together, then appointing either could spark infighting, which the Church didn't need.

Presiding Bishop William Preston offered Wilford and the Apostles another candidate—Joseph Don Carlos Young, one of Brigham's sons. Born in 1885, Don Carlos had been little more than a toddler when the coming of Johnston's army had marked the end of the Saints' isolation in Utah. When the boy had come of age, Brigham sent him to study at the Rensselaer Polytechnic Institute in New York, one of the finest engineering schools in the country. Brigham had hoped his son would bring his training back home to Salt Lake and teach at one of the schools there, and he was not disappointed. Don Carlos did indeed come home and was currently employed as a professor of architecture at the University of Deseret. He'd proven his skills by designing several notable buildings over the last several years, including the Bear Lake Stake Tabernacle

The Salt Lake Temple under construction, c. 1886.

in Idaho, the Brigham Young Academy in Provo, and the Templeton Building, where Zion's Bank would be housed. As for his personality, he was amiable and well-liked, though he apparently suffered from "a desponding nature"—perhaps mild depression—and was "apt to get low-spirited and think very little of himself."[67]

Bishop Preston told Wilford that he and his counselors in the Presiding Bishopric were decidedly in favor of Don Carlos's appointment. Wilford confessed that he was not familiar with the young man— Brigham had been father to some fifty-seven children, many adopted, so it would have been difficult for anyone outside the family to have known them all well. But the senior Apostle said that he was willing to call Don Carlos to the position based on Preston's recommendation. With that approval granted, the Apostles voted unanimously for his selection, with Truman Jr. and William Folsom again sustained as assistant architects.[68] One of Brigham's own sons would take on part of the burden of finishing the temple that his father had started so many years before.

The Church's lawyers presented their rebuttal to the government's lawsuit two days after Truman's passing. The hearings went on for several days as the counselors presented various technical, legal, and constitutional arguments, but it was for naught. On November 5, the three-judge panel—which included Charles Zane—ruled unanimously to appoint a government receiver to go after the Church's assets. The temple block and other properties were clearly worth far more than the $50,000 allowed, and so, the panel said, the appointment of a receiver was justified on those grounds alone.

Several judges had expressed interest in the appointment, but after a day of deliberation, the man chosen for the position was US Marshal Frank Dyer. He accepted the position with some hesitation, as he suspected—with some justification—that he was likely to meet with significant resistance from the Saints, who considered the entire legal action nothing more than persecution and outright theft. Many of the old-timers had watched Missouri mobbers rob them of all they owned and now felt that the US government was doing the same.

Once he took the post, Dyer showed the same zeal in pursuing Church property as he had shown in pursuing "cohabs." The day after he was sworn in as the government receiver, he seized the Tithing Office; the Historian's Office and the Gardo House followed a few days later; and then he took over the Perpetual Emigrating Fund Company to round out his first week on the job. The following week he went after the temple block, but as those clearly were buildings whose primary purpose was religious gatherings, he agreed to let the Church rent everything on the block for the cost of one dollar per month. That would let the Saints continue to use the Tabernacle and the Assembly Hall for meetings, but there were other problems regarding the temple.

The simple fact was that, with the Tithing Office and related assets seized, the Church had very little money with which to pay the stonecutters, the masons, the blacksmiths, and all of the other workmen trying to finish the house of the Lord. Many had always been willing to donate labor, but given that it could take weeks to carve, finish, raise, and lay a single stone under the best of circumstances, trying to assemble all of the men with the needed skills now become exceedingly difficult. Adding to their troubles, the marshals under Dyer's command were still hunting with great zeal the men who practiced plural marriage—a severe deterrent to skilled men willing to work for free. With the temple block under Dyer's control, such workmen would be placing themselves at great risk. The man who was empowered to oversee the disposition of the unfinished temple was the same man who could arrest any workman there if he suspected the person practiced plural marriage.

It was a risk that Wilford and the other Church leaders were no longer willing to let them take. On December 31, all of the workmen on the temple block were dismissed, and work on the Lord's house was officially suspended until further notice.

The walls of the temple were 160 feet high, just seven feet shy of the top.

CHAPTER 12

THE CAPSTONE IS NOW READY TO BE LAID

At the start of 1888, the Saints' circumstances were about as bleak as they had ever been. The road from the courts to the prison gates was practically a freeway, with men going in the latter as fast as they were coming out of the former. The number of Saints imprisoned swelled to the point that the territorial penitentiary had to construct new housing facilities, which opened in May to handle the growing number of inmates. The US government's push to end the institution of plural marriage was now one of the largest and longest running campaigns of criminal prosecution and civil disobedience the Western world would ever see. The Saints' faith that the Lord would deliver them remained unbroken, but until that happened, all they could do was endure and dread the possibility that the government would again increase the pressure.

By mid-July, Marshal Dyer and his men had taken control of Church assets valued on paper at just over $800,000, but the truth was that the value was surely far higher. Dyer had not tried to put a value on the temple block or the Office of the President of the Church, and many of the other assets were undervalued, such as the Gardo House, for which Dyer accepted a stipulated value of just $50,000. Regardless, the Church functionally had no cash on hand—in fact, under the complex negotiations worked out with Dyer, the Presiding Bishopric had to take out loans to pay off obligations and expenses. Tithing receipts were low because many of the tithe payers were sitting in prison with their businesses shuttered. Some who could have paid tithing hesitated to do so out of fear that the government would just seize the donations. The Church's debts mounted further when it was unable to pay the bank loans it had been forced to seek and the interest began compounding.[1]

Under Wilford Woodruff's direction, the Presiding Bishopric appealed the case to the Territorial Supreme Court, hoping that the judges would rule that the temple block, the Tithing Office, the Historian's Office, and the Gardo House were exempt from seizure. The buildings on the temple block, they argued, clearly had no purpose other than religious worship; the Church had constructed and used the Tithing Office for more than thirty years, predating even the Morrill Act, so its purpose was inarguably to further the Church's religious mission; and the Historian's Office and Gardo House were, the lawyers argued, parsonages. The court denied all of the Presiding Bishopric's appeals except one—the court agreed that the buildings on the temple block were purely religious in nature and should be returned to the Church, with the stipulation that it not use them in any other way or to encourage defiance of the law. That was a clear warning that the government could seize them again if Wilford or anyone else preached the doctrine of plural marriage from the Tabernacle pulpit.

But the temple was in the Saints' control again, and the challenge now was to find a way to pay laborers to work on it. That problem would have no easy resolution so long as Marshal Dyer was ready to seize any tithes or offerings that he saw fit to take. Until the Church could find a way out of its present predicament and become solvent again, the house of the Lord would sit mostly untouched and unfinished.

Adding to the Saints' woes, some of their most beloved leaders were being taken from them. Eliza R. Snow, arguably the most respected woman in the Church and the poetess who had penned some of the Saints' most beloved hymns, had passed away at her home in the Lion House the previous December. She was "one of the noblest, best and purest women that ever graced the earth," declared the *Deseret Evening News*. In her lengthy obituary, no compliment was considered too effusive, no praise of her character or talents too flattering. "Aunt Eliza," as many of the Saints called her, had been failing for a year, succumbing not to any particular ailment but simply to the ravages of age, and her death was a peaceful one. Her brother, Elder Lorenzo Snow, had been by her bedside when she went, and he felt her passing very keenly. "Between the brother and sister there has ever existed a most exquisite affection, that has never been interrupted by any incident during the long course of their lives," the paper noted.[2]

———— • • • ————

Wilford Woodruff and the Twelve made their way to Manti in secret in May 1888, where they had the joy of dedicating that house of the Lord, now finished. Wilford was overjoyed by the moment, a rare occurrence for him, given the times. "We visited the whole Temple from the font to the roof," he wrote the day before the dedication. "[It] is the finest Temple, best finished & most costly of any building the Latter-day Saints have ever built since the organization of the Church. It cost over one million dollars."[3] President Woodruff convened the ceremony on May 17, and it was kept private, with only selected members invited, to avoid any publicity that might draw the federal marshals to the event. "I felt to thank God that I had lived on the Earth to once more have the privilege of dedicating another Temple in the Rocky Mountains unto the Most High God," Wilford recorded, "and I pray God my Eternal Father that He will protect the Manti Temple and all other Temples we have built in them unto His Holy Name that they may never go into the hands of . . . our enemies to be defiled."[4]

That prayer for protection was made in earnest. The same day that he dedicated the temple in Manti, Wilford learned that Marshal Dyer had "made a demand for the Logan Temple, Tabernacle, Tithing Office & all Church property in Logan."[5] The government's receiver seemed determined to take away the temples as fast as the Saints could build them.

——— · · ———

The Saints had clear enough title to the Salt Lake Temple now to restart the work, at least as much as the Church's severely constrained cash flow would permit. Finances were still an ever-present concern, but they had never let that stop them before. They'd built the temples in Kirtland and Nauvoo during times when they had been strapped for funds, so for some of the old-timers, including Wilford, the current deficit of money may have made them feel like they were swimming in familiar waters. They would go forward as they always had and trust that the Lord would provide the means to finish. So the masons and stonecutters returned to the temple site in the spring of 1889, picked up their tools again for the first time in over a year, and started to lay down the final courses of the walls. They had only seven or so more feet to go, which would take only a few months at most.

It was time to address the issue of the roof. Wilford's decision to make the spires out of granite had created a bit of a quandary. The plans in Don Carlos Young's office called for the six spires to rise another forty feet into the air, and if they were to be made of granite, the masons would need the construction derricks to lift the stone. But the derricks they were using to lift the stones had been moved *inside* the temple walls years before, and neither the roof could go on nor the interior work could begin as long as those were in place. The derricks needed to be out of the way to assemble the roof, but the workers would always need at least one derrick to lift any heavy materials for the roof into place.

There was a solution, simple in theory but very inconvenient in practice. The masons and roof builders could have all the derricks they wanted so long as they weren't inside the temple walls. So the derricks inside the walls had to come down, and new ones had to be erected outside, one each on the east and west sides of the building. That would remove any impediments to putting the roof together, enable the masons to continue laying granite on the spires, and clear out the building so work on the interior could begin before the towers were finished. To outsiders, tearing down old derricks only to build new ones might have appeared to be tedious and repetitive work, but the Saints' idea of *tedious* had been seriously redefined. After thirty-six years of quarrying, hauling, and laying stone, a few months spent tearing down and putting up a few derricks hardly qualified as an annoyance.

That problem resolved, the other decision to be made was that of hiring a contractor. For that, Don Carlos Young and James Moyle approached one Amos Howe early in 1889. Howe was a New Yorker, fifty-nine years old, having been born the year that the Prophet Joseph had first organized the restored Church. Howe came to the valley in 1864 during the height of the Civil War and soon thereafter established a steel foundry—a prescient move, as the transcontinental railroad's arrival a few years later would both increase the demand for steel and provide the means to move it around the territory in bulk for cheap rates. A few years after that boom, Howe joined with a business partner to establish Davis, Howe & Company, Iron Founders and Machinists, fine providers of mining and milling machinery, in 1872.[6] The company's reputation earned Howe a contract to build the baptismal font for the St. George Temple, which job he'd executed in 1877 to Brigham Young's satisfaction. That success put Howe on the short list of steelworkers whom Church leaders trusted to work on a temple. Now Howe was called up again, and he agreed to erect the temple roof, which would be tin-coated sheet iron laid over a lattice of steel girders. The contract he hashed out called for his company to furnish the workers and steel; the Church would pay all expenses for labor and supplies; and Howe's firm would receive a percentage commission upon completion of the job. Compared to the protracted troubles, financial and logistical, involved in getting the

The Salt Lake Temple under construction, c. 1889.

stone walls up, buying a steel-and-iron ceiling through a contract must have seemed like child's play. So long as the Church could find the funds to pay Howe's expenses and commission, this would, in theory, be the easiest part of the entire project to date.[7]

Howe went to work and had the steel framework in place before the end of summer. Tile went down over that, followed by a layer of cement and the tin plating on top. He worked while the interior derricks came down, and by November the two new cranes were in place on the east and west ends of the temple.

◆ · ◆

Early that same year, Wilford began to feel impressed that it was time to reorganize the First Presidency. Only two years had passed since John Taylor had passed away, rather than the traditional three that the Quorum of the Twelve tended to wait before sustaining a new President of the Church, but Wilford felt it was time to move forward anyway.

A few days into April, the Saints sustained him by unanimous vote in general conference as the fourth President of the Church, with Elders George Q. Cannon and Joseph F. Smith as his counselors. Formally assuming the callings of Church President and prophet apparently led him to reflect on the hard duties and enormous troubles that he was facing. "This is the highest office ever conferred upon man in the flesh. And what a responsibility it places upon me or any other man in the same position," he wrote in his journal.[8]

Within a few days, Wilford quietly began denying permission for Saints to enter into further plural marriages. He made no announcement of the decision, nor did he say anything about it to his counselors. It was not an official change in Church policy or doctrine; it was simply what Wilford felt impressed to do when the requests came before him, but he apparently was turning away far more than he was granting (if indeed he was granting any requests at all). But two days after President Woodruff was sustained in his new position, Elder Franklin D. Richards conducted a marriage ceremony in the Endowment House for Hans Jesperson and Laura Alice Dean, who became the groom's second wife. Jesperson was subsequently arrested, convicted, and sentenced to five years in prison for polygamy and three additional years for adultery. The Church President didn't learn about the ceremony until October, when the word got out. He spoke publicly about the event in an attempt to limit that damage, and that was when he formally revealed to the world his decision not to grant his sanction to plural marriages going forward. "I have refused to give any recommendations for the performance of plural marriages since I have been president," he told a *New York Herald* reporter.[9] The problem was that, so far as the Church was concerned, the US public thought words were cheap. If Wilford wanted to convince the country that he was serious, some kind of more serious action would be necessary. He met with several Apostles to discuss the possibilities, and Elder Brigham Young Jr. suggested that the Endowment House should be torn down. President Woodruff considered the proposal—they had always known the Endowment House was a temporary facility that heaven permitted them to use because they had no permanent temple. Now they had three, so Saints who wished to marry for the first time or participate in other ceremonies could travel to a proper house of the Lord. Moreover, destroying the only structure in Salt Lake City where plural marriages were performed would certainly be a practical demonstration to even hardened critics that Wilford was serious about his change of course. The rest of the Twelve agreed, and the order was given. The demolition proceeded under the direction of James Moyle, now the construction superintendent on the temple block, and Don Carlos Young. By the end of the year, the "temple pro tem" was gone.

The performance of an unauthorized plural marriage was not Wilford's only headache that year connected with temple work. In early December, the First Presidency called Don Carlos Young, Superintendent James Moyle, and Presiding Bishop William B. Preston to a meeting to discuss the construction of a tunnel from the temple to a planned annex building. It was during that session that some hard feelings spilled out, with Young taking the role of accuser. Moyle, he said, was ignoring Young's instructions in favor of Bishop Preston's directions, and it was causing delays and other problems. Young groused that he'd wanted to get the temple windows installed before winter so the carpenters could work on the interior during the cold season, but that task remained unfinished thanks to Preston's interference.

Elder George Cannon tried to calm the rough waters between the three men, telling them that there should be no divisions among them on a matter so important as temple building. Preston and Moyle were in the wrong, Cannon noted, as "the Presiding Bishop was doing more in dictating the construction . . . than belonged to the Aaronic Priesthood. It is the Melchisedek Priesthood that has the direction of such matters, and not the Aaronic, and this was told to Bishop Preston some time ago by President Woodruff," Cannon advised. For that reason, the First

Presidency "held the Architect responsible for the building and for everything connected with it," and so Moyle needed to take his marching orders from Young. But Young did not entirely escape censure. He had been right on the merits of the argument, Cannon admitted, but he had been wrong in the way he had handled the affair.[10] Young was often abrasive and concerned about protecting his own authority. Criticizing others in anger and particularly in front of their leaders was corrosive to the unity that they needed to maintain when working for the Lord. Young needed to shed his pride and worry more about accomplishing the work than about whether other people were giving him the respect he thought he was owed.

Whether the three men made amends then and there, Cannon didn't record in his journal.

———— · · ————

The Saints turned the calendar page to 1890 a few weeks later, but the new year started with a bad omen. The first month was only halfway past when another Saint ended up giving his life while working on the temple. On January 18, Robert H. Ford was inside the building, standing on the interior scaffolding to hang canvas inside the upper tier of circular windows. The level he had to reach apparently was above his head, and he set a board on the window ledge to stand on. The end of the board was too close to the edge, and when Ford shifted his weight, the plank slipped off. Ford tumbled twelve feet down the interior wall and struck a timber, then fell another eighteen feet to the floor. The multiple impacts on the hardwood and stone knocked him senseless, broke his collarbone, shoulder, and right hip, and left him with severe internal injuries. The doctors examined their patient and could offer his family no hope for Ford's recovery. The damage to his organs was too severe, they said, and their diagnosis proved prophetic. Ford languished five days, unconscious most of the time, until he finally passed away on January 23.[11] He was the fifth man to die by accident working on the temple itself, four of them having fallen to their deaths.

———•·•·•———

Despite that depressing start to the season, the workmen on the temple block had made tremendous progress in the last few years. The roof was on, and if the laborers could sustain the same rate of progress they had managed in recent years, they would finish the spires in the next season or two, perhaps by the end of 1891, or early 1892 at the latest. It was, therefore, time to start on the interior, and some of the rooms were going to take years to complete.

For centuries, the walls and ceilings of Christian churches and cathedrals in Europe and later America had been adorned with stained-glass windows and paintings depicting biblical stories. These were not merely decorative—they were also instructional. Prior to the invention of the Gutenberg press, each new copy of the Bible had to be written by hand, which was a long and tedious process that ensured only a relative handful of new Bibles would become available in any given year. Most would go into churches for use by the clergy, while a few others went into the private collections of the very wealthy. It was just as well because most Europeans were illiterate and most Bibles were copied in Latin, which the commoners didn't understand anyway. Even after movable type was invented, several centuries would pass before books would become cheap enough for the average family to be able to buy a Bible. So having scenes taken from scriptures on the walls of a chapel or cathedral was useful for teaching the gospel to those who would never actually read a word from a Bible page in a language they knew.

Similarly, as the Saints participated in the endowment ceremony of the temple, they moved from room to room, receiving instruction in each one. President Woodruff and the Twelve had come to see how large murals on the walls could reinforce both the spirit and the message of related instruction in each room. So they wanted the instruction rooms decorated with scenes that would contribute to the teaching inside. Those rooms were very large, so the size of the "canvases" that the artists would need to cover was considerable. Moreover, the paintings themselves needed to be of sufficiently high quality that they would contribute to the ceremony, not detract from it by appearing poorly executed by amateurs or mediocre artists. This was the house of the Lord, and it deserved the best work the Saints could offer.

Wilford was therefore open to a proposal brought to the First Presidency by two young artists, John Hafen and Lorus Pratt. Hafen had been born in Switzerland in 1856 and joined the Church while he was still a boy. Pratt was the son of Apostle Orson Pratt, deceased now for nine years. Both men had shown an early aptitude for art and studied the subject at the University of Deseret (now the University of Utah). Both knew that Paris was the center of the art world and that the finest instruction was there. They also knew that, given their own finances, they would never get to study there unless someone sponsored them to go. With the temple nearing completion, Hafen saw an opportunity for his circle of artists and the Church to mutually benefit from such a sponsorship. Hafen wrote a letter to Elder George Cannon in late March and suggested that the Church provide a grant for a small group of Utah artists to travel, live, and study art in Paris for a year or more, with the amount estimated at $500 per student per year. In return, Hafen promised that the students would return to Utah and apply their improved skills and talents to the decoration of the temple's interior walls.[12]

Despite the Church's precarious finances, Wilford and his counselors thought it would be a worthy expense. They agreed to the proposal, the funds were appropriated, and in early June, Elder Heber J. Grant of the Quorum of the Twelve set apart Hafen, Pratt, and fellow artist John Fairbanks as full-time missionaries whose service would consist of studying their craft. George Cannon paid $500 out of his own pocket to subsidize the effort, thus becoming an official patron of the arts.[13]

The trio of artists left for France a few weeks later. In the coming year they would be joined by two more students from Utah, Edwin Evans and Herman Hugo Haag, and the young men wasted neither time nor their patrons' money. To take advantage of every moment, they kept a tiring schedule—they arose by 5:30 to study French and human anatomy. After breakfast they spent the day engaged in life drawing at the Académie Julian, a private art school. Dinner gave them a short break, and then they attended night classes until 10:00, when they retired for the night. When they did have any free time, they traveled around the region to sketch, paint, and visit museums to study the works of the masters. It was a brutal regimen, but they kept it up for two years, until it was time to come home and make good on their promise to Wilford and the First Presidency.[14]

Another young creative was starting work that season on a different part of the temple, which called for a very different kind of artwork. The baptistry in the temple's lowest level was going to require something more than paint, floorboards, and chairs to make it ready for use. That facility would take up a third of the entire basement, and in the center would be the font itself. Made of cast iron and shaped as an elongated bowl, it would be ten feet long, six wide, and four deep. Even empty, the font would be enormously heavy, but when full, the font would contain 400 gallons of water, adding another 3,300 pounds of weight. To support that load, the font would require an exceptionally strong and stable base on which to sit. That foundation would be twelve life-sized and lifelike statuary oxen, cast in iron and covered in bronze. The metal livestock would stand in a circle, facing outward in groups of three, with the font resting on their backs. To create the base, a sculptor had to create a model from which a mold would be made. That would be sent to the ironworks, where molten metal would be poured into the mold's cavity and then cooled to produce an iron duplicate of the prototype. Repeated twelve times, the statues could then be finished in copper—with other artistic touches applied as needed—and installed.

The person chosen to create the circle of oxen was Gavin Hamilton Jack, a thirty-year-old Saint from Edinburgh, Scotland, who had a gift for sculpture and a wandering artist's heart. He would spend most of his life outside the valley, traveling the world to study, practice, and hone his craft, never content to stay in any one place very long. But for the moment, he was right where Wilford needed him, and Jack's youth was no measure of his talent. He'd impressed the First Presidency with his prototype ox that would be used to create the mold for casting, and they had placed only one real constraint on him as he'd done his work. "We thought his model very good, and we all approved of its appearance," George Cannon wrote after the viewing. "The intention of getting this model is to have the whole of the legs of the oxen appear above the surface, and for the font to rest on the hips of the oxen, instead of the shoulders as at present were the oxen in the three temples already completed."[15] That was no great problem for the young Scot, and he delivered what the prophet and his counselor had asked.

———— • · • ————

The threat of escheatment reared its head again that summer. Marshal Frank Dyer had been dual-hatted as both marshal and US government receiver for years now, but the Republicans in Washington had always looked to get rid of him, as he was a Democrat. Their unhappiness with some of Dyer's handling regarding the Saints' property, including the deal he had struck allowing them to retain the temple block, was just more fuel for the discontent. So when Dyer was accused of malfeasance and self-dealing, enriching himself off the seized property, the Republicans pushed newly elected US President Benjamin Harrison to replace him. The president concurred, and Dyer was promptly relieved of both his jobs.

The new government receiver was Henry W. Lawrence. Heber C. Kimball's nephew-in-law and one-time business partner, Lawrence had been a Latter-day Saint until he fell in with a group called the Godbeites, so named for their leader, William S. Godbe.[16] The group had criticized Brigham's leadership and had tried to push the Church to embrace religious beliefs such as spiritualism. Brigham had tried personally to convince Lawrence to turn away from the group, but Lawrence refused to change course and so was excommunicated from The Church of Jesus Christ of Latter-day Saints in late 1869. Further alienating himself from his former people, Lawrence testified in open court about the contents of endowment ceremonies performed in the temples, which the Saints considered sacred.

President Harrison also appointed a new US Attorney for the Utah Territory: Charles S. Varian. Varian also believed that Dyer had been unreasonably generous in the terms he'd granted the Saints in leasing back some of their seized property, and, with Lawrence's support, he moved to correct that. His reasoning was simple and twofold. First, he claimed that the Church still taught plural marriage in the temples. If anyone questioned that, he could point to Henry Lawrence, his expert on temple ceremonies, though Lawrence surely hadn't been inside the Endowment House since 1869 and had never been inside the temples in St. George, Manti, or Logan.

Second, Dyer hadn't even placed a value on the temple block, but to Varian's eyes, it was clearly worth more than the $50,000 that the Edmunds-Tucker Act allowed the Church to hold in property. On that point, he was surely correct. The Tabernacle alone was obviously worth more than that, and the Church had spent far more on the unfinished temple. On either of those points, Varian was quite sure that he could convince the courts to let Lawrence take control of everything inside the walls of the temple block.

———•·•———

With their leaders having gone to ground for years now, many of the Saints in outlying settlements and surrounding states had had no interaction with the Church's General Authorities through all of the troubles caused by the government's campaign. President Woodruff decided that that could only be rectified by his going out among the people and ministering to their needs in person. For someone of his advanced age, such extended travel would be rigorous, but that did not deter him. He took George Cannon with him, boarded the train, and began the journey.

They stopped over in Brigham City, Logan, Sanpete, and Tooele. That was only the start, and Wilford kept going, traveling to Idaho, Southern Canada, New Mexico, Arizona, and Colorado, in each place teaching and counseling with the Saints and discussing the effects that the Edmunds-Tucker Act was having on their families, wards, and stakes. After traveling more than 2,300 miles,[17] he returned to Salt Lake for a few weeks in August, and then set out for California in September. He visited San Francisco and Sacramento and met with Saints and influential citizens in each city, then returned to Salt Lake City.

Wilford had been deeply sobered by all that he had seen and heard in the time since he had become the President of the Church. The suffering that the federal government's campaign had visited on the Saints had been immense. Many of the Latter-day Saint men and all of the women in Utah were disenfranchised, as were all of the Saints in Idaho. One judge had ruled that Church membership was sufficient reason to deny a foreign immigrant US citizenship. Lacking for funds, the Church was seriously crippled in its ability to function. It could not relieve the Saints' physical suffering, properly fund the workers building the Salt Lake Temple, or undertake any of a thousand other actions. Utah would never become a state in the Union so long as plural marriage existed there.

Another blow came while Wilford was touring the Western states. Senator George Edmunds and his fellow Republicans had been following the Utah Commission's reports for the past several years and decided that it was time to increase the pressure on the Saints again. The open question was what more they could do. Despite the fact that the Saints had almost no supporters in Washington, some legislators had already denounced the Edmunds-Tucker Act, and the more the Republicans pressed the limits of what the Constitution might allow, the more legislators and judges they risked losing in support of their campaign. They were all in uncharted territory here, Saints and government officials alike. There had to be a constitutional limit somewhere, though no one knew where it was. But Edmunds and other like-minded officials were willing to press forward into the legal mist. On April 11, Congressman Isaac Struble and now-Senator Shelby Cullom introduced a bill to disenfranchise all Latter-day Saints everywhere in the United States. Edmunds himself did the same a month later, on May 14. Utah's delegate to Congress, John Caine, noted that these new proposals would not affect Saints practicing plural marriage—they had already lost the right to vote, hold office, or serve on juries. So they would only affect Latter-day Saints who were not practicing plural marriage. Those men had committed no crime, and so Congress would, without question, be punishing Saints for their beliefs alone and not for their actions.

As if to give its blessing to the endeavor, the Supreme Court again ruled five days after Edmunds submitted his bill. In the case of *Late Corporation of the Church of Jesus Christ of Latter-day Saints v. U.S.*—another appeal by the Saints to overturn the government's seizure of Church property—the Supreme Court ruled six to three that the confiscation was constitutional and that Congress's authority over the territories was absolute. The Church's attempts to sell its own assets to its members were declared null and void because it was assumed that the property might still be used to enable the practice of plural marriage.[18]

If the Saints persisted in obeying God's commandment as they understood it and continued the institution of plural marriage, they faced the prospect of endless dispossession and the ever-escalating loss of what civil rights they had left. "Abide the penalty," indeed.

———— ◆ · · ◆ ————

The Church was at a breaking point, Wilford was sure. He had been thinking about plural marriage and the government's campaign against it for more than a decade—certainly since that night he'd received a heavenly vision among the San Francisco Peaks in northern Arizona. He had remained defiant of the government in the decade since that night, determined not to trade God's commands for US law. But while the Saints' situation had grown more dire, no solution had presented itself.[19] Wilford was certain that something had to be done, but he could not act solely at his own discretion. He needed to know the Lord's will in the matter. Exactly when he started seeking a revelation on the matter or how long he sought one, Wilford did not record in his journal, but he received his answer by the early fall, and the impression it left on him to act was very strong. "This morning, I found President Woodruff quite stirred up in his feelings concerning the steps taken by our enemies to malign us before the country and to make false statements concerning our teaching and action. He felt that it was his duty to get out some kind of manifesto," George Q. Cannon wrote on the twenty-third of September. Wilford dictated a public statement to Elder George Gibbs, secretary to the First Presidency, and then asked Elder Cannon to review it. "While it was not in exactly the proper shape to publish, it contained the ideas and was very good. I told him I felt it would do good," Cannon said.[20]

Wilford's own journal entries leading up to September 24 were uneventful, almost mundane, but on that day, he made a cryptic entry in his personal record that "I met with [three] of the Twelve & my counselors upon an important subject."[21] The truth was that he had gone to his office and there told the assembled group that he that been "struggling all night with the Lord about what should be done under the existing circumstances of the Church. And, he said, laying some papers upon the table, 'here is the result'."[22] Two pages long, handwritten in Wilford's strange block printing, was a declaration that the Church was no longer solemnizing plural marriages or teaching the principle, and that he intended to submit to federal law. He assured them that "the Lord had made it plain to him that this was his duty, and he felt perfectly clear in his mind that it was the right thing."[23]

It would be the largest change to any Church practice in a half century. Such moments in the past had sometimes resulted in disaffection among Church leaders—the Prophet Joseph had encountered that on several occasions. Wilford wanted to know the Apostles' feelings and to secure their unanimity if he could, to avoid creating a schism. His hopes that they would be united behind him were realized. They reviewed the Manifesto, discussed the contents and offered some changes, and then sustained the prophet's chosen course.

After returning home that evening, Wilford took out his journal and wrote one of his most poignant entries. "I have arrived at a point in the history of my life as the President of the Church of Jesus Christ of Latter-day Saints where I am under the necessity of acting for the temporal salvation of the Church," he wrote in his journal. "The United State[s] Government has taken a stand & passed laws to destroy the Latter-day Saints upon the subject of polygamy or Patriarchal Order of Marriage. And I have issued the following proclamation which is sustained by my counselors and the 12 Apostles. . . ."[24] He included the text of the Manifesto in his own record, which read:

To Whom It May Concern:

Press dispatches having been sent for political purposes, from Salt Lake City, which have been widely published, to the effect that the Utah Commission, in their recent report to the Secretary of the Interior, allege that plural marriages are still being solemnized and that forty or more such marriages have been contracted in Utah since last June or during the past year, also that in public discourses the leaders of the Church have taught, encouraged and urged the continuance of the practice of polygamy—

I, therefore, as President of The Church of Jesus Christ of Latter-day Saints, do hereby, in the most solemn manner, declare that these charges are false. We are not teaching polygamy or plural marriage, nor permitting any person to enter into its practice, and I deny that either forty or any other number of plural marriages have during that period been solemnized in our Temples or in any other place in the Territory.

One case has been reported, in which the parties allege that the marriage was performed in the Endowment House, in Salt

Lake City, in the Spring of 1889, but I have not been able to learn who performed the ceremony; whatever was done in this matter was without my knowledge. In consequence of this alleged occurrence the Endowment House was, by my instructions, taken down without delay.

Inasmuch as laws have been enacted by Congress forbidding plural marriages, which laws have been pronounced constitutional by the court of last resort, I hereby declare my intention to submit to those laws, and to use my influence with the members of the Church over which I preside to have them do likewise.

There is nothing in my teachings to the Church or in those of my associates, during the time specified, which can be reasonably construed to inculcate or encourage polygamy; and when any Elder of the Church has used language which appeared to convey any such teaching, he has been promptly reproved. And I now publicly declare that my advice to the Latter-day Saints is to refrain from contracting any marriage forbidden by the law of the land.[25]

WILFORD WOODRUFF
President of The Church of Jesus Christ
of Latter-day Saints.

Wilford published the Manifesto to the world on the twenty-fifth of September.

———•••———

The nation's reaction to the news was decidedly mixed and mostly disbelieving. The Saints had resisted giving up plural marriage for so long that some federal officials, convinced that no such manifesto would ever come, were at a loss as to how to respond now that it was here. A few embraced it, but most were skeptical. Western politicians who stood to suffer at the ballot box declared that it was purely a political maneuver to ensure Republicans would go down in defeat the following November. One even claimed that the Manifesto was a fraud on the grounds that President Woodruff had no authority to issue it, which surely caused some eye rolling among the Saints. To demand that the Church renounce plural marriage and then claim the Church President *couldn't* renounce it must have convinced many that there was just no way to appease the Saints' most hardened opponents.

The *Salt Lake Tribune* didn't go that far, but it did claim that the prophet had played word games to make the declaration sound binding while giving the Saints a wink-and-a-nod to carry on as before.[26] It wasn't an official pronouncement, they reasoned, because the Church President hadn't publicly declared that the Manifesto was a revelation and laid it before the Church claiming, "Thus saith the Lord," so the Saints could ignore it if they chose. Many critics grabbed onto that point. If President Woodruff *had* intended it to be binding on the Saints, shouldn't he have declared it from the pulpit of the Tabernacle instead of through the newspapers? The federal government certainly thought so. John Caine, Utah delegate to Congress, reported back that the government wouldn't accept the Manifesto unless the Saints formally sustained it in general conference.

If they were daring Wilford to take that step, they were frustrated. Wilford had no compunction whatsoever about presenting the Manifesto in general conference, which convened the following Saturday morning. Seven thousand Saints gathered in the Tabernacle on October 4, anticipating some discourse from the Church's President on the matter, but Wilford said nothing about it in his opening address that morning or the following day. None of the other speakers took up the subject either, perhaps not wanting to step out ahead of the prophet. It was during the third day of the conference that the Manifesto was finally laid before the Saints. At Wilford's direction, Bishop Orson F. Whitney read the text of the declaration. Elder Lorenzo Snow then asked the Saints to sustain President Woodruff as the man "fully authorized by virtue of his position to issue the manifesto" and to "accept his declaration concerning plural marriages as authoritative and binding." The vote to do so was unanimous.

The prophet finally stood to speak. "I want to say to all Israel,"

President Woodruff started, "that the step which I have taken in issuing this manifesto has not been done without earnest prayer before the Lord. . . . For me to have taken a stand in anything which is not pleasing in the sight of God . . . I would rather have gone out and been shot," he assured the audience. He then noted that this was not the first time the Lord had asked the Saints to carry out some work that they had been restrained from doing. He had told them to build temples in Jackson County and Far West, both in Missouri, and the mobs had prevented either from being constructed. "The Lord has given us commandments concerning many things, and we have carried them out as far as we could; but when we cannot do it, we are justified. The Lord does not require at our hands things that we cannot do," he concluded. They had done their duty, but it was not wisdom to fight the entire country any longer. The United States was in God's hands and He would settle all accounts in the end. As for the Saints, they had only to trust that the Apostles and the prophet were led by revelation from heaven. "The Lord will never permit me or any other man who stands as the President of this Church, to lead you astray. It is not in the program. It is not in the mind of God," he assured them. "If I were to attempt that, the Lord would move me out of my place." If any of the Saints had doubts about the Manifesto being the right course of action, they should take their questions to God in prayer and receive an answer for themselves.

With that, Wilford finished and took his seat.[27]

———— ·•·•· ————

Plural marriage had been part of their religion for almost half a century. The majority of Saints had never practiced it, but virtually all of those who didn't knew someone who did. The younger generation, born in the Salt Lake Valley, had never known a time when it wasn't practiced. What had been so hard for so many to accept in the beginning, when the Prophet Joseph had first taught it to a select few, had become a way of life, a part of their culture. For that reason, giving it up now would prove as hard for some as taking it up had been for many in the beginning. But the Lord had shown to Wilford the potential consequences if they did not. Knowing what that outcome looked like, Wilford traveled around the territory for more than a year to explain to the people why he had issued the Manifesto. He told one congregation that continuing on would have meant the entire destruction of the Church and its work. "I have had some revelations of late, and very important ones to me, and I will tell you what the Lord has said to me," President Woodruff said.

> The Lord showed me by vision and revelation exactly what would take place if we did not stop this practice. If we had not stopped it, you would have had no use for . . . any of the men in this temple at Logan; for all ordinances would be stopped throughout the land of Zion. Confusion would reign throughout Israel, and many men would be made prisoners. This trouble would have come upon the whole Church, and we should have been compelled to stop the practice. Now, the question is, whether it should be stopped in this manner, or in the way the Lord has manifested to us, and leave our Prophets and Apostles and fathers free men, and the temples in the hands of the people, so that the dead may be redeemed. . . .

> I saw exactly what would come to pass if there was not something done. I have had this spirit upon me for a long time. But I want to say this: I should have let all the temples go out of our hands; I should have gone to prison myself, and let every other man go there, had not the God of heaven commanded me to do what I did do; and when the hour came that I was commanded to do that, it was all clear to me. I went before the Lord, and I wrote what the Lord told me to write.[28]

Presenting the Manifesto to the Saints in general conference produced no immediate reversal of the government's campaign. Some officials claimed they had no faith that the Saints would abide by the change and so tried to carry on against the Church without breaking stride. They succeeded somewhat. Most federal officials adopted a wait-and-see attitude and so made no moves to repeal the Edmunds-Tucker

Act or reverse any of the actions the government had taken under the provisions of that law. But they had to offer the Saints some kind of olive branch. Wilford had done what the government had demanded for years. If the government now refused to relieve the pressure to some degree, the Saints could argue that the Act had always been a sham to seize Church property and give official license to open persecution. Most officials truly had no interest in hounding a religious minority that had promised to obey the law; Senator Edmunds himself had said that the Saints "had their citizenship in their own hands and when they chose to abjure polygamy, they would be citizens as much as anyone else."[29]

So the government began to pull back and engage in a kind of quiet détente. The raids and arrests decreased significantly, and even zealous old Judge Zane began doling out far more lenient punishments for the few men brought into his courtroom for the crime. He also ruled that membership in the Church was no longer a justification for denying citizenship. He had been among the first to declare his belief that the Manifesto was genuine, that the Saints would abide by it, and he changed his judicial approach accordingly. The Saints would never hold any real love for Judge Charles Zane in their hearts, but it seems that he did try to show that his zeal in punishing polygamy had been an expression of his dislike for the institution of plural marriage and not for the Saints who practiced it.

◆ · · ◆

News of that détente apparently did not reach the ears of US Attorney Charles Varian. Emboldened by the Supreme Court's decision to uphold the constitutionality of the Edmunds-Tucker Act's escheatment clause, Varian filed several lawsuits on November 5 in the Third District Court for the forfeiture of the temple block and of the temples in St. George, Manti, and Logan. He made no mention of the Church teaching plural marriage inside the temples or the Tabernacle. Grounding his suits on that argument would have required witness testimony to prove the point. He could have produced Henry Lawrence for that, but that man's knowledge of what happened in temples was stale by two decades. So Varian made the financial argument instead. Any fool could see that the Tabernacle, the temple, and other structures on the block were worth more than $50,000 together.[30] They were surely each worth more than $50,000 individually, in fact.

The disposition of the unfinished temple was now in the hands of the Third District Court of the Utah Territory, and it would be Judge Charles Zane who would decide whether it would remain in the Saints' hands or become the escheated property of the United States government.

———•··•———

Near the end of 1890, the First Presidency was grappling with ugly choices about how to address the Church's insolvency. In earlier years, the Church had been able to rely on tithing labor as a key resource in finishing a considerable number of projects, including building temples, with paid labor and monetary donations playing lesser, though still important, parts of the effort. The coming of the railroad had kicked off a transition in which donated labor began to play the lesser part, with paid labor funded by tithing becoming the preferred system. Now, with Henry Lawrence in control of the Church's assets, many Saints hesitated to pay tithing, and so the Church's coffers were dry. Much of the leadership's time was spent traveling, seeking loans and donations. Banks were more willing to extend them now that plural marriage was no longer an issue, but they often demanded usurious rates. The debts were mounting, and Wilford had to reduce the Church's expenses as much as possible. At the top of the list was the option to dismiss the workers on the temple block yet again.

Construction costs on the temples had always consumed an enormous part of the Church's budget. In 1880, ten years ago and before the Edmunds-Tucker Act had eviscerated its finances, the Church's income had stood at a little more than a million dollars. Of that, $235,000 had been allocated for temple construction—almost a quarter of the total.[31] During the last three years alone, the total spent had come to

$256,000[32]—almost exactly the same amount of money the Church had had to borrow to meet the receiver's demands a few years back, and an average of $85,000 annually.[33] They expected that amount to go up to $100,000 in the coming year as the interior work on the temple ramped up even as the exterior work approached completion.[34]

The First Presidency met with the Presiding Bishopric and Don Carlos Young to discuss whether to halt construction. George Cannon was disturbed by the thought, but there were few alternatives and none of them good.

> The brethren seemed to be in favor of discharging all the hands [temple laborers]. President Woodruff, feeling the embarrassment of the situation and the great need of means, was inclined at first to take this course. I could not in my feelings consent to this, although I said nothing for some time; but being appealed to know what my feelings were, I said that I could talk more understandingly about this if I knew the circumstances of the church better than I did—what our income was now compared with last year, and also what amount it would require to continue these hands. It seemed to me that if we yielded to the panic it would only increase the embarrassments, and by discharging a lot of workmen at the present time it would have an injurious effect on the public mind. [35]

After much discussion and study, the assembled counsel finally decided to continue building the temple, but given the math staring them in the face, it was an act of pure faith that the Lord would somehow provide.

———— • · • ————

The year closed as it began, with the unexpected death of one of their own. The unfortunate soul was not one of the masons or stonecutters—it was James Moyle, the superintendent. An otherwise healthy man with a strong constitution, Moyle had started to feel ill in November but had refused to limit his activities. When most around him were relaxing on Thanksgiving Day, he chose to climb Ensign Peak instead. The cold fall air did nothing to help his condition, and he "was finally compelled to retire to his bed." He refused to stay there and insisted on going to the temple block the next week to attend to business, but his strength finally abandoned him. By December 5, he was laid out in bed. The disease had gotten into his lungs and developed into pneumonia. He died at his home on December 8 at a little past eight-thirty in the evening. He was only fifty-five years old.

It was a stunning loss to the men who "universally held [Moyle] in the highest esteem," the *Deseret News* observed. "They feel that in his departure they have lost a brother and a friend." The Church's leadership concurred, with some admitting that "it would be difficult to find a person to fill the position on the public works made vacant by his demise."[36] But the temple's construction would be stopped by no man's death, and they had to choose a replacement.

The man they chose was Charles Livingston, the younger brother of the Little Cottonwood Canyon quarry superintendent, James Livingston. Charles's own history matched that of his brother in most particulars, and just as their past had forged one brother into the right kind of man to run the quarry, it had developed the other into the kind of man the Church needed to become superintendent of the temple block. The Livingston brothers had joined the Church together back in Scotland and worked together cutting granite for the temple. Both had stood against Johnston's army, and both had been lawmen. Their history together finally diverged in a serious way in 1860 when Charles left to take up farming in Fairview, Sanpete County, but he gave up the pastoral life when the coming of the railroad brought "a very great amount of crime such as murders, garreters, gamblers, hurdy-gurdy harasses and all the worst criminal element" to Utah.[37] The territorial government needed experienced policemen to reign in the growing number of hardened villains, and Charles was both able and willing.[38] His second turn at law enforcement brought him first to Ogden and then back to Salt Lake City, but he gave it up again in 1881, when he accepted the posting of supervisor of streets. He held that job for

The Salt Lake Temple under construction, c. 1891.

a decade and through it became known and well-liked throughout Salt Lake City, enough so to earn him the name of "Uncle Charlie." Then the Church asked him to succeed the much-loved James Moyle. He accepted. Working in tandem with his brother James again, Charles Livingston would be the final superintendent of the temple block, leading the workmen there until the house of the Lord was complete.

The Livingstons were a family of stonecutters, so it may have been ironic to call Charles Livingston to the superintendency as the interior work began to ramp up. But the outside was not finished yet, though they were very, very close. That first month of 1891, Joseph Don Carlos Young produced the final drawings for the final stonework courses to be laid for the spires.[39] There was no question about it now. Barring some disaster, they could finish the spires with another season of labor. Their enemies were trying hard to produce such a disaster—the very first week of the year saw *The Illustrated American* publish a pair of scandalous articles, allegedly written by a longtime member of the Church, which repeated numerous claims designed to inflame the country against the Saints. "This is one of the most villainous plots that I have ever known," George Cannon observed. "Coming from a professed Mormon, it is a most extraordinary communication; yet anyone familiar with our history will see that the writer is not a Mormon, for he betrays his ignorance of many points that a Mormon would understand. There is no doubt that these articles have been prepared by our enemies here."[40] But the temple workmen just kept their heads down and let the prophet and the Apostles fend off the outside world.

———•·•———

They lost another of those Apostles a few weeks later when Daniel H. Wells succumbed to pleurisy and pneumonia in late March at the age of seventy-six. He had been the first superintendent of public works, and there had never been a time when he had not been near to the project until he was called to preside over the Manti Temple. They buried him on the twenty-ninth of the month, and his funeral in the Tabernacle drew one of the largest crowds ever seen in Salt Lake City. The building was decked out in white, matching the color of the casket that was the final home for the Apostle. President Woodruff delivered the eulogy before an assembly that he estimated at 10,000 people, which would have left standing room only inside the building. He could only hope that no one had to stand outside. "It was a very stormy day," Wilford wrote, "the worst day for a funeral I ever attended."[41]

———•·•———

Besides the five artists studying their craft in Paris and Gavin Jack working to cast oxen for the baptistry in iron, there was another artist at work on one element of the building that would go on to become an icon as recognizable as the temple itself. Cyrus Edwin Dallin was born in Springville, Utah, in November 1861, but he was not a member of the Church. His parents had been early pioneers, but they quit the Church and became Presbyterians before his birth. They remained in Utah through his childhood, so young Cyrus was no doubt familiar with the

Church and its teachings, but he did not unite himself with the Saints. He studied sculpture in Boston and, while there, at the age of twenty-one, he beat out several notable sculptors in a major competition to produce a statue of the city's famous Revolutionary patriot Paul Revere. But after he had received the commission, his early models were rejected, and he would ultimately struggle fifty-eight years to finish the sculpture that now sits west of Boston's Hanover Street on the Paul Revere Mall.

Seeking to support himself while he wrestled with the Revere project, Dallin wrote to then-President of the Church John Taylor, told him of his plan to return to Utah and open a studio, and proposed that the Church commission him to create a memorial to the Prophet Joseph. "I would gladly erect it at my own expense; but I am sorry to say my life has been through the barren walks of life, and I have to still 'struggle for existence,'" he explained.[42] Nothing came of that letter so he tried again four months later, with no better result. Disappointed, he soon made his way back to the East Coast and then to Paris, where, like the five artists later funded by the Church, he attended the Académie Julian. His work drew critical acclaim, and with his résumé thus improved, he returned to the United States to again seek work.

He went back home to Utah and there was able to secure a job producing busts of the First Presidency—Wilford Woodruff, George Q. Cannon, and Joseph F. Smith. His work impressed the prophet, and Wilford offered Dallin a commission to produce a statue of an angel to be placed atop the almost-finished temple's center spire on the eastern side. Dallin declined at first on the grounds that he was neither a member of the Church nor a believer in angels, but the prophet was insistent. Dallin visited his mother in Springville, and she counseled him to accept the commission. She urged him to study the Bible and the Book of Mormon for inspiration, and he found it in the book of Revelation.

> And I saw another angel fly in the midst of heaven, having the
> everlasting gospel to preach unto them that dwell on the earth, and
> to every nation, and kindred, and tongue, and people,

Saying with a loud voice, Fear God, and give glory to him; for the hour of his judgment is come: and worship him that made heaven, and earth, and the sea, and the fountains of waters.[43]

Thus persuaded, Dallin accepted the commission and set to work sketching designs for a statue. He presented his proposed drawings for the statue to the First Presidency, Church Architect Don Carlos Young, and the Presiding Bishopric of William B. Preston and John R. Winder on July 21. They liked what they saw, and Wilford gave his approval for Dallin to proceed. The sculptor had a forty-inch plaster model of the proposed statue ready to view at the Salt Lake Fair on October 4, where the public reception was overwhelmingly favorable. After that preview was complete, Dallin made a full-size model and shipped it to W. H. Mullins and Company in Salem, Ohio, a metalworking firm that had gotten its start manufacturing sinks and cabinets. The company was equal to the task and in short order used the plaster model to produce a metal twin, cast in copper. The final product was then covered in polished 22-karat gold, packaged up, and shipped back to Salt Lake City, where it awaited its final placement atop a temple spire that was not yet quite finished.[44]

The angel statue, or at least its silhouette, would go on to become for years the de facto logo symbol of The Church of Jesus Christ of Latter-day Saints, as closely identified with it as the sign of the cross is to Christianity or the Star of David to Judaism. It is another of the ironies of the Salt Lake Temple story that one of the great iconic symbols of the Church was created by a man who not only was not a Latter-day Saint, but whose parents had left the faith before he was even born.

Cyrus Dallin returned to Salt Lake City and Temple Square some years later. Elder Levi Edgar Young of the Quorum of the Seventy, president of the Temple Square Mission and an old friend of Dallin's, recognized the artist touring the site, greeted him warmly, and took on the role of escort and tour guide. The two men spent the day together looking at the statuary around the square and taking in the Sunday organ recital at the Tabernacle. Afterward, sitting on the curb around the

Seagull Monument, Dallin looked up at Moroni and made an admission to his friend. "I consider that my 'Angel Moroni'[45] brought me nearer to God than anything I ever did. It seemed to me that I came to know what it means to commune with angels from heaven," Dallin said. Then he added, "We can only create in life what we are and what we think."[46]

———•••———

It was finally all coming together. The laborers on the temple block had made enough progress by late September to predict with confidence that they could lay the capstone atop the last spire that season if the First Presidency so chose. They would not be ready for that step by the October general conference, but it would not be long after.

President Woodruff and his counselors pondered that one. Thirty-nine and a half years of work deserved some kind of special celebration, did it not? Did not the Saints deserve some kind of public ceremony to commemorate all of the obstacles that they'd passed through to get here? They'd endured the crickets and near famine; Johnston's army; the massive destruction of the Arsenal Hill explosion; hostile federal officials, mass arrests, and incarceration; and all of the heat, cold, rain, and snow that had beaten down on them as they'd dug out the foundation, excavated a failed canal, quarried and hauled thousands of tons of granite and sandstone, and laid hundreds of miles of railroad track. Or should they simply put on the capstone and be done with it? Why delay an event one more day that had been so long in coming?

Wilford decided that, yes, the moment deserved some pomp and ceremony. "The question has been before us for a day or two concerning the capstone, when it should be laid, and whether it should be laid with ceremonies," wrote George Cannon.

> We have decided that it should be laid with appropriate ceremonies, and I suggested that . . . we defer the laying of the capstone until next April Conference, which will be the completion of the 40 years since the foundation stone was laid. . . . This proposition President Woodruff thought well of, and it was so decided.[47]

There was, however, the matter of money, which was still scarce, courtesy of the United States government. Don Carlos Young estimated that they would have to raise at least $100,000, and perhaps as much as $150,000, to finish the temple. There was also some concern that Wilford's decision to delay placing the capstone might cost him his own chance to see it happen. Would Wilford himself live to see it? He was, after all, eighty-four years old, older than either Brigham Young or John Taylor had been when they had passed away.

The prophet was not deterred by numbers, related either to money or to age. As far as Church finances and building the temple were concerned, the Saints had been pushing ahead on faith for some time now, and the money had come when they'd needed it. And if the Lord saw fit to take him before the temple was done, as He'd done with the two preceding Church presidents, so be it. That would be heaven's prerogative, and Wilford's successor would get the privilege of finishing the building. Others in the room agreed on both counts.

> The question of completing the Temple came up, and Brother F[rancis] M. Lyman related a manifestation which he had concerning its completion, and that President Woodruff would live to see it. President Woodruff also spoke of the manifestations he had had concerning the Temple while on a mission in Boston many years ago. The feeling was manifested to raise the necessary amount by donation. It was thought that a hundred men could be found who would put in $1000 each, the architect having intimated that $100,000 would complete the building. It was suggested, however, that it would be wiser to raise $150,000, and that it should not be confined to the rich, but that all should have the opportunity of contributing according to their means and their faith towards the completion of the building. There was a most excellent spirit manifested concerning this.[48]

Legal observers might have thought Wilford was being premature in planning a capstone ceremony for the temple. US Attorney Charles Varian's lawsuit to escheat the entire temple block and the temples of St. George, Manti, and Logan had been pending before Judge Zane's Third District Court for a year. The delay was unusual. Past rulings from the courts approving escheatment had usually come within a few months. The Supreme Court itself had moved more quickly on the issue. But whether Varian had grown nervous during the intervening months waiting on Judge Zane, he never said. Maybe the Chief Justice had simply been taking his time investigating whether the disputed properties should be seized . . . or maybe not. Zane was a believer that Wilford had been sincere in publishing the Manifesto, so perhaps he had been giving the Saints time to prove that they were going to abide by it.

Whatever the reason for the delay, Zane finally issued two rulings, the first on October 27, the second on November 11. The Tithing Office, the Gardo House, the Historian's Office, and the Church farm in Salt Lake qualified for confiscation. The other properties that Varian had requested, including the temple block, were exempt and beyond the government's reach. The temples, including the unfinished house of the Lord in Salt Lake City, would remain in the Saints' hands.[49]

- - • - -

The six months passed with many of the Saints' former troubles taking on a hopeful aspect. The First Presidency and the Twelve drafted a petition to President Harrison pleading for executive clemency—and, to their joy, both the territorial governor and Judge Zane endorsed it in writing. "We have no doubt of its sincerity, and no doubt that it is tendered in absolute good faith," they wrote. "The signers . . . are men who not lightly pledge their faith and honor to the Government, or subscribe to such a document, without having fully resolved to make their words good in letter and spirit."[50] It was read to Congress in February in support of a "home rule" bill proposing that Utah be allowed to become a state at last. After fifty years of applications for statehood, and with plural marriage removed as a bone of contention, the federal legislature was finally disposed to give the matter serious consideration. The bill actually passed out of committee in the House of Representatives on March 30, 1892, the first sign that Utah might soon be allowed to join the Union as an equal member in the family of states.

Wilford was, as Elder Lyman had predicted, still alive, but his health had given him trouble during the late fall and winter. He'd endured bouts of bilious colic that had left him bedridden for days at a time. Looking to ease his load, the General Authorities of the Church decided that individual recommends to enter a temple no longer needed Wilford's personal signature. It was common for him to sign several dozen each day when he was in his office, and it was clear that that requirement of the prophet's individual endorsement wasn't going to scale up any further. If the policy didn't change as the Church grew, signing temple recommends would soon be all that the prophet had time to do. Having the prophet sign each recommend did convey how seriously each member should take his or her personal preparation and worthiness to enter the house of the Lord—but the Church was now so large that local leaders of stakes and wards were in a far better position to evaluate whether any given member was ready. So they published a circular that "it [was] no longer being necessary to send Temple Recomm[en]ds to Pres[iden]t Woodruff for his endorsem[e]nt. The names of the Bishop & Pres[iden]t of Stake being all that is necessary to admit to the Temples . . ."[51]

◆·◆·◆

The date for laying the capstone of the Salt Lake Temple was drawing near. To educate the Saints on the importance of the event, the *Deseret News* ran a series of historical articles tracing the development of temples throughout history, from Moses's tabernacle in the desert to Solomon's and Herod's temples in Jerusalem, to Kirtland, Nauvoo, and the three temples now finished in Utah. But the lengthy essays could hardly have increased the Saints' excitement for the event. Men who had been young in 1852 and helped dig out the foundation were now old and gray. Others were young enough that they'd never known a time when the Salt Lake Temple hadn't been under construction. Many who had given their time and labor hadn't lived to see this day—including Brigham Young, Truman Angell, Daniel H. Wells, Heber C. Kimball, and John Taylor. Many of the women who had supported the work through the years with their talents, donations, and every other kind of aid they could render had passed on also—Eliza R. Snow and Phebe Woodruff, to name just two. Others, like Sarah M. Kimball and Zina D. H. Young, were widows, but they were still as active in their support of the Church as old age allowed.

It promised to be a day to remember, and the people began to arrive in Salt Lake City days before general conference was scheduled to start. They came by every means available, with the train now allowing Saints to come from all over the territory in less than a day.

The weather looked uncooperative during the week before the event, and there were fears that nature itself might become an obstacle. Wilford noted in his journal that the valley received "a hard snow storm" on March 30, just a week before the capstone laying, and cold storms rolled through the valley much of that week.[52] But the skies were fair on April 6, the last day of the four-day conference, for which the people must have been grateful. An enormous crowd gathered outside the gates to the temple block hours before conference was set to begin that morning, and it was apparent early on that most would have to stay outside. The exact number who attended is unknown, but later estimates put the number at 40,000. Once the gates opened, "the multitude pressed in and filled the Tabernacle . . . the aisles and doorways [and] the space surrounding the Tabernacle was filled and thousands more unable to get near enough to hear anything went into the temple yard and got in position to witness the ceremonies that should be conducted there when the Tabernacle services should be ended."[53] More watched from nearby rooftops and windows.

It was the sixty-second anniversary of the Church's founding, and

Wilford later described it as "the most interesting day in some respects the Church has ever seen since its organization."[54] For that conference session, the priesthood holders of the Church assembled by quorums within the Tabernacle. The General Authorities, stake presidencies, high councils, and bishoprics took places on the stand under the shadow of the great pipe organ. Other priesthood quorums were seated in the center aisle, with the general public taking up the rest of the seating throughout the building. Crowds pressed as near to the Tabernacle doors and windows as they could manage, hoping that the speakers' voices might carry far enough for them to listen.[55]

The session began at ten o'clock that morning with all the Saints singing a hymn written by one of their own, William Clayton, while the Saints had been crossing the plains. It had become an anthem to the Saints over the decades, a song that was very much their own.

> Come, come, ye Saints, no toil nor labor fear,
> But with joy wend your way;
> Though hard to you this journey may appear,
> Grace shall be as your day.
> 'Tis better far for us to strive
> Our useless cares from us to drive;
> Do this, and joy your hearts will swell—
> All is well! All is well!
>
> Why should we mourn or think our lot is hard?
> 'Tis not so; all is right.
> Why should we think to earn a great reward
> If we now shun the fight?
> Gird up your loins; fresh courage take.
> Our God will never us forsake;
> And soon we'll have this tale to tell—
> All is well! All is well!
>
> We'll find the place which God for us prepared,
> Far away in the West,
> Where none shall come to hurt or make afraid;

There the Saints will be blessed.
We'll make the air with music ring,
Shout praises to our God and King;
Above the rest these words we'll tell—
All is well! All is well!

And should we die before our journey's through,
Happy day! All is well!
We then are free from toil and sorrow, too;
With the just we shall dwell!
But if our lives are spared again
To see the Saints their rest obtain,
Oh, how we'll make this chorus swell—
All is well! All is well!![56]

George Q. Cannon of the First Presidency offered some opening re-marks before retaking his seat. Then Elder Lorenzo Snow of the Twelve stepped forward to "[instruct] the congregation as to the order of cere-mony at the laying of the capstone of the Temple." As he did so, he in-troduced them to a new action that the First Presidency desired them to perform at the appropriate moment. "The words of the shout 'Hosanna,' to be uttered upon, or after, the laying of the capstone today were intro-duced by President Joseph Smith at the Kirtland Temple," he explained.

> This is no ordinary order, but is—and we wish it to be dis-tinctly understood—a sacred shout and employed only on extra-ordinary occasions like the one now before us. We wish it also to be distinctly understood that we want the brethren and sisters not only to express the words, but that their hearts shall be full of thanksgiving to the God of heaven, who has accomplished, through our agency, this mighty and extraordinary labor.

To perform the "Hosanna Shout," the Saints were to repeat three times the words, "Hosanna, Hosanna, Hosanna to God and the Lamb. Amen, amen, and amen." And they were to repeat them at such a volume that "every house in this city may tremble, the people in every portion of this city hear it, and it may reach to the eternal worlds."[57]

———— + · · + ————

President Woodruff stood and made his way to the pulpit. He looked over the congregation assembled before him, and his feelings spilled out.

> If there is any scene on the face of this earth that will attract the attention of the God of heaven and the heavenly host, it is the one before us today. . . . My brethren and sisters and friends, we want to finish this Temple; we want to dedicate it unto God as soon as we can, so that the vast host who dwell in this region of country may go into it and attend to their ordinances for their living and for their dead. I hope we shall all lay this to heart and try to furnish means so far as we can, in order that the building may be speedily completed. We are able, as a people to do this. I realize that there are many calls upon the Latter-day Saints for the work and purposes of the Church and kingdom of God upon the earth; but this work now before us is a most important event—the most important that we have upon our hands.

He reached back into his memory and told the Saints that he remembered the very day and hour when the Prophet Joseph had revealed the doctrine of the salvation for the dead. "We have the power to go into these Temples of our God and redeem our progenitors," he assured them.

> They never heard the Gospel; they never enjoyed the blessings which you and I have in our day and time through the mercy of God. We are their posterity. They are on the other side of the vail, shut up in prison, and will remain there until their sons and daughters go into these holy places and redeem them, as Jesus went to preach to the spirits in prison.

Some of those ancestors had waited thousands of years for their descendants to save them, Wilford said, and there were unimaginable blessings waiting for those who performed that work.

Wilford finished his discourse and took his seat. George Q. Cannon closed the meeting with prayer, and then, at eleven-thirty, the procession to the temple began as the attendees filed out of the Tabernacle by quorums, with the prophet leading the way.

In a single day, workmen had erected three stands on the south side of the temple. The main stand was by the southwest corner, eight feet high and decorated with red, white, and blue bunting. President Woodruff and the First Presidency took their places there, followed by the Twelve; John Smith, the Patriarch of the Church; the Presidency of the Seventy; the Presiding Bishopric; and the stake presidents and their counselors. The Tabernacle Choir filed onto another platform to the left. The rest of the Church leaders climbed onto the third by the southeast corner of the temple. Several minutes passed before everyone was in place, and then the crowds moved in and surrounded the elevated platforms, some 40,000 people come to see the event.

With everyone settled, a band performed a new piece written for the day's ceremony titled "The Capstone March,"[58] followed by the Choir, which sang a new hymn also composed for the occasion, "The Temple Anthem."

Glorious God, Eternal Father,
In the name of Christ we pray
Thou wilt bless us with Thy presence,
While this crowning stone we lay;
Let thy favor rest upon it,
Let thy hand protect these tow'rs
May thy peace brood o'er this temple,
It is thine, O Lord, not ours,
It is thine, It is thine,
It is thine, O Lord, not ours.

Chorus:
Glory, Glory, hallelujah,
Heav'n and earth and angels sing.

Choirs celestial join the chorus,
Praise Him, praise Him, Christ our King.

Shout hosanna, shout hosanna!
Glory be to God our head
For his everlasting mercies
To the living and the dead;
Joy now reigns where once was sadness
'Midst the prison's dreadful gloom,
Millions hail with joy and gladness
Victory over hell and tomb!
Victory, victory, victory over hell and tomb.

Sound throughout his vast creations,
All his wondrous heavenly host,
Glory be to God the Father,
Jesus Christ and Holy Ghost;
Sing ye bright seraphic legions
Loud as thunder in the sky,
Pealing through celestial regions,
Glory be to God on high,
Glory, glory, glory be to God on high.[59]

The Choir fell silent, and Joseph F. Smith stepped forward to offer an invocation. He offered gratitude on behalf of all the Saints that they were now privileged to lay the capstone and pleaded for God's approbation of the product of their thirty-nine years of work. "May it go down in the memories of those that are assembled here, and may it be retained in the memories of the young—the children that are here in our midst—that they may carry it to their latest day." And then he expressed a sentiment that must have risen up from deep inside his own memory: "We thank Thee that there are a few of us here that were privileged to behold the laying of the corner stone of this building," he exclaimed, "and that Thou hast preserved us through years that have passed and brought us to this present time under so favorable circumstances as those which surround us." It was a striking comment, given the dark hardships of the

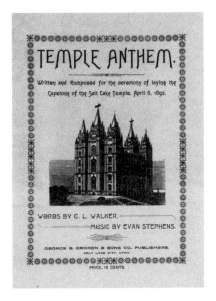

last decades that had only recently started to recede, but he did not dwell upon the difficulties that were now past. Instead, he asked for blessings on those who had labored on the temple and who yet had some work to do on it and inside it. Then, as he moved toward the end of his prayer, he combined a request and an expression of thankfulness together into an unusual conclusion. "Bless Thine aged servant President Woodruff and sanctify to him the honor which is due unto him, O God, of laying the capstone by the instrumentality of electricity, that great agency, the discovery of which has been granted unto the people of this generation." With a final plea for divine acceptance of the building, the builders, and their labors, Joseph F. Smith ended his prayer.

The Choir sang another hymn—"Grant Us Peace"—and then all was silent.

From 200 feet above the crowd, standing on the scaffolding surrounding the central spire of the eastern wall, Joseph Don Carlos Young stood with several men, ready to lower the capstone into place. The

Laying the capstone on the Salt Lake Temple, April 6, 1892.

lower half of the sphere was already fixed, its upper half hanging suspended a few feet above it, ready to descend and complete the whole.

It was actually more than just a capstone—it was also a record stone. Inside the lower half of the sphere was a shelf that ran around the circumference to hold the books, pictures, and other documents chosen for preservation. Charles Livingston recorded that he was honored to place the records inside,[60] which consisted of the music and lyrics for the "Capstone March" and "Temple Anthem" performed a few minutes earlier; the standard works of the Church; a hymnal; books and missionary tracts, including Parley P. Pratt's *Voice of Warning* and *Key to the Science of Theology*; some kind of renderings of Joseph and Hyrum Smith; photographs of Brigham Young, John Taylor, Wilford Woodruff and his two counselors, and the Salt Lake Temple as it presently stood. Also set inside was a polished brass dedication plaque upon which the Saints had recorded key names and dates of the temple's history:

HOLINESS TO THE LORD.

THE TEMPLE BLOCK CONSECRATED AND GROUND BROKEN FOR FOUNDATION OF THIS TEMPLE, FEBRUARY 14TH, 1853.

THE CORNER STONES WERE LAID APRIL 6TH, 1853, COMMENCING AT THE SOUTHEAST CORNER.

General Church Authorities:

April 6th, 1853.

FIRST PRESIDENCY.
Brigham Young, Heber C. Kimball, Willard Richards.

TWELVE APOSTLES
Orson Hyde, Amasa Lyman, Parley P. Pratt, Ezra T. Benson, Orson Pratt, Charles C. Rich, Wilford Woodruff, Lorenzo Snow, John Taylor, Erastus Snow, George A. Smith, Franklin D. Richards.

PATRIARCH TO THE CHURCH.
John Smith, son of Asael.

FIRST SEVEN PRESIDENTS OF SEVENTIES.
Joseph Young, Zera Pulsipher, Levi W. Hancock, A. P. Rockwood, Henry Herriman, Jedediah M. Grant, Benjamin L. Clapp.

PRESIDING BISHOP.
Edward Hunter.

April 6th, 1892.

FIRST PRESIDENCY.
Wilford Woodruff, George Q. Cannon, Joseph F. Smith.

TWELVE APOSTLES
Lorenzo Snow, Franklin D. Richards, Brigham Young, Moses Thatcher, Francis M. Lyman, John H. Smith, George Teasdale, Heber J. Grant, John W. Taylor, Marriner W. Merrill, Anthon H. Lund, Abraham H. Cannon.

PATRIARCH TO THE CHURCH.
John Smith, son of Hyrum.

FIRST SEVEN PRESIDENTS OF SEVENTIES.
Jacob Gates, Seymour B. Young, C. D. Fjelsted, John Morgan, B. H. Roberts, George Reynolds, Jonathan G. Kimball.

PRESIDING BISHOP.
William B. Preston, R. T. Burton, John R. Winder, Counselors.

T. O. Angell, Joseph D. C. Young, Architects.
THE CAPSTONE WAS LAID APRIL 6TH, 1892, BY PRESIDENT WILFORD WOODRUFF.

Wilford had wanted the senior leaders of the Church to climb the scaffolding to direct the laying of the capstone, but, on the day before the ceremony, George Cannon asked four of the Apostles[61] to inspect the platforms and give their opinion of that plan. They fulfilled that assignment, and all four concluded that it would be "impracticable" to go up. Whether they were concerned about the challenge and risk it would have presented for Wilford, Cannon didn't record, but that would have been a reasonable worry. Given Wilford's age, such a climb would have been difficult for him, if not downright dangerous. Several men had died falling off the temple, and no one would be anxious for the prophet to become a casualty. But Don Carlos Young suggested that electricity offered a suitable alternative. He could connect a cable holding the capstone to an electric motor and rig a switch on the speaker's platform to activate it. President Woodruff would need only to close the switch and complete the circuit to lower the stone. Young, along with Charles Livingston and others, would be on the scaffolding, 200 feet above the crowd, ready to guide the stone as it came down and ensure that it fit into its final resting place. Cannon approved of the plan, and the architect had the entire system in place within a day.

Now, as the Choir's voices faded to silence, Young yelled out in his loudest voice, "The capstone is now ready to be laid." At that cue, Wilford returned to the podium and addressed the assembly before him. "Attention, all ye house of Israel and all ye nations of the earth," he said. "We will now lay the top stone of the temple of our God, the foundation of which was laid and dedicated by the Prophet, Seer and Revelator, Brigham Young." He activated the switch, the motor rumbled to life, and the capstone descended down and landed in its place. Lorenzo Snow stood and signaled the congregation to offer up the "sacred shout" that he had taught them earlier. The people yelled, "Hosanna, hosanna, hosanna, to God and the Lamb, Amen, Amen, and Amen." This they did three times, waving white handkerchiefs.

The Tabernacle Choir stood again and broke out into a hymn—"The Spirit of God Like a Fire Is Burning."[62] First written by William W. Phelps in 1835, it was sung at the dedication of the Kirtland Temple and every house of the Lord dedicated since. The Union Glee Club then followed the congregation by singing another composition, "The Temple Ode."

> *All hail this glorious day,*
> *This grand, auspicious day.*
> *The vale resound, the mountain ring,*
> *The capstone on the Temple bring,*
> *With gladsome peal, united sing,*
> *Of truth's still widening way.*
>
> *The time is near at hand,*
> *When Christ shall come and claim His own.*
> *And 'mid his Saints erect that throne,*
> *Which on the earth must stand.*
>
> *All hail that glorious day,*
> *The shadows melt away;*
> *The skies are bright,*
> *Soon truth and right,*
> *Shall come to earth from Zion's light.*
> *And man redeemed at last shall shine,*
> *Our Father's image, all divine.*[63]

With the singing done for the moment and the crowd settled enough that a speaker could be heard again, Elder Francis Lyman of the Quorum of the Twelve walked to the podium. Lyman, fifty-two years old, was the son of Amasa Lyman, also an Apostle, and counselor to Joseph Smith in the First Presidency when the Prophet had been killed at Carthage. Amasa had brought his family across the plains to the valley in 1848, with eight-year-old Francis helping drive the family wagon and livestock. Francis had been a young teenager when he watched Brigham Young lay the temple cornerstones. Now an Apostle himself, he stood to issue a call to the Saints to "gird up their loins" and perform a work that some would consider impossible.

The crowd, finally hushed, listened as Francis explained that, in a meeting of the Church's leaders six months before, Wilford had expressed his desire to live to see the temple dedicated. Given his advanced age, it was questionable whether that was possible. He was already well past the normal life expectancy of the times and could, quite literally, die any day—and the temple was enormous. It would surely have been more sensible to do what they had done with the Nauvoo Temple and dedicate it in sections. Perhaps the baptistry might be made ready soon enough to guarantee that Wilford would see at least some part of the building finished and brought into service before he died.

Neither President Woodruff nor his counselors and the Apostles were satisfied with that. Elder Lyman issued a challenge to the Saints that was ambitious to say the least: "I propose that this assemblage pledge themselves collectively and individually, to furnish, as fast as it may be needed, all the money that may be required to complete the Temple at the earliest time possible, so that the dedication may take place on April 6th, 1893," he said. If they succeeded, they would be able to fully dedicate the building on the fortieth anniversary of the day they had laid the cornerstones.

Elder Lyman put the resolution to the congregation. It was accepted by unanimous vote in a deafening shout as tens of thousands of people cried "aye!"

The Tabernacle Choir stood and performed the fourth new song of the day, titled "Song of the Redeemed." George Q. Cannon offered the benediction, and the conference was declared adjourned for six months' time.

———— • • • ————

Some of the crowd began to move away, but many remained to watch the laborers high above on the scaffolding perform one more task. Cyrus Dallin's angel statue had been completed some time before and shipped to Salt Lake City, where it had remained stored until needed. Twelve feet, five inches tall, the finished copper statue weighed more than one ton and possibly as much as two.[64] The angel was now raised up above the capstone and ready to be fixed in place. The workmen had inserted a vertical rod that ran twenty-seven feet down through the spire to a 4,000-pound counterbalance weight below that would hold the statue firmly in place.[65] At about three o'clock, they lowered the statue and affixed its feet to the rod. Once attached, the statue was unveiled to the crowd below. "The figure is admirably proportioned, and its pose is graceful. It is gilded with pure gold leaf, and surmounting its crown is an incandescent lamp of one hundred candle-power," the *Deseret News* reported matter-of-factly. When the statue was lit and the rest of the temple illuminated by the lights placed on the other five towers, the reporter could not resist adding a personal opinion to his description of the scene. "Its effect is beautiful."

Wilford had stayed to watch the statue take its place on the temple capstone. Cyrus Dallin, the sculptor, sat next to him. Both men sat in silence until Moroni was unveiled. Then Wilford leaned over to the Gentile sculptor who had once tried to turn down the commission because he didn't believe in heavenly beings. "Now, Mr. Dallin, do you believe in angels?" Wilford asked him.

"Yes," Dallin replied. "My mother is an angel."[66]

—— ◆ · · ◆ ——

The stone walls and spires of the Salt Lake Temple were, at long last, finished.

CHAPTER 13

THERE WAS GLADNESS AMONG THE SANCTIFIED IN HEAVEN

The crowd dispersed, which took considerable time, as the assembly was so large that it was difficult for anyone to move. But the temple continued to draw visitors back for days after, with many climbing up to the temple's highest spire to see the view of the city and mountains around. It quickly became a tradition for those making the ascent to insert a dime into the seam running horizontally between the capstone and its base—even Wilford and his family did so. The prophet insisted on going up with his daughter Emma and two of his grandchildren to see the view, and they left coins, as so many of the other visitors had.[1] But the tradition was short-lived. Those pilgrimages to the top of the house of the Lord soon ended as the workers began removing the scaffolding from the towers. Soon there was no sign of construction on the exterior of the building, its appearance now final.

The inside was another matter entirely. The temple was not an empty shell, as it had been just three years earlier before Amos Howe had finished installing the roof, but there was a tremendous amount of work to do, and by all rights it should have taken years. The architect's plans called for the temple to have four major floors covering just over a quarter-million square feet of floor space. The walls and ceilings in some rooms were two stories high, all of which would need painting, detailed molding, and other decoration. Lighting fixtures and chandeliers needed to be wired up and hung. Workmen had installed flooring, and some walls were up. John Hafen, one of the Paris art missionaries, had come home from France after only a year because his family in Salt Lake had been suffering financial difficulties; he had made the best of it and gotten an early start on painting the frescoes in one of the instruction rooms.[2] The rest of the Saints studying in Paris would soon be summoned home to help their friend finish the artistic task that would reimburse the Church for their tuition to the Académie Julian. To give them their own head start, Young would send them the dimensions of the rooms they were to paint so they could start sketching designs long before they made their way to Salt Lake City. Soon after, Wilford and his counselors in the First Presidency sent them a letter asking them to return by the fall so they could begin work, and offering them some encouragement. "We would like to get the benefit of the best artistic skill now in the Church in the decoration of this grand building," they told the students. It was time for the Church to recoup its investment in the young men.[3]

The frescoes were not the only artwork that the Saints wanted for the building. They wanted paintings to beautify the hallways and stained-glass windows to illuminate the rooms. They wanted custom doorknobs and escutcheons, fine carpets, hardwood handrails, and crystal chandeliers. Most of these could not be bought in Utah, at least not of the kinds that met the high standards the Saints insisted upon for this building. Those pieces would need to be purchased and shipped, which could take months, depending on their ports of origin. For others, craftsmen would have to bring the raw materials and fashion and assemble them on site. As always with temples, all of the fixtures and the workmanship involved in placing them were expected to be of the highest possible quality.

With quality came cost. The First Presidency was always appreciative of Saints willing to lend their skills, and some men with the appropriate level of skill were hired. But, given the timeline, the leadership decided to hire contractors to perform most of the interior work. Contractors would be obligated to finish by short deadlines and to redo the work as many times as necessary to ensure it was done properly and to a high standard. They would also doubtless charge a handsome price for those requirements, and at a time when the Church was heavily in debt. Wilford and his counselors were already spending much, if not most, of their time just trying to secure funds to keep the Church operating. So a more conservative accountant might have suggested that they stop the work until Wilford could get the Church on a more stable financial footing, or at least slow down and spread the cost of the work over several years. But that was no option for the Saints. They had pledged themselves to finish by April, and they would raise the money required, no matter how much was needed. To that end, the First Presidency set apart Sunday, May 1, as a general fast day for the members to give their offerings to the temple fund. Wilford was not one to ask for what he would not give himself. He and both of his counselors gave a thousand dollars each. The Saints responded with generosity and, when the receipts were counted, $160,000 had been raised.[4] It was not all that they would need to finish the temple, but it was a very good start.

———— • • • ————

Armchair critics are never happy, so it was no surprise that complaints about the slow pace of construction were soon replaced by grumbling that they were now trying to do too much too fast. But more optimistic Saints believed that they could do the work, and that the long delays getting to this point were actually a sign of providence. "[A] little reflection will demonstrate that many advantages are consequent upon this feature of deferred completion," wrote one. "First came the railroad, then, as the walls rose to the square, came also available scientific methods of heating, lighting and sanitary arrangements, such as would have seemed impossible years ago."[5] "It is surprising what changes have occurred through inventions since the first plan of the Temple was drawn out," said another.

> Brother Truman O. Angell provided holes for stove-pipes, and no provisions were made for closets or any conveniences of that character. Now the building is heated throughout with hot water, and any part of it can be heated separately from the whole. Instead of climbing stairs, elevators are being provided. Instead of depending on candles for light, as had to be done when the Temple was designed, we now have the place well supplied with wires for electricity, which will make the interior very brilliant when lighted up.[6]

Electricity on demand was a relatively new development, but one that was becoming indispensable because of its most immediate and useful application—powering the incandescent bulb. Inventors, including Thomas Edison, had demonstrated the first filament lightbulbs some thirteen years before, and from that point on there was no question that electric lights would eventually illuminate the world. People would be freed from the sun's schedule and the danger of lit fires inside buildings to work past dark. Lighting up a building the size of the temple, though, would require bulbs by the hundreds, and that would require a generator capable of producing a significant amount of electricity. Eventually adding onto that power load would be two elevators destined for the central western tower. Manual and steam-powered elevators had been around for more than a half century, so their use in the Lord's house had been anticipated for some time, and the first elevators that went into it were hydraulic. The electric elevator was a newer creation, newer than the filament lightbulb, but it was an invention that the Saints would one day be happy to adopt. The temple had its roots in ancient history, but there was no reason at all that it couldn't have the most modern conveniences.

To power the building, an underground machine room was excavated west of the temple to house the generators. The Saints purchased four engines—two seventy-five horsepower and two twenty-five horsepower—which they connected to four Edison dynamos. Once installed and running, the entire system could power 2,000 lights—enough to light all of Temple Square, the Tabernacle, and the Assembly Hall—with enough to spare for water pumps and boilers.[7] The latter were housed in a boiler house that the workmen erected 300 feet northwest of the temple. Water heated to steam inside that facility flowed into the temple through a twelve-inch pipe that ran up to the attic, where a massive tank was installed. The steam could then be pumped through pipes that ran throughout the building to heat the rooms without the need for any open fire inside. It was a more complex system than trying to keep a fire burning in a fireplace in every room, but it was cleaner, safer, and far more efficient. And when the weather turned hot in the summer and the boiler wasn't needed, temple workers could press a button to open transoms and start up sixteen electric fans, one-half horsepower each, to circulate air throughout the building.[8] The hope was that the system would keep the temperature inside at tolerable, if not entirely comfortable, levels—but in that, they would be disappointed. As it would turn out, the temple would get uncomfortably warm in the summertime.

The boiler house was almost trivial to put up compared to the other support building they needed to construct. Wilford, his counselors, and Don Carlos Young had been planning for an annex to the temple for more than two years. The annex would serve as a kind of reception center for those visiting the house of the Lord. It would be the primary entrance to the temple—which would connect to it by way of a tunnel—and have a sizable waiting area for those arriving early for a coming endowment session or other ceremonies. Given how long that wait could be, it would also include a kitchen and dining area for patrons' refreshment. (Early designs even included apartments where patrons could lodge overnight, which would have made the annex a full hotel, but that idea was soon dropped.) The waiting area could also be used as a small assembly hall for teaching, particularly for temple workers who needed instruction in how to perform the ceremonies in the Lord's house. Wilford wanted the annex finished and available for use the day the temple opened. So while

One of Joseph Don Carlos Young's interior elevation sketches for the first temple annex.

carpenters and painters and other tradesmen were laboring inside the temple, many were called to work outside on an entirely separate edifice that needed to be built and furnished in the same year.

Don Carlos Young's blueprints described a building that was radically different in appearance from the temple. Where the house of the Lord looked like a gothic fortress, the annex building plans called for a structure that looked downright Islamic—"Moorish" was the term later used to describe it. The annex ceilings would be domes with round gables on every side and tall, thin minarets at every corner. On paper, it looked like nothing else on the temple block, or possibly in all of Salt Lake City, for that matter. But between the temple and the great dome-shaped Tabernacle, the temple block was a place for unusual architecture, and the First Presidency approved the plans. So on May 1, three weeks and four days after the capstone ceremony, Charles Livingston's men broke ground for the temple annex.

The short schedule, the very long list of tasks to finish inside the temple, and now the exterior and interior construction of a second large building had created a tremendous load for Don Carlos Young to carry. It was a burden that likely would have killed his predecessor. Truman Angell Sr., with his persistently weak health and strained nerves, almost certainly would have folded under the load. So perhaps his death a few years before had not been a tragedy but a divine release from his calling at the precise time the workload was about to finally exceed his capacity. That was no comfort to Young. The current architect could not count on death to save him from his responsibilities. The only way out was through, but Wilford did not leave him to do the work alone. The Church's senior leaders had set expectations very high for what Young had to accomplish in the next year, and the Saints were doing their part. If the temple was not ready by the deadline and they failed to dedicate it on the fortieth anniversary of the laying of the cornerstone, the public disappointment would be intense. It would not be fair for Young take the blame for failing to meet a short deadline that hadn't been his to set.

So Wilford called Bishop John R. Winder, first counselor in the Presiding Bishopric, to assist the architect. They might have given him the Presiding Bishop, William Preston, but he and Young had clashed before, and any repeats of that conflict would almost certainly throw them behind schedule and abolish any hope of finishing by next April. So they gave him Winder instead, to split the load and also to help shoulder the backlash of failure if it came to that. "I look upon [Winder's calling], though I did not say so to [Young] that the appointment of Bishop Winder was a benefit to him and would be a protection, so that blame could not fall upon him alone," Cannon wrote in his journal. Young probably needn't have worried, as there would be plenty of blame for everyone if the worst happened.

To put some additional force behind the appointment, the prophet took Bishop Winder and several of the Apostles to the temple on the fifteenth of April to introduce the new supervisor to the men. More than a hundred men assembled to hear President Woodruff as he tried "to endeavor to infuse into the breasts of all . . . the importance of diligence and union and of cultivating the other graces of the Gospel, as well as industry, so that the Temple might be completed for dedication by the 6th of April next."[9] It was not enough to merely work hard, he told them. The men would need the Lord's help to accomplish the goal—and to receive that, they had to strive for righteousness in all aspects of their lives.

All of the Apostles addressed the men, as did Don Carlos Young and Bishop Winder. It was a scene that would become frequent over the next year as the Church President, his counselors, and the Twelve would visit the site frequently. Of all the issues they had to manage over the year, the temple remained one of their highest priorities. The prophet remained intimately involved in the process at every point, exhorting and directing the workers. He did not micromanage the work, but his was the final word when any question arose. His declaration that he wanted to see the building dedicated had been no idle claim, and he proved his emotional investment in it by spending as much time in the house of the Lord as his health and other responsibilities allowed.

To further assist, Wilford appointed a committee of twelve people to oversee the selection and procurement of the fineries that would beautify the building. Wilford would prove to have strong feelings on such matters throughout the year, but he was not an interior designer, and his workload was already quite heavy. Don Carlos Young and Bishop Winder were both assigned to the committee, though both men would be occupied with all of the other aspects of the labor as well. Other members included Hiram B. Clawson, Brigham Young's former business manager, and his son Spencer, also a businessman with contacts in New York; Willard Young, a former member of the First Presidency; and several other men. Three women were also chosen for the committee to ensure that the sisters of the Church had a voice in the temple's decoration—Lillie Staines, P. P. Jennings, and Caroline Elizabeth Dye, a milliner and businesswoman.[10] That Wilford thought twelve people would be necessary was a sign of the magnitude of their responsibilities. There was hardly a square inch of the temple interior that didn't fall under their purview, and Wilford expected them to be meticulous in their labor to furnish the Lord's own house. They were a talented group with considerable business experience, but despite their skills and numbers, they would be as busy as anyone trying to procure the goods needed from all over the country during the next year.

In the midst of this push to the finish, an unexpected bit of news arrived on June 19 in the form of a telegram from Washington, addressed to Wilford Woodruff and George Cannon. The president of the United States was considering a general pardon for all Saints previously convicted of polygamy under the Edmunds-Tucker Act. Politician that he was, Benjamin Harrison wanted to take the nation's temperature before signing such a proclamation, and he hoped that Wilford might assist him. Harrison wanted the prophet to nominate forty or fifty people to receive amnesty, and if that did not "call down too much abuse on him from the nation he [would] grant general amnesty immediately after." The Saints' delegate in Washington was skeptical, thinking it was "continued humiliation imposed upon [the Saints] in return for demands for mere justice"; but Harrison and other leading politicians were sure that it would "show to the nation that polygamy is dead in Utah, and satisfy any argument which may be brought up by enemies and pave the way to statehood."[11] These were bold promises and beyond the president's actual power to keep. Moreover, such a declaration would have no practical effect on anyone already released from the penitentiary except in one area—it would restore their right to vote. That was a worthy prize, as it would allow the Saints to again have their voices heard in full measure at the ballot box. So, after a week of discussions, the First Presidency forwarded the names of their candidates to receive the president's clemency.[12]

Four months along, the workers had made good progress on the temple interior, but it was apparent that they had put only a dent in the overall amount that needed to be done. There was no point in pushing everyone hard and spending large sums of money when the Church was in serious debt if there was actually no chance that they could get the Lord's house ready by next April. So Wilford called for a council to discuss whether the fortieth anniversary was still a practical deadline. On August 4, he called together the First Presidency and as many of the Twelve as were available—eight men, as it turned out—to discuss the question.[13] It was an ambitious aim, certainly, but the Church's senior leaders decided that, yes, they still wanted to keep the April 6 goal.

That settled, Wilford raised the issue of the actual dedication ceremony. The planning for the capstone ceremony had been left practically to the last minute. It had come off very well, but the prophet decided that they should address the matter early this time. As they discussed what form the program should take, Wilford thought they should plan on repeating it as many times as necessary to accommodate all the Saints who wanted to come. The prophet was determined that "all the worthy Saints [should] have the privilege of visiting the temple [dedication]," no matter how many sessions they needed to convene.[14] That would be a serious commitment of time for this group. They estimated that the Assembly Room that took up the temple's uppermost floor would seat perhaps 4,000 people, but more than 40,000 people had come to the capstone ceremony. If a similar number wanted to attend the dedication, Wilford and the rest would have to conduct a dozen sessions at least, and perhaps more. Each meeting would last hours, so they would likely be able to manage two each day. By that math, the General Authorities would have to oversee an entire week of dedication sessions. That would be a serious strain on eighty-six-year-old Wilford, but he was adamant. "It was thought that nothing short of this would be satisfactory."[15]

◆ · ◆ · ◆

The rest of the Paris art missionaries had made their way home by then, and Wilford knew that the artists would need to start on the enormous frescoes destined to cover the endowment room walls if there was to be any hope of finishing them by the deadline. Wilford hosted one of the artists, Lorus Pratt, on August 5 to talk it over. Pratt expressed his readiness to proceed, but the prophet did something surprising—he told the young man to slow down. With every other aspect of the interior work, Wilford had been pushing everyone to move forward with all due haste, but he was wise enough to know that art of the highest quality could not be rushed, and nothing less would do here. So he told the young man that "under the circumstances it would be better probably . . . not to push the artistic work in the Temple, but to do it leisurely and in such a way that it would give us pleasure in years to come, and if it was necessary to dedicate the Temple without it that we could do so, and leave this to be done afterwards." Pratt, perhaps somewhat relieved, agreed with the prophet. The temple was going to stand forever, or at least "through the millennium," as Brigham had always hoped, so the frescoes would have his and the other artists' names attached to them for at least that long. And like any artist who took pride in his work, Pratt did not want to turn in subpar work that countless Saints would see for generations to come.

The October general conference marked the halfway point of the Saints' year-long effort. A number of the speakers addressed the desire to finish the temple, but one key audience for that message was absent—the woodcarvers. They were so zealous to finish their part of the project that they decided as a group to skip the general conference and stay on the job. So while the First Presidency and the Quorum of the Twelve were exhorting the people to give of their time, money, talents, and whatever else they could spare, the woodcarvers were inside the temple attacking wooden pilasters, moldings, and hand railings.[16]

The Saints had given no small amount of money to the effort, and so they deserved a report on the results of their generosity thus far. Wilford asked Bishop John R. Winder to deliver one. Taking to the pulpit on the afternoon of October 8, Bishop Winder told the audience that the temple was on track to be ready for dedication as planned. Between 200 and 300 people were laboring on the Lord's house daily now, and the bishop promised that all of the funds the Saints had raised were being managed and spent with care. But having taken stock of what was left still to do, the leaders estimated that they would need another $150,000 beyond what the Saints had already pledged complete the building. "The work now being done was of a costly character," he told the congregation, "but when finished it would be most beautiful for the Saints to look upon."[17] Winder had to increase that projection by another $25,000 a few days later.[18]

There was nothing for it but to put out another call for funds, and the Saints responded again. Money came in, enough to keep the work moving and to purchase the fineries that Wilford's twelve-person committee were looking to buy. Everything was of the best quality, and no detail was being spared. The tile for the baptistry floor was marble, the lining for the washtubs was porcelain, and for the washbasins, onyx.[19] Custom stained-glass windows depicting biblical and other scenes were ordered from Tiffany & Co. in New York City. The doors acquired for the building were solid oak, custom-made, with "beveled plate glass in the transoms and upper panels, and graceful grills in the form of beehives on the lower panels."[20] The fixtures and handles for both doors and windows were custom-made and cast in different metals according to the floor where they would be installed—in the basement, they were all of brass; on the first floor, plated gold; on the second, plated silver; on the third, old silver; and above that, bronze.[21] All of the doorknobs had intricate designs drawn in the metal, a beehive with the words "Holiness to the Lord" above it, and they were mounted in extravagant doorplates with equally complex carvings on them. Grand chandeliers were purchased to be hung in all of the larger rooms. Rich carpets were installed, the colors changing with the themes of the rooms in which they were laid down.

The artwork for the instruction rooms, however, had barely started. John Hafen had done some preliminary work, but if the murals were to have any chance of being completed without undue haste degrading the final products, the artists needed to get fully engaged in the work very soon. A few weeks after the October conference, Wilford called in Don Carlos Young, Bishop John Winder, and Lorus Pratt again to come up with a plan to start painting the garden and telestial rooms as soon as possible.[22] Young responded by calling for "a committee of our home artists to take up the work of painting in the Garden and the World [telestial] Rooms, and go ahead as rapidly as possible, as the time is now short, there only being five months yet before dedication."[23]

More progress was being made on the paintings to be framed and hung in the hallways. One artist, Alfred Lambourne, presented Wilford with a painting of the Hill Cumorah, where the Prophet Joseph had received the golden plates from Moroni that contained the ancient record translated into the Book of Mormon. Wilford and his counselors suggested some minor changes to the scene, but overall, they were quite taken with the work. "The scene is a very beautiful one," George Cannon wrote. "The sun is shining in the east, but to the right there are clouds of thick darkness, and lightning. In [Lambourne's] written description, which is very poetical, he says this is a symbolism of the powers of darkness. We were all suited with the picture."[24] They decided to hang it in the celestial room, the room that represented the very kingdom where the Saints believed that God dwells.[25]

Lambourne also had another painting in progress, this one of Adam-ondi-Ahman, a place that the Prophet Joseph had identified as the location where Adam and Eve had lived after their expulsion from the Garden of Eden and where a significant gathering of the righteous would occur prior to the Second Coming of Christ. He asked Wilford to name his price for the two paintings, Cumorah and Adam-ondi-Ahman, but the prophet demurred, perhaps unsure how to place a dollar figure on art. After some negotiation, they settled on those two and three future paintings for a total of $2,500, with the Church paying expenses for canvas, paints, brushes, and studio.[26]

—————•··•—————

They had made enormous progress in six months, but the amount of work remaining to be done was "immense."[27] Whether they would make the deadline was an open question, but spirits remained high among the General Authorities and the laborers—among everyone, it seemed, except for the Church architect. The enormous strain was finally getting to Don Carlos Young. He answered to Wilford, but the success or failure of the endeavor rested on him, and, as is often the case when one is overburdened, the enormous stress began to manifest itself as a shortened temper and hard words directed at those who did not see things Young's way. Even Wilford and his counselors were not immune to the fallout. Near the end of the year they met with Young to discuss some matters and found themselves on the receiving end of his sharpened tongue. Wilford was not usually one to disparage others in his journal, but the interaction was so sour that even he could not avoid recording it in his personal diary. "I think his conversation to us was very unchristianlike," he noted.[28] In an attempt to be patient and long-suffering, the First Presidency tried again the next day, perhaps hoping that a night's sleep might have softened Young's mood. If so, they were disappointed, and the second discussion went about as well as the first. "We had another conversation this morning with Joseph Don Carlos [Young] and it appears he is a very bad man to manage," Wilford wrote.[29]

The load on Young did not get lighter as the new year arrived. They were running out of time to make the April 6 deadline, and the architect truly began to crumple under the load. His health declined, and he almost stopped going to the temple to oversee the work.[30] Finally he asked Wilford to release him from his calling and his duties if the prophet thought another man could better carry the load and hasten the work.

The prophet declined the request. There was no one else who had Don Carlos Young's training, experience, and intimate knowledge of the temple and the annex that were nearing completion. Contrary to hastening the work, to lose the architect at this late date might well have destroyed their chances to be ready before the April general conference. The Saints needed him to see it through. But Wilford did give him one piece of advice—Young needed to learn to delegate more. "I told him . . . to do what he could [and] others must do the rest."[31]

That raised the question of how those "others" were doing. Wilford decided that the turn of the new year was a good time to take stock of the laborers' progress and see whether and where additional help might be required. On January 3, 1893, with three months to go, Wilford took George Q. Cannon to the temple, and the two men spent three hours going through the building with the contractors. They interrogated each one as to "how long it would take them to finish their part." To a man, they all promised that they could complete their part of the whole by the deadline.[32] Wilford and Cannon felt somewhat better after the meeting, and the prophet accepted the workmen's assurances—but Wilford began visiting the temple more frequently from that point on to assure himself that the work remained on schedule. The prophet's age and responsibilities kept him from engaging in any of the labor himself, such as he had performed when he was a younger man. All he could do was direct and exhort, and he kept himself available to do that whenever it was needed and helpful.

The one area where labor was still truly and stubbornly deficient was the painting of the murals for the instruction rooms—the former missionaries whom the Church had sent to Paris had yet to start work on them in a serious way. The First Presidency called them in to talk about the reasons for the delay. At least one of the reasons, it turned out, was money. The artists wanted $17,500 to do the work. It was an astonishingly high request—exactly one-tenth of the entire amount that the Church was now trying to raise to finish the building—and one that surely must have seemed ungrateful, given that the Church had funded their studies at one of the finest art academies in Europe. There is no proof that the artists hoped the looming deadline might leave the First Presidency and Quorum of the Twelve feeling pressured to accept the demand, though the lateness of the request itself is notable. But the men sitting across the table from the artists were having none of it. George Q. Cannon, Joseph F. Smith, Heber J. Grant, and Francis M. Lyman "thought this figure exorbitant, and there was quite a plain talk given to the artists."[33] All four of the Church leaders took turns addressing the young men, and Wilford entered the room and joined the discussion at some point. What he and the Apostles said is unknown, but surely they reminded the creatives that even poor Saints were donating money to the effort in small amounts they could hardly afford to spare. For the artists to try to profit now by charging extortionist prices late in the day would be an offense to those who were casting in all the living that they had.[34]

At the end of the discussion, the Apostles told the artists to withdraw their proposition and make another one. The young men returned with more modest demands, and Wilford "finally agreed to give them $300 a month."[35] The artists left the meeting poorer but perhaps wiser for having learned that while Apostles are charitable men, they can drive hard bargains when spending the widow's mite.

———— • • • ————

Along with difficult artists and an overstressed architect, the new year also brought with it happy news. On January 4, President Benjamin Harrison made good on his promise to extend the nation's forgiveness to all the Saints who had been convicted or were presently under indictment for plural marriage. Noting Wilford's Manifesto and the Saints' adherence to it, the chief executive signed Proclamation 346—Granting Amnesty and Pardon for the Offense of Engaging in Polygamous or Plural Marriage to Members of the Church of Latter-day Saints.

I, Benjamin Harrison, President of the United States, by virtue of the powers in me vested, do hereby declare and grant a full amnesty and pardon to all persons liable to the penalties of said act by reason of unlawful cohabitation under the color of polygamous or plural marriage who have since November 1, 1890, abstained from such unlawful cohabitation, but upon the express condition that they shall in the future faithfully obey the laws of the United States hereinbefore named, and not otherwise. Those who shall fail to avail themselves of the clemency hereby offered will be vigorously prosecuted.[36]

It was a kind gesture, but it was met among the Saints with a kind of collective shrug. Wilford noted the event in his journal, but added that it was "of little benefit to the people."[37] As a former convict under the Edmunds-Tucker Act, George Cannon might have been expected to be more enthusiastic about the amnesty, but his opinion was similar to the prophet's.

It has been a long time coming, and now that it has come it brings comparatively little benefit to our people, though it would not be wise for us to belittle it. I suggested that we find no fault with it, but claim for it all the benefits that we ought to receive under it. Its value in my opinion consists in the moral effect it will have on the country, and it also shows the drift of public sentiment. Each act of this kind has the effect to alleviate existing conditions.[38]

They might have been more enthusiastic had the president found a way to return all the escheated Church property that the government had seized over the years. Given the financial troubles that Wilford was wrestling with and the constant need to raise funds to finish the temple, he truly could have put those funds and assets to good use. As it was, he acknowledged President Harrison's generosity and then went back to work.

------ • · • ------

By late February, the temple was practically all-consuming to Wilford. The dedication was now only six weeks away. The workmen were laboring virtually nonstop six days a week and every holiday, but they were still far from the goal. The prophet noted with some resignation that "there is still a great deal of work to be done there before the finish."[39] He, George Cannon, and Joseph F. Smith toured the building repeatedly, examining every detail in every room as time permitted. Despite the considerable work left to do, they were still hopeful that they would make it. "We are in hopes to get it ready for Dedication," Wilford said, "but it is a load upon us."[40]

That load was, in fact, getting heavier for Don Carlos Young by the day. His responsibilities had grown so burdensome that his health started to fail, and he was unable to provide the guidance necessary to keep the work going at the necessary pace. Wilford moved quickly to solve that problem. On February 7, he "appointed Joseph F. Smith, Lorenzo Snow, and [Abraham] H. Cannon a committee to see to the finish of the temple, to employ architects to furnish patterns and specifications for the workmen."[41]

The First Presidency was starting to feel impressed that not all of the preparations to be made for the dedication had to do with woodcarving and finishing and painting. Rather, they had to do with that always-divisive pastime called politics. In earlier years, most men who had run for office in Utah had done so without vowing allegiance to any particular political faction. That had worked well enough until 1870, when a group calling itself the Liberal Party—composed largely of non–Latter-day Saints—had arisen. The Saints had formed their own group, which they called the People's Party, so named to convey the idea that Utah was not ruled by any religious tyrant (namely Brigham Young). It had dominated state elections even after the US government had disenfranchised both women and anyone practicing plural marriage.

Now that the Manifesto had been issued, the Saints were again entertaining hopes of statehood, but the People's Party had become a problem. Both the Democrats and Republicans were wary of granting Utah that status if the dominant force in politics was going to be a home-grown organization that would elect senators and representatives with no allegiance to the major national parties. So the Church's leadership disbanded the People's Party in June 1891 and encouraged the Saints to put their energy equally behind the major parties. It wouldn't do for all of the Saints to throw their support behind one party, as that would just be recasting the People's Party under a different name.

But whom to support? Given the Republicans' thirty-year history driving the campaign against the Saints to eliminate plural marriage, it was no surprise that the "Grand Old Party" had rarely ever found a vote among the Saints. The Democratic Party had had more success in that regard over the years, but it had done nothing to help relieve the Saints' suffering over the last decade, so they weren't feeling particularly grate-ful toward that faction, either. Both parties were vying for the votes of a people who felt that neither group had done much to earn them.

The result, much to Wilford's chagrin, was growing partisan divi-sions among the people. No small amount of political vitriol was cours-ing through the city, and it pained the Church's senior leaders to see and hear it. Such feelings were entirely incompatible with the unity that the prophet believed should exist among the Saints, and with the spirit that he felt should permeate the temple. "If ye are not one, ye are not mine," the Lord had said in one of the Prophet Joseph's revelations;[42] if they were not one, as the Lord's people should have been, how then could they dedicate a house to Him and expect Him to accept it?

George Cannon suggested that they might publish an epistle to the Saints calling on them as a people to repent. He, Wilford, and Joseph F. Smith counseled together and decided that Cannon's proposal was wise. Wilford approved the idea, and they spent several days drafting the epistle.

> We feel now that a time for reconciliation has come; that be-fore entering into the Temple to present ourselves before the Lord

in solemn assembly, we shall divest ourselves of every harsh and unkind feeling against each other; that not only our bickerings shall cease, but that the cause of them shall be removed, and every sentiment that prompted and has maintained them shall be dispelled; that we shall confess our sins one to another, and ask forgiveness one of another; that we shall plead with the Lord for the spirit of repentance, and, having obtained it, follow its promptings; so that in humbling ourselves before Him and seeking forgiveness from each other, we shall yield that charity and generosity to those who crave our forgiveness that we ask for and expect from heaven.

Thus may we come up into the holy place with our hearts free from guile and our souls prepared for the edification that is promised! Thus shall our supplications, undisturbed by a thought of discord, unitedly mount into the ears of Jehovah and draw down the choice blessings of the God of Heaven![43]

To prove their own sincerity in the matter, the First Presidency said that they wanted all who held a grievance against them, as either private individuals or Church officers, to come forward and make it known. Such persons would get a hearing, and the members of the First Presidency would do all they could to restore friendship and affection.

If there is a single member of the Church who has feelings against us, we do not wish to cross the threshold of the Temple until we have satisfied him and have removed from him all cause of feeling, either by explanation or by making proper amends and atonement; neither would we wish to enter the sacred portals of that edifice until we have sought an explanation, or amends, or atonement, from any against whom we may have either a real or fancied grievance.[44]

To encourage the people to act on the call for general repentance and reconciliation, the Presidency asked the Saints to make the twenty-fifth of March a day of fasting, prayer, and confession to their leaders and each other. As they had with the other calls to action issued by Wilford and their leaders, the Saints did as they were asked. Special meetings for that purpose were held on the designated Saturday, and many stood, admitted their faults, and asked forgiveness. Hard feelings do not always disappear so easily and quickly, especially when they've been allowed to fester, but many went home that day with kinder feelings toward others than they'd brought in with them. Many recorded in their journals that their meetings were filled with a happy spirit, and some recorded an outpouring of spiritual manifestations like those seen among Christ's disciples on the day of Pentecost. President Woodruff was pleased with the result. The fast and testimony meetings "throughout Utah . . . [did] a great deal of good," he concluded.[45]

The day was scheduled for general conference to begin, and the Saints had all but run out of time to finish the temple. The crowds had been building in Salt Lake for some weeks now in anticipation of the dedication. Saints, tourists, government officials, and curiosity seekers were coming in droves, assisted by the Union Pacific Railroad, which knew a marketing opportunity when it saw one. The company published a twenty-four-page booklet to generate interest, then reduced its fares, gave away some free tickets to the poor, and ran additional trains to Salt Lake City to meet the demand. With that kind of assistance, the people had started arriving weeks before, and the rate at which they came increased by the day. The Associated Press reported that "large delegations [are] arriving on every train. Excursion trains are arriving hourly. The principal streets are packed with visiting saints and visitors from all directions."[46] One train derailed near Juab, midway between Fillmore and Provo, courtesy of a broken rail. Four passenger cars jumped the track, and one crashed down onto its side, but the passengers escaped with nothing more than bruises.[47] Other Saints came as they had since the first pioneers had entered the valley in '47—by foot, horseback, buggy, or wagon. The numbers surged past what Wilford and the other leaders had expected, and it became apparent very quickly that they would have to convene additional dedication sessions if they truly wanted to accommodate every Saint who wanted to attend one.

The conference opened on April 4, 1893, and both the Tabernacle and the Assembly Hall were filled to overflowing. Wilford was the first to speak, and he was in a reflective mood. He confessed that he had lived to see this day by the prayers of the Saints and the power of God, and he was thankful for them both. Then he began to talk of the early days forty-plus years ago when he and the first pioneers had come to an empty valley. It was "to him a marvel and a wonder" what they had accomplished since that time.[48] He spoke of the many settlers who had since passed on, particularly Brigham, now dead almost sixteen years. Wilford was sure that his old friend and all the others who had worked to build the temple just across the way before their deaths were "in the spirit world today . . . deeply interested and rejoicing in the work in which the Latter-day Saints were engaged on this special occasion."[49] They had reason to celebrate. The Saints had kept their promise of the year before. "No call, he believed, had ever been made upon any people upon the face of the earth which had met with such a hearty and universal response as that for means to finish the Salt Lake Temple."[50] They had been blessed in their efforts because it was the work of God and not of men, he assured the congregation, so they should do their duty despite all troubles and tribulations "during the little time we have to live here on earth."[51]

As during the previous conference, laborers continued working throughout the first day and into the second, and their efforts produced several milestones on April 5. Most important, the contractors finished their work on the temple interior. They had needed every single day of the year, Sundays only excepted, to finish the task, and it had come down very nearly to the final hour, but the house of the Lord was ready. Even the young artists who had not started their work until a few months before had completed the murals in the garden and world rooms. They would return to the temple after the dedication to do some additional work in other rooms, and another mural would be added to the creation room in 1915 when then-future prophet Joseph F. Smith would hire Norwegian artist and Latter-day Saint Frithjof Weberg to turn the white walls of that room into his canvas. And there were other small jobs that needed finishing, but nothing that would detract from the temple's appearance or function in any serious way.

The annex one hundred feet to the north was also completed that day, which was practically a miracle in its own right. From groundbreaking to completion, the workmen had done with the annex in one year what had taken forty for the temple it would serve. The structure, classified as a Victorian adaptation of Byzantine architecture, would be the temple entrance for patrons, a reception center for visitors, and a small assembly hall for meetings and instruction for workers and patrons. Now finished, it would be dedicated with the temple and ready to serve the day the temple opened to the Saints for ordinance work.

With both of those projects completed, it was time for many of those involved to rest. The carpenters and contractors were finally released. Most notably, Don Carlos Young was finally given the release from his calling as Church architect that he had sought months before. He had finished what Truman Angell had started and done it on time. George Q. Cannon extended the release in general conference. He praised the architect's work and called on the congregation to extend him a vote of thanks. The response in favor was unanimous, and, despite his short temper and sharp tongue of recent months, he had earned it.

Then, that evening, Wilford surprised both the Saints and gentile visitors alike. It had been decided some weeks before that no one would be allowed to enter a dedication session without a signed temple recommend, but that night, before the Lord's house was dedicated, selected visitors who were not Saints were invited to enter and tour the temple. Guides would escort them and answer their questions. It was a stunning gesture and the first open house for a temple that had ever been arranged. Several hundred responded and went through the building that evening, among them some of the Saints' most vocal critics in Salt Lake

City. The response was overwhelmingly positive, and even the antagonistic *Salt Lake Tribune* published a complimentary piece on the temple and the tour.

It was ironic that after all those decades of work and the many times that outsiders had stopped the temple's construction or brought it to a near halt, the first people to tour the building would be people of other faiths. There was no list kept of those who went through that evening, but it would have been a very interesting tour if George Cannon or Lorenzo Snow had escorted Judge Charles Zane through the temple and taught him about the sealing ordinance of marriage for time and eternity.

———— · · ————

There was very little sunlight filtering down through the canyons into the valley on the morning of Thursday, April 6. The skies were dark with lowering clouds, and a steady, strong breeze was blowing in from the northwest.

A large crowd of almost 3,000 people had formed at the south gate of the temple block before eight-thirty. Wilford had thought it fitting to extend invitations for the first dedication session to "all of the Presiding Priesthood that could gain ingress, and also some of the families of the Church authorities, both of those who were living and those who were dead."[52] Cards had been mailed out a week before to the latter group, notably to the widows of Apostles and others who had played important roles in the temple's construction. "Dear Sister," they began—

> The dedication of the great Temple in Salt Lake City is an event of unique importance. We desire your presence on that occasion and cordially invite you to attend. We cannot forget the part which your noble husband, now deceased, took in contributing to its erection and the lively interest which he always felt in the progress of the building and in its completion. We feel sure that you will appreciate the ceremonies, and therefore desire your presence.[53]

Salt Lake City, Utah Territory,
March 29th, 1893.

Mrs. Josephine R. Taylor

Dear Sister:

The dedication of the great Temple in Salt Lake City is an event of unique importance. We desire your presence on that occasion and cordially invite you to attend. We cannot forget the part which your noble husband, now deceased, took in contributing to its erection and the lively interest which he always felt in the progress of the building and in its completion. We feel sure that you will appreciate the ceremonies, and therefore desire your presence.

It will be proper for you to be at the south gate of the Temple Block between half past eight and half past nine o'clock on Thursday morning, April 6th, 1893.

Very respectfully, your Brethren,
WILFORD WOODRUFF,
GEORGE Q. CANNON,
JOSEPH F. SMITH,
First Presidency of the Church of Jesus Christ of Latter-day Saints.

Invitation to the dedication of the Salt Lake Temple.

The invitations were addressed to each widow individually and went out over the names of Wilford Woodruff, George Cannon, and Joseph F. Smith.

The requirements for entry had been published in advance. All attendees had to have temple recommends; no person would be allowed to enter without one, and no children under the age of eight would be admitted so as to preserve the peace of the ceremony. The gates were opened at eight-thirty, and the people began to file in. They entered the temple and followed a guided route up to the Assembly Room on the temple's top floor. It took almost two hours for the congregation to reach their seats in the hall, and the wind outside steadily increased in speed and force as they made their way in. It soon was obvious that the Assembly Room would not be able to accommodate everyone. It could hold a few more than 2,200. Even with many people left standing, some 400 disappointed people who had come just a little later than the rest had to be turned away for lack of space. Knowing their disappointment, Wilford decided to convene an extra third session the following evening specifically for those who had qualified to attend the first session but could not be seated. In the meantime, those left outside were invited to attend a service in the Tabernacle, during which speakers recounted the history of the temple's construction and those in the congregation were allowed to stand and share their testimonies of the gospel with the crowd.

The wind continued to pick up outside, until it was audible inside the building.

The General Authorities of the Church were all there in the Assembly Room, everyone dressed in white suits—the First Presidency, the Quorum of the Twelve, the Church Patriarch, the Presiding Council of Seventies, and the Presiding Bishopric. (Only Moses Thatcher of the Twelve was absent.) It was the first time in many years that all of those leaders had been assembled in one room. Between their responsibilities and the government's campaign over the last decade, they had been scattered. Some had been in hiding and exile, others living abroad. Even had the temple dedication not taken place that morning, just having all of the Church leadership in the same room would have been a remarkable event by itself.

The attendees were all seated by shortly after ten o'clock, and the dedication ceremony was ready to begin. Almost precisely at that hour, the wind became a near-hurricane. "From that hour until noon it seemed as if 'the prince of the power of the air'"—Satan himself—"was giving vent to his fiercest wrath," an observer later wrote.[54] Roofs were torn off homes, chimneys were toppled, and the air turned cold. "The temperature must have fallen in the two or three hours fully 25 degrees," recalled another witness to the event.[55] Rain and snow blew horizontally through the city. The *Deseret Evening News* later reported that the wind speed had peaked at sixty miles per hour, the "highest velocity ever recorded at the Salt Lake [weather] station."[56]

——— • · • ———

Inside the temple, all was calm. George Q. Cannon called the meeting to order and then announced the opening hymn. A 300-voice choir stood and sang, "Let Israel Join and Sing," under the direction of Elder Evan Stephens and accompanied by a large pipe organ built for the occasion.

Then the prophet stood. This was the moment for which he had waited for more than forty years, since the day that Brigham had put his cane in the ground and declared it the spot for this very temple. Wilford had been a young Apostle then; he had been there at the start, had given his labor, his time, and every talent he could lend to the building of this temple, and now he was here as the prophet to complete the work started decades before. He offered some introductory remarks to the assembly, speaking only a few minutes. Then he knelt down on a low cushioned stool and offered up the dedicatory prayer of the temple. The prayer was long, just over 5,000 words (it took up two full pages of the *Deseret News* when it was reprinted the following day).[57] If President Woodruff spoke at the average rate of a little more than a hundred words per minute, he would have prayed for some forty minutes. When he was finished, he stood up and took his seat. Lorenzo Snow stepped forward and, as he had done a year earlier, he led the Saints, waving white handkerchiefs, in the Hosanna Shout.

> Hosanna, Hosanna, Hosanna to God and the Lamb. Amen, amen, and amen.
>
> Hosanna, Hosanna, Hosanna to God and the Lamb. Amen, amen, and amen.
>
> Hosanna, Hosanna, Hosanna to God and the Lamb. Amen, amen, and amen.

Silence settled in the room. Then, at the direction of Evan Stephens, the choir sang "The Hosanna Anthem," which Stephens had composed for occasion. When that song was finished, the conductor directed the congregation to join the choir in singing "The Spirit of God Like a Fire Is Burning," the hymn without which, by then, no temple dedication would be complete.

The Spirit of God like a fire is burning!
The latter-day glory begins to come forth;
The visions and blessings of old are returning,
And angels are coming to visit the earth.

Chorus:
We'll sing and we'll shout with the armies of heaven,
Hosanna, hosanna to God and the Lamb!
Let glory to them in the highest be given,
Henceforth and forever, Amen and amen!

The Lord is extending the Saints' understanding,
Restoring their judges and all as at first.
The knowledge and power of God are expanding;
The veil o'er the earth is beginning to burst.

We'll call in our solemn assemblies in spirit,
To spread forth the kingdom of heaven abroad,
That we through our faith may begin to inherit
The visions and blessings and glories of God.

How blessed the day when the lamb and the lion
Shall lie down together without any ire,
And Ephraim be crowned with his blessing in Zion,
As Jesus descends with his chariot of fire![58]

When the music faded to quiet again, George Cannon stood. He spoke for an hour, but with difficulty at first. "My feelings almost choked me," he recalled.

My words were entirely too feeble to express my thoughts. After speaking a few minutes, however, I obtained control of myself. . . . I felt to praise the Lord for the union He had given us and the results of the course which the First Presidency had taken in asking the people to fast and pray. . . . The First Presidency knew by the Spirit of the Lord which He had revealed to them that the course they had taken was from Him, and that they had been guided by the revelations of Jesus in taking it.[59]

He was followed by President Woodruff. The prophet looked out over the congregation and then uttered a prophecy that must have been received with great emotion by the older Saints who had endured so much over the years, some of them having been old enough to remember the persecution in Missouri and Nauvoo. He prophesied that the Saints would see a change in affairs, that "from now on our enemies should not prevail against us, and that the power of Satan would in a great measure be bound and the Saints be blessed and prosper."[60]

He returned to his chair, and his other counselor stood to speak. Addressing the congregation was even more emotional for Joseph F. Smith, nephew of the Prophet Joseph and son of Hyrum Smith, than it had been for George Cannon. "He wept like a child and all that were present wept with him," a witness said. The Apostle spoke for a time and then ended by calling "upon all who felt that the Lord had accepted of the House to say, Aye! A united shout went up. And for all who felt the House was not accepted of God to say, No! But not a single response was made."[61]

The choir sang the concluding hymn, "Arise, Ye Saints." Lorenzo Snow then offered the benediction, and the first dedication session of the temple was over. It was about twelve-thirty in the afternoon.

Outside the temple, at that same moment, the storm died. The sun broke through, and the remainder of the day was clear of rain or snow and devoid of wind.

Then they did it all over again that day starting at two o'clock;

Ticket for the dedication of the Salt Lake Temple.

three times the day after that; and two times daily every day afterward, Sundays excepted, for weeks. The average attendance at each session was 2,260 persons, meaning the Assembly Room of the temple was practically filled to capacity every time. Not every session was identical to the first. Not all of the General Authorities were able to attend every session, and the prophet missed six of them due to illness—the strain of the month weakened him, and he suffered an attack of bilious colic that very nearly killed him. The special Friday evening session that President Woodruff had arranged for that first group turned away had some real excitement when Sister Emma Bennett went into labor during the meeting. She was led from the Assembly Room to a private room in the temple, where she gave birth to a son. She and her husband, Benjamin, returned to the temple eight days later on April 15 and asked Joseph F. Smith to name the baby and give it a blessing. The Apostle took the child in his arms and did as requested—perhaps feeling just a little bit cheeky, he named the boy Joseph Temple Bennett.

There were no dedicatory sessions held on April 19. Instead, President Woodruff convened a unique meeting in the Assembly Room in which General Authorities and other leaders were asked to share their testimonies of Jesus Christ. One hundred fifteen people shared their deepest convictions with each other for three hours before adjourning for a bit and then returning in the afternoon to continue for five hours more. The following day, they met in the celestial room of the temple and joined in prayer and partaking of the sacrament. Then they held another meeting in which they shared their memories of the early history of the Church. Of the one hundred fifteen there, only thirty-six had seen the laying of the temple cornerstones forty years before. Thirty-three had actually known the Prophet Joseph, and just ten had attended any meeting in the first temple in Kirtland.[62]

The following two days, April 21 and 22, were designated as "Sunday School services." Children under the age of eight had not been permitted to attend the regular sessions so as to preserve the peace of the meetings, but Wilford did not want the children excluded from the dedication services altogether. The Savior Himself had said, "Suffer the little children to come unto me, and forbid them not; for of such is the kingdom of God."[63] So the sessions on those days were shortened and customized for the children to attend so they could join in the celebration and gain some understanding of the temple's importance. Being smaller than their parents, almost 3,000 children were able to be seated in the Assembly Room. Twelve thousand little children and their teachers attended those sessions over the two days.

Finally, on Monday, April 24, the Saints concluded all of it with the *thirty-first* dedication session of the house of the Lord. More than 70,000 Saints had participated during the two weeks and four days that the sessions were held.

It was done. After forty years, the temple was finished.

——— • • • ———

After the last service ended and the visitors and tourists had dispersed and gone home, Wilford took a month to organize the temple staff. He called Elder Lorenzo Snow to be the first president of the Salt Lake Temple. Bishop John R. Winder became his first assistant and Adolph Madson his second. To take charge of the female temple workers,

Wilford called Zina D. H. Young as president, with Bathsheba W. Smith and Minnie J. Snow as her assistants. Other staff were called, from the temple recorder—to track the records of the ordinances performed—to the doorkeepers and janitors. The temple finally opened its doors to the Saints for ordinance work on May 23, and Temple Square settled into the routines that would become normal for the decades to come.

* * *

Wilford had lived long enough to finish the temple that his friend Brigham had started, but he was certain that his friend and all the prophets who had come before him knew that the task was finally complete—and they were glad. During one of the dedication sessions on April 7, Wilford told the congregation in the Assembly Room that he had received a revelation from heaven since the first day's meetings.

> [He] arose and said the Lord had made it manifest to him that there was gladness among the sanctified in heaven and that all the prophets of this dispensation, Joseph, Brigham and John Taylor, and the prophets of ancient days among the Nephites and Israelites led by the Son of God all rejoiced exceedingly at the dedication of this Temple, and it was accepted of God.[64]

Even as the Saints were celebrating the Salt Lake Temple's completion, there was, he assured the Saints, another celebration taking place on the other side of the veil that separates mortality from eternity.

For his part, Wilford was content that he had done what heaven had called him to do. He had known for most of his life that this was one of the major parts of his earthly mission to fulfill. He had known it since before the Saints had ever left Nauvoo for the mountains, before Brigham had ever put his cane in the ground of the barren valley soil. Whether Wilford shared it with others is unknown, but he recorded it in his journal, which he kept without fail for sixty-five years.

> Near[ly] fifty years ago while in the city of Boston I had a vision of going with the Saints to the Rocky Mountains, building a

temple and I dedicated it. Two nights in succession before John Taylor's death [in 1887], President Brigham Young [who died in 1877, a decade earlier] gave me the keys of the temple and told me to go and dedicate it . . .

And then this humble phrase, a fitting close to that mortal duty: ". . . which I did." [65]

THE DEDICATORY PRAYER OF THE SALT LAKE TEMPLE

FIRST OFFERED ON APRIL 6, 1893, BY PRESIDENT WILFORD WOODRUFF

Our Father in heaven, Thou has created the heavens and the earth, and all things that are therein; Thou most glorious One, perfect in mercy, love, and truth, we, Thy children, come this day before Thee, and in this house which we have built to Thy most holy name, humbly plead the atoning blood of Thine Only Begotten Son, that our sins may be remembered no more against us forever, but that our prayers may ascend unto Thee and have free access to Thy throne, that we may be heard in Thy holy habitation. And may it graciously please Thee to hearken unto our petitions, answer them according to Thine infinite wisdom and love, and grant that the blessings which we seek may be bestowed upon us, even a hundred fold, inasmuch as we seek with purity of heart and fullness of purpose to do Thy will and glorify Thy name.

We thank Thee, O Thou Great Eloheim, that Thou didst raise up Thy servant, Joseph Smith through the loins of Abraham, Isaac and Jacob, and made him a Prophet, Seer, and Revelator, and through the assistance and administrations of angels from heaven, Thou didst enable him to bring forth the Book of Mormon, the stick of Joseph, in the hand of Ephraim, in fulfillment of the prophecies of Isaiah and other prophets, which record has been translated and published in many languages. We also thank Thee, our Father in heaven, that Thou didst inspire Thy servant and give him power on the earth to organize Thy Church in this goodly land, in all its fullness, power and glory, with Apostles, Prophets, Pastors and Teachers, with all the gifts and graces belonging thereto, and all this by the power of the Aaronic and Melchizedek Priesthood, which Thou didst bestow upon him by the administration of holy angels, who held that Priesthood in the days of the Savior. We thank Thee, our God, that Thou didst enable Thy servant Joseph to build two temples, in which ordinances were administered for the living and the dead; that he also lived to send the gospel to the nations of the earth and to the islands of the sea, and labored exceedingly until he was martyred for the word of God and the testimony of Jesus Christ.

We also thank Thee, O our Father in heaven, that Thou didst raise up Thy servant Brigham Young, who held the keys of the Priesthood on the earth for many years, and who led Thy people to these valleys of the mountains, and laid the corner-stone of this great Temple and dedicated it unto Thee; and who did direct the building of three other temples in these Rocky Mountains which have been dedicated unto Thy holy name, in which temples many thousands of the living have been blessed and the dead redeemed.

Our Father in heaven, we are also thankful to Thee for Thy servant John Taylor, who followed in the footsteps of Thy servant Brigham, until he laid down his life in exile.

Thou hast called Thy servants Wilford Woodruff, George Q. Cannon, and Joseph F. Smith to hold the keys of the Presidency and priesthood this day, and for these shepherds of Thy flock we feel to give Thee thanksgiving and praise. Thy servant Wilford is bound to acknowledge Thy hand, O Father, in the preservation of his life from the hour of his birth to the present day. Nothing but Thy power could have preserved him through that which he has passed during the eighty-six years that Thou hast granted him life on the earth.

For the raising up of the Twelve Apostles, we also thank Thee, our God, and for the perfect union which exists among us.

We thank Thee, O Lord, for the perfect organizations of Thy Church as they exist at the present time.

O Lord, we regard with intense and indescribable feelings the completion of this sacred house. Deign to accept this the fourth temple which Thy covenant children have been assisted by Thee in erecting in these mountains. In past ages Thou didst inspire with Thy Holy Spirit Thy servants, the prophets, to speak of the time in the latter days when the mountain of the Lord's house should be established in the tops of the mountains, and should be exalted above the hills. We thank Thee that we have had the glorious opportunity of contributing to the fulfillment of these visions of Thine ancient seers, and that Thou hast condescended to permit us to take part in the great work. And as this portion of Thy servants' words has thus so marvelously been brought to pass, we pray Thee, with increased faith and renewed hope, that all their words with regard to Thy great work in gathering Thine Israel and building up Thy kingdom on earth in the last days may be as amply fulfilled, and that, O Lord, speedily.

We come before Thee with joy and thanksgiving, with spirits jubilant and hearts filled with praise, that Thou hast permitted us to see this day for which, during these forty years, we have hoped, and toiled, and prayed, when we can dedicate unto Thee this house which we have built to Thy most glorious name. One year ago we set the capstone with shouts of Hosanna to God and the Lamb. And today we dedicate the whole unto Thee, with all that pertains unto it that it may be holy in Thy sight; that it may be a house of prayer, a house of praise and of worship; that Thy glory may rest upon it; that Thy holy presence may be continually in it; that it may be the abode of Thy Well-Beloved Son, our Savior; that the angels who stand before Thy face may be the hallowed messengers who shall visit it, bearing to us Thy wishes and Thy will, that it may be sanctified and consecrated in all its parts holy unto Thee, the God of

Israel, the Almighty Ruler of Mankind. And we pray Thee that all people who may enter upon the threshold of this, Thine house, may feel Thy power and be constrained to acknowledge that Thou hast sanctified it, that it is Thy house, a place of Thy holiness.

We pray Thee, Heavenly Father, to accept this building in all its parts from foundation to capstone, with the statue that is on the latter placed, and all the finals and other ornaments that adorn its exterior. We pray Thee to bless, that they decay not, all the walls, partitions, floors, ceilings, roofs and bridging, the elevators, stairways, railings and steps, the frames, doors, windows, and other openings, all things connected with the lighting, heating, and sanitary apparatus, the boilers, engines, and dynamos, the connecting pipes and wires, the lamps and burners, and all utensils, furniture and articles used in or connected with the holy ordinances administered in this house, the veils and the altars, the baptismal font and the oxen on which it rests, and all that pertains thereto, the baths, washstands and basins. Also the safes and vaults in which the records are preserved, with the records themselves, and all books, documents, and papers appertaining to the office of the recorder, likewise the library with all the books, maps, instruments, etc., that may belong thereto. We also present before Thee, for Thine acceptance, all the additions and buildings not forming a part of the main edifice, but being appendages thereto; and we pray Thee to bless all the furniture, seats, cushions, curtains, hangings, locks, and fastenings, and multitudinous other appliances and appurtenances found in and belonging to this Temple and its annexes with all the work or ornamentation thereon, the painting and plastering, the gilding and bronzing, the fine work in wood and metal of every kind, the embroidery and needlework, the pictures and statuary, the carved work and canopies. Also the materials of which the buildings and their contents are made or composed—the rock, lime, mortar and plaster, the timbers and lath, the wood of various trees, the gold and silver, the brass and iron, and all other metals, the silk, wool, and cotton, the skins and furs, the glass, china, and precious stones, all these and all else herein we humbly present for Thine acceptance and sanctifying blessing.

Our Father in heaven, we present before Thee the altars which we have prepared for Thy servants and handmaidens to receive their sealing blessings. We dedicate them in the name of the Lord Jesus Christ, unto Thy most holy name, and we ask Thee to sanctify these altars, that those who come unto them may feel the power of the Holy Ghost resting upon them, and realize the sacredness of the covenants they enter into. And we pray that our covenants and contracts which we make with Thee and with each other may be directed by Thy holy Spirit, be sacredly kept by us, and accepted by Thee, and that all the blessings pronounced may be realized by all Thy Saints who come to these altars, in the morning of the resurrection of the just.

O Lord, we pray Thee to bless and sanctify the whole of this block or piece of ground on which these buildings stand, with the surrounding walls and fences, the walks, paths and ornamental beds, also the trees, plants, flowers and shrubbery that grow in its soil; may they bloom and blossom and become exceedingly beautiful and fragrant; and may Thy Spirit dwell in the midst thereof, that this plot of ground may be a place of rest and peace, for holy meditation and inspired thought.

Preserve these buildings, we beseech Thee, from injury or destruction by flood or fire; from the rage of the elements, the shafts of the vivid lightning, the overwhelming blasts of the hurricane, the flames of consuming fire, and the upheavals of the earth-quake, O Lord, protect them.

Bless, we pray Thee, Heavenly Father, all who may be workers in this house. Remember continually Thy servant who shall be appointed to preside within its walls; endow him richly with wisdom of the Holy Ones, with the spirit of his calling, with the power of his Priesthood, and with the gift of discernment. Bless, according to their calling, his assistants and all who are associated with him in the performance of the ordinances—baptisms, confirmations, washings, anointings, sealings, endowments, and ordinations which are performed herein, that all that is done may be holy and acceptable unto Thee, Thou God of our salvation. Bless the recorders and copyists, that the records of the Temple may be kept perfect, and without omission and errors, and that they may also be accepted of Thee. Bless, in their several positions, the engineers, watchmen, guards, and all others who have duties to perform in connection with the house, that they may perform them unto Thee with an eye single to Thy glory.

Remember also in Thy mercy all those who have labored in the erection of this house, or who have, in any way, by their means or influence aided in its completion; may they in no wise lose their reward.

O Thou God of our fathers, Abraham, Isaac, and Jacob, whose God Thou delightest to be called, we thank Thee with all the fervor of overflowing gratitude that Thou hast revealed the powers by which the hearts of the children are being turned to their fathers and the hearts of the fathers to the children, that the sons of men, in all their generations can be made partakers of the glories and joys of the kingdom of heaven. Confirm upon us the spirit of Elijah, we pray Thee, that we may thus redeem our dead and also connect ourselves with our fathers who have passed behind the veil, and furthermore seal up our dead to come forth in the first resurrection, that we who dwell on the earth may be bound to those who dwell in heaven. We thank Thee for their sake who have finished their work in mortality, as well as for our own, that the prison doors have been opened, that deliverance has been proclaimed to the captive, and the bonds have been loosened from those who were bound. We praise Thee that our fathers, from last to first, from now, back to the beginning, can be united with us in indissoluble links, welded by the Holy Priesthood, and that as one great family united in Thee and cemented by Thy power we shall together stand before Thee, and by the power of the atoning blood of Thy Son be delivered from all evil, be saved and sanctified, exalted and glorified. Wilt Thou also permit holy messengers to visit us within these sacred walls and make known unto us with regard to the work we should perform in behalf of our dead.

And, as Thou has inclined the hearts of many who have not yet entered into covenant with Thee to search out their progenitors, and in so doing they have traced the ancestry of many of Thy Saints, we pray Thee that Thou wilt increase this desire in their bosoms, that they may in this way aid in the accomplishment of Thy work. Bless them, we pray Thee, in their labors, that they may not fall into errors in preparing their genealogies; and furthermore, we ask Thee to open before them new avenues of information, and place in their hands the records of the past, that their work may not only be correct but complete also.

O Thou Great Father of the spirits of all flesh, graciously bless and fully qualify those upon whom Thou hast placed a portion of Thine authority, and who bear the responsibilities and powers of the priesthood which is after the order of Thy Son. Bless them all from first to last from Thy servant who represents Thee in all the world to the latest who has been ordained to the Deacon's office. Upon each and all confer the spirit of their calling, with a comprehension of its duties and a loving zeal to fulfill them. Endow them with faith, patience and understanding. May their lives be strong in virtue and adorned with humility; may their ministrations be effectual, their prayers be availing and their teachings the path of salvation. May they be united by the Spirit and power of God in all their labors, and in every thought, word and act, may they glorify Thy name and vindicate the wisdom that has made them kings and priests unto Thee.

For Thy servants of the First Presidency of the Church we first of all pray. Reveal, in great clearness, Thy mind and will unto them in all things essential for the welfare of Thy people; give them heavenly wisdom, abounding faith, and the power and gifts necessary to enable them to preside acceptably unto Thee over the officers and members of Thy Church. Remember in love Thy servant whom Thou hast called to be a Prophet, Seer, and Revelator to all mankind, whose days have been many upon the earth; yet lengthen out his span of mortal life, we pray Thee, and grant unto him all the powers and gifts, in their completeness, of the office Thou hast conferred upon him; and in like manner bless his associates in the Presidency of Thy Church.

Confer upon Thy servants, the Twelve Apostles, a rich endowment of Thy Spirit. Under their guidance may the gospel of the kingdom go forth into all the world, to be preached to all nations, kindreds, tongues, and people, that the honest in heart in every land may hear the glad tidings of joy and salvation. Overrule, we pray Thee, in the midst of the governments of the earth, that the barriers that now stand in the way of the spread of Thy truths may be removed, and liberty of conscience be accorded to all peoples.

Remember in loving kindness Thy servants, the Patriarchs. May they be full of blessings for Thy people Israel. May they bear with them the seeds of comfort and consolation, of encouragement and blessing. Fill them with the Holy Spirit of promise, and be graciously pleased to fulfill their words of prophecy, that Thy name may be extolled by the people of Thy Church and their faith in Thee and in the promises of Thy ministering servants be increasingly strengthened.

With Thy servants of the Twelve, bless their associates, the Seventies; may they be powerful in the preaching of Thy word and in bearing it to the four quarters of the earth. May an ever-widening way be opened before them until they shall have raised the gospel standard in every land and proclaimed its saving truths in every tongue, that all the islands and the continents may rejoice in the testimony of the great work Thou art in these later days performing on the earth.

Bless abundantly, O Lord, the High Priests in all the varied duties and positions to which Thou hast called them. As standing ministers of Thy word in the multiplying Stakes of Zion wilt Thou endow them richly with the spirit of their exalted callings. As Presidents, Counselors, Bishops, members of High Councils, and in every other office which their Priesthood gives them the right to fill may they be righteous ministers of Thy holy law, loving fathers of the people, and as judges in the midst of the Saints may they deal out just and impartial judgment tempered with mercy and love.

So also, in their various callings, confer precious gifts of wisdom, faith and knowledge upon Thy servants, the Elders, Priests, Teachers, and Deacons, that all may diligently perform their parts in the glorious labors Thou hast called Thy Priesthood to bear.

Forget not, we beseech Thee, Thy servants the missionaries, who are proclaiming the saving truths that Thou hast revealed for man's redemption to the millions who are now overshadowed by deep spiritual darkness. Preserve them from all evil, deliver them from mob violence, may they want no good thing, but be greatly blessed with the gifts and powers of their ministry. Remember also their families, that they may be sustained and comforted by Thee and be cherished and cared for by Thy Saints.

We pray Thee for the members of Thy Holy Church throughout all the world, that Thy people may be so guided and governed of Thee, that all who profess to be and call themselves Saints may be preserved in the unity of the faith, in the way of truth, in the bonds of peace, and in holiness of life. Strengthen the weak, we pray Thee, and impart Thy Spirit unto all.

Our Father, may peace abide in all the homes of Thy Saints; may holy angels guard them; may they be encompassed by Thine arms of love; may prosperity shine upon them, and may the tempter and the destroyer be removed far from them. May the days of Thy covenant people be lengthened out in righteousness, and sickness and disease be rebuked from their midst. May the land they inhabit be made fruitful by Thy grace, may its waters be increased and the climate be tempered to the comfort and need of Thy people; may drought, devastating storms, cyclones, and hurricanes be kept afar off, and earthquakes never disturb the land which Thou hast given us. May locusts, caterpillars and other insects not destroy our garden and desolate our fields; but may we be a people blessed of Thee in our bodies and spirits, in our homes and habitations, in our flocks and herds, in ourselves and our posterity, and in all that Thou hast made us stewards over.

Now we pray for the youth of Zion—the children of Thy people; endow them richly with the spirit of faith and righteousness and with increasing love for Thee and for Thy law. Prosper all the institutions that Thou hast established in our midst for their well-being. Give to our Church Schools an ever-increasing power for good. May the Holy Spirit dominate the teachings given therein and also control the hearts and illumine the minds of the students. Bless marvelously Thy servants, the General Superintendent, and all the principals, teachers and other officers, and also those from the General Board of Education of Thy Church. Remember, likewise in Thy loving kindness the Sunday Schools, with all who, either as teachers or scholars, belong thereto; may the influence of the instruction given therein broaden and deepen, to Thy glory and the salvation of Thy children, until the perfect day. Bless the members of the General Board of the Deseret Sunday School Union with the wisdom necessary for the proper fulfillment of their duties, and for the accomplishment of the purposes for which this board was created.

We also uphold before Thee the Young Men's and Young Ladies' Mutual Improvement Associations, with all their officers, general and local, and the members. May they be prospered of Thee, their membership be enlarged, and the good that they accomplish increase with every succeeding year. For the Primaries and Religion Classes we also seek Thy constant blessing and guiding care; may the spirit of instruction be poured out upon the presidents and associate officers and the teachers. May they keep peace with the rest of the educational establishments in Thy Church; so that from their earliest years our children may be diligently brought up in the ways of the Lord, and Thy name be magnified in their growth in virtue and intelligence.

Nor would we forget, O Lord, the normal training classes among Thy people, whether these classes be connected with the Church Schools, the Improvement Associations, or the Sunday Schools. Grant that these classes may be the means of spreading true education throughout all the borders of the Saints by the creation of a body of teachers who will not only be possessed of rare intelligence but be filled also with the spirit of the gospel and be powerful in the testimony of Thy truth and in implanting a love for Thee and Thy works in the hearts of all whom they instruct.

We would hold up before Thee, O Lord, the Relief Societies, with all their members; and all those who preside in their midst according to their callings and appointments, general or local. Bless the Teachers in their labors of mercy and charity, who, as ministering angels, visit the homes of the sick and the needy, bearing succor, consolation and comfort to the unfortunate and sorrowful. And bless, we beseech Thee, most merciful Father, the poor of Thy people, that the cry of want and suffering may not ascend unto Thee from the midst of Thy Saints whom Thou hast blessed so abundantly with the comforts of this world. Open up new avenues by which the needy can obtain a livelihood by honest industry, and also incline the hearts of those blessed more abundantly, to give generously of their substance in this respect, less favored brethren and sisters, that Thou mayest not have reason to chide us for the neglect of even the least among Thy covenant children.

O God of Israel, turn Thy face, we pray Thee, in loving kindness toward Thy stricken people of the House of Judah. Oh, deliver them from those that oppress them. Heal up their wounds, comfort their hearts, strengthen their feet, and give them ministers after Thine own heart who shall lead them as of old, in Thy way. May the days of their tribulation soon cease, and they be planted by Thee in the valleys and plains of their ancient home; and may Jerusalem rejoice and Judea be glad for the multitude of her sons and daughters, for the sweet voices of children in her streets, and the rich outpouring of Thy saving mercies upon them. May Israel no more bow the head, or bend the neck to the oppressor, but may his feet be made strong on the everlasting hills, never more, by violence, to be banished therefrom, and the praise and the glory shall be Thine.

Remember in like pity the dwindling remnants of the House of Israel, descendants of Thy servant Lehi. Restore them we pray Thee, to Thine ancient favor, fulfill in their completeness the promises given to their fathers, and make of them a white and delightsome race, a loved and holy people as in former days. May the time also be nigh at hand when Thou wilt gather the dispersed of Israel from the islands of the sea and from every land in which Thou hast scattered them, and the ten tribes of Jacob from their hiding place in the north, and restore them to communion and fellowship with their kinsmen of the seed of Abraham.

We thank Thee, O God of Israel, that Thou didst raise up patriotic men to lay the foundation of this great American government. Thou didst inspire them to frame a good constitution and laws which guarantee to all of the inhabitants of the land equal rights and privileges to worship Thee according to the dictates of their own consciences. Bless the officers, both judicial and executive. Confer abundant favors upon the President, his Cabinet, and Congress. Enlightened and guided by Thy Spirit may they maintain and uphold the glorious principles of human liberty. Our hearts are filled with gratitude to Thee, our Father in heaven, for Thy kindness unto us in softening the hearts of our fellow citizens, the people of this nation, toward us. That which Thou hast done has been marvelous in our eyes. We thank Thee that Thou didst move upon the heart of the President of our nation to issue a general amnesty. Thou hast removed prejudice and misunderstanding from the minds of many of the people concerning us and our purposes, and they are disposed to treat us as fellow citizens, and not as enemies. In this holy house we feel to give Thee glory therefore, and we humbly ask Thee to increase this feeling in their hearts. Enable them to see us in our true light. Show unto them that we are their friends, that we love liberty, that we will join with them in upholding the rights of the people, the Constitution and laws of our country; and give unto us and our children an increased disposition to always be loyal, and to do everything in our power to maintain Constitutional rights and the freedom of all within the confines of this great Republic.

Remember in mercy, O Lord, the kings, the princes, the nobles the rulers, and governors and the great ones of the earth, and likewise all the poor, the afflicted and the oppressed, and indeed, all people, that their hearts may be softened when Thy servants go forth to bear testimony of Thy name, that their prejudices may give way before the truth, and Thy people find favor in their eyes. So control the affairs of the nations of the earth, that the way be prepared for the ushering in of a reign of righteousness and truth. We desire to see liberty spread throughout the earth, to see oppression cease, the yoke of the tyrant broken, and every despotic form of government overthrown by which Thy children are degraded and crushed, and prevented from enjoying their share of the blessings of the earth, which Thou hast created for their habitation.

O God, the Eternal Father, Thou knowest all things. Thou seest the course Thy people have been led to take in political matters. They have, in many instances, joined the two great national parties. Campaigns have been entered upon, elections have been held, and much party feeling has been engendered. Many things have been said and done which have wounded the feelings of the humble and the meek, and which have been a cause of offense. We beseech Thee, in Thine infinite mercy and goodness, to forgive Thy people wherein they have sinned in this direction. Show them, O Father, their faults and their errors, that they may see the same in the light of Thy Holy Spirit, and repent truly and sincerely, and cultivate that spirit of affection and love which Thou art desirous that all the children of men should entertain one for another, and which Thy Saints, above all others, should cherish. Enable Thy people hereafter to avoid bitterness and strife, and to refrain from words and acts in political discussions that shall create feeling and grieve Thy Holy Spirit.

Heavenly Father, when Thy people shall not have the opportunity of entering this holy house to offer their supplications unto Thee, and they are oppressed and in trouble, surrounded by difficulties or assailed by temptation and shall turn their faces towards this Thy holy house and ask Thee for deliverance, for help, for Thy power to be extended in their behalf, we beseech Thee, to look down from Thy holy habitation in mercy and tender compassion upon them, and listen to their cries. Or when the children of Thy people, in years to come, shall be separated, through any cause, from this place, and their hearts shall turn in remembrance of Thy promises to this holy Temple, and they shall cry unto Thee from the depths of their affliction and sorrow to extend relief and deliverance to them, we humbly entreat Thee to Turn Thine ear in mercy to them; hearken to their cries, and grant unto them the blessings for which they ask.

Almighty Father, increase within us the powers of that faith delivered to and possessed by Thy Saints. Strengthen us by the memories of the glorious deliverances of the past, by the remembrance of the sacred covenants that Thou hast made with us, so that, when evil overshadows us, when trouble encompasses us, when we pass through the valley of humiliation, we may not falter, may not doubt, but in the strength of Thy Holy name may accomplish all Thy righteous purposes with regard to us, fill the measure of our creation, and triumph gloriously, by Thy grace, over every besetting sin, be redeemed from every evil, and be numbered in the kingdom of heaven amongst those who shall dwell in Thy presence forever.

And now, our Father, we bless Thee, we praise Thee, we glorify Thee, we worship Thee, day by day we magnify Thee, and give Thee thanks for Thy great goodness towards us, Thy children, and we pray Thee, in the name of Thy Son Jesus Christ, our Savior, to hear these our humble petitions, and answer us from heaven, Thy holy dwelling place, where Thou sittest enthroned in glory, might, majesty, and dominion, and with an infinitude of power which we, Thy mortal creatures, cannot imagine, much less comprehend. Amen and Amen.

ACKNOWLEDGMENTS

Writing any history book is always a team effort, and so I want to recognize the help and assistance of those who made this book both possible and better:

My dear wife, Janna, who always deserves the first place on the list. Her willingness to take on so many burdens so that I can have time to research and write makes this book hers just as much as it is mine. Janna, I love you more than I can tell you.

My mother, Lynne Henshaw, who always believed me capable of writing books worth reading. She supported my efforts to write this one in so many ways. I love you, Mom, and I'm very proud to be your son.

Kinde Brinton, my "first reader," and her husband, Chris, who readily supported her efforts to go through the manuscript week after week. She was meticulous and not afraid to tell me when I was flying off on unimportant tangents and burying the reader under details at the expense of telling the tale. Kinde saved me from many embarrassing errors, and her suggestions improved the storytelling in so many ways and places. Any readers who enjoy this book will owe her and Chris a debt of gratitude, as I do.

Brad Wilcox, who has been a family friend for twenty years now and without whose assistance my wife and I never would have married. He seized on the idea of a narrative history of the Salt Lake Temple's construction when I first suggested it, immediately moved to put the proposal before his own editor at Deseret Book, and gave it his full-throated support. He is a force for good in this world.

Lisa Roper, my product director at Deseret Book, who has believed in the project from the start. She has been a joy to work with, even when her edits drew some literary blood from the author. Her diligence and experience ensured the book was as good as it could be coming from me.

Dr. Jacob Wayne Olmstead of the Church History Library, who is the current authority on the history of the Salt Lake Temple. Where others made sure the story was told well, he ensured it would be told accurately and kept me from errors that would have turned this narrative history into a work of historical fiction. In particular, I would have had no hope of understanding the issues surrounding the temple's foundation without his patient explanations. For anyone looking for an expert on the temple's history, Jacob should be the first name on the list.

Anne Berryhill, formerly of the Church History Library, for her patient assistance in showing me the ins and outs of retrieving materials in the archive and helping me to identify photographs and other materials to improve the work.

Jason Yarn, my literary agent, for his willingness to humor me in taking a break from spy novels to write a history book for Latter-day Saints. Trust me, Jason, it was the right thing to do.

Sister missionaries Hannah Smith of Mesa, Arizona, and Calle Whitmarsh of Sydney, Australia, who were my guides to the Salt Lake Tabernacle during my research trip. Both will have finished their missionary service and returned home by the time this book is published. Thank you, sisters, for answering my questions about that amazing building. (Do you remember what I told you about acknowledgment pages and people who help authors?)

Warren and Carolyn Brunson and Gail and Lanning Porter,

extended family members who supported me during my research trip to Salt Lake City. Your willingness to feed and lodge a boarder (and listen to extended rambling about temple history) is forever appreciated. I love you all.

Wilford Woodruff, Andrew Jenson, B. H. Roberts, and every other Church historian, past and present, who worked so hard to preserve all of the records that make writing this kind of book possible. We Latter-day Saints enjoy an embarrassment of riches in that regard, both in the sheer amount of primary materials available and in how much of it is now online. Anyone who has access to the internet has access to an enormous volume of material on Church history, with more being uploaded by the day. I think the blessings we now enjoy from those records pale in comparison to what is to come from them in the future.

And finally, to every man, woman, or child who ever turned a spade of dirt, hammered on a granite block, drove an ox team, laid a train rail, or did anything, no matter how small, to help build the Salt Lake Temple or to support those who did. The vision, faith, and stubbornness in enduring to the end that they displayed over forty years will always be a model for the rest of us to follow.

LIST OF ABBREVIATIONS USED IN NOTES

CHL: Church History Library, The Church of Jesus Christ of Latter-day Saints, Salt Lake City, UT.

GPO: US Government Printing Office, Washington, D.C.

GQCJ: George Q. Cannon Journal. George Q. Cannon was an Apostle and member of the First Presidency who kept an extensive journal totaling some 2.5 million words. The Church History Library has recently made a complete transcript of the journal available online. Accordingly, all citations will refer to the web pages where the cited entries are located. Dates for the entries are included in the citations to help readers find them should the URLs to the cited pages change over time. Cited as: George Q. Cannon, The Journal of George Q. Cannon (Salt Lake City: Church Historian's Press, n.d.). Online only. https://churchhistorianspress.org/george-q-cannon.

HBLL: Harold B. Lee Library, Brigham Young University, Provo, UT.

HOTC: *History of the Church*. This is not the more-famous *History of the Church* compiled by Elder Brigham Henry (B. H.) Roberts, which has errors that make it problematic as a historical reference. Instead, this is the history of the Church compiled by the Church Historian's Office that covers the time from the Church's founding to the early period of John Taylor's tenure as Church President (1839–1882). Cited as: Historian's Office, *Historian's Office History of the Church, 1839–circa 1882*. CR 100 102. CHL.

JD: *Journal of Discourses* is a compilation of sermons given by members of the Church's First Presidency and Quorum of the Twelve from 1854 to 1886. The Church does not consider the *Journal* to be an authoritative doctrinal source by itself, and all quotations cited in the narrative are included for their historical value only. Cited as: *Journal of Discourses*, 26 vols. (London: LDS Booksellers Depot, 1854–1886).

JHC: *Journal History of the Church.* Commonly referred to simply as the *Journal History*, it is a chronological scrapbook composed of periodical clippings, typed notes, and other material assembled by Church historians. The Church has scanned and posted online the *Journal History* at https:// catalog. churchofjesuschrist.org/record? id= 3ffad93a-5200-4a7e-9d68 -2f4e42a13188 (accessed August 24, 2019).

JSP: The Joseph Smith Papers. Edited by Dean C. Jessee, Ronald K. Esplin, and Richard Lyman Bushman (Salt Lake City: Church Historian's Press). Various volumes or online entries are cited specifically within individual notes.

MHBY: *Manuscript History of Brigham Young, 1847–1850.* Cited as: Brigham Young, *Manuscript History of Brigham Young, 1847–1850.* Edited by William S. Harwell. (Salt Lake City: Collier's Publishing Co., 1997).

OR: U. S. War Department, *The War of the Rebellion: A Compilation of the Official Records of the Union and Confederate Armies*, 128 parts in 70 vols. and atlas (Washington: Government Printing Office, 1880–1901). The *Official Records* contain transcripts of the original battle reports, military correspondence, and other records from the governments and militaries of both the United States and the Confederate states for the duration of the Civil War (1861–1865). A major supplement of additional records has recently been made available in print by Broadfoot Publishing of Wendell, NC, but no material from the supplement was cited in this volume.

WWJ: Wilford Woodruff, *Wilford Woodruff Journals, 1833–1898*, MS 1352, Church History Library, The Church of Jesus Christ of Latter-day Saints, Salt Lake City, UT. A typescript version of the *Wilford Woodruff Journals* spanning several volumes is available from Signature Books, but the Church has recently scanned and posted the complete set of original journals on the Church History Library's website at https://catalog.churchofjesuschrist.org /record?id=400c3266-ede2-43cf-9a24-50153adebbeb&compId =8c4f3058 -5de9-4278-be3c-7d02713f2dd2 (accessed August 22, 2019).

NOTES

CHAPTER 1: HERE WILL BE THE TEMPLE OF OUR GOD

1. Egan, *Pioneering the West*, 95. Egan, a member of Young's vanguard company, reported in his July 12 journal entry that "President Young was taken sick this forenoon. After resting two hours all the camp, except eight wagons, proceeded on their journey. President Young not being able to go on, Brother Kimball's three wagons remained behind."
2. Aldous, "Mountain Fever in the 1847 Mormon Pioneer Companies," 52–59.
3. Erastus Snow, "Discourse on the Utah Pioneers," 45.
4. Egan, *Pioneering the West*, 95.
5. WWJ, *1847 January–1853 December*, July 24, 1847.
6. HOTC, *1847 January 1–December 29*, July 24, 1847.
7. Woodruff, "Zion's Camp, Mormon Battalion, Pioneers," 23.
8. Exodus 25–27; 35–40.
9. JD, 2:31.
10. Rigdon, "Oration Delivered by Mr. S. Rigdon on the 4th of July 1838," 12.
11. A digital image of the original handwritten order can be viewed at https://en.wikipedia.org/wiki/Missouri_Executive_Order_44#/media/File:Extermination_order.gif (accessed November 13, 2019).
12. D&C 124.
13. Joseph Smith and Elias Higbee, "Letter to Hyrum Smith and Nauvoo, Illinois, High Council, 5 December 1839," 85; in Godfrey, et al., eds., JSP, *Documents, Volume 7: September 1839–January 1841*, 85–88. The original letter is not extant; the copy reproduced from Joseph Smith's

Letterbook in the Joseph Smith Papers is in the handwriting of Howard Coray. The facsimile is also available online at https://www.josephsmith papers.org/paper-summary/letter-to-hyrum-smith-and-nauvoo-illinois-high -council-5-december-1839/1 (accessed November 13, 2019).

14. Smith and Higbee, "Letter to Hyrum Smith."

15. Church member Albert P. Rockwood first coined the term "Mormon War" to describe the series of violent clashes between the Saints and their Missouri neighbors. For an excellent summary of those events, see the historical introduction to "Part 3: 4 November 1838–16 April 1839," in Ashurst-McGee et al., eds, JSP, *Documents, Volume 6: February 1838–August 1839*, 265–78.

16. Van Buren lost the 1840 election to William Henry Harrison, but he did carry the state of Missouri.

17. Joseph Smith—History 1:23.

18. Spencer and Harmer, *Brigham Young at Home*, 16–17.

19. "An Overland Journey XXI—Two Hours with Brigham Young," *New York Tribune*, August 20, 1859.

20. Leonard J. Arrington, *Brigham Young: American Moses*, 30.

21. JD, 4:297–98.

22. Young, *Manuscript History of Brigham Young*, chap. 2 "1836."

23. Young, *Manuscript History of Brigham Young*, chap. 2 "1836."

24. Young, *Manuscript History of Brigham Young*, chap. 2 "1836."

25. Young, *Manuscript History of Brigham Young*, chap. 8, "1844."

26. JD, 2:32.

27. JD, 13:85–86.

28. Kane, "The Mormons," 21.

29. Polk, *Polk: The Diary of a President 1845–1849*, 109.

30. Brigham Young letter to James K. Polk, August 9, 1846. Kane family papers, Vault MSS 792, L. Tom Perry Special Collections, Nineteenth Century Western & Mormon Manuscripts, HBLL.

31. JHC, 18 Jan. 1847.

32. JHC, 12–14 April 1847.

33. JD, 5:226.

34. Snow, "Discourse on the Utah Pioneers," 46.

35. Woodruff, "Zion's Camp, Mormon Battalion, Pioneers," 23.

36. Bullock, *Thomas Bullock journals, 1843–1849*, July 25, 1847.

37. Woodruff, "Zion's Camp, Mormon Battalion, Pioneers," 23.

38. Bancroft, *History of Utah 1540–1886*, 258–59.

39. "Pioneer's Day," *Deseret Evening News*, July 26, 1880.

CHAPTER 2: SHALL WE NOT BUILD THE LORD A HOUSE?

1. Spencer and Harmer, *Brigham Young at Home*, 285.
2. Dirkmaat et al., eds., JSP, *Documents, Volume 3: February 1833–March 1834*, 121–30.
3. WWJ, *1847 January–1853 December*, July 28, 1847.
4. MHBY, 64.
5. MHBY, 66.
6. Jenson, *Church Chronology*, 35.
7. Bancroft, *History of Utah 1540–1886*, 262.
8. MHBY, 63.
9. WWJ, *1847 January–1853 December*, August 5, 1847.
10. JD, 1:210.
11. MHBY, 62.
12. Bancroft, *History of Utah 1540–1886*, 263.
13. MHBY, 67–68.
14. Smith wrote nothing about the injury in his journal entry for that day.
15. MHBY, 67–68.
16. Spencer and Harmer, *Brigham Young at Home*, 270.
17. MHBY, 65.
18. Jenson, *Church Chronology*, 34; Egan, *Pioneering the West*, 121.
19. JHC, August 12, 1847.
20. MHBY, 67.
21. WWJ, *1847 January–1853 December*, 15 August 1847.
22. JHC, August 11, 1847.
23. Egan, *Pioneering the West*, 125.
24. Jenson, *Church Chronology*, August 22, 1847.
25. MHBY, 64.
26. Jenson, ed., "The Pioneers of 1847," 100.
27. MHBY, 68.
28. Jenson, ed., "The Pioneers of 1847," 100.
29. MHBY, 70.
30. MHBY, 70.
31. MHBY, 74.
32. MHBY, 74.
33. MHBY, 75–76.
34. J. Earl Arrington, "Williams Weeks, Architect of the Nauvoo Temple," 346.
35. Kelly, ed., *Journals of John D. Lee*, 132–33.
36. J. Earl Arrington, "Williams Weeks, Architect of the Nauvoo Temple," 355–56.
37. Bullock, *Thomas Bullock journals*, July 8, 1848.

38. J. Earl Arrington, "William Weeks, Architect of the Nauvoo Temple," 356.

39. Young, et al., *General Epistle from the Council of the Twelve Apostles*, 5.

40. Young, et al., *General Epistle from the Council of the Twelve Apostles*, 5.

41. Young, et al., *General Epistle from the Council of the Twelve Apostles*, 5.

42. B.F. Cummings, Jr., "Education," in *The Utah Pioneers: Celebration of the Entrance of the Pioneers into Great Salt Lake Valley*, 30–31.

43. B.F. Cummings, Jr., "Education," in *The Utah Pioneers: Celebration of the Entrance of the Pioneers into Great Salt Lake Valley*, 30–31.

44. D&C 88:118; see also D&C 109:14.

45. D&C 109:14.

46. D&C 93:36.

47. *Doctrine and Covenants*, 1835 ed., 39; reproduced as a facsimile in Jenson, Turley, and Lorimer, eds. JSP, *Revelations and Translations, Volume 2: Published Revelations*, 349.

48. *Doctrine and Covenants*, 1835 ed., 36; reproduced as a facsimile in Jenson, Turley, and Lorimer, eds. JSP, *Revelations and Translations, Volume 2: Published Revelations*, 346.

49. D&C 130:18.

50. Young, et al. *General Epistle from the Council of the Twelve Apostles*, 7.

51. D&C 107:23.

52. MHBY, 79.

53. Miller's Hollow would later be renamed Kanesville after Thomas Kane, the friend to the Saints who had intervened in Washington to find them lands to settle after their eviction from Nauvoo; it was renamed again in 1853 to Council Bluffs.

54. Historian's Office general Church minutes, 1839–1877; 1846-1850; Pottawattamie settlements, 1847 December 23-27; Orson Pratt, 17; Amasa Lyman, 18; https://catalog.churchofjesuschrist.org/record?id=0e53d68-5d7c-4f37-83d4-b6dd8fcdadf8&compId=1d7bde13-c3bc-4e38-b8fd-d81555f59259&view=browse (accessed: November 24, 2019).

55. MHBY, 89–93.

56. Bancroft, *History of Utah 1540–1886*, 275.

57. Bancroft, *History of Utah 1540–1886*, 276.

58. MHBY, 89–93.

59. Bancroft, *History of Utah 1540–1886*, 277.

60. Bancroft, *History of Utah 1540–1886*, 262.

61. Bancroft, *History of Utah 1540–1886*, 280–81.

62. Andrew Jenson, ed., "The Nauvoo Temple," *Historical Record* 8, no. 1 (June 1889): 872–73.

63. JD, 14:124.

64. MHBY, 134–35.

65. Hedges, Smith, and Anderson, eds., JSP, *Journals, Volume 2: December 1841– April 1843*, 53–54. See the entry for May 4, 1842, in which Joseph Smith records that Brigham was among those present in the meeting where the prophet gave "certain instructions concerning the priesthood."

66. Parley P. Pratt, "To President Orson Pratt, and the Saints in Great Britain," *Latter-day Saints' Millennial Star,* vol. 11, no. 2 (January 15, 1849): 24.

67. JHC, March 12, 1849.

68. Constitution of the State of Deseret. *Deseret* is a word found in the Book of Mormon, translated as "honeybee"; see Ether 2:3. The honeybee was chosen as being symbolic of "industry and its kindred virtues," which the Saints felt they had exemplified in their establishment of Great Salt Lake City.

69. Constitution of the State of Deseret.

70. Morgan, "State of Deseret," 118–19.

71. Morgan, "State of Deseret," 126–27.

72. For more on the subject of Utah first receiving territorial status instead statehood, see Rogers, *Unpopular Sovereignty,* chapter 1.

73. John M. Bernhisel to Millard Fillmore, September 16, 1850. Brigham Young office files, 1832–1878 (bulk 1844–1877); Utah Delegate Files, 1849–1872; John M. Bernhisel to Brigham Young, 1849–1866; 1850 July–November; John M. Bernhisel letter; CHL; https://catalog.churchofjesuschrist.org /assets?id=fb4be51d-a1a3-447d-9959-428d41597849&crate=0&index=5 (accessed September 28, 2019).

74. Tullidge, *Life of Brigham Young,* 199.

75. *Church History in the Fulness of Times,* 354.

76. HOTC, *1851 January 6–December 29,* September 7, 1851.

77. Reported in *Latter-day Saints' Millennial Star,* 14:33–34.

78. WWJ, *1847 January–1853 December,* September 8, 1851.

79. WWJ, *1847 January–1853 December,* September 8, 1851.

80. WWJ, *1847 January–1853 December,* September 8, 1851.

81. HOTC, *1851 January 6–December 29,* September 8, 1851.

82. Brigham Young to Isaac Morley, September 10, 1851. Brigham Young office files, 1832–1878 (bulk 1844–1877); General Correspondence, Outgoing, 1843–1876; 1851 September–December; CHL; https://catalog.churchofjesus christ.org/assets?id=cdbf59af-e4dd-4611-8a1c-5896c7cf2801&crate=0&index =1 (accessed September 28, 2019).

83. JHC, September 19, 1851; see also HOTC, *1851 January 6–December 29,* September 19, 1851.

84. Perry Brocchus to Brigham Young, September 19, 1851. Brigham Young office files, 1832–1878 (bulk 1844–1877); Governor's Office Files,

1850–1867; Executive Files, 1850–1858; Communications with Territorial Officers (Justices), 1851–1856; Perry E. Brocchus, 1851; Perry E. Brocchus letter; CHL; https://catalog.churchofjesuschrist.org/assets?id=df3317e1 -6751-41c4-9214-9ca7991c23e9&crate=0&index=1 (accessed September 28, 2019).

85. JHC, September 20, 1851.

86. JHC, September 20, 1851.

87. House of Representatives, Exec. Doc. No. 25, 23–24.

88. House of Representatives, Exec. Doc. No. 25, 24–27.

89. House of Representatives, Exec. Doc. No. 25, 29.

90. House of Representatives, Exec. Doc. No. 25, 28–32.

91. House of Representatives, Exec. Doc. No. 25, 31.

92. House of Representatives, Exec. Doc. No. 25, 21.

93. Spencer and Harmer, *Brigham Young at Home*, 278.

94. Spencer and Harmer, *Brigham Young at Home*, 278.

95. Jenson, *Church Chronology*, 42.

96. Jenson, *Church Chronology*, 42–43.

97. Angell, *Autobiography, 1810–1887*, 17.

98. Paul L. Anderson, "Truman O. Angell: Architect and Saint," 133–73.

99. https://history.lds.org/overlandtravel/companies/1/brigham-young-pioneer -company (accessed September 20, 2018).

100. Angell, *Journal, 1851 December-1856 April*, 4. This page reference is for the original handwritten journal. Truman's handwriting is almost illegible, so it is fortunate that the original journal has a transcript of the entire work appended at the end. The reader is encouraged to see page 1 of the appended transcript for a more readable version.

101. Angell, *Journal, 1851 December-1856 April*, 4.

102. Angell, *Journal, 1851 December-1856 April*, 30; see entry for April 5, 1852.

103. Jenson, *Church Chronology*, May 21, 1851; JHC, May 21, 1851.

104. JD, 1:376.

105. JD, 1:376.

106. JD, 1:376.

107. "Minutes of the General Conference of the Church of Jesus Christ of Latter Day Saints, held at the New Tabernacle, Great Salt Lake City, April 6, 1852, 10 a.m., Prest. Brigham Young, presiding," *Deseret News*, April 17, 1852.

108. "Discourse By President Young, in the afternoon of the third day of Conference, April 8, 1852," *Deseret News*, January 1, 1854.

109. J. Earl Arrington, "William Weeks, Architect of the Nauvoo Temple," 357.

110. "A Special Conference of the Elders of the Church of Jesus Christ of Latter-day Saints . . . ," *Deseret News* (Extra), September 14, 1852.

111. "A Special Conference of the Elders of the Church of Jesus Christ of Latter-day Saints . . . ," *Deseret News* (Extra), September 14, 1852.

112. Andrew Jenson, ed., "Plural Marriage," *Historical Record* 6, no. 3 (May 1887): 232–33; Bachman, "New Light on an Old Hypothesis," 22.

113. Quoted in Hales, "Encouraging Joseph Smith to Practice Plural Marriage," 58.

114. JD, 3:266.

115. "Plural Marriage in Kirtland and Nauvoo," Gospel Topics Essays, The Church of Jesus Christ of Latter-day Saints (website), https://www.lds.org/topics /plural-marriage-in-kirtland-and-nauvoo (accessed August 9, 2019).

116. "A Special Conference of the Elders of the Church of Jesus Christ of Latter-day Saints . . . ," *Deseret News* (Extra), September 14, 1852.

117. D&C 132.

118. "Minutes of the General Conference of the Church of Jesus Christ of Latter Day Saints, held in the Tabernacle, Great Salt Lake City, Commencing October 6th, 1852, 10 a.m., Prest. Brigham Young, presiding," *Deseret News*, October 16, 1852.

119. JD, 1:296.

120. JD, 1:296.

121. JD, 1:160.

122. JD, 1:162.

123. JHC, October 9, 1852.

124. JD, 1:218.

125. JD, 1:220.

CHAPTER 3: THE VISION OF IT WAS THERE

1. JD, 21:299–300; Wilford delivered this discourse on August 1, 1880.

2. D&C 28:6.

3. Brigham Young to Amasa Lyman and Charles C. Rich, October 17, 1852. Brigham Young office files, 1832–1878 (bulk 1844–1877); General Correspondence, Outgoing, 1843–1876; 1852 September–October; CHL; https:// catalog.churchofjesuschrist.org/assets?id=6185a1e6-512e-4dea-bdaa -7e705502afa7&crate=0&index=45 (accessed September 29, 2019).

4. "Who Designed the Temple?" *Deseret News*, April 23, 1892.

5. "Who Designed the Temple?" *Deseret News*, April 23, 1892.

6. Angell, *Journal, 1851 December–1856 April*, 52–53 (transcript 12–13).

7. Angell, *Journal, 1851 December–1856 April*, 52–53 (transcript 12–13).

8. Truman O. Angell, "The Temple," *Deseret News*, August 17, 1854.

9. JHC, May 1 and 2, 1852.

10. "The Temple," *Deseret News*, February 19, 1853.

11. JD, 1:277.

12. JD, 1:277.

13. JD, 1:277.

14. JD, 1:278–79.

15. JD, 1:279.

16. JD, 1:279.

17. "The Temple," *Deseret News*, February 19, 1853.

18. "The Temple," *Deseret News*, February 19, 1853.

19. WWJ, *1847 January–1853 December*, February 14, 1853.

20. "The Temple," *Deseret News*, February 19, 1853.

21. "The Temple," *Deseret News*, February 19, 1853.

22. "The Temple," *Deseret News*, February 19, 1853.

23. WWJ, *1847 January–1853 December*, February 14, 1853.

24. Franklin D. Richards from George Albert Smith, July 31, 1854; reprinted as "Description of the Temple," *Millennial Star* 26, no. 40 (October 7, 1854): 635.

25. JHC, February 21, 1853; see also Brigham Young office files, 1832–1878 (bulk 1844–1877); Journals, 1832–1877; President's Office Journals, 1852–1863; *Journal, 1853 February 11–July 12, 1855, November 8–1856 December 20* (CHL): 4 (entry for March 24, 1853), https://catalog.churchofjesuschrist.org/assets?id=be0abad5-7e4a-4546-a6b8-fe9aa528db5b&crate=0&index=9.

26. *Deseret News*, February 19, 1853; the quote is taken from a miscellaneous untitled notice on p. 2, column 5.

27. JHC, February 28, 1853. They likely didn't have to haul the dirt too far. Because the temple block was on a gradual slope, much of it was probably unloaded just a few hundred feet to the west, at the site where the Tabernacle now sits, to level the ground.

28. WWJ, *1847 January–1853 December*, February 21, 1853.

29. WWJ, *1847 January–1853 December*, February 21, 1853.

30. Angell, *Journal, 1851 December–1856 April*, 53–54 (transcript 13).

31. WWJ, *1847 January–1853 December*, February 21, 1853; see also JHC, February 21, 1853, and March 24, 1853.

32. JD, 1:279.

33. Raynor, *Everlasting Spires*, 86.

34. Brigham Young office files, 1832–1878 (bulk 1844–1877); Journals, 1832–1877; President's Office Journals, 1852–1863; *Journal, 1853 February 11–July 12, 1855 November 8–1856 December 20* (CHL): 6 (entries for March 28–29, 1853), https://catalog.churchofjesuschrist.org/assets?id=be0abad5-7e4a-4546-a6b8-fe9aa528db5b&crate=0&index=11 (accessed September 29, 2019).

35. JHC, April 2, 1853.

36. "Ninth General Epistle of the Church of Jesus Christ of Latter-Day Saints,

from Great Salt Lake Valley, to the Saints Scattered Abroad Through the Earth," *Deseret News*, April 16, 1853. The wording of the epistle is inconsistent with other examples of Brigham's own writings, suggesting he did not write it; however, it was published over his name and those of Heber C. Kimball and Willard Richards, his counselors in the First Presidency of the Church, certainly with his approval of the contents.

37. "To the Saints," *Deseret News*, April 16, 1853.
38. "To the Saints," *Deseret News*, April 16, 1853.
39. "Type of flag Utah settlers flew lost to history," *Deseret News*, June 14, 2008. The "Kingdom of God" flag's exact design is lost to history.
40. "Minutes of the General Conference," *Deseret News*, April 16, 1853.
41. "Minutes of the General Conference," *Deseret News*, April 16, 1853.
42. "Minutes of the General Conference," *Deseret News*, April 16, 1853.
43. "Minutes of the General Conference," *Deseret News*, April 16, 1853.
44. "Minutes of the General Conference," *Deseret News*, April 16, 1853.
45. "Minutes of the General Conference," *Deseret News*, April 16, 1853.
46. Snow, *Eliza R. Snow: The Complete Poetry*, 230.
47. "Minutes of the General Conference." *Deseret News*, April 16, 1853.
48. "Minutes of the General Conference." *Deseret News*, April 16, 1853.
49. "Minutes of the General Conference." *Deseret News*, April 16, 1853.
50. "Minutes of the General Conference." *Deseret News*, April 16, 1853.
51. "Minutes of the General Conference." *Deseret News*, April 16, 1853.
52. LDS Church History website, "Early Mormon Missionaries" at https://history .lds.org/missionary/individual/ george-b-wallace-1817; also LDS Church History website, "Mormon Pioneer Overland Travel," "Abraham O. Smoot - George B. Wallace Company (1847)" at https://history.lds.org/overlandtravel /companies/276/abraham-o-smoot-george-b-wallace-company-1847.
53. "Minutes of the General Conference." *Deseret News*, April 16, 1853.
54. "Minutes of the General Conference." *Deseret News*, April 16, 1853.
55. Pratt, *Autobiography of Parley P. Pratt*, 37–38.
56. Pratt, *Autobiography of Parley P. Pratt*, 37–38.
57. Isaiah 8:19; Pratt was actually quoting from the Book of Mormon, 2 Nephi 18:19, which is a direct quotation of the aforementioned verse from the Bible.
58. "Minutes of the General Conference," *Deseret News*, April 16, 1853.
59. "Minutes of the General Conference," *Deseret News*, April 16, 1853.
60. "Minutes of the General Conference," *Deseret News*, April 16, 1853.
61. "Minutes of the General Conference," *Deseret News*, April 16, 1853.
62. "Minutes of the General Conference," *Deseret News*, April 16, 1853.
63. "General Conference in G.S.L. City," *Millennial Star* 15, no. 30 (July 23, 1853): 486.

64. JD, 1:132.

65. JD, 1:132.

66. JD, 1:133.

67. JD, 1:133.

CHAPTER 4: THE WORKS OF THE ANCIENTS

1. "Mails," *Deseret News*, June 18, 1853.

2. HOTC, *1853 January –December 30*, June 2, 1853.

3. Historical Department office journal, 1844–2012; Volume 16, 1853 January 17–1854 April 12; see entry for June 12, 1853. CHL; https://catalog .churchofjesuschrist.org/assets?id=4666c251-bb52-434d-9819-6333a8a c86a4&crate=0&index=95 (accessed September 30, 2019).

4. Historical Department office journal, 1844–2012; Volume 16, 1853 January 17–1854 April 12; see entry for June 11, 1853.

5. Talmage, *House of the Lord*, 139–40.

6. "Ninth General Epistle of the Church of Jesus Christ of Latter-Day Saints, from Great Salt Lake Valley, to the Saints Scattered Abroad Through the Earth," *Deseret News*, April 16, 1853.

7. JD, 1:106.

8. JD, 1:106.

9. "Proclamation by the Governor," *Deseret News*, April 30, 1853.

10. Brigham Young to William Wall, April 25, 1853; https://catalog.churchofjesus christ.org/ assets?id=432cd6c0-be3d-49c3-aefc-d13c1910c9ac&crate=0 &index=0 (accessed September 29, 2019).

11. "Proclamation by the Governor," *Deseret News*, April 30, 1853.

12. "History, 1838–1856, volume D-1 [1 August 1842–1 July 1843]," JSP website, https://www.josephsmithpapers.org/paper-summary/history-1838-1856 -volume-d-1-1-august-1842-1-july-1843/140 (accessed November 22, 2018).

13. JD, 1:106.

14. Historical Department office journal, 1844–2012; Volume 16, 1853 January 17–1854 April 12; see entry for July 19, 1853.

15. Brigham Young, "An account of the massacre of Captain J. W. Gunnison and Seven of his part on the Sevier River on the 26th of October 1853," Brigham Young office files: Governor's Office Files, 1850–1867, Executive Files, 1850–1858, *Governor's letterbook, 1853 October 31–1858 June 16*, 22–29, CHL.

16. Livingston, *Short Extracts*, 1.

17. Livingston, *Short Extracts*, 1.

18. Brigham Young Office Emigrating Companies Reports, 1850–1862; Reports, 1853–1855; Appleton M. Harmon Company report, 1853, CR 1234 5, CHL;

https://catalog.lds.org/assets/82d17689-8958-421a-b2f3-f97e6adf59cf/0/5 (accessed September 14, 2019).

19. Watt, "Dry Goods and Groceries," 64–69.

20. See Bennett, *Temples Rising* , 149, 166, for a more extended discussion of Brigham's decision to build another facility to attend to temple ordinances.

21. Raleigh, *Alonzo H. Raleigh journal*, 79.

22. Angell, *Journal, 1851 December–1856 April*, 74 (transcript 18).

23. Angell, *Journal, 1851 December–1856 April*, 74–75 (transcript 18).

24. "The Temple," *Deseret News,* August 17, 1854.

25. "The Temple," *Deseret News,* August 17, 1854.

26. "The Temple," *Deseret News,* August 17, 1854.

27. Angell, *Journal, 1851 December–1856 April*, 89–90 (transcript 22).

28. Angell, *Journal, 1851 December–1856 April*, 102 (transcript 25).

29. HOTC, August 21, 1855.

30. Angell, *Journal, 1851 December–1856 April*, 105 (transcript 25).

31. Historian's Office general Church minutes, 1839–1877; 1851–1855; Salt Lake City, Endowment House, May 5, 1855; CHL; https://catalog.churchofjesus christ.org/assets?id=93fd0820-a0b1-4c10-91ea-dad5b0e52a13&crate=0 &index=0 (accessed September 30, 2019).

32. Leonard Arrington, *Great Basin Kingdom,* 148–52.

33. George A. Smith, *Rise, Progress and Travels,* 17.

34. "Remarks by President Brigham Young, Tabernacle, p.m. of March 16, 1856," *Deseret News,* March 26, 1856.

35. "Canal and Land Notice," *Deseret News,* February 1, 1855.

36. Brigham Young office files, Journals, 1832–1877, President's Office Journals, 1852–1863, *Journal, 1853 February 11–July 12, 1855 November 8–1856 December 20,* CHL; 163. Also HOTC, *1856 January 4-December 31,* April 1, 1856.

37. Angell, *Journal, 1856 April–1857 May,* Introduction.

38. Angell, *Journal, 1856 April–1857 May,* Introduction.

39. Angell, *Journal, 1856 April–1857 May,* April 11, 1856.

40. Angell, *Journal, 1856 April–1857 May,* Introduction.

41. Truman Angell to Brigham Young, April 20, 1856. Brigham Young office files, 1832–1878 (bulk 1844–1877); General Correspondence, Incoming, 1840–1877; General Letters, 1840–1877, Ad-An, 1856. Truman O. Angell letter (4 of 4), CHL.

42. Angell, *Journal, 1856 April–1857 May,* April 22, 1856.

43. Angell, *Journal, 1856 April–1857 May,* May 3–8, 1856.

44. Angell, *Journal, 1856 April–1857 May,* July 2, 1856.

45. Angell, *Journal, 1856 April–1857 May,* July 13, 1856.

46. Angell, *Journal, 1856 April–1857 May,* July 23, 1856.

47. Angell, *Journal, 1856 April–1857 May*, July 25–26, 1856.

48. Angell, *Journal, 1856 April–1857 May*, August 12, 1856.

49. Angell, *Journal, 1856 April–1857 May*, August 12, 1856.

50. Angell, *Journal, 1856 April–1857 May*, August 16, 1856.

51. The Crystal Palace was destroyed by fire in 1931.

52. Angell, *Journal, 1856 April–1857 May*, August 22, 1856.

53. Angell, *Journal, 1856 April–1857 May*, August 22, 1856.

54. Angell, *Journal, 1856 April–1857 May*, August 25–27, 1856.

55. Angell, *Journal, 1856 April–1857 May*, August 22, 1856.

56. Angell, *Journal, 1856 April–1857 May*, October 13, 1856

57. Truman Angell to Brigham Young, Oct 23, 1856. Brigham Young office files, 1832–1878 (bulk 1844–1877); General Correspondence, Incoming, 1840–1877; General Letters, 1840–1877, Ad-An, 1856. Truman O. Angell letter (2 of 4), CHL.

58. Angell, *Journal, 1856 April–1857 May*, November 3, 1856.

59. Angell, *Journal, 1856 April–1857 May*, November 4, 1856.

60. Angell, *Journal, 1856 April–1857 May*, November 4, 1856.

61. Angell, *Journal, 1856 April–1857 May*, November 19, 1856.

62. Angell, *Journal, 1856 April–1857 May*, November 21, 1856.

63. Angell, *Journal, 1856 April–1857 May*, November 15, 1856.

64. Angell, *Journal, 1856 April–1857 May*, November 29, 1856.

65. Angell, *Journal, 1856 April–1857 May*, December 1, 1856. There is no "Oxgud Castle" on the island of Jersey. Truman may have been referring to the Mont Orgueil castle, as he recorded the locals' contention that the construction of the castle in question "commenced in the year 1120 (so they say)." Of the three castles and many forts on the island, only Mont Orgueil's construction can be established as having started within a century of that year, around 1200 CE.

66. Angell, *Journal, 1856 April–1857 May*, December 1, 1856.

67. Angell, *Journal, 1856 April–1857 May*, December 6, 1856.

68. Angell, *Journal, 1856 April–1857 May*, January 31, 1857.

69. Angell, *Journal, 1856 April–1857 May*, January 27, 1857.

70. Brigham Young to Orson Pratt, October 30, 1856. Brigham Young office files, General Correspondence, Outgoing, 1843–1876, 1856 October, CHL; https://catalog.churchofjesuschrist.org/assets?id=709d6710-d058-455d-b8b8 -1160f21b24bd&crate=0&index=69 (accessed September 19, 2019).

71. Angell, *Journal, 1856 April–1857 May*, February 12–13, 1857.

72. Angell, *Journal, 1856 April–1857 May*, February 12–13, 1857.

73. Angell, *Journal, 1856 April–1857 May*, May 29, 1857.

74. Angell, *Journal, 1856 April–1857 May*, May 29, 1857.

75. "Big Cottonwood Canal," *Deseret News,* March 25, 1857.

76. JD, 4:309.

77. HOTC, *1857 January 1–December 31,* March 9, 1857.

78. JD, 4:309.

79. HOTC, *1857 January 1–December 31,* June 18, 1857.

80. HOTC, *1857 January 1–December 31,* June 18, 1857.

81. "Fourteenth General Epistle of the First Presidency," *Millennial Star* 19, no. 16 (April 18, 1857): 246.

82. HOTC, *1857 January 1–December 31,* July 27, 1857. The official count was 2,587 persons arriving in 464 wagons and carriages drawn by 1,028 horses and mules. They also brought 332 oxen and cows.

83. Spencer and Harmer, *Brigham Young at Home*, 88.

84. WWJ, *1854 January–1859 December,* July 24, 1857.

85. Spencer and Harmer, *Brigham Young at Home*, 89.

86. Spencer and Harmer, *Brigham Young at Home*, 88.

87. Spencer and Harmer, *Brigham Young at Home*, 89.

88. WWJ, *1854 January–1859 December,* July 24, 1857.

89. JD, 5:226.

90. Spencer and Harmer, *Brigham Young at Home*, 90.

CHAPTER 5: TRUST IN GOD AND KEEP YOUR POWDER DRY

1. President James Buchanan, *First Annual Message to Congress on the State of the Union,* December 8, 1857, https://www.presidency.ucsb.edu/node/202407 (accessed September 8, 2019).

2. Klein, *President James Buchanan*, 254.

3. Brooks was arrested, tried and convicted of assault, and a fine of $300 was imposed. He resigned his office to let his constituents hold a special election as a referendum on his action. He was reelected, and admirers throughout the South gifted him hundreds of canes. Sumner was unable to resume his senate duties for three years, and he suffered crippling pain for the rest of his life.

   For his part in the attack, Keitt was censured by the House of Representatives, and he resigned in protest. Like Brooks, he was promptly reelected. Also like Brooks, he assaulted a fellow member of Congress two years later when Pennsylvania Representative Galusha Grow would insult him as a "negro driver." The House's motion to censure Edmundson failed to pass.

4. William M. F. Magraw to James Buchanan, October 3, 1856; included in House of Representatives No. 35—Exec. Doc. 71, 2–3.

5. Magraw to Buchanan, October 3, 1856.

6. "The Modern Sodom," *Daily National Intelligencer,* April 21, 1857.

7. William W. Drummond to Jeremiah S. Black, March 30, 1857; included in House of Representatives No. 35—Exec. Doc. 71, 212–14.

8. Drummond to Black, March 30, 1857.

9. Douglas, "Remarks of the Honorable Stephen A. Douglas on Kansas, Utah, and the Dred Scott Decision," June 12, 1857.

10. Auchampaugh, *Robert Tyler, Southern Rights Champion*, 180–81.

11. US Army, General Orders #12, June 30, 1857, Brigham Young office files 1832–1878 (bulk 1844–1877), Federal and Local Government Files 1844–1876, CR 1234 1, CHL.

12. Gen. Winfield Scott to the Adjutant General, Quartermaster General, Commissary General, Surgeon General, Paymaster General, and Chief of Ordnance, May 28, 1857; included in House of Representatives No. 35—Exec. Doc. 71, 4–5.

13. John B. Floyd to James Buchanan, August 5, 1858, in MacKinnon, *At Sword's Point*, 151–52. The original letter is deposited in the James Buchanan Papers, Historical Society of Pennsylvania, Philadelphia.

14. U.S. War Department, *Official Correspondence of Brig. General W. S. Harney*, 5.

15. Reavis, *Life and Military Services of General William Selby Harney*, 276–79.

16. James Buchanan to Robert J. Walker, July 12, 1857; included in House of Representatives No. 36–648, 112–13.

17. In MacKinnon, *At Sword's Point*, 183–84. The original letter is deposited in the Records of Adjutant General's Office, Letters Received (RG 94), National Archives.

18. In MacKinnon, *At Sword's Point*, 183–84.

19. US War Department, General Orders No. 12, August 29, 1857. A copy is located at Brigham Young office files, 1832–1878 (bulk 1844–1877); Federal and Local Government Files, 1844–1876; *United States Army, general orders, No. 12, 1857 June 30*; CHL; https://catalog.churchofjesuschrist.org/assets?id=ac9fd8f6 -8e29-4b22-9819-bfbb19a6805c&crate=0&index=0 (accessed October 1, 2019).

20. Col. Robert E. Lee to Col. Albert Sidney Johnston, August 1, 1857, in Roland, *Albert Sidney Johnston*, 185. The original letter is located in the Albert Sidney and William Preston Johnston papers, Manuscripts Collection 1, Louisiana Research Collection, Howard-Tilton Memorial Library, Tulane University, New Orleans.

21. Lt. Col. George W. Lay to Gen. William S. Harney, June 29, 1857; included in House of Representatives No. 35—Exec. Doc. 71, 7–9.

22. Lay to Harney, June 29, 1857.

23. Lay to Harney, June 29, 1857.

24. HOTC, *1858 January 1–December 31*, April 13, 1858.

25. HOTC, *1858 January 1–December 31,* April 13, 1858.

26. HOTC, *1858 January 1–December 31,* April 12, 1858.

27. JD, 5:232.

28. Young, *Proclamation by the Governor.*

29. Young, *Proclamation by the Governor.*

30. Young, *Proclamation by the Governor.*

31. Exodus 14:13.

32. D&C 124:55–60.

33. Lewis Bidamon, second husband of Joseph's widow Emma, opened the Nauvoo House cornerstone in 1882, a few years after Emma's death. He found that some three-quarters of the original Book of Mormon manuscript had been destroyed by water damage and mold. The Church of Jesus Christ of Latter-day Saints now owns virtually all that remains of the original manuscript, minus some minor fragments in private hands. The Church History Department is planning to publish a typographical facsimile of the extant pages with accompanying transcriptions as volume 5 in the Revelations and Translations series of the Joseph Smith Papers.

34. WWJ, *1854 January–1859 December,* August 13, 1857.

35. WWJ, *1854 January–1859 December,* August 13, 1857.

36. WWJ, *1854 January–1859 December,* August 13, 1857. An unknown person recorded the list of works included in the records stone in Wilford's journal and clearly did so with his knowledge, as the list is included neatly between Wilford's journal entries for August 13 and 14. Also, the list is written in a neat and elegant English roundhand style, confirming another author, and not in Wilford's own crude block printing, which resumes in the next entry.

37. WWJ, *1854 January–1859 December,* August 13, 1857. Regrettably, Brigham's prayer was not answered as he had hoped. The stone's exact location was lost to history until 1993, the centennial anniversary of the temple's dedication. In a bid to find the stone before the celebration, the Church Historical Department directed construction workers to excavate around the area and perform test drillings. Once the stone was identified, a larger hole in the stone was opened and the contents were extracted. Unfortunately, tiny fractures in the stone box had allowed moisture to enter, which had destroyed most of the paper contents over the 136 years they remained inside. Church historians could identify only about half of the items listed in the original inventory from the fragments recovered. See "Salt Lake Temple site held 1847 artifacts," *Deseret News,* August 21, 2009: https://www.deseretnews.com /article/700082424/Salt-Lake-Temple-site-held-1847-artifacts.html (accessed August 12, 2019). The headline is erroneous, but the article is correct—the site held artifacts from 1857, not 1847.

38. JHC, March 21, May 19, August 7, and December 31, 1857; February 23, 1858; March 22, 1860.

39. James Cummings and R.J. Burton to Daniel H. Wells, August 31, 1857, Brigham Young office files 1832–1878 (bulk 1844–1877), Federal and Local Government Files 1844–1876, Young's Correspondence with Nauvoo Legion Regarding U.S. Expedition Against Utah, 1857 July–September, CHL; https://catalog.churchofjesuschrist.org/assets?id=bb27574a-9890-41bb-9748 -bbab9465725a&crate=0&index=10 (accessed September 19, 2019). Van Vliet did not know that Colonel Johnston had replaced General Harney as the Utah Expedition commanding officer just two days before.

40. HOTC, *1857 January 1–December 31*, September 8, 1857.

41. "Obituary of Gen. Stewart Van Vliet," *New York Times*, March 29, 1901.

42. Capt. Stewart Van Vliet to Capt. Alfred Pleasanton, September 16, 1857; included in House of Representatives No. 35—Exec. Doc. 71, 24–26.

43. WWJ, *1854 January–1859 December*, September 9, 1857.

44. Gen. William S. Harney to Brigham Young, July 28, 1857. Brigham Young office files 1832–1878 (bulk 1844–1877), Federal and Local Government Files 1844–1876, CR 1234 1, Governor Young's Correspondence with Nauvoo Legion Regarding U.S. Expedition Against Utah, 1857, July–September, CHL.

45. Minutes of an interview between the First Presidency, Twelve Apostles, and Captain Van Vliet, Asst. Quarter Master & Commissary, U.S. Army, September 9, 1857. Historian's Office collected historical documents, circa 1851–1869; *Minutes of an interview, Great Salt Lake City, 1857* September 9; CHL; https://catalog.churchofjesuschrist.org/assets? id=4a97b6b6-b966 -4510-9b7e-229b57d2c3d0&crate=0&index=0 (accessed October 1, 2019).

46. Van Vliet to Pleasanton, September 16, 1857.

47. Van Vliet to Pleasanton, September 16, 1857.

48. Col. Edmund B. Alexander to Col. Samuel Cooper, October 9, 1857; included in House of Representatives No. 35—Exec. Doc. 71, 30–32.

49. Van Vliet to Pleasanton, September 16, 1857.

50. Spencer and Harmer, *Brigham Young at Home*, 93.

51. Van Vliet to Pleasanton, September 16, 1857.

52. Alexander to Cooper, October 9, 1857.

53. Report of Gen. William S. Harney, August 8, 1857; included in House of Representatives No. 35—Exec. Doc. 71, 17.

54. *Church History in the Fulness of Times*, 373–74.

55. Capt. H. F. Clarke to Maj. Fitz John Porter, November 4, 1857; included in House of Representatives No. 35—Exec. Doc. 71, 63.

56. Col. E. B. Alexander to the officers of the United States Army commanding

forces en route to Utah, October 8, 1857, included in House of Representatives No. 35—Exec. Doc. 71, 38–40.

57. Col. A. S. Johnston to Maj. Irvin McDowell, October 13, 1857; included in House of Representatives No. 35—Exec. Doc. 71, 29–30.

58. Col. A. S. Johnston to Maj. Irvin McDowell, October 18, 1857; included in House of Representatives No. 35—Exec. Doc. 71, 35–38.

59. Johnston to McDowell, October 18, 1857.

60. Col. A. S. Johnston to Maj. Irvin McDowell, November 30, 1857; included in House of Representatives No. 35—Exec. Doc. 71, 77–79.

61. Gove, *Utah Expedition, 1857–1858*, 92.

62. Johnston to McDowell, November 30, 1857.

63. Johnston to McDowell, November 30, 1857.

64. Tullidge, *History of Salt Lake City*, 197–99.

65. HOTC, December 2, 1857.

66. President James Buchanan, *First Annual Message to Congress on the State of the Union*, December 8, 1857, https://www.presidency.ucsb.edu/node/202407 (accessed September 8, 2019).

67. For an in-depth study of Kane's life and his contribution to a peaceful resolution of the Utah Expedition, see Grow, *Liberty for the Downtrodden*.

68. MacKinnon, "'Full of Courage:' Thomas L. Kane," 105.

69. HOTC, February 25, 1858.

70. WWJ, *1854 January–1859 December*, February 25 and 27, 1858. Kane met privately with Brigham for about a half hour the evening of the twenty-fifth, then talked with Wilford on the twenty-seventh about what they'd discussed.

71. Brigham Young to Elder W. I. Appleby, 6 Jan. 1858. Brigham Young office files: Letterbooks, 1844–1877, *Letterbook, v. 3, 1856 August 20–1858*, 944–47, CHL.

72. HOTC, March 21, 1858.

73. HOTC, March 23, 1858.

74. HOTC, March 25, 1858.

75. Tullidge, *History of Salt Lake City*, 205.

76. Lewis Cass to James Buchanan, February 3, 1858; included in House of Representatives No. 35—Exec. Doc. 71, 1–2.

77. Cass to Buchanan, February 3, 1858.

78. *Congressional Globe*, 35th Congress, 1st Session, 1431–32 (1858).

79. James Buchanan, "Proclamation—Rebellion in the Territory of Utah," April 6, 1858. Available online at The American Presidency Project, https://www.presidency.ucsb.edu/node/202635 (accessed September 14, 2019).

80. Tullidge, *History of Salt Lake City*, 206–7.

81. Tullidge, *History of Salt Lake City*, 208.

82. Tullidge, *History of Salt Lake City*, 212.

83. Brigham Young to John M. Bernhisel, May 6, 1858. Brigham Young office files: Letterbooks, 1844–1877, *Letterbook, v. 4, 1858 January 2–1858 November 22*, 148, CHL.

84. Young to Bernhisel, May 6, 1858.

85. HOTC, May 17, 1858.

86. HOTC, June 10, 1858.

87. Young to Bernhisel, May 6, 1858.

88. Tullidge, *History of Salt Lake City*, 217.

89. HOTC, June 12, 1858.

90. HOTC, June 12, 1858.

91. "Cessation of Difficulties in Utah," House of Representatives No. 35—Exec. Doc. 138, 1.

92. Tullidge, *History of Salt Lake City*, 223–24.

93. *Atlantic Monthly*, vol. 3, no. 18, 490.

94. Merrill, *Spurs to Glory*, 102.

95. HOTC, June 26, 1858.

96. Merrill, *Spurs to Glory*, 102.

97. *Atlantic Monthly* vol. 3, no. 18, 490.

98. HOTC, June 30, 1858.

99. HOTC, July 1, 1858.

CHAPTER 6: THIS IS MY REVELATION

1. HOTC, March 8, 1859.

2. HOTC, March 22, 1859.

3. HOTC, March 8, 1859.

4. HOTC, March 26, 1859.

5. Brigham Young to John M. Bernhisel, May 6, 1858. Brigham Young office files: Letterbooks, 1844–1877, *Letterbook, v. 4, 1858 January 2–1858 November 22*, 143–48, CHL.

6. WWJ, *1854 January–1859 December*, December 7, 1859.

7. WWJ, *1854 January–1859 December*, December 7, 1859.

8. HOTC, May 26, 1860.

9. Raynor, *Everlasting Spires*, 69.

10. Livingston, *Short Extracts*, 1.

11. Roland, *Albert Sidney Johnston*, 219–20.

12. "Report of the Secretary of War," *Deseret News*, January 25, 1860.

13. McPherson, *Battle Cry of Freedom*, 1:214–21.

14. HOTC, May 1, 1860; see also WWJ, *1860 January–1865 October*, May 1, 1861.

15. L. P. Walker to Gen. P. G. T. Beauregard, April 10, 1861, OR 1, 1:297.

16. Godfrey et al., eds. *Documents, Volume 2: July 1831–January 1833*, 328–31; see also D&C 81:1–4.

17. Godfrey et al., eds. *Documents, Volume 2: July 1831–January 1833*, 355; see 344–55 for a more detailed recitation.

18. Godfrey et al., eds. *Documents, Volume 2: July 1831–January 1833*, 345; see also D&C 88:119.

19. Foote, *Civil War: A Narrative*, 49–50.

20. WWJ, *1860 January–1865 October*, April 21, 1861.

21. JD, 10:38–39.

22. Brigham Young office files: *Journals, 1832–1877,* President's Office Journals, 1852–1863, *Journal, 1863 June 18–September 30, 1858 August 8–1862 May 19*, 272, CHL. See entry for July 9, 1861.

23. Julia Dent Grant, *Personal Memoirs,* 150.

24. Leonard J. Arrington, *Great Basin Kingdom,* 198–99.

25. William Clayton to George Q. Cannon, July 16, 1861, published in *Millennial Star*, vol. 23, no. 35, 566.

26. George Q. Cannon, "Passing Thoughts," *Woman's Exponent* (15 April and 1 May 1893): 157.

27. HOTC, December 18, 1861.

28. Truman O. Angell to Brigham Young, September 20, 1858. Brigham Young office files, 1832–1878 (bulk 1844–1877); General Correspondence, Incoming, 1840–1877; General Letters, 1840–1877; A, 1858; CHL. https://catalog.churchofjesuschrist.org/assets?id=530ed7f4-22f9-42f0-a7e8-8c655e931674&crate=0&index=0 (accessed September 15, 2019).

29. Truman O. Angell to Brigham Young, January 2, 1860. Brigham Young office files, 1832–1878 (bulk 1844–1877); General Correspondence, Incoming, 1840–1877; General Letters, 1840–1877; A-Bi, 1860; CHL. https://catalog.churchofjesuschrist.org/assets?id=f6d74a3f-8d1a-49d3-bc34-5d1b2dcf7d9d&crate=0&index=0 (accessed September 15, 2019).

30. Anderson, "William Harrison Folsom," 241–44.

31. Anderson, "William Harrison Folsom," 241–44.

32. Anderson, "William Harrison Folsom," 241–44.

33. Bowles, *Across the Continent*, 103.

34. "Semi-Annual Conference," *Deseret News,* October 23, 1861.

35. Raleigh, *Alonzo H. Raleigh diary*, 1–2. See entry for February 22, 1861.

36. Raleigh, *Alonzo H. Raleigh diary*, 1–2. See entry for February 22, 1861.

37. William H. Folsom to Brigham Young, June 2, 1862. Brigham Young office files, 1832–1878 (bulk 1844–1877); General Correspondence, Incoming, 1840–1877; General Letters, 1840–1877; Ev-Ga, 1862; William H. Folsom letter; CHL; https://catalog.lds.org/assets/e58d63dc-7a46-4df8-8236

-e3ddd733b3aa/0/0 (accessed September 15, 2019). A "spall" is a small, flat rock, almost certainly the stone shims that were inserted in the defective foundation in an attempt to level the ashlars.

38. Daniel H. Wells to Brigham Young, May 29, 1862. Brigham Young office files, 1832–1878 (bulk 1844–1877); General Correspondence, Incoming, 1840–1877; Letters from Church Leaders and Others, 1840–1877; Daniel H. Wells, 1861–1862; Daniel H. Wells letter; CHL; https://catalog.lds.org /assets/96b22306-9529-4173-8f35-5957530ecf16/0/0.

39. Truman O. Angell to Brigham Young, May 29, 1862. Brigham Young office files, 1832–1878 (bulk 1844–1877); General Correspondence, Incoming, 1840–1877; General Letters, 1840–1877; A-Bo, 1862; Truman O. Angell letter; CHL; https://catalog.lds.org/assets/ad86d8f7-25b8-46b9-b7f2 -43f7fc3cf09a/0/0.

40. Hughes, *Life of Archibald Gardner*, 133–34.

41. WWJ, *1860 January–1865 October*, June 1, 1862. See also Gibbons, *Wilford Woodruff*, 249.

42. JD, 10:254.

43. JD, 10:254.

44. JD, 10:254.

45. Brigham Young to Daniel H. Wells, June 4, 1864. Brigham Young office files: *Letterbooks, 1844–1877, Letterbook, v. 6, 1861 November 2–1864 April 1*. CHL; https://catalog.churchofjesuschrist.org/assets?id=0c8e23c5-4d6a-446f-8d81 -108a52bd39c4&crate=0&index=297 (accessed: September 15, 2019).

46. JHC, June 6, 1862.

47. WWJ, *1860 January–1865 October*, June 10, 1862.

48. WWJ, *1860 January–1865 October*, December 31, 1862.

49. Gen. P. G. T. Beauregard to Army of the Mississippi, April 10, 1862, OR, 1:10, part 2: 408–9.

50. Freeman, *R. E. Lee: A Biography*, 2:462.

51. Pease and Randall, eds., *Diary of Orville Hickman Browning*, 1:600.

52. "The Completion of the Telegraph," *Deseret News*, October 23, 1861.

53. JD, 10:295.

54. P. Edw. Connor to Maj. O. C. Drum, October 20, 1862, OR 1:50, part 2: 119.

55. Connor to Drum, February 19, 1863, OR 1:50, part 2:319–20.

56. Connor to Drum, October 20, 1862, OR 1: 50, part 2:119.

57. *Congressional Globe*, April 9, 1862, 1581.

58. Atherton, "Legislative Career of Justin S. Morrill," speech, November 14, 1900.

59. Greeley, *Proceedings of the First Three National Republican Conventions*, 43.

60. House of Representatives 391, 37th Cong. (1862).

61. The statement "if [they] will leave me alone" appears to originate in a letter from T.B.H. Stenhouse to Brigham dated June 7, 1863; see Brigham Young office files, 1832–1878 (bulk 1844–1877); General Correspondence, Incoming, 1840–1877; General Letters, 1840–1877; St, 1863; Thomas B. H. Stenhouse letter; CHL; https://catalog.churchofjesuschrist.org/assets?id=7dc3acd0-c720 -4aa2-83f2-1826b038a413&crate=0&index=0 (accessed September 14, 2019). Brigham recounted the story in his own words as follows during a sermon in June 1864: "This reminds me of what I was told the President of the United States said to a gentleman who is a preacher and a member of Congress. He took our President to task for not destroying both 'the twins' together, that is, polygamy as well as slavery. After he had laid the whole matter before the President in an elaborate manner, showing him the necessity of destroying this people who believed in polygamy, the President said, 'It makes me think of a little circumstance that happened with me in my younger days. I was ploughing a piece of newly cleared land, and by and by I came to a big log; I could not plow over it, for it was too high, and it was so heavy I could not move it out of the way, and was so wet I could not burn it; I stood and looked at it and studied it, and finally concluded to plow around it.' It looks as though they were trying to plow around Mormonism" ("Remarks," *Deseret News*, June 22, 1864).

62. WWJ, *1860 January–1865 October*, May 20, 1863.

CHAPTER 7: MAKE THE EVERLASTING HILLS TO TREMBLE BEFORE THEM

1. Livingston, *Short Extracts*, 2.
2. Kuhre, *Recollections of temple quarry*, 2.
3. Raynor, *Everlasting Spires*, 70–74.
4. Livingston, *Short Extracts*, 2.
5. Livingston, *Short Extracts*, 3.
6. Livingston, *Short Extracts*, 3.
7. Livingston, *Short Extracts*, 3.
8. Livingston, *Short Extracts*, 3.
9. P. Edw. Connor to Maj. O. C. Drum, March 15, 1863, OR 1:50, part 2:370.
10. Connor to Drum, March 15, 1863.
11. D&C 87:5.
12. McPherson, *Battle Cry of Freedom*, 2:665.
13. JD, 9:239–40.
14. Raynor, *Everlasting Spires*, 88.
15. Kuhre, *Recollections of temple quarry*, 2–3.
16. Kuhre, *Recollections of temple quarry*, 6.

17. "A Trip to the Quarry in Little Cottonwood Canyon," *Deseret Evening News*, July 2, 1877.

18. Raynor, *Everlasting Spires*, 72.

19. Kuhre, *Recollections of temple quarry*, 2–5.

20. Raynor, *Everlasting Spires*, 73.

21. Raynor, *Everlasting Spires*, 75.

22. Raynor, *Everlasting Spires*, 73; see also "Church Quarry," *Deseret Evening News*, June 9, 1876.

23. Kuhre, *Recollections of temple quarry*, 6.

24. Raynor, *Everlasting Spires*, 73–74.

25. Raynor, *Everlasting Spires*, 72.

26. Raynor, *Everlasting Spires*, 72.

27. "A Disastrous Snow Slide," *Deseret News*, April 6, 1864.

28. Kuhre, *Recollections of temple quarry*, 3.

29. Raynor, *Everlasting Spires*, 76.

30. Raynor, *Everlasting Spires*, 76–80.

31. Kuhre, *Recollections of temple quarry*, 5.

32. Raynor, *Everlasting Spires*, 79.

33. Kuhre, *Recollections of temple quarry*, 5–6.

34. "A Trip to the Quarry in Little Cottonwood Canyon," *Deseret Evening News*, July 2, 1877.

35. Raynor, *Everlasting Spires*, 79.

36. Raynor, *Everlasting Spires*, 79–81.

37. Raynor, *Everlasting Spires*, 88.

38. "A Trip to the Quarry in Little Cottonwood Canyon," *Deseret Evening News*, July 2, 1877.

39. Sharp, "Temple Recollections," 199, 228. The "staple" is a metal band placed around the yoke between the two bows that rest on the oxen's necks. A metal ring connected to the staple hangs under the yoke, to which a rope, pole, chain, or other connector ties the yoke to the next yoke on the pair of oxen behind or to the wagon. So when Joseph Sharp's oxen "went right through their ox staples as if they were matches," they snapped the metal band connecting their yoke to the wagon and ran ahead, leaving the wagon and its load behind.

40. Sharp, "Temple Recollections," 228–29.

41. Raynor, *Everlasting Spires*, 88.

42. Raynor, *Everlasting Spires*, 88.

43. Raynor, *Everlssting Spires*, 88.

44. Robinson and Dixon, "Design and Construction," 143.

45. Spencer and Harmer, *Brigham Young at Home*, 281–82.

46. Dr. Jacob Wayne Olmstead (Curator of Historic Sites, Church History

Department), in discussion with the author, April 2019. It has been commonly claimed that the Tabernacle was constructed without any nails or other metal fasteners. That claim was disproven conclusively in 2006 when engineers recovered numerous original nails from the superstructure during a seismic upgrade of the building.

47. For a detailed review of the Tabernacle's construction using the most recent documentation available, see Robison, *Gathering as One*.

48. Chesnut, *Diary from Dixie*, 327.

49. Lt. Gen. Ulysses S. Grant to Maj. Gen. Henry W. Halleck, July 14, 1864, OR series 1, vol. 40, part 3:223.

50. Sheridan to Grant, OR series 1, vol. 43, part 1:30–31.

51. *Millennial Star* 25, no. 30 (July 25, 1863): 476.

52. Brigham Young to John Sharp, August 15, 1864. Brigham Young office files: General Correspondence, Outgoing, 1843–1876, 1864. CHL; https://catalog .churchofjesuschrist.org/assets?id=f7501284-69cd-4218-a68f-e6eea1e0fad0 &crate=0&index=15 (accessed September 15, 2019).

53. Jenson, *Church Chronology*, 72.

54. Bancroft, *History of Utah, 1540–1886*, 624.

55. "Home Items," *Deseret News*, March 8, 1865.

56. Bancroft, *History of Utah, 1540–1886*, 625.

57. Stanton to Dix, OR series 1, vol. 46, part 3:683.

58. "Assassination of President Lincoln," *Deseret News*, April 19, 1865.

59. "Home Items," *Deseret News*, April 19, 1865.

60. Tullidge, *History of Salt Lake City*, 337.

61. Bowles, *Across the Continent*, 83.

62. Bowles, *Across the Continent*, 84.

63. Bowles, *Across the Continent*, 102–3.

64. Bowles, *Across the Continent*, 86.

65. Bowles, *Across the Continent*, 110–11.

66. Bowles, *Across the Continent*, 112–13.

67. Bowles, *Across the Continent*, 107.

68. *Millennial Star* 25, no. 30 (July 25, 1863): 476.

69. Raynor, *Everlasting Spires*, 125–26.

70. This is based on the author's personal experience; the readers' experience may vary.

71. Raynor, *Everlasting Spires*, 121.

72. Grow, "One Masterpiece, Four Masters," 180.

73. Angell, *Journal, 1867 April–1868 April*, 18–19.

74. Angell, *Journal, 1867 April–1868 April*, 18–19.

75. Angell, *Journal, 1867 April–1868 April*, 19–20.

76. Truman O. Angell to Brigham Young, March 31, 1867. Brigham Young office files, 1832–1878 (bulk 1844–1877); General Correspondence, Incoming, 1840–1877; General Letters, 18401877; A-Bi, 1867; Truman O. Angell letter, March 31, 1867; CHL; https://catalog.churchofjesuschrist.org/assets ?id=9f4e314c-8524-4dbb-8726-633d9fa5ce56&crate=0&index=0 (accessed September 15, 2019).

CHAPTER 8: THE WHISTLE AND THE PUFFING OF THE IRON HORSE

1. McPherson, *Battle Cry of Freedom*, 1:12.
2. "The Completion of the Telegraph," *Deseret News*, October 23, 1861.
3. US Department of the Interior, *Guidebook of the Western United States*, 1n.
4. McPherson, *Battle Cry of Freedom*, 1:12.
5. Pacific Railroad Act of 1862 (12 Stat. 489); to see subsequent legislative modifications, see the Pacific Railroad Act of 1863 (12 Stat. 807); Pacific Railroad Act of 1864 (13 Stat. 356); Pacific Railroad Act of 1865 (13 Stat. 504); and Pacific Railroad Act of 1866 (14 Stat. 66).
6. Bain, *Empire Express*, 148.
7. Morton and Watkins, *History of Nebraska*, 484.
8. JD, 12:290.
9. JD, 12:293.
10. Bowles, *Our New West*, 260.
11. JD, 1:279.
12. Bain, *Empire Express*, 364–65.
13. *Millennial Star* 30, no. 2 (11 January 1868): 27.
14. Athearn, "Contracting for the Union Pacific," 17–18.
15. *Millennial Star* 30, no. 2 (11 January 1868): 27.
16. Bain, *Empire Express*, 364.
17. Union Pacific Railroad contract with Brigham Young, May 20, 1868; Brigham Young office files, 1832–1878 (bulk 1844–1877); Union Pacific Railroad Contract Files, 1868–1872; CHL; https://catalog.churchofjesuschrist.org /record?id=02e985d2-0e16-45c3-8891-986d21e20b37&compId=79dd1d2e -6a63-4927-9ee4-a37fe4221477&view= browse&subView=arrangement (accessed September 17, 2019).
18. Union Pacific Railroad contract with Brigham Young, May 20, 1868.
19. Sabin, *Building the Pacific Railway*, 167.
20. *Millennial Star* 30, no. 27 (4 July 1868): 428.
21. "The Mass Meeting," *Deseret News*, June 17, 1868.
22. "The Mass Meeting," *Deseret News*, June 17, 1868.
23. "The Mass Meeting," *Deseret News*, June 17, 1868.
24. "The Mass Meeting," *Deseret News*, June 17, 1868.

25. "Demise of President Heber C. Kimball," *Deseret News*, June 24, 1868.

26. "Demise of President Heber C. Kimball," *Deseret News*, June 24, 1868.

27. "Obsequies of President Heber C. Kimball," *Deseret News,* July 1, 1868.

28. Sabin, *Building the Pacific Railway*, 158.

29. Quoted in Union Pacific Railroad Company, *Progress of the Union Pacific Railroad*, 9–10. The original author of this famous quote is unknown.

30. Sabin, *Building the Pacific Railway*, 191.

31. Sabin, *Building the Pacific Railway*, 179–80; "Mr. Reed" was Samuel Reed, the superintendent who was popular among the Saints working on the railroad.

32. Livingston, *Short Extracts*, 2.

33. Livingston, *Short Extracts*, 2.

34. Kuhre, *Livingston Family*, November 2, 1935.

35. Livingston, *Short Extracts*, 2.

36. Livingston, *Short Extracts*, 1–2.

37. Livingston, *Short Extracts*, 2.

38. Brigham Young to Samuel B. Reed, September 7 and September 22, 1868. Brigham Young office files, 1832–1878 (bulk 1844–1877); Letterbooks, 1844–1877; Letterbook, v. 11, 1868 August 27–1870 February 9; CHL; https://catalog.lds.org/assets/967db140-f060-437f-b583-794f7affa2d0/0/132 (accessed September 17, 2019).

39. John Sharp to Brigham Young, May 5, 1870. Brigham Young office files, 1832–1878 (bulk 1844–1877); General Correspondence, Incoming, 1840–1877; General Letters, 1840- 1877; Sa-Sn, 1870; John Sharp letter; CHL; https://catalog.churchofjesuschrist.org/assets?id=a9c29c5d-03e2-4c72-86a2-d6e5e0bb5398&crate=0&index=0 (accessed September 17, 2019).

40. Sabin, *Building the Pacific Railway*, 198.

41. Sabin, *Building the Pacific Railway*, 203.

42. Bowman, "Driving the Last Spike," 90.

43. Bowman, "Driving the Last Spike," 94–101. All of the ceremonial spikes were removed from their auger holes after the ceremony and replaced with common metal spikes. Doubtless someone would have stolen the gold and silver spikes had they been left in place.

CHAPTER 9: EDUCATION AND AGITATION ARE OUR BEST WEAPONS

1. JD, 8:355–56.

2. WWJ, *1865 October-1872 December*, August 22, 1869.

3. HOTC, August 22, 1869.

4. "Local and Other Matters," *Deseret News*, September 1, 1869.

5. "Visits to This City and Their Effects," *Deseret Evening News*, August 25, 1869.

6. "Visits to This City and Their Effects," *Deseret Evening News*, August 25, 1869.

7. Jenson, *Church Chronology*, 81.

8. Colfax and Taylor, "The Mormon Question," see pages 3–4 of the transcript.

9. Cowan, "Steel Rails and Utah Saints," 190.

10. Livingston, *Short Extracts*, 2.

11. A Bill in Aid of the Execution of the Laws in the Territory of Utah, and for Other Purposes, House of Representatives 696, 41st Cong., 2nd Sess. (1870).

12. Kimball, "Greeting," 139.

13. "Minutes of a Ladies Mass Meeting," Jan. 6, 1870, Fifteenth Ward, Salt Lake Stake, Relief Society Minutes and Records, 1868–1968, vol. 1, 1868–1873, 139–42; CHL; https://catalog.churchofjesuschrist.org/assets?id=b0d3ab4a -9810-46cd-99fc-53c482bff1b4&crate=0&index=156 (accessed September 17, 2019); also Derr, et al., *First Fifty Years of Relief Society*, Document 3.13.

14. JHC, January 13, 1870.

15. "Proceedings in Mass Meeting of the Ladies of Salt Lake City, to Protest against the Passage of the Cullom's Bill." Public meeting held in Salt Lake City, UT, January 14, 1870: 8. The report notes that the ladies held this meeting in the "old" tabernacle, but that building could only seat about 2,500 people. If the number of attendees at this meeting truly exceeded five thousand, it could only have been held in the newer tabernacle, as that was the only building in the city that could have accommodated anything close to that number of people.

16. "Proceedings in Mass Meeting," 1.

17. "Proceedings in Mass Meeting," 1.

18. "Proceedings in Mass Meeting," 4–5.

19. "Proceedings in Mass Meeting," 7–8.

20. "Proceedings in Mass Meeting," 7.

21. "The Ladies' Mass Meetings—Their True Significance," *Deseret News*, Mar. 9, 1870; see also Derr et al., *First Fifty Years of Relief Society*, Document 3.13.

22. Richard L. Forstall, ed., *Population of States and Counties of the United States: 1790–1990 from the Twenty-one Decennial Censuses* (Washington, DC: GPO, 1996): 163.

23. Jenson, *Encyclopedic History of the Church*, 907.

24. "Further Proceedings," *Salt Lake Daily Herald*, October 3, 1871.

25. "Further Proceedings," *Salt Lake Daily Herald*, October 3, 1871.

26. D&C 128:15.

27. "Semi-Annual Conference of the Southern Mission," *Deseret News*, November 4, 1871.

28. JHC, November 9, 1871.

29. Townsend, *Mormon Trials*, 15.

30. *Clinton v. Englebrecht*, 80 U.S. 434 (1871).

31. "In the Supreme Court," *Millennial Star* 34:349–50.

32. JD, 14:370.

33. "Local and Other Matters," *Deseret News*, August 28, 1872. See the subsection titled "An Event."

34. "The Wasatch and Jordan Valley Railroad," *Deseret News*, April 5, 1873.

35. "The Wasatch and Jordan Valley Railroad," *Deseret News*, April 5, 1873.

36. Raynor, *Everlasting Spires*, 105.

37. "The Wasatch and Jordan Valley Railroad," *Deseret News*, April 16, 1873.

CHAPTER 10: JOSEPH! JOSEPH! JOSEPH!

1. "General Conference," *Deseret News*, April 16, 1873.

2. Brigham Young to the 43rd Annual Conference of The Church of Jesus Christ of Latter-day Saints, April 6, 1873. Brigham Young office files, 1832–1878 (bulk 1844–1877); General Correspondence, Outgoing, 1843–1876; 1873–1876; CHL.

3. Sloan, *Gazeteer of Utah and Salt Lake City Directory 1874*, 45.

4. "The Temple," *Deseret Evening News*, August 16, 1873.

5. "The Temple," *Deseret Evening News*, August 16, 1873.

6. "The Temple," *Deseret Evening News*, August 16, 1873.

7. "The Temple," *Deseret News*, September 17, 1873.

8. Jenson, *Church Chronology*, 91.

9. Leonard J. Arrington, *Great Basin Kingdom*, 278.

10. "The St. George Temple," *Deseret Evening News*, April 2, 1874.

11. Brigham Young to John Willard Young, October 26, 1874. In Jessee, ed., *Letters of Brigham Young to His Sons*, 109–11.

12. Holzapfel, *Every Stone a Sermon*, 22.

13. Poland Act of 1874 (18 Stat. 253, sec. 4).

14. "A Genuine Polygamy Indictment," *Deseret Evening News*, October 26th, 1874; see also George Reynolds journals, 1861–1881; *Journal, 1872 April–1881 January*, 78, CHL.

15. George A. Smith papers, 1834–1877; Autobiographical Writings; *Journal, 1874 October–1875 June*, 15, CHL; https://catalog.churchofjesuschrist.org/assets?id=460579a0-c179-4102-a2a0-ee8252c79d4a&crate=0&index=14 (accessed September 19, 2019); see also JHC, November 12, 1874.

16. George A. Smith papers, 1834–1877; Autobiographical Writings; *Journal, 1874 October–1875 June*, 15.

17. JHC, November 12, 1874.

18. George A. Smith papers, 1834–1877; Autobiographical Writings; *Journal, 1874 October-1875 June*, 23.

19. George A. Smith papers, 1834–1877; Autobiographical Writings; *Journal, 1874 October-1875 June*, 18.

20. George A. Smith papers, 1834–1877; Autobiographical Writings; *Journal, 1874 October-1875 June*, 25.

21. "Judicial Discretion, Moderation, and Insight Wanted in Utah," *Deseret Evening News*, March 31, 1875.

22. "Judicial Discretion, Moderation, and Insight Wanted in Utah," *Deseret Evening News*, March 31, 1875.

23. "Polygamy Case," *Deseret Evening News*, March 31, 1875.

24. "The Reynolds Indictment Quashed," *Deseret Evening News*, June 19, 1875.

25. Chernow, *Grant*, 958.

26. Chernow, *Grant*, 20.

27. Grant, *Personal Memoirs of Julia Dent Grant*, 185.

28. Grant, *Personal Memoirs of Julia Dent Grant*, 185.

29. "Departure of the Presidential Party," *Deseret Evening News*, October 5, 1875.

30. "The Presidential Visit," *Deseret Evening News*, October 5, 1875.

31. Jenson, *Church Chronology*, 95.

32. "Terrible Disaster," *Deseret Evening News*, April 6, 1876.

33. "Terrible Disaster," *Deseret Evening News*, April 6, 1876.

34. "Terrible Disaster," *Deseret Evening News*, April 6, 1876.

35. "Terrible Disaster," *Deseret Evening News*, April 6, 1876.

36. JD, 18:190.

37. Besides Taylor, there had been three other men in the upper room of Carthage Jail on June 27, 1844, the day of the martyrdom: Joseph Smith, his older brother Hyrum Smith, and Willard Richards. Joseph and Hyrum were killed in the attack. Richards escaped unharmed; he died of "dropsy" in 1854 in Utah. While recovering from his wounds, Taylor wrote the announcement of the martyrdom that was later canonized as D&C 135.

38. JD, 18:201.

39. JD, 18:201.

40. "In St. George," *Deseret Evening News*, May 10, 1876.

41. "In St. George," *Deseret Evening News*, May 10, 1876.

42. "Visited the Temple," *Deseret Evening News*, May 11, 1876.

43. "President Young and Party," *Deseret Evening News*, June 12, 1876.

44. "The Temple," *Deseret Evening News*, August 16, 1876.

45. "The Temple," *Deseret Evening News*, August 16, 1876.

46. "The Temple," *Deseret Evening News*, August 16, 1876.

47. Brigham Young to Alfales Young, August 17, 1876. Brigham Young office files, 1832–1878 (bulk 1844–1877); Letterbooks, 1844–1877; Letterbook, v. 14, 1875 November 15–1877 July 13, CHL; https://catalog.churchofjesuschrist

.org/assets?id=8ee2bf6f-8a90-4bd6-943d-532c27f3aae2&crate=0&index=560 (accessed September 19, 2019).

48. George Reynolds to Brigham Young, November 29, 1876. Brigham Young office files, 1832–1878 (bulk 1844–1877); General Correspondence, Incoming, 1840–1877; General Letters, 1840- 1877; P-Re, 1876; George Reynolds letter; CHL. Making the walls "safe for the winter" usually involved either covering the exposed tops with a protective layer of mortar or putting shedlike wooden roofs over them. Workers would also try to remove newly fallen snow from the walls as quickly as they could after a storm.

49. "The Temple," *Deseret News*, December 6, 1876; see also First Presidency, "*To the bishops, seventies, high priests and elders. Dear brethren: It is expected, in accordance with a circular issued some time ago, that the labor upon the Temple here will continue to be pushed forward by those now engaged in it,*" viz.: the seventies', elders' and high priests' quorums / [signed] John W. Young, Daniel H. Wells of the First Presidency; John Taylor, in behalf of the Twelve Apostles [Salt Lake City]: The First Presidency, [1876?], https://catalog.lds.org/record/e078b42a -bbbd-44d3-a0aa-94b5f4cd3408.

50. Formerly Brigham's First Counselor, Elder George A. Smith had passed away on September 1, 1875. Brigham called John W. Young, one of his sons, to succeed Elder Smith as the First Counselor in the First Presidency. Elder Young was sustained in that calling on October 8, 1876.

51. Daniel H. Wells to Brigham Young, November 15, 1876. Brigham Young office files, 1832–1878 (bulk 1844–1877); General Correspondence, Incoming, 1840–1877; Letters from Church Leaders and Others, 1840–1877; Daniel H. Wells, 1874–1876; Daniel H. Wells letter; CHL; https://catalog.lds.org/assets /cfb8e57f-bae1-4a04-88e9-dc8b101be3e5/0/1 (accessed May 5, 2019).

52. Daniel H. Wells to Brigham Young, September 24, 1876. Brigham Young office files, 1832–1878 (bulk 1844–1877); General Correspondence, Incoming, 1840–1877; Letters from Church Leaders and Others, 1840–1877; Daniel H. Wells, 1874–1876; Daniel H. Wells telegram; CHL.

53. WWJ, *1873 January–1880 February*, November 10, 1876.

54. WWJ, *1873 January–1880 February*, December 11, 1876.

55. WWJ, *1873 January–1880 February*, December 25, 1876.

56. WWJ, *1873 January–1880 February*, January 1, 1877.

57. WWJ, *1873 January–1880 February*, March 1, 1877.

58. JD, 18:357.

59. Isaiah 24:5.

60. Ephesians 4:5.

61. "Remarks of Prest. Brigham Young," *Deseret Evening News*, May 5, 1877.

62. "Remarks of Prest. Brigham Young," *Deseret Evening News*, June 16, 1877.

63. JD, 1:133.

64. Turner, *Brigham Young: Pioneer Prophet,* 407.

65. WWJ, *1873 January–1880 February,* August 27–28, 1877.

66. Richard Whitehead Young, 1858–1919; *Richard W. Young diary,* 17; https://catalog.lds.org/assets/e3e29aad-61a0-4bdc-946e-16f917c42b41/0/18 (accessed May 7, 2019).

67. "Obituary," *Deseret Evening News,* August 30, 1877; see also Gates and Widtsoe, *Life Story of Brigham Young,* 362.

68. WWJ, *1873 January–1880 February,* September 2, 1877.

69. WWJ, *1873 January–1880 February,* September 2, 1877.

70. Truman O. Angell to John Taylor, September 25, 1877. First Presidency (John Taylor) correspondence, 1877–1887; Letters, 1877; Truman O. Angell letters, 1877; CHL; https://catalog.lds.org/assets?id=957d9481-4f00-4792-b992-729889e28b4d&crate=0&index=0 (accessed October 1, 2019).

71. JHC, August 16, 1878.

72. John D. T. McAllister to John Taylor and Wilford Woodruff, August 16, 1878. First Presidency (John Taylor) correspondence, 1877–1887; Letters, 1878; John D. T. McAllister letters, 1878; CHL; https://catalog.churchofjesuschrist.org/assets?id=b14cdf7d-6325-4bc9-9247-26be5cb5f5a1&crate=0&index=0 (accessed October 1, 2019).

CHAPTER 11: PREPARED TO ABIDE THE PENALTY

1. Truman O. Angell to John Sharp and Committee, February 12, 1878. First Presidency (John Taylor) correspondence, 1877–1887; Letters, 1878; Truman O. Angell letters, 1878; CHL.

2. Total count of stonecutters taken from First Presidency (John Taylor) correspondence, 1877–1887; Letters, 1878; Truman O. Angell letters, 1878; Truman O. Angell letter, Salt Lake City, Utah, to John Taylor and Council; CHL; https://catalog.lds.org/assets/9cee64c0-8ccf-4d8e-ab61-b469c4d26b07/0/0 (accessed May 9, 2019).

3. Jenson, *Church Chronology,* 53.

4. "Fatal Accident," *Deseret Evening News,* September 27, 1878.

5. "The Reynolds Case," *Salt Lake Herald,* November 15, 1878.

6. "Women's Mass Meeting," *Deseret Evening News,* November 16, 1878.

7. "The Ladies' Topic," *Salt Lake Herald,* November 16, 1878.

8. Thomas Jefferson to Messrs. Nehemiah Dodge and Others, a Committee of the Danbury Baptist Associations in the State of Connecticut, January 1, 1802. In Peterson, ed. *Thomas Jefferson: Writings,* 510.

9. *Reynolds v. United States,* 98 U.S. 145 (1878), 164.

10. *Reynolds v. United States,* 98 U.S. 145 (1878), 167.

11. "The 'Mormon' Question in the Cabinet—The Reynolds Case Receives Attention," *Deseret Evening News,* June 14, 1879.

12. George Reynolds journals, 1861–1881; *Journal, 1872 April–1881 January;* CHL; https://catalog.lds.org/assets? id=b3166034-46c1-41a0-ae75 -0a84901f5798&crate=0&index=247 (accessed September 21, 2019).

13. George Reynolds journals, 1861–1881; *Journal, 1872 April–1881 January;* CHL; https://catalog.lds.org/assets?id=b3166034-46c1-41a0-ae75 -0a84901f5798&crate=0&index=252 (accessed September 21, 2019).

14. George Reynolds journals, 1861–1881; *Journal, 1872 April–1881 January;* CHL; https://catalog.lds.org/assets?id=b3166034-46c1-41a0-ae75 -0a84901f5798&crate=0&index=256 (accessed September 21, 2019).

15. WWJ, *1873 January–1880 February,* January 26, 1880.

16. JD, 22:39.

17. JD, 22:39.

18. "One or Two More," *Deseret Evening News,* January 21, 1881.

19. George Reynolds journals, 1861–1881; *Journal, 1872 April-1881 January;* CHL; https://catalog.lds.org/assets?id=b3166034-46c1-41a0-ae75 -0a84901f5798&crate=0&index=305 (accessed September 121, 2019). Elder Reynolds's *A Complete Concordance to the Book of Mormon* would total 851 pages when it was finally published in 1900.

20. "The Salt Lake Temple," *Deseret Evening News,* June 10, 1881.

21. "Acting-President Arthur," *Chicago Tribune,* July 3, 1881.

22. President Chester A. Arthur, *First Annual Message,* December 6, 1881, The American Presidency Project, https://www.presidency.ucsb.edu/documents /first-annual-message-13 (accessed September 10, 2019).

23. "Report of the Utah Commission, August 31, 1882," Utah Commission, *The Edmunds Act,* 7.

24. "The Temple," *Deseret News,* November 14, 1883.

25. Hamilton, *Salt Lake Temple,* 54–55.

26. Hamilton, *Salt Lake Temple,* 54–55.

27. Truman O. Angell to John Taylor and Counsel, March 11, 1885. First Presidency (John Taylor) correspondence, 1877–1887; Letters, 1885; Truman O. Angell letters, 1885; CHL; https://catalog.lds.org/assets?id=d680ad3f -7608-4841-bc5b-5954d49ce5b5&crate=0&index=1 (accessed May 30, 2019)

28. "General Conference," *Deseret Evening News,* April 7, 1879.

29. "Another Martyr for the Truth," *Deseret Evening News,* July 22, 1879.

30. "The Indictment for Polygamy," *Deseret News,* May 7, 1884.

31. "Court Proceedings," *Deseret Evening News,* October 16, 1884.

32. Some of the procedural judicial minutiae, including objections and decisions

rendered on them by Judge Zane, have been omitted to keep the narrative's focus on the actual testimony.

33. "The Polygamy Trial," *Deseret Evening News*, October 18, 1884.

34. JD, 26:155.

35. JD, 26:157.

36. "Ransacking the Temple," *Deseret Evening News*, May 26, 1887.

37. "Deputy Marshals Visit the Temple Block," *Deseret Evening News*, April 24, 1885.

38. "A Shocking Fatality," *Deseret Evening News*, June 24, 1885.

39. "A Shocking Fatality," *Deseret Evening News*, June 24, 1885.

40. "Utah County Notes," *Deseret News*, June 27, 1888.

41. The stories claim that John Rowe Moyle resumed his weekly commute on foot to and from the temple block after acquiring his wooden leg. While he may have walked some of the distance, given his advanced age, one wonders why he wouldn't have ridden a horse instead. It also seems likely that, at the very least, he would have caught the occasional ride from wagon drivers traveling in his direction.

42. "Death of James Moyle," *Deseret Weekly*, December 13, 1890.

43. "The Thumbscrews," *Salt Lake Herald*, September 17, 1885.

44. "Apostle Snow Arrested," *Deseret Evening News*, November 20, 1885.

45. *Snow v. United States*, 118 U.S. 346, 354 (1885).

46. "Governor West at the Penitentiary," *Deseret News*, May 14, 1886.

47. "Response of the 'Mormon' Prisoners," *Deseret Evening News*, May 26, 1886.

48. "Reception to Hon. Morrison R. Waite," *Deseret Evening News*, September 15, 1886.

49. "Chief Justice Waite," *Salt Lake Tribune*, September 15, 1886.

50. Jenson, *Church Chronology*, 137. See entry for September 15, 1886.

51. For an example of such an interview, see Lorenzo Snow to family, October 9, 1886. Snow, Lorenzo 1814–1901. Folder contents: (1) Journal, circa 1841–1847. Folder contents: (2) Correspondence, circa 1868–1894. https://catalog.churchofjesuschrist.org/assets?id=6f0cc8ab-27d7-4888-970f-f5f290d2bdfa&crate=0&index=34 (accessed September 21, 2019). Elder Snow wrote this letter just a few weeks after his interview with the Chief Justice.

52. *In re Snow*, 120 U.S. 274 (1887).

53. Alexander Ramsey et al. to Hon. H. M. Teller, Secretary of the Interior, August 24, 1883. Utah Commission, *The Edmunds Act*.

54. Leonard J. Arrington, *Great Basin Kingdom*, 361.

55. Congressional Record—Senate, January 8, 1886, 562.

56. GQCJ, July 8, 1887.

57. GQCJ, July 18, 1887.

58. GQCJ, July 25, 1887.

59. GQCJ, July 26, 1887.

60. GQCJ, August 15, 1887.

61. "To Fleece the 'Mormon'," *Deseret Evening News*, July 30, 1887.

62. Hamilton, *Salt Lake Temple*, 56.

63. "Truman O. Angell, Sr., Dead," *Salt Lake Herald*, October 17, 1887.

64. "Death of T. O. Angell, Sr.," *Deseret Evening News*, October 17, 1887.

65. "Death of T. O. Angell, Sr.," *Deseret Evening News*, October 17, 1887.

66. WWJ, *1880 February-1885 December*, February 4, 1884.

67. GQCJ, February 16, 1888.

68. GQCJ, February 16, 1888.

CHAPTER 12: THE CAPSTONE IS NOW READY TO BE LAID

1. Leonard J. Arrington, *Great Basin Kingdom*, 370–72.

2. "Death of Sister E. R. Snow Smith," *Deseret Evening News*, December 5, 1887.

3. WWJ, *1886 January–1892 December*, May 15, 1888.

4. WWJ, *1886 January–1892 December*, May 17, 1888.

5. WWJ, *1886 January–1892 December*, May 17, 1888.

6. "Amos Howe Dies," *Salt Lake Herald*, June 17, 1908.

7. Nuttall, *In the President's Office*, 325–26.

8. WWJ, *1886 January–1892 December*, April 7, 1889.

9. "A Strange Interview," *Salt Lake Daily Tribune*, October 20, 1889.

10. GQCJ, December 3, 1889. The priesthood organization of The Church of Jesus Christ of Latter-day Saints has two major division: the Melchizedek Priesthood, named after the Old Testament priest and king of Salem who blessed Abraham in Genesis 14; and the Aaronic Priesthood, named after the brother of Moses who acted as his mouthpiece, assistant, and later as the high priest in the tabernacle. The Aaronic Priesthood is considered the "lesser" priesthood and acts under the guidance and direction of the Melchizedek or "higher" priesthood.

11. "Fell Thirty Feet," *Deseret Weekly*, January 25, 1890.

12. Florence, "Harvesting the Light," 35.

13. GQCJ, June 20, 1890.

14. Wolff, "When young Mormon artists went to Paris."

15. GQCJ, November 12, 1890.

16. For a detailed history of the "Godbeite" movement, see Walker, *Wayward Saints*.

17. WWJ, *1886 January–1892 December*, August 24, 1890.

18. *The Late Corporation of the Church of Jesus Christ of Latter-Day Saints v. United States; Romney et al. v. United States.* 136 U.S. 1 (1890).

19. The Manifesto's origins are complex and have been the subject of considerable research. For a shorter study of events leading to the drafting and publication of the Manifesto, see Alexander, "Odyssey of a Latter-day Prophet," 169–206. For a longer exploration, see Alexander, *Things in Heaven and Earth*, chapters 11–13.

20. GQCJ, September 23, 1890.

21. WWJ, *1886 January–1892 December,* September 24, 1890.

22. *Church History in the Fulness of Times*, 440.

23. GQCJ, September 24, 1890.

24. WWJ, *1886 January–1892 December,* September 25, 1890.

25. D&C, Official Declaration—1, *Excerpts from Three Addresses by President Wilford Woodruff Regarding the Manifesto.*

26. "That Manifesto," *Salt Lake Tribune*, September 26, 1890.

27. "Remarks by President George Q. Cannon and President Wilford Woodruff," *Deseret Evening News*, October 11, 1890.

28. D&C, Official Declaration—1, *Excerpts from Three Addresses by President Wilford Woodruff Regarding the Manifesto.*

29. "The Idaho Campaign," *Salt Lake Herald*, September 28, 1890.

30. "Confiscation," *Deseret Weekly*, November 22, 1890.

31. Leonard J. Arrington, *Great Basin Kingdom*, 353.

32. Raynor, *Everlasting Spires*, 61.

33. Raynor, *Everlasting Spires*, 59–60.

34. Nuttall, *In the President's Office*, 452–53.

35. GQCJ, December 23, 1890.

36. "Death of James Moyle," *Deseret News*, December 13, 1890.

37. Charles Livingston, "Brief Synopsis from Memory."

38. "Chas. Livingston Dies Suddenly," *Salt Lake Herald-Republican*, June 18, 1908.

39. Raynor, *Everlasting Spires*, 161.

40. GQCJ, January 3, 1891.

41. WWJ, *1886 January–1892 December,* March 29, 1891.

42. Cyrus Dallin to John Taylor, September 11, 1883; First Presidency (John Taylor) correspondence, 1877–1887; Letters, 1883; Letters, 1883 D; CHL; https://catalog.lds.org/assets? id=111e32b8-5d6c-480e-a669-8ba230d82948&crate=0&index=0 (accessed September 10, 2019).

43. Revelation 14:6–7.

44. Zobell, "Cyrus Dallin and the Angel Moroni Statue," 5–6.

45. The statue atop the Salt Lake Temple was not identified as Moroni at the time Wilford Woodruff commissioned Dallin to create the piece. That association took place later.

    According to Joseph Smith, Moroni was the angel who appeared to him in 1823 and first told him of an ancient record inscribed on gold plates buried in a hill near Joseph's home. Moroni had charge over the record because, during his mortal life, he had been the final historian and author to work on it and, after completing the record, had been the one to bury it in the hill where it would wait some fourteen hundred years to be recovered. See Joseph Smith—History 1:27–54, 59.

46. Levi Edgar Young, "The Angel Moroni and Cyrus Dallin," 234.

47. GQCJ, September 24, 1891.

48. GQCJ, October 7, 1891.

49. "Confiscation Suits Dismissed," *Deseret Evening News,* October 27, 1891; "Decision in the Church Suits," *Deseret Evening News,* November 11, 1891.

50. "Application for Amnesty," *Deseret Evening News,* February 15, 1892.

51. Nuttall, *In the President's Office,* 479.

52. WWJ, *1886 January–1892 December,* March 30, 1892.

53. Joseph H. Dean journals, 1876–1944; 1892 February–1892 December; CHL; https://catalog.lds.org/assets?id=fd828603-ee2a-4020-9122-d572a6e1fc5c&crate=0&index=40; 41–42.

54. WWJ, *1886 January–1892 December,* April 6, 1892.

55. Please note that all of the capstone ceremony events described in this chapter not otherwise cited were drawn from "At the Tabernacle," *Deseret Evening News,* April 6, 1892.

56. "Come, Come, Ye Saints," by William Clayton, in *Hymns,* 30.

57. This instance of the Hosanna Shout is especially notable for two reasons. First the guidance given by Joseph F. Smith marked the beginning of the standardization of the Shout. All instances of it since that day have followed the pattern Smith established here: a member of the Twelve instructs the congregation on how it occurs, including the wording; the wording is now fixed; and handkerchiefs are waved. Second, this was the first instance in which handkerchiefs were used instead of simply a waving of hands in the air. For a detailed review of the Shout's history, see Olmstead, "From Pentecost to Administration," 7–37.

58. Charles John Thomas composed both the lyrics and music for "The Capstone March." "At the Tabernacle," *Deseret Evening News,* April 6, 1892.

59. Susa Young Gates papers, circa 1870–1933; General Correspondence; Alphabetical Subject Files; Temple dedications and correspondence; Salt Lake Temple dedication, Temple anthem, 1892; CHL; https://catalog.churchof jesuschrist.org/assets?id=ff867dd7-ac93-47aa-b470-d8720e5da0df&crate =0&index=2 (accessed August 11, 2019); lyrics by Charles Lowell Walker, music by Evan Stephens; see Charles Lowell Walker, *Diary,* 2:736.

60. Charles Livingston, "Brief Synopsis from Memory."

61. The four apostles were John. H. Smith, Heber. J. Grant, John W. Taylor (son of the third President of the Church) and Anton H. Lund. GQCJ, April 4, 1892.

62. "The Spirit of God," by W. W. Phelps, in *Hymns*, 2.

63. Holzapfel, *Every Stone a Sermon*, 47. Lyrics by Henry W. Naisbitt, music by Charles John Thomas.

64. The Moroni statue's precise weight is still unknown. Experts can only estimate it based on the weights of similar Moroni statues made later.

65. "Temples of the Church of Jesus Christ of Latter-day Saints: Salt Lake Temple," https://churchofjesuschristtemples.org/salt-lake-temple (accessed September 10, 2019).

66. Quoted in Hawkins, *Mountain of the Lord*, 97–98.

CHAPTER 13: THERE WAS GLADNESS AMONG THE SANCTIFIED IN HEAVEN

1. WWJ, *1886 January–1892 December*, April 11, 1892.

2. Florence, "Harvesting the Light," 37–39.

3. Cope, "'With God's Assistance,'" 143. The original First Presidency letter may be found at Wilford Woodruff, George Q. Cannon, and Joseph F. Smith to J. W. Clawson, Lorus Pratt, John Fairbanks, Henry Evans, Herman Haag, April 18, 1892, Lorus Pratt Collection, Springville Museum of Art.

4. Walker, *Diary of Charles Lowell Walker*, 2:738; also WWJ, *1886 January-1892 December*, April 24, 1892.

5. Naisbitt, "Temple Building," 253.

6. GQCJ, September 8, 1892.

7. Anderson, "The Salt Lake Temple," 287.

8. Anderson, "The Salt Lake Temple," 287.

9. GQCJ, April 15, 1892.

10. Anderson, "The Salt Lake Temple," 291. See also "Death of a Well-Known Lady," *Salt Lake Herald-Republican*, February 28, 1895.

11. GQCJ, June 20, 1892.

12. GQCJ, June 28, 1892.

13. WWJ, *1886 January–1892 December*, August 4, 1892.

14. WWJ, *1886 January–1892 December*, August 4, 1892.

15. GQCJ, April 15, 1892.

16. Holzapfel, *Every Stone a Sermon*, 52.

17. "Third Day of Conference," *Deseret Evening News*, October 8, 1892.

18. GQCJ, October 10, 1892.

19. GQCJ, July 18, 1892.

20. Cannon, *House of the Lord*, 14.

21. Anderson, "The Salt Lake Temple," 291–92.

22. GQCJ, October 20, 1892.

23. Holzapfel, *Every Stone a Sermon*, 52.

24. GQCJ, November 16, 1892.

25. GQCJ, November 29, 1892.

26. GQCJ, January 6, 1893.

27. GQCJ, November 23, 1892.

28. WWJ, *1886 January–1892 December*, December 20, 1892.

29. WWJ, *1886 January–1892 December*, December 20, 1892.

30. WWJ, *1893 January–1897 April*, January 17, 1893.

31. WWJ, *1893 January–1897 April*, February 9, 1893.

32. WWJ, *1893 January–1897 April*, January 3, 1893.

33. GQCJ, January 20, 1893.

34. See Luke 21:1–4.

35. WWJ, *1893 January–1897 April*, January 12, 1893.

36. President Benjamin Harrison, *Proclamation 346—Granting Amnesty and Pardon for the Offense of Engaging in Polygamous or Plural Marriage to Members of the Church of Latter-Day Saints*, January 04, 1893; The American Presidency Project, https://www.presidency.ucsb.edu/node/205484 (accessed September 10, 2019).

37. WWJ, *1893 January–1897 April*, January 5, 1893.

38. GQCJ, January 5, 1893.

39. WWJ, *1893 January–1897 April*, February 23, 1893.

40. WWJ, *1893 January–1897 April*, March 18, 1893.

41. WWJ, *1893 January–1897 April*, February 7, 1893.

42. D&C 38:27.

43. First Presidency, *An address to the officers and members of the Church of Jesus Christ of Latter-day Saints* (Salt Lake City: The Church of Jesus Christ of Latter-day Saints, 1893); https://catalog.lds.org/assets?id=2c7e4e8c-9fd6-4267-b242 -e42f96a6ff42&crate=0&index=0 (accessed September 10, 2019).

44. First Presidency, *An address to the officers and members.*

45. WWJ, *1893 January–1897 April*, March 25, 1893.

46. "A Hard Road," *Los Angeles Times*, April 6, 1893.

47. "Conference Train Accident," *Deseret Evening News*, April 5, 1893.

48. "General Conference," *Deseret Evening News*, April 4, 1893.

49. "General Conference," *Deseret Evening News*, April 4, 1893.

50. "General Conference," *Deseret Evening News*, April 4, 1893.

51. "General Conference," *Deseret Evening News*, April 4, 1893.

52. Anderson, "The Salt Lake Temple," 286.

53. For an example of one of these invitations, see Maude Frances Smeath Weight, 1900–1998. F. H. Weight scrapbook items, https://catalog.lds.org

/assets?id=2acf817b-8d1c-4b0c-b5b5-b717c6d2a0f5&crate=0&index=9 (accessed September 10, 2019).

54. Anderson, "The Salt Lake Temple," 292.

55. Joseph H. Dean journals, 1876–1944; *1893 January–1893 November*, 66 (April 6, 1893); CHL; https://catalog.churchofjesuschrist.org/assets?id=1ec035fc-02fa-40ee-98ff-a543e134c065&crate=0&index=0.

56. "Work of the Wind," *Deseret Evening News*, April 6, 1893.

57. For the complete text of the dedicatory prayer, see the appendix.

58. "The Spirit of God," by W. W. Phelps; in *Hymns*, 2.

59. GQCJ, April 6, 1893.

60. Joseph H. Dean journals, *1893 January–1893 November*, 64–65 (April 6, 1893).

61. Joseph H. Dean journals, *1893 January–1893 November*, 64–65 (April 6, 1893).

62. Cowan, *Temples to Dot the Earth*, 114.

63. Mark 10:14; see also Matthew 19:14; Luke 18:16.

64. GQCJ, April 7, 1893.

65. WWJ, *1893 January–1897 April*, synopsis of 1893 events (immediately follows Wilford's December 21, 1893 entry).

BIBLIOGRAPHY

ARTICLES

Aldous, Jay A. "Mountain Fever in the 1847 Mormon Pioneer Companies." *Nauvoo Journal* 9, no. 2 (Fall 1997): 52–59.

Alexander, Thomas G. "The Odyssey of a Latter-day Prophet: Wilford Woodruff and the Manifesto of 1890." *Journal of Mormon History* 17, no. 1 (1991): 145–68.

Anderson, James H. "The Salt Lake Temple." *The Contributor* 14, no. 6 (April 1, 1893): 243–303.

Anderson, Paul L. "William Harrison Folsom: Pioneer Architect," *Utah Historical Quarterly* 43, no 3: 241–44.

Arrington, J. Earl. "William Weeks, Architect of the Nauvoo Temple." *BYU Studies Quarterly* 19, no. 3 (Spring 1979), article 6: 337–60.

Athearn, Robert J. "Contracting for the Union Pacific." *Utah Historical Quarterly* 37, no. 1 (Winter 1969): 16–40.

Bachman, Danel W. "New Light on an Old Hypothesis: The Ohio Origins of the Revelation on Eternal Marriage." *Journal of Mormon History* 5, no. 1 (1978): 19–32.

Bowman, J. N. "Driving the Last Spike at Promontory, 1869." *Utah Historical Quarterly* 37, no. 1 (Winter 1969): 76–101.

Brown, Lisle G. "'Temple Pro Tempore': The Salt Lake City Endowment House," *Journal of Mormon History* 34, no. 4 (Fall 2008): 1–68.

Cannon, Annie Wells. "Passing Thoughts." *Woman's Exponent* 21, nos. 20–21 (April 15 and May 1, 1893): 157–58.

Cope, Rachel. "'With God's Assistance I Will Someday Be an Artist': John B.

Fairbanks's Account of the Paris Art Mission." *BYU Studies* 50, no. 3 (2011): 133–59.

Cowan, Richard O. "Steel Rails and Utah Saints." *Journal of Mormon History* 27, no. 2 (Fall 2001): 177–96.

Florence, Giles H. "Harvesting the Light: The 1890 Paris Art Mission." *Ensign* 18, no. 1 (October 1988): 34–41.

Grow, Nathan D. "One Masterpiece, Four Masters: Reconsidering the Authorship of the Salt Lake Tabernacle." *Journal of Mormon History* 31, no. 3 (2005): 170–97.

Hales, Brian C. "Encouraging Joseph Smith to Practice Plural Marriage: The Accounts of the Angel with a Drawn Sword." *Mormon Historical Studies* 11, no. 2 (Fall 2010): 55ff.

MacKinnon, William P. "'Full of Courage': Thomas L. Kane, the Utah War, and BYU's Kane Collection as Lodestone." *BYU Studies Quarterly* 48, no. 4 (October 2009): 89–119.

Morgan, Dale L. "The State of Deseret." *Utah Historical Quarterly* 8, nos. 2, 3, 4 (April–October 1940).

Naisbitt, Henry W. "Temple Building." *The Contributor* 13, no. 6 (April 1, 1892).

Olmstead, Jacob W. "From Pentecost to Administration: A Reappraisal of the History of the Hosanna Shout." *Mormon Historical Studies* 2, no. 2 (Fall 2001): 7–37.

———. "Mormon Political Schism and the Salt Lake Temple Dedication." Unpublished manuscript. Microsoft Word file.

———. "Why is there a wall around the Salt Lake Temple? The answer might surprise you." Unpublished manuscript. Microsoft Word file.

———, and W. Randall Dixon. "'Here will be the temple of our God': Reconciling the Two Location-Identification Narratives for the Salt Lake Temple." Unpublished manuscript. Microsoft Word file.

Richards, Paul C. "The Salt Lake Temple Infrastructure: Studying It Out in Their Minds." *BYU Studies Quarterly* 36, no. 2 (1996–97): 202–25.

Robison, Elwin C., and W. Randall Dixon. "Design and Construction of the Great Tabernacle Arches." *BYU Studies Quarterly* 52, no. 3 (2013): 143–59.

Sharp, James P. "Temple Recollections." *Improvement Era* 46, no. 4 (April 1943): 199, 228–29.

Smith, Joseph Fielding. "The Salt Lake Temple." *Improvement Era* 56, no. 4 (April 1953): 223–24, 294–95.

"The Utah Expedition: Its Causes and Consequences [Part I]." *The Atlantic Monthly* 3, Issue 17 (March 1859): 361–75.

"——— [Part II]." *The Atlantic Monthly* 3, Issue 18 (April 1859): 474–91.

"——— [Part III]." *The Atlantic Monthly* 3, Issue 19 (May 1859): 570–84.

Watt, Ronald G. "Dry Goods and Groceries in Early Utah: An Account Book View of James Campbell Livingston." *Utah Historical Quarterly* 47, no. 1 (Winter 1979): 64–69.

Young, Levi Edgar. "The Angel Moroni and Cyrus Dallin," *Improvement Era* 56, no. 4 (April 1953): 234–35, 268.

Zobell, Albert L. "Cyrus Dallin and the Angel Moroni Statue," *Improvement Era* 71, no. 4 (April 1968): 4–7.

BOOKS, TRACTS, AND PAMPHLETS

Anderson, Paul L. "Truman O. Angell: Architect and Saint," in *Supporting Saints: Life Stories of Nineteenth-Century Mormons*. Provo, UT: Religious Studies Center, Brigham Young University, 1985, 133–73.

Arrington, Leonard J. *Brigham Young: American Moses*, 1986 ed. Chicago, IL: University of Illinois Press, 1986.

———. *Great Basin Kingdom: An Economic History of the Latter-day Saints, 1830–1900*. Lincoln, NE: University of Nebraska Press, 1966.

Auchampaugh, Philip G. *Robert Tyler, Southern Rights Champion*. Duluth, MN: Himan Stein, 1934.

Bain, David Haward. *Empire Express: Building the First Transcontinental Railroad*. New York: Viking Penguin, 1999.

Bancroft, Hubert Howe. *History of Utah 1540–1886*. Vol. 26 of *The Works of Hubert Howe Bancroft*. San Francisco, CA: The History Company, 1889.

Bennett, Richard. *Temples Rising: A Heritage of Sacrifice*. Salt Lake City: Deseret Book, 2019.

Bowles, Samuel. *Across the Continent: A Summer's Journey to the Rocky Mountains, the Mormons, and the Pacific States, with Speaker Colfax*. Springfield, MA: Samuel Bowles & Company, 1868.

———. *Our New West: Records of Travel Between the Mississippi River and the Pacific Ocean*. Hartford, CT: Hartford Publishing Company, 1869.

Buchanan, James. *The Works of James Buchanan*, vol. 10. Edited by John Bassett Moore. Philadelphia: J. B. Lippincott Company, 1910.

Cannon, George Q. *House of the Lord*. Salt Lake City: George Q. Cannon & Sons Co, 1897.

Chernow, Ron. *Grant*. New York: Penguin Books, 2017.

Church History in the Fulness of Times, 2nd ed. Salt Lake City: The Church of Jesus Christ of Latter-day Saints, 2003.

Clark, James R., ed. *Messages of the First Presidency of the Church of Jesus Christ of Latter-day Saints, 1833–1964*. 6 vols. Salt Lake City: Bookcraft, 1965–75.

Clayton, William. *The Latter-Day Saints' Emigrants Guide*. St. Louis: Chambers & Knapp, 1848.

Cowan, Richard O. *Temples to Dot the Earth.* Salt Lake City: Bookcraft, 1994.

Cowley, Matthias F. *Wilford Woodruff: History of His Life and Labors.* Salt Lake City: Deseret News, 1909.

Derr, Jill Mulvay, Carol Cornwall Madsen, Kate Holbrook, and Matthew J. Grow, eds. *The First Fifty Years of Relief Society: Key Documents in Letter-day Saint Women's History.* Salt Lake City: Church Historian's Press, 2016.

The Doctrine and Covenants of the Church of Jesus Christ of Latter-day Saints. Salt Lake City: Intellectual Reserve Inc., 2013.

———, 1835 ed. Edited by Joseph Smith, Jr., Oliver Cowdery, Sidney Rigdon, and Frederick G. Williams. Kirtland, OH: F. G. Williams & Co., 1835.

Foote, Shelby. *The Civil War: A Narrative, vol 1: Fort Sumter to Perryville.* New York: Vintage, 2011.

Freeman, Douglas Southall. *R. E. Lee: A Biography.* 4 vols. New York: Charles Scribner's Sons, 1934–35.

Fremont, Capt. John Charles. *Report of the exploring expedition to the Rocky Mountains in the year 1842: and to Oregon and north California in the years 1843–44.* Washington: Gales and Seaton, 1845.

Gates, Susa Young, and Leah D. Widtsoe. *The Life Story of Brigham Young.* New York: Macmillan & Co., 1930.

Gibbons, Francis M. *Wilford Woodruff: Wondrous Worker, Prophet of God.* Salt Lake City: Deseret Book, 1988.

Gove, Jesse A. *The Utah Expedition, 1857–1858; Letters of Capt. Jesse A. Gove, 10th Inf., U. S. [. . .].* Edited by Otis G. Hammond. Concord, NH: New Hampshire Historical Society, 1928.

Grant, Julia Dent. *The Personal Memoirs of Julia Dent Grant.* Edited by John Y. Simon. New York: G. P. Putnam's Sons, 1975.

Grant, Ulysses S. *Memoirs and Selected Letters.* New York: Library of America, 1990.

Greeley, Horace. *Proceedings of the First Three National Republican Conventions of 1856, 1860, 1864.* Minneapolis: Charles W. Johnson, 1893.

Grow, Matthew J. *Liberty for the Downtrodden.* New Haven, CT: Yale University Press, 2009.

Hamilton, C. Mark. *Nineteenth-Century Mormon Architecture & City Planning.* New York: Oxford University Press, 1995.

———. *The Salt Lake Temple: A Monument to a People*, 5th ed. Salt Lake City: University Services Corporation, 1983.

Hawkins, Chad S. *The Mountain of the Lord.* Salt Lake City: Deseret Book, 2010.

Holzapfel, Richard Neitzel. *Every Stone a Sermon.* Salt Lake City: Bookcraft, 1992.

Hughes, Delilah Gardner. *Life of Archibald Gardner, Utah Pioneer of 1847*, 2nd ed. West Jordan, UT: Alpine Publishing Co., 1970.

Hymns of The Church of Jesus Christ of Latter-day Saints, 2nd ed. Salt Lake City: Intellectual Reserve, Inc., 2002.

Jenson, Andrew. *Church Chronology: A Record of Important Events Pertaining to the History of the Church of Jesus Christ of Latter-day Saints*, 2nd ed. Salt Lake City: The Deseret News, 1899.

———. *Encyclopedic History of the Church.* Salt Lake City: Deseret News Publishing Company, 1941.

Jessee, Dean C., ed. *Letters of Brigham Young to His Sons.* Salt Lake City: Deseret Book, 1974.

Journal of Discourses. 26 vols. London: LDS Booksellers Depot, 1854–86.

Klein, Philip Shriver. *President James Buchanan.* University Park, PA: Pennsylvania State University Press, 1962.

MacKinnon, William P. *At Sword's Point, Part 1: A Documentary History of the Utah War to 1858.* Norman, OK: University of Oklahoma Press, 2008.

McBride, Matthew, and James Goldberg, eds. *Revelations in Context: The Stories behind the Sections of Doctrine and Covenants.* Salt Lake City: Intellectual Reserve, Inc., 2016.

McPherson, James M. *Battle Cry of Freedom.* 2 vols. Norwalk, CT: Easton Press, 1988.

Merrill, James M. *Spurs to Glory: the Story of the United States Cavalry.* Chicago, IL: Rand McNally, 1966.

Morton, J. Sterling, and Albert Watkins. *History of Nebraska: From the Earliest Explorations of the Trans-Mississippi Region.* Lincoln, NE: Western Publishing and Engraving Company, 1918.

Nutall, Leonard James. *In the President's Office: The Diaries of L. John Nuttall, 1879–1892.* Edited by Jedediah S. Rogers. Salt Lake City: Signature Books, 2007.

Olmstead, Jacob Wayne. *How We Got the Salt Lake Temple.* Unpublished manuscript. Microsoft Word file.

Packer, Boyd K. *The Holy Temple.* Salt Lake City: Bookcraft, 1980.

Pease, Theodore C., and James G. Randall, eds. *The Diary of Orville Hickman Browning.* 2 vols. Springfield, IL: Trustees of the Illinois State Historical Library, 1927–33.

Peterson, Merrill D., ed. *Thomas Jefferson: Writings: Autobiography/Notes on the State of Virginia/Public and Private Papers/Addresses/Letters.* New York: Library of America, 1984.

Pratt, Parley P. *The Autobiography of Parley P. Pratt.* Edited by Parley P. Pratt, Jr. Chicago, IL: Law, King & Law, 1888.

Raynor, Wallace A. *The Everlasting Spires: The Story of the Salt Lake Temple.* Salt Lake City: Deseret Book, 1965.

———. "History of the Construction of the Salt Lake Temple." Master's thesis, Brigham Young University, 1961.

Reavis, Logan U. *The Life and Military Services of General William Selby Harney*. St. Louis, MO: Bryan, Brand & Co., 1878.

Robison, Elwin C. *Gathering as One: The History of the Mormon Tabernacle in Salt Lake City*. Provo, UT: BYU Studies, 2013.

Rogers, Brent M. *Unpopular Sovereignty: Mormons and the Federal Management of Early Utah Territory*. Lincoln, NE: University of Nebraska Press, 2017.

Roland, Charles P. *Albert Sidney Johnston: Soldier of Three Republics*, 3rd paperback ed. Austin, TX: University of Texas Press–Austin, 1994.

Sabin, Edwin. *Building the Pacific railway; the construction-story of America's first iron thoroughfare between the Missouri River and California* . . . Philadelphia, PA: J. B. Lippincott Company, 1919.

Simon, John Y., ed. *The Personal Memoirs of Julia Dent Grant (Mrs. Ulysses S. Grant) and The First Lady as an Author*. New York: G. P. Putnam's Sons, 1975.

Sloan, Edward L., ed. *Gazeteer of Utah and Salt Lake City Directory, 1874*. Salt Lake City: Salt Lake Herald Publishing Company, 1874.

Smith, George A. *The Rise, Progress and Travels of the Church of Jesus Christ of Latter-day Saints*. Salt Lake City: Deseret News Offices, 1869.

Snow, Eliza R. *Eliza R. Snow: The Complete Poetry*. Compiled and edited by Jill Mulvay Derr and Karen Lynn Davidson. Provo: Brigham Young University Press, and Salt Lake City: University of Utah Press, 2015.

Spencer, Clarissa Young, and Mabel Harmer. *Brigham Young at Home*. Whitefish, MT: Kessinger Publishing, LLC, 2004.

Talmage, James E. *The House of the Lord*. Salt Lake City: The Church of Jesus Christ of Latter-day Saints, 1912.

Temple Souvenir Album, April, 1892, Illustrated with Portraits of the Architects, Views of the Building, Plan of Electric Lights, Engine-House and Grounds, Including Views of Logan, Manti, Nauvoo, and Kirtland Temples, and Places of Interest in Salt Lake City. Salt Lake City: Magazine Printing, 1892.

Townsend, George Alfred. *The Mormon Trials*. New York: American News Company, 1871.

Tullidge, Edward W. *History of Salt Lake City*. Salt Lake City: Star Printing Company, 1886.

———. *Life of Brigham Young: or Utah and Her Founders*. New York: Tullidge & Crandall, 1876.

Union Pacific Railroad Company. *Progress of the Union Pacific Railroad west from Omaha, Nebraska*. New York: Union Pacific Railroad Company, 1868.

The Utah Pioneers: Celebration of the Entrance of the Pioneers into Great Salt Lake

Valley. Salt Lake City: Deseret News Printing and Publishing Establishment, 1880.

Wadsworth, Nelson B. *Set in Stone, Fixed in Glass: The Great Mormon Temple and Its Photographers*. Salt Lake City: Signature Books, 1992.

Walker, Ronald W. *Wayward Saints: The Godbeites and Brigham Young*. Champaign, IL: University of Illinois Press, 1998.

Welch, Thomas Weston. "Early Mormon Woodworking at Its Best: A Study of the Craftsmanship in the First Temples of Utah." Master's thesis, Brigham Young University, 1983.

Woodruff, Wilford. *Leaves from My Journal*. Salt Lake City: The Church of Jesus Christ of Latter-day Saints, 1881.

Young, Brigham. *Manuscript History of Brigham Young, 1801–1844*. Compiled by Elden Jay Watson. Salt Lake City: Smith Secretarial Service, 1969.

———. *Manuscript History of Brigham Young, 1847–1850*. Edited by William S. Harwell. Salt Lake City: Collier's Publishing Co., 1997.

———, et al. *General Epistle from the Council of the Twelve Apostles to the Church of Jesus Christ of Latter-day Saints, Abroad, Dispersed through the Earth*. Liverpool: R. James, 1847.

GOVERNMENT DOCUMENTS

An Act to aid in the construction of a railroad and telegraph line from the Missouri river to the Pacific ocean, and to secure to the government the use of the same for postal, military, and other purposes. 12 Stat. 489 (1862).

Acts, Resolutions, and Memorials Passed by the First Annual and Special Sessions of the Legislative Assembly of the Territory of Utah. Great Salt Lake City: Brigham H. Young, 1851.

Admission of Utah Into the Union: Memorial of the Convention to Frame a Constitution for the Admission of Utah Into the Union as a State. Salt Lake City: n.p., February 19, 1872.

Buchanan, James. *Message of the President of the United States*. 35th ed. GPO: June 10, 1858.

———. *Presidential Proclamation 74 by President James Buchanan Relating to Rebellion in Utah and Granting Pardons Under Conditions*. GPO: April 6, 1858.

Citizens of Utah Territory. *Memorial to Congress*. Salt Lake City, n.d.

Congressional Globe.

Constitution of the State of Deseret. State of Deseret, n.d.

Cooke, Philip Saint George, Col. *Report from the Secretary of War, Communicating, in Compliance with a Resolution of the Senate, of the 21st February, 1849, a Copy of the Official Journal of Lieutenant Colonel Philip St. George Cooke, From Santa Fe to San Diego, &C*., GPO: 1849.

Edmunds-Tucker Act of 1887, 48 U.S.C. ch. 10 § 1461 (1887).

Fillmore, Millard. "Utah Message from the President of the United States, Transmitting Information in Reference to the Condition of Affairs in the Territory of Utah, January 9, 1852." GPO: January 9, 1852.

Forstall, Richard L., ed. *Population of States and Counties of the United States: 1790–1990*. Department of Commerce, US Bureau of the Census, Population Division. Washington, DC, March 1996. https://www.census.gov/population/www/censusdata.

Harding, Stephen S., and William H. Seward. "Affairs in Utah." Salt Lake City, n.d.

House of Representatives, Exec. Document No. 25, 32nd Congress, First Session, January 9, 1852.

Morrill Anti-Bigamy Act, Pub. L. No. 37-126, 12 Stat. 501 (1862).

Poland Act of 1874 (18 Stat. 253).

Porter, Richard H. to Hon. Salmon P. Chase. GPO: May 27, 1861.

Ramsey, Alex. "Report of the Utah Commission to the Secretary of the Interior." Salt Lake City, October 28, 1885.

Salt Lake City Government. *Ordinances of Salt Lake City*. Salt Lake City: Salt Lake City (Government), October 1, 1894.

———. *Ordinances Passed by the Legislative Council of Great Salt Lake City, and Ordered to Be Printed*. Salt Lake City: Salt Lake City (Government), February 24, 1849.

Thompson, John. *Mormonism—Increase of the Army*. Washington, DC: Buell & Blanchard, January 27, 1858.

US Department of the Interior. *Guidebook of the Western United States: Part B. The Overland Route with a Side Trip to Yellowstone Park*. GPO: 1916.

US War Department. *Official Correspondence of Brigadier General W. S. Harney, USA and First Lieutenant George Ihrie, USA with the War Department and Subsequent Personal Correspondence, 1861*. GPO: April 1, 1861.

———. *The War of the Rebellion: A Compilation of the Official Records of the Union and Confederate Armies*. 128 parts in 70 vols. and atlas. GPO: 1880–1901.

Utah Commission. *The Edmunds Act, Reports of the Commission, Rules, Regulations and Decisions, and Population, Registration and Election Tables, &c*. Salt Lake City: Tribune Printing and Publishing Company, 1883.

———. "Utah Statehood: Reasons Why It Should Not Be Granted." Salt Lake City: Tribune Print, 1887.

Windom, William. *Ex-Governor Brigham Young*. Vol. 38. GPO: February 19, 1864.

Young, Brigham. "Governor's Message, Salt Lake City." Salt Lake City, December 2, 1850.

———. Letter to James K. Polk. 1846 August 9. Vault MSS 792; Kane family papers; L. Tom Perry Special Collections; 19th Century Western & Mormon

Manuscripts; 1130 Harold B. Lee Library; Brigham Young University; Provo, Utah 84602.

———. *Proclamation by the Governor.* Salt Lake City, 1857. https://catalog.church ofjesuschrist.org/assets?id= 9e15470b-9902-459a-a4e0-f02e9aa7231f &crate=0&index=0.

HISTORICAL COLLECTIONS, DIARIES, JOURNALS, LETTERS, AND PAPERS

Angell, Truman Osborn (1810–1887). *Autobiography, 1810-1887.* MS 12334, CHL.

———. *Journal, 1851 December–1856 April.* MS 626, CHL. https://catalog.churchof jesuschrist.org/assets?id=626b24e6-5a44-4300-888e-041c1732213b.

———. *Journal, 1856 April–1857 May.* Daughters of Utah Pioneers collection, 1828–1963. MS 8795, CHL.

———. *Journal, 1867 April–1868 April.* Daughters of Utah Pioneers collection, 1828–1963. MS 8795, CHL.

Ashurst-McGee, Mark, David W. Grua, Elizabeth Kuehn, Alexander L. Baugh, and Brenden W. Rensink, eds. *Documents, Volume 6: February 1838–August 1839.* Vol. 6 of the Documents series of The Joseph Smith Papers, edited by Ronald K. Esplin, Matthew J. Grow, and Matthew C. Godfrey. Salt Lake City: Church Historian's Press, 2017.

Bullock, Thomas (1816–1885). *Thomas Bullock journals, 1843–1849;* MS 2737 Box 65, 43, CHL.

Cannon, George Q. *The Journal of George Q. Cannon.* (Salt Lake City: Church Historian's Press, n.d.). Online only. https://churchhistorianspress.org/george -q-cannon.

Chesnut, Mary Boykin. *A Diary from Dixie.* Edited by Isabella D. Martin and Myrta Lockett Avary. New York: D. Appleton and Company, 1905.

Davidson, Karen Lynn, David J. Whittaker, Mark Ashurst-McGee, and Richard L. Jensen, eds. *Histories, Volume 1: Joseph Smith Histories, 1832–1844.* Vol. 1 of the Histories series of The Joseph Smith Papers, edited by Dean C. Jessee, Ronald K. Esplin, and Richard Lyman Bushman. Salt Lake City: Church Historian's Press, 2012.

Dean, Joseph Henry (1855–1947). *Joseph H. Dean journals, 1876–1944.* MS 1530, CHL.

Dirkmaat, Gerrit J., Brent M. Rogers, Grant Underwood, Robert J. Woodford, and William G. Hartley, eds. *Documents, Volume 3: February 1833–March 1834.* Vol. 3 of the Documents series of The Joseph Smith Papers, edited by Ronald K. Esplin and Matthew J. Grow. Salt Lake City: Church Historian's Press, 2014

Egan, Howard R. *Pioneering the West.* Richmond, UT: Howard R. Egan Estate, 1917.

Godfrey, Matthew C., Mark Ashurst-McGee, Grant Underwood, Robert J. Woodford, and William G. Hartley, eds. *Documents, Volume 2: July*

1831–January 1833. Vol. 2 of the Documents series of The Joseph Smith Papers, edited by Dean C. Jessee, Ronald K. Esplin, Richard Lyman Bushman, and Matthew J. Grow. Salt Lake City: Church Historian's Press, 2013.

——, Spencer W. McBride, Alex D. Smith, and Christopher James Blythe, eds. *Documents, Volume 7: September 1839–January 1841.* Vol. 7 of the Documents series of The Joseph Smith Papers, edited by Ronald K. Esplin, Matthew J. Grow, and Matthew C. Godfrey. Salt Lake City: Church Historian's Press, 2018.

Hedges, Andrew H., Alex D. Smith, and Richard Lloyd Anderson, eds. *Journals, Volume 2: December 1841–April 1843.* Vol. 2 of the Journals series of The Joseph Smith Papers, edited by Dean C. Jessee, Ronald K. Esplin, and Richard Lyman Bushman. Salt Lake City: Church Historian's Press, 2011.

Historian's Office (1842?–1972). *Historian's Office history of the Church, 1839–circa 1882.* CR 100 102, CHL.

Historical Department (1972–2000). *Historical Department journal history of the Church, 1896–2001 July,* CR 100 137, CHL.

Jenson, Robin Scott, Richard E. Turley Jr., and Riley M. Lorimer, eds. *Revelations and Translations, Volume 2: Published Revelations.* Vol. 2 of the Revelations and Translations series of The Joseph Smith Papers, edited by Dean C. Jessee, Ronald K. Esplin, and Richard Lyman Bushman. Salt Lake City: Church Historian's Press, 2011.

Kelly, Charles, ed. *Journals of John D. Lee, 1846–47 and 1859.* Salt Lake City, UT: Western Printing Company, 1938.

Kimball, Heber C. *Journal of Heber C. Kimball.* Edited by Robert Blashel Thompson. 1st ed. Nauvoo, IL: Robinson & Smith, 1840.

Kuhre, William Dobbie (1863-1960). *The Livingston family, 1935 November 2.* CR 100 102, CHL. https://catalog.churchofjesuschrist.org/record?id=c03129d6-c1f8 -4cae-9603-569ee418f73f.

——. *Recollections of temple quarry, Little Cottonwood Canyon, and old Granite (City),* undated. MS 13729, CHL. https://catalog.churchofjesuschrist.org /record?id=1f27c331-6d1b-4f98-a219-a965e01ff24f.

Livingston, James Campbell (1833–1909). *Short Extracts Taken from the Autobiography of James Campbell Livingston . . .* Undated. MS 11798, CHL. https://catalog.churchofjesuschrist.org/assets?id=12c64281-30ee-4aa1-afa9 -ab79df507e48&crate=0&index=0.

McAllister, Joseph W. *Diary and Account Book of Joseph W. McAllister 1882–1885.* San Marino, CA: [s. n.] [n.d.].

Polk, James K. *Polk: The Diary of a President 1845–1849.* Edited by Allan Nevins. New York: Longmans, Greed and Co., 1952.

Raleigh, Alonzo Hazelton (1818–1901). *Alonzo H. Raleigh autobiography.* MS

11438, CHL. https://catalog.churchofjesuschrist.org/assets?id=4f1d10e0-2bd4
-41eea27e-01c79398ef7f&crate=0& index=0.

———. *Alonzo H. Raleigh diary, 1861 February–1886 February.* MS 13912, CHL.
https://catalog.churchofjesuschrist.org/record?id=0d1ac2b5-4a36-4f1c
-8854-c909717588de&compId= b85b6d08-30fe-4675-85e9-412b04c41adf
&view=browse&subView=arrangement.

———. *Alonzo H. Raleigh journal.* MS 13912, CHL. https://catalog.churchofjesus
christ.org/assets?id=99d9ea67-b774-415a-8039-8a9c9a79d33a&crate=0
&index=0.

Walker, Charles Lowell, *Diary of Charles Lowell Walker,* vol. 2. Logan, UT: Utah
State University Press, 1980.

Woodruff, Wilford (1807–1898). *Wilford Woodruff journals and papers, 1828–1898,*
MS 1352, CHL.

Young, Brigham. *Brigham Young Office. Brigham Young office files, 1832–1878 (bulk
1844–1877).* CR 1234 1, CHL. https://catalog.churchofjesuschrist.org/record
?id=02e985d2-0e16-45c3-8891-986d21e20b37&compId=ec2fb3e4-b093
-4545-aa2a-f41fd89d5454.

NEWSPAPERS AND MAGAZINES

Alexandria Gazette. Alexandria, VA. 1834–1974.

Atlantic Monthly. Washington, DC. 1857–Present.

Christian Science Monitor. Boston, 1908–Present.

Contributor. Salt Lake City. 1879–1896.

Daily National Intelligencer. Washington, DC. 1800–1869.

Deseret Evening News. Salt Lake City. 1867–1920.

Deseret News. Salt Lake City. 1850–Present.

Deseret Weekly, Salt Lake City. 1888–1898.

Ensign. Salt Lake City. 1971–Present.

Historical Record. Salt Lake City. 1882–1890.

Improvement Era. Salt Lake City. 1897–1970.

Latter-day Saints' Millennial Star. Liverpool, Manchester, England. 1840–1970. (For
all citations to this periodical, note that the Church's President of the British
Mission was typically listed as the editor of the *Millennial Star.*)

New York Daily Tribune. New York City. 1841–1862.

New York Times. New York City. 1851–Present.

Philadelphia Sunday Mercury. Philadelphia. 1860–1863.

Salt Lake Herald. Salt Lake City. 1870–1909.

Salt Lake Tribune. Salt Lake City. 1871–Present.

Washington Evening Star. Washington, DC. 1852–1981.

Woman's Exponent. Salt Lake City. 1872–1914.

BIBLIOGRAPHY

SPEECHES

Atherton, George W. "The Legislative Career of Justin S. Morrill." Address delivered at New Haven, Connecticut, November 14, 1900.

Colfax, Schuyler, and John Taylor. "The Mormon Question." Debate held at the Townsend House, Salt Lake City, UT, October 5, 1869.

Curtis, Samuel R. "The Mormon Rebellion and the Bill to Raise Volunteers." Speech delivered in the U. S. House of Representatives, March 10, 1858.

Douglas, Stephen A. "Remarks of the Hon. Stephen A. Douglas, on Kansas, Utah, and the Dred Scott Decision." Speech given at the State House, Springfield, IL, June 12, 1857.

Kane, Thomas L. "The Mormons." Speech given in Philadelphia, PA, to the Historical Society of Pennsylvania, March 26, 1850.

Pratt, Orson, and Dr. J. P. Newman. "The Bible and Polygamy." Debate held at the Tabernacle, Salt Lake City, UT, August 12, 1870.

"Proceedings in Mass Meeting of the Ladies of Salt Lake City, to Protest against the Passage of the Cullom's Bill." Public meeting held in Salt Lake City, UT, January 14, 1870. https://archive.org/details/proceedingsinmas00saltrich (accessed August 23, 2019).

Rigdon, Sidney. "Oration Delivered by Mr. S. Rigdon on the 4th of July 1838 at Far West, Caldwell County, Missouri." See "Appendix 3: Discourse, circa 4 July 1838." The Joseph Smith Papers, https://www.josephsmithpapers.org /paper-summary/appendix-3-discourse-circa-4-july-1838/1. Accessed November 13, 2019.

Snow, Erastus. "Discourse on the Utah Pioneers." In *The Utah Pioneers: Celebration of the Entrance of the Pioneers into Great Salt Lake Valley* (Salt Lake City: Deseret News Printing and Publishing Establishment, 1880), 41–50.

Woodruff, Wilford. "Zion's Camp, Mormon Battalion, Pioneers." In *The Utah Pioneers: Celebration of the Entrance of the Pioneers into Great Salt Lake Valley* (Salt Lake City: Deseret News Printing and Publishing Establishment, 1880), 17–24.

———, George Q. Cannon, and Franklin Dewey Richards. "President Woodruff's Manifesto." Speech given in the Tabernacle, Salt Lake City, UT, October 6, 1890.

WEBSITES

The Church of Jesus Christ of Latter-day Saints; Gospel Topics Essays; https://www .churchofjesuschrist.org/study/manual/gospel-topics-essays/essays.

The Joseph Smith Papers. http://josephsmithpapers.org.

INDEX

legislation against, 284–85, 508n15; supported by Latter-day Saint women, 285–90, 339–40, 508n15; federal prosecution of, 291–92, 295–96, 307–10, 314, 319, 339–40, 357–59, 361–68, 370, 383, 384, 503n61; and Poland Bill, 306–7; George Reynolds imprisoned for, 341–42, 346; Wilford Woodruff exiled for, 342–43; Arthur opposes, 348–49; and Edmunds Anti-Polygamy Act, 349–50, 357, 363, 368; Rudger Clawson indicted for, 353–57; and Edmunds-Tucker Act, 368–70, 438; and seizure of Church property, 374–75, 381–82, 383–84, 386, 395–96, 398, 405–6, 415; end of, 389–90, 398–404; federal pardons for, 438, 445–46

Poland, Luke, 307

Poland Bill, 306–7

Political disagreements, 447–49

Polk, James K., 17

Popular sovereignty, 128, 129

Powell, Lazarus, 165–66

Powers, Orlando, 363

Pratt, Lorus, 393–94, 440

Pratt, Orson, 2–3, 36, 57, 58–59, 110

Pratt, Parley P., 40, 85–87

Preston, William B., 390–91

Priesthood organization, 515n10

Proclamation 346—Granting Amnesty and Pardon for the Offense of Engaging in Polygamous or Plural Marriage to Members of the Church of Latter-day Saints, 445–46

Provo, Cradlebaugh's "reign of terror" in, 170–72

Pullen, William, 346–47

Railroads: need for, 105, 106, 249–50, 278–79; benefits of, 251–52. *See also* Central Pacific Railroad; Transcontinental railroad; Union Pacific Railroad; Utah Central Railroad; Utah Southern Railroad

Raleigh, Alonzo, 101, 172, 191–92

Rathbone, Henry, 236, 237

Read, James, 278

Red Butte Canyon Company, 74–75

Red Butte Canyon quarry, 74–75, 91, 97

Reed, Samuel B., 262, 277

Relief Society, 285

Religion, freedom of, 58–59

Repentance, Saints called to, 448–50

Republican Party, 176–77, 203, 448

Reynolds, George A., 307–10, 314, 319, 321, 339, 341–42, 346

Reynolds v. United States (1879), 339–41

Richards, Willard, 11, 35–36, 41, 510n37

Rigdon, Sidney, 7

Rockwell, Orrin Porter, 123

Rockwood, Albert P., 484n15

Rocky Mountain spotted fever, 1–2

"Runaway Officials" scandal, 45–49

Salt Lake City: Ulysses S. Grant visits, 310–14; Morrison Waite visits, 367. *See also* Salt Lake Valley

Salt Lake Tabernacle: conception and design of, 228–30; construction of, 230–31, 234–35, 244–46, 504–5n46; Julia Grant on, 313. *See also* Adobe Tabernacle

Salt Lake Temple: site selection for, 19–20, 21–22; architects for, 29–31, 51–52, 190–91, 247–48, 334–35, 379–80, 414, 452; construction of wall and Council House, 38; Brigham Young on construction of, 54–55, 88–89, 316–17; proposals for construction of, 59–62; materials for, 61–62, 63–65, 74–75, 104–7, 258; visions of, 64–65, 89, 332, 461–62; design of, 65–66, 73–74, 99–100, 430–31; spires of, 66, 89, 100, 303, 335, 351, 353, 375–77, 386–87, 409; groundbreaking for, 66–72; excavation for, 72–73, 490n27; foundation of, 74–76, 90–91, 97–98, 101–2, 119–20, 157–58, 172–73, 185–86, 191–96, 206; cornerstones of, 76–88, 142–44, 422–23, 497n37; wall surrounding, 91; suspension of work on, 103–4, 382; basement of, 120–21; and Utah Expedition, 141–42, 157–58,